Women and the United States Constitution

Women and the United States Constitution

HISTORY,
INTERPRETATION,
AND PRACTICE

Edited by Sibyl A. Schwarzenbach *and* Patricia Smith

Columbia University Press   New York

Columbia University Press
Publishers Since 1893
New York   Chichester, West Sussex

Copyright © 2003 Columbia University Press

Library of Congress Cataloging-in-Publication Data
Women and the United States Constitution : history, interpretation,
and practice / edited by Sibyl A. Schwarzenbach and Patricia Smith.
p.   cm.
Includes bibliographical references and index.
ISBN 0–231–12892–4 (cloth : alk. paper)—
ISBN 0–231–12893–2 (paper : alk. paper)
1. Women—Legal status, laws, etc.—United States—History.
2. Women's rights—United States.   3. Constitutional history—United States.
4. Equal rights amendments—United States.   5. Feminist jurisprudence—
United States.   I. Schwarzenbach, Sibyl A.   II. Smith, Patricia.

KF478.A5W654 2004
342.73'0878—dc21
2003055252

∞

Columbia University Press books are printed on permanent and
durable acid-free paper.

Printed in the United States of America

c 10 9 8 7 6 5 4 3 2 1
p 10 9 8 7 6 5 4 3 2 1

In Memory of Dr. Margaret van Wylick Froelicher
January 3, 1909—August 10, 1994

and for Hilary, Lauren, Mara, and Lee

Contents

Preface

Feminism lacks a theory of the United States Constitution, as well as an account of political legitimacy within the framework of democracy.[1] The following collection of essays—we believe among the first of its kind—does not presume to supply such a full-blown theory. What it does purport is to provide some of the groundwork for such a theory (or, better, group of theories) by giving various analyses of what it is that the United States Constitution may be lacking insofar as women were nowhere among its original authors. Indeed, women were rarely among any of its authors or interpreters in the intervening two hundred years. This "lack," or the lacuna of the representation of women in our constitutional tradition, emerges as twofold: on the one hand, it refers to the specific rights and to the political status of women, which, as the following essays all reveal, are still far from equal in the United States. On the other hand, the reference is to the *general* character of the U.S. Constitution and to its glorification and protection of activity that all too often emerges as traditionally and characteristically "male."

Nearly all the essays in this volume, moreover, attempt to locate both the weaknesses and the strengths of our constitutional tradition in light of the possibility of future feminist practice: not only for a better understanding of how women might gain greater political control over their own lives but also of how their growing participation in law and government might effect and even redirect future constitutional practice itself. Finally, the hope is that women in other countries, in different circumstances, and under very different types of regimes, may yet learn from our struggles within the specific legal tradition of a particular country—especially from the struggles within such a powerful country as the United States that often presumes to export its ideas and institutions worldwide.

When referring to "the United States Constitution," scholars refer in both narrower and broader senses. In the narrowest sense, the term refers to the actual *physical* document of 1787, signed by many of the American founding fathers, a parchment residing (by day) in a massive, bulletproof, and oxygen deprived glass case in the National Archives' rotunda in Washington D.C. (at night it is lowered into a vault of reinforced concrete and steel twenty-two feet deep). Reference to this piece of parchment may not even include the first ten amendments (the so-called Bill of Rights) added in 1791, and it certainly does not include reference to all future twenty-two amendments, nor to more than two centuries of constitutional interpretation and judicial practice. But today many of these latter documents are standardly regarded as part of the Constitution considered qua *legal* document.

In the title of this volume we are referring to the U.S. Constitution in an even wider and more inclusive sense, however. For it is not clear that the legal sense would include the prior Declaration of Independence, and it certainly would not include all the underlying social, political, and philosophical arguments and theories to be found in the writings of the *Federalist Papers*, nor in those of their anti-Federalist critics, in the debates (and notes taken) at the Continental Congress, nor in the writings of all future judges, etc. For many of these theories, arguments, and opinions simply contradict one another. Which one of them should be considered a *legitimate* part of our system of constitutional law thus ends up being not just a matter of legal debate but of moral and political theory as well. As numerous constitutional scholars have by now carefully argued, no legal text is self-interpreting; particularly one so sparse and ambiguous as the U.S. Constitution, however, requires us to use moral argument and appeal to principles external to that text itself. On such a legal "constructivist" approach, moral theory, in conjunction with interpretative history, plays an essential role in understanding the American constitutional tradition.[2]

In this constructivist vein we have gathered together recent work, not only by feminist legal theorists but also by historians, political scientists, philosophers as well as by activists, with the aim of better understanding the U.S. constitutional tradition in general, in light of its liabilities and potential for women in particular. In taking this cross-disciplinary approach, moreover, we are stressing what might be called the fluid or dynamic nature of this tradition. That the U.S. Constitution be viewed as a moving, living document—and not as some frozen structure burdened with all the weight of its two-hundred-year-old past—is of the utmost importance for women (indeed, for all those who have been excluded from its historical theory and practice). For it is only if the U.S. Constitution can *evolve* that women and their concerns will ever be fully included—or so at least runs a major assumption of this volume. And, indeed, issues and concerns that were once historically seen as "outside" the constitutionally protected sphere have frequently and repeatedly moved "inward" due to their central importance, either by way of explicit amendment or through a more refined interpretation and application to new domains of the Constitution's central tenets.

The most important example of the first form of change—of outright amendment—is surely the cluster of the Thirteenth, Fourteenth, and Fifteenth (the so-called Reconstruction) Amendments in the nineteenth century. What was once legally viewed as mere private property—namely the African slave—and largely regulated by the interstate commerce clause, emerges via the Reconstruction Amendments as a Freedman with all the privileges and immunities of a citizen. At least in theory. And a similar story can be told in the case of the Nineteenth Amendment, which granted women the right to vote.

An example of the second type of constitutional change—by way of extension, application, and a more refined interpretation of constitutional principles themselves—is provided by the case of abortion. What was once a (for the most part legitimate) practice regulated by common law moved to the center of fierce legal and constitutional debate, leading to and including the explicit right to abortion in the 1973 Supreme Court decision *Roe v. Wade*. Similarly, the interpretation of the Equal Protection Clause of the 14th Amendment, as one including the prohibition of discrimination on the basis of sex and not merely of race, is an instance of the evolution of meaning in the U.S. Constitution that changes the legal status of some activities from constitutionally unprotected to protected, or vice versa.

For this reason the following collection includes—beyond treating what today are considered straightforward U.S. constitutional issues such as federalism, gender discrimination, basic rights, privacy, abortion, etc.—further areas of central concern to contemporary women: areas that have not *as of yet* been considered a part of constitutional law strictly speaking. For example, this collection includes a number of papers on the nature of women's traditional *labor* and on its unique character. Is it possible that such a new and growing concern on the part of women with the nature and conditions of their laboring activity (both with their own traditional work in the home and with other forms) just might contribute to a greater recognition in the future of an emerging constitutional *right* of each citizen to decent work, or to a certain amount of leisure time, or perhaps even to a guaranteed basic income? We cannot know the possibilities until we have explored such issues.

The following collection does not presume to be an adequate history or interpretation of the relation of women to the U.S. Constitution. Such would entail scores of volumes if not more. Nor can this collection claim to be a particularly "balanced" view of women's struggles with American constitutional law and its social and political background institutions. Too many issues and perspectives—from ongoing debates regarding pornography, to feminist work in environmental law, to the role and rights of women in immigrant or religious communities, etc.—could not be included. But in attempting to understand just a few of the varied obstacles, contradictions, and potentialities that women face in their struggle to be equal as well as respected and fully participating members of the United States democratic and constitutional tradition, the following collection is, we would like to think, a start.

Sibyl A. Schwarzenbach
Patricia Smith

NOTES

1. See Tracy E. Higgins, "Democracy and Feminism," *Harvard Law Review* 110, June 1997, no. 8: 165–1703 for a discussion of this claim.

2. The constructivist approach is best exemplified in the writings of such legal theorists as Ronald Dworkin, David Richards, and Cass Sunstein among others; see the discussion by Schwarzenbach (this volume, chapter 1).

Acknowledgments

We wish to thank various people who were crucial in helping this volume reach fruition. Professors Lexa Logue and Myrna Chase, former dean and current dean, respectively, of the Weissman School of Arts and Science, provided both moral and financial support for the original three-day conference on Women and the U.S. Constitution held at Baruch College, CUNY in January 2001. This conference afforded feminist scholars from around the country the opportunity to meet and to discuss many of the issues included here. We are also grateful to Alan Grose, to Rob Landsman, as well as to our students Matthew Chin, Denis Giron, Sherrie Panikoff, Bommasamudram Raghu, and Vanessa Witenko, all of whom supplied invaluable organizational aid. Similarly, Professor Sylvia Law of New York University generously offered her extensive knowledge of the field in rounding up participants and in contacting scholars whose expertise we tapped for this volume. The Stanford Humanities Center supplied me with the time and a beautiful as well as stimulating setting to do the final editing. Finally, thanks must also go to Jeffrey Bliss for his patience and technical wizardry in helping the editors overcome the myriad confusions, viruses, and formatting incompatibilities that inevitably accompany, it seems, a collaborative project of twenty-one different authors each using her own personal computer in our modern technological age.

Women and the United States Constitution

Sibyl A. Schwarzenbach

CHAPTER 1

Women and Constitutional Interpretation

The Forgotten Value of Civic Friendship

For what is government itself but the greatest of all reflections on human nature?
—JAMES MADISON

Until recently feminists have approached the U.S. Constitution in a some-what piecemeal fashion. With but a few exceptions they have focused on specific areas of constitutional doctrine, for instance, on the First Amendment in their fight against pornography,[1] or on the Due Process and Equal Protection Clauses of the Fourteenth Amendment in their attempts to defend abortion.[2] But they have less often approached the Constitution as a whole. That is, less emphasis has been given to *general* constitutional interpretation: to the significance of the fact that this document was written over two hundred years ago and wholly by men, that it never refers to women explicitly (in fact it uses the masculine pronoun thirty times), and that it all too often (especially when enumerating the rights of citizens) originally excluded them.[3] So too, under it, women for scores of years were denied the right to vote, could typically not hold property on their own, and were relegated to the domestic field out of view of public life and largely subject to the whims of their fathers and husbands. What kind of document, we might ask, is this? How can women's allegiance to it and its history be maintained? Why should we not go with some other version of constitution as presented in various other countries? In short, feminism (as was noted earlier in the preface) lacks a philosophical theory of the U.S. Constitution, as well as a well-defined theory of political legitimacy within the framework of democracy.

In this chapter I speak for myself alone. I propose what might be called one analysis or hypothesis of what it is that our Constitution and its tradition of interpretation may be lacking insofar as women have rarely been among any of its authors or interpreters since its eighteenth-century inception. Although my project builds on the work of other feminist political and legal theorists—including on the work of many in this volume—my account will also differ in significant ways from their positions. Thus I hope to provide—as well as legitimate—one novel, feminist interpretation by which we may approach our Constitution as a whole and judge the history of its development.

The Analysis of What Is Lacking

Perhaps the central criticism feminists have proffered of the liberal political tradition in general, and of our constitutional regime in particular, is that the conception of the individual presupposed is quintessentially "male"; it does not match descriptions women give of their own selves and agency. The abstract legal person, bearer of universal rights against the state, is often assumed to be separate, autonomous, self-determining, and self-interested.[4] Feminists, by contrast, are surprisingly united in their characterization of women's experience as far more circumscribed. Women tend to see themselves as largely defined by their particular and concrete relations, as more "connected" with or focused on others, and—as Carol Gilligan has most famously argued—far from immediately resorting to the language of rights in moral dilemmas, they tend to stress their responsibility and duties to particular others first.[5] This has led many to claim that women possess a different perspective or standpoint, even that they speak in a "different voice."

A consensus on the nature of this difference, of course—indeed on whether there even is such a difference—remains outstanding. The following essay gives but one interpretation of what this difference might amount to, as well as its possible relevance for contemporary political and legal theory. Without entering into numerous ongoing debates, I will propose we simply look far more carefully at the underlying forms of *social labor* men and women have traditionally performed. I do not thereby necessarily deny other accounts focusing on women's biological or sexual differences (their capacity for pregnancy, mothering, emotional abilities, etc.). I only stress that a fuller analysis of women's traditional "reproductive" activity—especially considering the enormous role the concept of free "productive" labor has played in the modern period—is crucial. For, as we shall see, in early American debates regarding which types of labor and activity should be allowed and nurtured by the new government (whether it should encourage agricultural, wage, commercial, slave, or free) the very nature of the modern state is at issue. By offering a contrasting account of the historical labor typical of women, therefore, we will be in a better position to approach the philosophy behind the U.S. Constitution anew and see more clearly what might be absent insofar as women were nowhere among its original architects. Finally, and perhaps most importantly, greater light may be shed on how best to delineate the nature of government — including its underlying aims, legitimate functions, and practices.

Let us begin by noting an uncontroversial but significant discovery of twentieth-century anthropology: in the known societies both past and present, and but for the rarest exceptions, men *as a group* have not been the primary care takers of young children.[6] This is not to say that men have not also performed child care (although to a far lesser degree), nor is it to claim that such an activity is a part of women's "nature" or grounded in her "biology"; history, social institutions, and simple chance have surely all played their part. My claim is simply that the "reproductive" labor involved in child care has traditionally been woman's lot. It is my contention, moreover, that (unlike in much feminist theory) we must distinguish not just between a *biological* and an *ethical* sense of the term "reproduction" but between a *personal* and a *civic* form.[7]

Unlike biological reproduction, which refers to those largely unconscious, material processes that work to reproduce another member of the species (processes such as menstruation, production of semen, pregnancy, etc.), what I am calling *ethical* reproduction is a distinctively normative category: the activity seeks the maintenance and reproduction of human persons and their relationships. In taking care of a child, for instance, my aim is not (normally speaking) simply to keep it alive but to have the child grow to maturity — to flourish and fend for itself in a specific moral, social, and political climate. Ethical reproductive activity, in the best case, encourages the autonomy and the equality of the other. But as such, we might note, the activity need not be confined to child care strictly speaking but can apply as well to the support and care of the aged, the sick, and even to the loving care of those in their prime.

Ethical reproductive activities are thus not only "ethical" in the minimal sense of necessarily involving conscious choice and being imbued with reason and foresight (*logos*), they are also ethical in a thicker normative sense. Such activities may (in the worst case) reproduce the hierarchical relations of slave and arbitrary master or (in the best case) aim to reproduce equal and flourishing human relationships as ends in themselves — what I call (with Aristotle) relations of *philia* or friendship. Indeed, I henceforth use the term "ethical reproductive activity" in this full normative sense. The term refers to *all* those rational, deliberative activities (thinking about particular others and their needs, caring for them, cooking their meals, teaching them, encouraging their abilities, etc.) that seek in the best case to "reproduce" (develop, maintain, or enhance) relationships of genuine *philia* as ends in themselves.

A few words of explanation are still in order. I use the Greek term *"philia"* because it is broader than the English "friendship" (or the German *"Freund-schaft"*) and, as Aristotle has argued, it includes the relations not just between good parents and children, siblings as well as lovers, but also between fellow citizens.[8] It is important to note what all these relations have in common. In each case, genuine friends may be said reciprocally (1) to be aware of and to recognize the other as some form of moral equal, (2) to wish the other well for that other's sake (and not just for their own), and (3) materially or practically to do things for that other. Moreover, my claim is not only that ethical repro-ductive activity in the best case aims at *philia* or friendship but also that women have played a central role in maintaining such. All the many activi-ties the good mother performs for her family members for their sake, for in-stance, Aristotle would consider instances of *philia.*[9] The virtuous mother and child can even be said reciprocally to *aim* at each other's good—including at each other's autonomy and equality—when the relationship is conceived *over a complete life* (thus the child often helps the parent in old age, etc.). Final-ly, insofar as women have been educated de facto for the primary role of eth-ical reproductive activity in the home—far more so than men—they have si-multaneously been educated to further the virtue of *philia* in the ideal case.

The nature of ethical reproductive activity, however, is best understood by contrasting it with what it is not—a causal *production* model of labor. This production model, which ascends to prominence in the seventeenth century, is best conceived, I believe, by recalling John Locke's famous metaphor whereby man in the state of nature rightfully "owns" that with which he has "mixed his labor."[10] Central characteristics of this model are as follows: first, labor is primarily conceived as a technical mastery over the physical world (whether in agriculture, artisan labor or even in a factory still). More impor-tant, all such labor is a form of what the Ancients called "production" or "making" (*poiesis*). That is, the activities are done primarily for the sake of a "product" or end result and not performed for their own sake (what the An-cients called *praxis*). Finally, particularly in the modern period where com-modity production becomes the norm, such individual labor (in contrast to that of the ancient slave or serf) characteristically ushers in a private right to the object produced (or at least to some equivalent). That is, under modern circumstances, the *goal* of productive labor is typically some individual ben-efit to the self or private property.

The structure of reproductive activity, by contrast, is very different (which is one reason it has been overlooked as a form of labor—necessary and a cre-ator of use values—in the first place). On this model, a subject typically "mixes her labor" not in the first instance with a material object but with an-other subject that is her concern: the young, the aged, the beloved. Such reproductive labor is thus not merely "indirectly" social or other-directed but *directly* so; its proper end is the need satisfaction of the other and the encouragement of their abilities.

Please do not misunderstand me here. I am not claiming that women are necessarily any less greedy, self-seeking, etc. than men; my point is structural not psychological. Unless the mother or caretaker in deed looks after the child (the aged, etc.), the latter will not flourish. Moreover, at least in the case of the mother (or friend) such work is not pure self-sacrifice; the activity often entails great personal satisfaction. This may be explained, I believe, by again viewing the "reward" in such instances as the establishment (maintenance, furtherance) of a relationship. As Aristotle noted, *philia* in its genuine form is an end in itself. But the reward is thus not only *not* here conceived as exclusive private property, it is conceived as its antithesis: the reward may be called a "shared appropriation of the human world." Ethical reproductive activity emerges in the best case as a form of *praxis*: that type of activity that is its own end. [11]

The important point is that there exists a category of ethical reproductive *praxis*—traditionally performed by women in the home—which has been neglected by political philosophers in modern times. It is not the same as the category of *paideia* (rearing) or education, as many activities of friendship have no didactic purpose at all but, rather, aim at "fun and games." Nor is it simply the category of "care" recently stressed by feminists (although it usually includes the latter) for *unlike* simple care, activities of genuine friendship necessarily aim at reciprocally maintaining or enhancing the autonomy and equality of the other wherever possible. [12]

Finally, and critically, as Aristotle also noted (and as the modern period appears to have forgotten), there is a public *political* counterpart of such personal reproductive *praxis*. Political reproductive *praxis* includes all those public activities that are done for the sake of flourishing civic relations as ends in themselves, that is, simply for the sake of civic friendship (*politike philia*). Such activities can range anywhere from simply not begrudging your tax dollars for publicly subsidized meals (a favorite of Aristotle's) or for basic health care for all, to volunteering your services when fellow citizens are in trouble, to actively fighting for their rights and for just social institutions generally. Indeed, in Aristotle's view, the political legislator's activity should be viewed as a political extension—not of productive activity—but of this type of ethical *praxis*; the good legislator should concern himself more with the relations between citizens than with property or things (*Politics* 1259b).

Aristotle is emphatic on this point. He even believes that legislators should be more concerned with maintaining the friendship between citizens than with justice itself (*NE*.1155a22). And the reason, he suggests, is that in a society lacking in civic friendship—that is, in a generalized atmosphere of hostility, distrust, indifference, or fear—citizens may still *perceive* themselves to be un-justly treated even if justice in some narrow sense is being adhered to.[13] Again, if a general background of reciprocal awareness, good will, and practical doing—as evidenced in a country's constitution, its general laws and social in-stitutions, as well as in the everyday habits of its people—is *absent*, citizens will be unable to recognize or freely accept in practice the concrete *burdens* justice imposes in any particular case; they will very simply be unable to obtain to the flexible 'give and take' true justice requires. Civic friendship is a necessary con-dition for genuine justice, because without it *what we call justice* soon collaps-es into nothing more than the imposition of the will of the stronger.

Elsewhere I have argued that Aristotle's thesis holds as much today for the modern state as it did for the ancient *polis*, despite the modern state's far greater size, the ascendancy of the production model of market activity, and despite the disappearance of the language of friendship from public life. And it can still hold in a state of 175 million because civic friendship (unlike per-sonal) operates by way of institutions, laws and social practices.[14] Certain modern doctrines of universal individual rights, for instance—universally em-bodied and recognized in a nonpartisan practice of respect for persons—can be interpreted as embodying a fundamental regard, if not love, for the special interests of every human being. In fact, such public doctrines—always inclu-sive of the labor and education required to realize such rights in practice—may be considered one of the highest expressions of a *modern* form of civic friendship. Or at least so I have argued elsewhere.

The critical point is not that men have not also performed ethical repro-ductive activity or *praxis* in the intended sense; they clearly have. Although they rarely as a group have taken responsibility for young children, such pro-fessions as teaching, ministering, the arts and (at least in the ancient view) rul-ing and legislating, reveal ethical "reproductive" *praxis* in varying degrees; they all aim, in the best case, at the reproduction of the best of human rela-tionships. My point is only that women, not only in the past but in the midst of our advanced capitalist market-oriented present, continue to perform such labor and activity to an extraordinary degree. Moreover, a political version of it, as we have just seen, is a necessary prerequisite for justice.

Not surprisingly, just as the ancient category of reproductive *praxis* is gen-erally neglected by modern theorists, it is also rarely viewed by the American founding fathers as a widespread and integral part of the modern political state. Indeed, the modern liberal conception of the citizen, as we shall see, becomes intimately tied with the performance of—not *praxis* as for Aristo-tle—but free productive labor. It is thus also not surprising that there is so lit-tle explicit appeal to a friendship between citizens in the American tradi-tion—certainly none in the 1787 Constitution. Before we turn to an analysis of the philosophy behind this specific constitution, however, allow me still a few words on the general issue of constitutional interpretation.

Constitutional Interpretation and the Method of Reflective Equilibrium

Scholars have distinguished at least four different interpretative approaches to the U.S. Constitution: what might be called the appeal to authoritative historical exemplars, to convention, to moral reality, and a "constructivist" approach.[15] The first two approaches (although not without their distinguished defenders) have been widely criticized as inadequate and they hardly seem capable in addition of rectifying the lacuna of representation of women in our tradition. The first, which appeals in questions of interpretation to the founding fathers "intentions" in drafting the Constitution, begs the very issue at question: why should women listen to this group of men holding a convention more than two hundred years ago in which women had no participation? What *grounds* the moral authority of the "original intentions" of these men (even if one could make determinate sense of this notion)? The second approach, the appeal to a positivist conventionalism, should strike women as suspect for similar reasons. The view that law is neutrally given to us by a conventional legal authority independently of any need for interpretation does nothing to *justify* the authority of these conventions—particularly when they all too frequently neither defended women's interests nor worked for their good. Thus it appears we are left with one of the latter two approaches: the direct appeal to moral reality or to some form of legal constructivism.

The direct appeal to moral reality is tempting, for we all tend to think we have a good grasp of it. This school of constitutional interpretation advocates reading the text and its history in light of the best moral theory available, revising and even excising the text where necessary.[16] Such an approach might also appear particularly appealing to women who have historically suffered so from exclusion within the legal tradition. Why not simply reject the U.S. Constitution altogether? Why should women not hold their own convention, write a new constitution, and pledge their allegiance to this new constitution's now-more-friendly-to-women principles?

Beyond the practical difficulty of such a move, this approach suffers from two major problems. The first is that women have no unified moral and political theory that they jointly endorse (and they perhaps never will). The danger in this instance is one of forsaking the somewhat uncomfortable "known" for the radically unknown that could be far worse. But the second reason for not attempting this move is even more important; such an approach eschews the lessons of history. It views moral insight not as something that is garnered from long experience and interaction with others—as something importantly also embodied in customs and practices—but as the product of some individual's (or group of individuals') reflection alone. Where the first two approaches are uncritically accepting of the historical given, this third way (in Hegel's words) tries to leap over its own shadow—it is neglectful of its own sociohistorical presuppositions.

So it appears we are left with a position midway between a simple deference to the founding fathers' words or a conventionalism, on the one hand, and direct individualistic appeals to moral reality on the other. That is, we are left with the necessity of *interpreting* the Constitution and its history and hence with some form of legal "constructivist" approach. This final approach is best exemplified in the writings of such male legal theorists as Ronald Dworkin, David Richards, or Cass Sunstein.[17] Moreover, whatever the particular differences in the legal constructivist positions, the general approach can be traced back to John Rawls's method of reflective equilibrium. What is this method and what is its promise for feminist constitutional theory?

In the words of Rawls, the method of reflective equilibrium is that method of philosophical reflection whereby sincere moral agents seek a match or "equilibrium" between their particular considered moral judgments (formed through concrete observation and practice) and a set of general principles that purports to generate them.[18] Such "back and forth" reflection between particular judgments and general principle operates first between the individual's own set of moral convictions (narrow reflective equilibrium) and then between his or her unified convictions and an ever widening circle of others (wide reflective equilibrium). It is important to note that, according to Rawls, there exists the possibility of a *political* or *legal* reflective equilibrium whereby theorists elaborate "the basic intuitive ideas" and the "implicitly recognized principles" embedded in "the public political culture" of a society and seek to resolve particular historical conflicts.[19] The aim is to generate a set of fundamental moral principles on which all (or at least most) can agree.

Thus, in contrast to both classical rationalist (formalist) and empiricist (utilitarian) approaches, the search for a reflective equilibrium is viewed as the search for *a moral-practical consensus*: one addressed in the first instance to other human beings with whom we disagree and to whom we need to justify ourselves, and in terms that all can accept. The aim of theory, in this view, is not to mirror some independent ethical order but to *construct* or extend the range of an already existing moral consensus. Such a "reconciliatory" view of the nature of moral theory, we should note, appears particularly appropriate to the workings of a democracy.

Similarly, in the case of a legal reflective equilibrium, the goal will be to arrive at the best interpretation of the Constitution with the aim of forging common ground in areas where discord now reigns. In this legal instance, the particular judgments appealed to will include not only those embodied in the text of the Constitution itself but also those found in the history of its construction, ratification, as well as interpretation over the past two centuries (e.g., the Declaration of Independence, the *Federalist Papers*, the Court Opinions, the thousands of statutes enacted, the various rules and principles appealed to, etc.). This legal database (as it were) is then subjected to differing general interpretations, which aim not only to "fit" and organize the data but to present the Constitution in its best light—that is, to make it a sounder and more just document.

If we are convinced of something like the appropriateness of the constructivist method for U.S. constitutional interpretation, we are left with numerous difficulties if our concern is the lacuna of women's representation in this tradition. Most important, if reflective equilibrium must begin with the particular judgments and "basic intuitive ideas" of our "public political culture," it is difficult not to notice that this public culture has been (until lately) composed almost entirely of males. Women were typically denied the right to vote, to go to university, to hold public office, to own private property on their own, to speak or even to appear at many public gatherings, and this often well into the twentieth century.[20] It is thus highly unlikely that many of the particular, considered moral convictions *shared by women*—by those traditionally confined to the private, familial sphere and who performed the preponderance of reproductive labor—found their way into the delicate balancing act of a public and legal reflective equilibrium. What sort of distortion in our conception of the political state does this absence lead to?

Two points should be stressed here. First, regarding method, it is clear that if feminists are to overcome the male bias in even the best of legal constructivist thought, they cannot rest content with examining only the public texts and the history of their interpretation, for these public texts have largely ignored women's traditional concerns. For a more adequate public reflective equilibrium (including a more adequate constitutional theory), the vast repertoire of particular, moral convictions hitherto relegated to the so-called private, nonpolitical, and noneconomic sphere—whether it be the diaries of the housewife, the manifestos of the slave or the rantings of the abolitionist—must now be drawn into the original data pool from which a societywide reflective equilibrium at least *begins*.

Second, the project of extending a reflective equilibrium into the so-called private domains promises to shed new light in a number of areas. Not only will light be shed on background conceptions of the person (the different assumptions regarding gendered social roles), not only will we be able better to understand and to evaluate those social conditions upon which our modern political state in the narrow sense—and our U.S. Constitution in particular—until now rests, but if allowed adequate development, such a project may even work toward offering a new standpoint from which to evaluate tradition-al notions of the state. That is, we may consciously begin to construct a new and more adequate original position—this time from the perspective of the *ethical reproduction of persons*—from which to evaluate traditional legal and political theory. Perhaps we might even make good the demand that a central function of the new state be not merely the maintenance of law and order and a military prepared for war, nor simply a policing of citizenry and productive competition, but the furtherance of the conditions of the possibility of civic friendship as well.

The Founding Period and "Friends of Mankind"

Having sketched an interpretation of a critical "difference" (politically speaking) between men and women, and having indicated my departure in method from established approaches in constitutional theory, it is time to proffer my feminist reading of the U.S. Constitution. I hope the thesis will at least be intriguing. My claim is that the best way to view the U.S. constitu-tional tradition—from the Declaration of Independence, the *Federalist Papers* and ratification debates, through Reconstruction, the New Deal, and up to the Civil Rights and present women's movement—is to view the (zigzag) moral evolution of the document, not simply as an elaboration of the basic concepts of freedom and equality between persons (as is often claimed) but as an evolution in the awareness of the critical value of "civic friendship" as well. (I reject "fraternity" for the obvious reason that, strictly speaking, it holds be-tween brothers or men alone.) Further, I wish to claim that *only* some such reading—one that finds central room for the independent and distinct politi-cal value of *philia*—will afford the genuine, equal inclusion of women in the modern state, whether theoretically or practically.

It is generally recognized that there are at least three great "transforma-tive" periods in the history of the U.S. Constitution, periods where crucial substantive change was brought about: the Founding, Reconstruction, and the New Deal.[21] These were not only times in which profound changes in popular opinion gained authoritative constitutional recognition; they are ar-guably also times of growing inclusiveness and a diminished inequality. In-deed, I believe these periods may be described as ones in which it is ac-knowledged (even if vaguely and begrudgingly) that the political state at least *ought* to be an expression of a political friendship between citizens too. That is, Aristotle's thesis is by no means dead. Although for reasons of space I will here only touch upon the Founding period—including a brief discussion of the *Federalist Papers*—I will suggest application of my thesis to the later two transformations.[22]

The great eighteenth-century slogan "Liberté, Égalité, Fraternité" rang out across Europe and surely (to some extent) inspired the American revolutionaries. Oddly enough, however, unlike the first two terms of the famous triad, the latter notion of "fraternity" did not work its way into the Declaration of Independence nor into the new U.S. Constitution (although it does appear in the earlier Articles of Confederation).[23] Nor does the notion of friendship— at least at first sight—appear to play any significant role in the *Federalist Papers*. Nonetheless, I wish to argue that the new American republic implicitly furthered the value of fraternity along with that of equality and liberty, and this to an extent the world had rarely known.

For one, the Declaration of Independence publicly proclaims that "all men are created equal" and the founding fathers clearly sought (again, only to some extent) to embody this self-evident truth in the new republic. The above claim is *more* than simply an appeal to the value of equality, however. For, when I deny that the aristocrat or any other man is better than I am (politically speaking), or when, in doing so, I further deny that any man has authority over me without good reason, I appeal to "equality." I can thus further the value of equality *by promoting only my own* (let us call this strategic or "Hobbesian" equality). The case is quite different, however, if I sincerely proclaim "all are equal." For here I simultaneously grant that those *traditionally beneath me* are my equals as well. Here ipso facto I grant or extend my position of equality to others, and *that*, I want to say, is furthering the value not just of equality but of friendship as well. For one of the distinguishing marks of genuine friendship is *wanting the other to be equal too*. Similarly, the most minimal friendship characteristically requires providing the other with good reasons and not resorting to force, fraud, or subterfuge.

If we consider the attempt to embody a doctrine of universal equality between citizens into legal institutions of right (again attempted in the Constitution), we have a clear instance of what I am calling "civic friendship." Here I do not personally know the vast majority of these others, nor am I ever going to; nonetheless, I wish them well. I seek a general system whereby any rights and privileges that I seek for myself are granted to them also (including even my personal enemies). I seek a public order in which I relinquish my superiority at the same time as I refuse my subordination, and which thus embodies a reciprocity of principle upon which I act.

The important point is that modern proclamations of universal right, if genuinely realized in practice, can prevent the civic union from degenerating into a mere partial "friendship politics" (for which the ancient world was rightly criticized): that is, into a power play of private sects and hostile, opposing factions. Moreover, in efforts to uphold the rule of law and to realize these universal rights in practice, citizens reciprocally acknowledge and express their general concern and goodwill toward the specific interests of each individual in the concrete—what might be called a modern *impartial* form of civic friendship. Surely the U.S. Constitution's enunciation of various rights—from the personal rights of freedom of thought and religion to the more political rights of free speech and the press, of assembly, due process, the denial of the legitimacy of ex post facto laws, etc.—publicly acknowledges and protects central concerns of each citizen and aims to establish new and higher standards of public civic behavior.

Of course, as we all know, in the case of the resulting 1787 Constitution such expressions of civic friendship were quite limited: titles of nobility were explicitly prohibited, a basic set of rights and civic equality was proclaimed, but full citizenship was granted in practice only to a relatively small group of propertied, white males.[24] Thus the *scope* of early American fraternity did not extend far and its *content* was relatively homogeneous. Still, by the lights of the time the new nation repudiated inherited privilege, attempted to establish a "republic of reasons" over arbitrary privilege (Sunstein), and allowed the extension of equality to a rare degree.

So why is there so little appeal to "fraternity" by the founding fathers, whether in the *Federalist Papers*, the ratification debates, or in the U.S. Constitution itself? In accordance with my general thesis regarding political liberalism, much of the absence can be explained by noting the rise and pervasive influence of a production model of labor—the founding fathers are simply no exception. That is, unlike for the ancients and in the face of the emerging modern market, the category of reproductive labor tends to be reduced either to its mere biological meaning or to a form of servitude (viewed as appropriately done by women, not fully human slaves, or servants) or—in its civic sense—it comes to be seen as supererogatory (expected of only a virtuous few). In neither case is it viewed as a widespread and integral part of the modern political state. On the contrary, it is the capacity for production (in the ancient world performed primarily by illiterate artisans, foreigners, and slaves) that now, in addition to military service, becomes tied to active citizenship itself.[25] Even the state comes to be viewed according to the production model. When Hobbes writes, for example, that "By Art is created that great Leviathan called a Common-wealth or State," he does not merely assert that the state is a rational product of man (*poiesis*). Rather, Hobbes claims something more; the state is now instrumental to other ends (e.g., security, acquisition, power, etc.)—that is, to ends *beyond* the political reproduction of flourishing human relations for their own sake.

In the *Federalist Papers*, that authoritative explanation and defense of the 1787 U.S. Constitution, the central arguments presented by Madison, Hamilton, and Jay (alias *Publius*)—regarding the advantages of a strong national government, the analysis of factions, the role of commerce, the necessary checks and balances of government, etc.—all assume that personal reproductive activity (childcare, household and local duties, etc.) will continue to be performed primarily by women, servants, or slaves; such activity is neither problematized in these papers nor considered a form of rational activity at all. If one searches for any equivalent of what we have been calling civic reproductive *praxis*—the distinguishing mark of Aristotle's full citizen—it does emerge, but the category remains sketchy and appears restricted in the new republic to a small group of elected representatives. That is, in Madison's theory of "enlightened" and indirect representation, representatives have the job of deliberating about the interests of others and regarding the body politic *as a whole*. These enlightened men are chosen by other citizens, not so much to do the latter's bidding but to "deliberate the public good" by way of "refining and enlarging the public views."[26] It is clear that for Madison, these elected men should exhibit a "civic virtue" and a "love of justice" to a high degree (*Fed.* #10). Interestingly enough, he even refers to such men as "the friends of mankind" (*Fed.* #40). Moreover, it is one of the central benefits of a large republic, in Madison's view, that less worthy candidates will find it more difficult to gather widespread support and be elected; a large republic thus reduces the danger of unfit, self-interested men, as well as factious majorities, from ruling (*Fed.* #10).

Because such "friends of mankind" are so rare, however, whereas the "unfriendly passions" and "the propensity of mankind to fall into mutual animosities" so great, a general strategy of dividing government against itself, of controlling the effects of the factious spirit by checks and balances, and of using "auxiliary precautions" such as restricting popular participation, is the ultimate route advocated (*Fed.* #10, #51). It is thus clear (at least for Madison) that the proposed Constitution is far more than a mere set of ground rules for interest-group struggles pursuing their private self-interest. The *Federalist Papers* reveal repeated appeals to civic virtue, to public service, and to "friends of popular government" as well as to "friends of liberty," "of faith," and "of mankind" (*Fed.* #10, #40). The great *weakness* of these famous papers is that they provide us no institutional way of reproducing such friends; these virtuous men presumably spring up here and there like mushrooms. Again, whereas there is much institutional provision made by *Publius* (and by extension the tradition) for countering the effects of public hostility, animosity, and faction, there is little or no provision made for the institutional reproduction of friendly civic relations. These crucial relationships will presumably just "take care of themselves."

Indeed, if one seeks positive provisions, one is far more likely to find them in the American *Anti*-Federalist writings that criticized the new 1787 Constitution: in *Brutus'* discussions of greater popular "participation" as a check against corruption and greed, in *Cato's* claim that political participation is "an education in virtue," in *Federal Farmer's* call for more direct and "substantial representation" by the people and in his awareness of the "expense and time" needed for it, in *Dewitt's* insistence that "the means of education" should continue to be attended to and "the fountains of science brought within the reach of poverty" and of "every child," and in *Cato's* claim that "public service is the only honor" but "the framer's have departed from this democratic principle" by, for instance, leaving men in office for so long, etc.[27] These distinguished critics presumably "lost the debate," but it was central to their criticism that civic reproductive *praxis* be institutionally embodied in any political state genuinely calling itself "democratic." And their writings underscore this original lack.

If we take one final look at perhaps the most famous passage in the *Federalist Papers*—No. 10 where Madison discusses the causes of faction among men and pronounces the solution to lie in the "checks and balances" of power—this original inadequacy is only driven home. Madison writes:

> The diversity in the faculties of men, from which the rights of property originate, is not less an insuperable obstacle to a uniformity of interests. The protection of these faculties is the first object of government.

It is quite certain that Madison here, in discussing the origins of faction, has in mind the diverse faculties of those who perform the productive labor. That is, the deliberative and emotional "faculties" of women—or of those primarily involved in ethical reproductive *praxis*—are not being included, and this for reasons that, if spelled out, are quite illuminating. It is obvious, first, that the traditional work of women is not here being included because, at this point in history, women's reproductive labor (or for that matter any of her labor) ushered in no property rights at all. Whatever work the women did in the home (or outside of it) typically belonged to her father or husband (under Blackstone's Community of Persons).[28]

Second, it would be odd to draw attention to ethical reproductive labor as an "insuperable obstacle" to a uniformity of interest for (as we have seen) it is often that type of labor that characteristically seeks to forge or further a unity of interests—in the best case freely and autonomously. Finally, as we also noted earlier, the proper end or *telos* of reproductive *praxis* is not private property at all but what was called a "shared appropriation of the human world." The type of ownership such activity or labor ushers in, therefore, would hardly be the institution of private property, but something closer to a joint stew-ardship or common possession.[29]

In the above passage Madison clearly has different types of (male) produc-tive activities in mind: individual farming or large-scale agriculture, small- or large-scale manufacture, different branches of commercial activity, banking, and so forth. The issue for him is how to protect these different branches of competitive, productive industry without the civic body being rent by faction. The question *for us* becomes: why is it the nature of government that it should protect the different (productive) faculties of men and not those of ethical re-productive activity?

The answer more than two hundred years later can only be: *it is not*. Inso-far as reproductive labor and *praxis* are acknowledged as of crucial impor-tance—not only for the ethical reproduction of persons but for the justice of civic relations—it is impossible any longer to believe that such forms of labor lie "outside" the public's concern. Of course, the modern state has always has been implicated in this type of labor from the start by promoting, discourag-ing, or simply tolerating different forms: whether forced, slave, gendered, or private. What it has not so far done is to perceive its involvement or role in the reproduction of citizen relations as an explicit public—and specifically democratic—responsibility.

At least two points may be gleaned from our brief survey of the founding pe-riod. First, while recognizing the necessity that other-directed "friends of mankind" must legislate in order to preserve peace and afford genuine justice, when it comes time to provide for the education or reproduction of such civic friends—and of positive civic relations generally—the Federalists (as well as much of the ensuing tradition) have little to say. There is little recognition of the affirmative political obligation or the necessary cooperative *praxis* required for creating or sustaining such fair and equal background civic relations. Thus it is not surprising, I believe, that we have hardly avoided injurious "faction" today at the beginning of the twenty-first century. On the contrary, the gap in the United States today between the haves and the have-nots is greater than at any point since 1929 (the Great Depression), with corporate executives of the top companies earning over one thousand times the wage of the average work-er.[30] We have a ruling corporate culture that is hierarchical, secretive, and tyrannical—anything but open and democratic[31]—at the same time as the electorate is so apathetic that roughly 50 percent of eligible citizens do not even bother to vote.[32] We are perhaps the most violent of advanced industrial nations, with gun ownership still enshrined in our Constitution, with one out of every thirty-two adults behind bars or on probation or parole,[33] and with a military expenditure that already outstrips that of the next eight largest military powers in the world combined.[34] And yet, despite all our super wealth and power, we are among the most pusillanimous of advanced industrial nations in terms of the public granting of welfare or benefits.[35] We are one of the very few without universal health care (and with over four million persons uninsured); we have a system of inadequate family leave plans and one of short-term, punitive welfare benefits, our public schools are failing, and our aid to foreign countries has fallen to as little as 0.1 percent of our rich economy (much of it for armaments).[36] Simply put, our awareness and positive concern for fellow citizens—and our practical or material doing for them—is shockingly *low*.

A second point: once we view ethical reproductive labor and *praxis* as a distinct form of rational activity—and acknowledge its importance—it becomes the duty of a just government to protect, promote, and distribute it fairly, in the same manner as it protects and promotes manufacturing or farming or any other form of productive labor. And indeed, when we look to the subsequent history of the U.S. Constitution over the next two centuries, we perceive extraordinary periods where this awareness dawns ever so slowly on future generations—although hardly without struggle, and certainly not without strenuous opposition.

For instance, the second great transformation in American constitutional law typically cited by scholars, is the change leading up to and culminating in the Thirteenth, Fourteenth, and Fifteenth (the so-called Reconstruction) Amendments.[37] On the reading I am offering here, this legal transformation—which officially freed the confederate slaves and constitutionally guaranteed all citizens equal protection of the laws—may be described as one whereby the American political system begins to acknowledge its complicit role in the *reproduction of citizens*. That is, the Reconstruction Amendments are one of the first indications that the state explicitly recognizes a duty, however imperfectly, to engage in civic reproductive activity and to promote the conditions of a civic equality among its inhabitants. During this tumultuous time, moreover, all the necessary criteria of our definition of civic friendship were being expressed, some even embodied in law.

For instance, awareness of the evils of the system of slavery (and the brutal Black Codes of the Jacksonian era) as well as sympathy with the downtrodden African-American became widespread with the abolitionist movement, and to this movement is even attributed the novel idea of an American people "unbounded by race" not to be found in the original 1787 document.[38] As Angelina Grimké (daughter of a Southern Carolina slaveholder and a prominent abolitionist and feminist) wrote, the crusade against slavery is the nation's preeminent "school in which *human rights* . . . are investigated."[39] Thus not only a widespread *awareness*, but the *desire* for the other (the slave) to be legally equal, backed by a committed *practical doing* (including the great fratricidal conflict known as the American Civil War) led to one of the greatest extensions of the system of individual rights in American history. We even obtain a glimpse of an alternative conception of the state emerging as well. Union armies did not just win the war, but General Sherman's men entered the South to protect and enforce the rights of the newly emancipated slave, a Freedman's bureau was established in 1865, and Congress (at the behest of Thaddeus Stevens, Charles Sumner, and other radical Republicans) authorized the president to confiscate rebel lands with plans of providing "forty acres and a mule" to every adult male freedman enabling him to begin life anew as an independent farmer. And more than thirty thousand acres of farmland were in fact set aside, before the reaction set in.[40]

Reconstruction is often viewed as the most radical, progressive, enlightened, corrupt, even "unconstitutional" time in American history, depending upon one's ultimate point of view. Here I note only that many of the above actions (I exclude the atrocities committed by Sherman's armies) do not sound radical from a feminist perspective—or at least not from a feminist perspective that stresses the value of ethical reproductive *praxis*. That the political state—after more than four score years of complicity in one of the worst crimes known to all of humanity (equaled only by the slaughter of America's native inhabitants)—seeks redress for its victims, and actually *works* to establish the conditions for the possibility of just social relations free of all prejudice, would appear merely the natural realization of the value of civic friendship. And I believe a similar story can be told about the legal revolution of 1937—that third great transformation in American constitutional law known as the New Deal—but this is a story I here leave for others to tell.[41] I shall only note that, as scholars have generally indicated, the end of the Lochner era and the turn to a national welfare state is often considered to begin with *Nebbia v. New York*, 291 U.S. 502 (1934) where the Supreme Court cites the simple principle that "[n]either property rights nor contract rights are absolute; for government cannot exist if the citizens may at will use his property to the detriment of his [*sic*] fellows."

Beneath the surface of the values of liberty and equality in the American constitutional tradition, there lurks the necessary requirement of a minimal friendship between citizens as well. Civic friendship, we might say, is a vaguely perceptible subtheme of this tradition. The hope presented here is that it might become an explicit and even dominant theme as well, as women gain their rightful place within the spheres of philosophy, politics, and law.

If I am correct, we have before us a novel way of viewing the normative development—as well as the lapses—of the U.S. constitutional tradition: as a growing awareness of the necessity of not merely the political values of liberty and equality but those of friendship as well. It is an interpretation that, I believe, does no major violence to the historical texts, at the same time as it centrally includes women and their traditional activity in its evolution; women are no longer conceived as mere afterthoughts. But we should note as well that we have before us a novel way (or at least a renewed way) of conceiving of democracy itself. That is, most contemporary democratic theorists account for the superiority of democracy as a political form in terms of the value of freedom or of equality or of both.[42] The suggestion here, by contrast, is that a central value of democracy is in fact political or civic friendship. And the reason is this: we can appeal to the freedom and equality of others (and not just to our own) until the cows come home, but if no one cares for these others, if no one is motivated to help them when they are down or to check them when they grow arrogant, all appeals to freedom and equality — and particularly to justice — are in vain. Civic friendship points to that necessary prior *motivation* for democracy and to its ultimate source in satisfying and equal human relationships for their own sake. Genuine democracy is the political extension of friendship too, and if democracy violates this fundamental value, it compromises its nature. The U.S. constitutional tradition has skirted around and about this value for more than two centuries — it is high time to look it squarely in the face.

NOTES

1. See, e.g., Catherine MacKinnon, *Toward a Feminist Theory of the State* (Cambridge: Harvard University Press, 1989).

2. E.g., Sylvia Law, "Rethinking Sex and the Constitution," *University of Pennsylvania Law Review* 132 (1984): 987–1013. An important exception to this general rule, is e.g., Robin West, *Progressive Constitutionalism* (Durham, N.C.: Duke University Press, 1994).

3. Although Jan Lewis, in a novel take on the original Constitutional Convention, argues that women's concerns were implicitly included by the American founding fathers (chapter 2, this volume).

4. See, for instance, the collection of articles in Patricia Smith, ed., *Feminist Jurisprudence* (Oxford: Oxford University Press, 1993).

5. Carol Gilligan, *In a Different Voice* (Cambridge: Harvard University Press, 1982).

6. See, for instance, the early collection by R. Reiter, ed., *Toward an Anthropology of Women* (London and New York: Monthly Review Press, 1975).

7. The following discussion of "reproduction" draws from my "A Political Reading of the Reproductive Soul in Aristotle," *History of Philosophy Quarterly* 9, no. 3 (July 1992): 243–64.

8. See Aristotle's discussion in his *Nicomachean Ethics*, bks. 8–9. All references to Aristotle's works will be to the revised Oxford translation of *The Complete Works of Aristotle*, ed. J. Barnes, 2 vols., (Princeton: Princeton University Press, 1984) and cite the pagination of the Greek text.

9. Cf. my (1992) account.

10. John Locke, *The Second Treatise of Government*, in P. Laslett, ed., *Two Treatises of Government* (Cambridge: Cambridge University Press, 1960), para. 27.

11. At this point, in order to avoid confusion, let us distinguish clearly between reproductive *labor* and reproductive *praxis*. If the activity is done for private benefit (for example, in day care performed primarily for a wage), I will refer to such as reproductive *labor*. The term "reproductive *praxis*," by contrast, I reserve for reproductive activity that is done for its own sake. Many actual actions, of course, will be a mixture of these two categories.

12. And this care need not necessarily do. On this point—that friendship necessarily *aims* at equality—I differ also from Aristotle who tends to argue that genuine friendship already *presupposes* equality, whereas I wish to argue that it *aims* at equality. See Schwarzenbach (1992).

13. This is my reading of Aristotle's claim that "when men are friends they have no need of justice, while when they are just they need friendship as well, and the truest form of justice is thought to be a friendly quality" (*NE*.1155a22–28).

14. See my "On Civic Friendship," *Ethics* 107 (October 1996): 97–128.

15. I here follow David Richards, *Foundations of American Constitutionalism* (Oxford: Oxford University Press, 1989), ch. 1.

16. John Hart Ely's *Democracy and Distrust: A Theory of Judicial Review* (Cambridge: Harvard University Press, 1980) is often cited as an instance.

17. See Ronald Dworkin, *Taking Rights Seriously* (Cambridge: Harvard University Press, 1979), ch. 5; Richards (1989); and Cass R. Sunstein, *The Partial Constitution* (Cambridge: Harvard University Press, 1993).

18. John Rawls, *A Theory of Justice* (Cambridge: Harvard University Press, 1971), 20, 46–53, 130–135.

19. See Rawls, *Political Liberalism* (New York: Columbia University Press, 1993), lecture 1.

20. See Eleanor Flexner, *Century of Struggle: The Women's Rights Movement in the United States* (Cambridge, MA: Belknap Press, 1959).

21. See Bruce Ackerman, *We the People: Foundations* (Cambridge: Harvard University Press, 1991), 81–103.

22. For a fuller account, see my *On Civic Friendship* (forthcoming), ch. 7; see also chapters 5–8, this volume.

23. The Articles of Confederation aimed to create a "firm league of friendship" between the separate state republics for purposes of "defense, the security of their Liberties, and their mutual and general welfare" (Article III).

24. Importantly, the 1787 Constitution left the matter of defining who was to be a citizen to the individual states, and consequently women, blacks, the propertyless, Native Americans, Orientals, and others were largely excluded for the majority of U.S. history. See Rogers M. Smith, *Civic Ideals* (New Haven: Yale University Press, 1997), 15.

25. Nowhere is this clearer than in Kant's *Metaphysics of Morals* where Kant distinguishes between "active" citizens (he gives the example of the wig-maker) from "passive" citizens (he cites the barber) according to whether the individual produces

an independent "product" (para. 46). For application of this modern prejudice to the American case, see Judith Sklar, *American Citizenship* (Cambridge: Harvard University Press, 1992).

26. Federalist Paper #10, in C. Rossiter, ed., *The Federalist Papers: Hamilton, Madison, Jay* (New York: Penguin, 1961).

27. See *Brutus* 18 (October 1787): 270ff; *Cato*, Letter V, 320–21; *Federal Farmer*, 8 October 1787, 264ff; and *DeWitt* "Essay I," 190, in R. Ketcham, ed., *The Anti-Federalist Papers and the Constitutional Convention Debates* (New York: Penguin, 1986).

28. See n. 20.

29. See my discussion in "Rawls and Ownership: The Forgotten Category of Reproductive Labor," *Canadian Journal of Philosophy* 13 (1987).

30. David Cay Johnston, "More Get Rich and Pay Less in Taxes" *New York Times*, 7 February 2002; Alexander Cockburn, "The Hog Wallow," *The Nation*, August 5, 2002; Paul Krugman, "For Richer," *New York Times Magazine*, October 20, 2002.

31. See Kate Jennings, "The Hypocrisy of Wall Street Culture," *New York Times*, July 14, 2002.

32. Douglas J. Amy, *Real Choices, New Voices: The Case for Proportional Elections in the United States* (New York: Columbia University Press, 1993), 5.

33. J. D. Salant, "Corrections Census Reaches Record High," *Times Union*, August 26, 2002.

34. Timothy G. Ash, "The Peril of Too Much Power,"*New York Times*, April 9, 2002.

35. See especially chapters 7 and 8, this volume.

36. Joesph Kahn and Tim Weiner, "World Leaders Rethinking Strategy on Aid to Poor," *New York Times*, March 18, 2002.

37. See n. 21.

38. Eric Foner, "The Strange Career of the Reconstruction Amendments," *Yale Law Journal* 108 (July 1999): 2003.

39. Larry Ceplair, ed., *The Public Years of Sarah and Angelina Grimke: Selected Writings, 1835–1839* (New York: Columbia University Press, 1989), 194.

40. For a more nuanced discussion, see Aiyetero (chapter 6, this volume).

41. See Sunstein (1993); also the discussions by Fox Piven and Smith (chapters 7 and 8, this volume).

42. See, for instance, Josh Cohen and Joel Rogers, *On Democracy* (New York: Penguin, 1983); the collection of essays in J. Bohman and W. Rehg, eds., *Deliberative Democracy* (Cambridge: MIT Press, 1997) or in D. Copp, J. Hampton, and J. Roemer, eds., *The Idea of Democracy* (Cambridge: Cambridge University Press, 1993); Robert Dahl, *Democracy and Its Critics* (New Haven: Yale University Press, 1989); Carol Gould, *Rethinking Democracy* (Cambridge: Cambridge University Press, 1988); Ian Shapiro, *Democracy's Place* (Ithaca, N.Y.: Cornell University Press, 1996), to name but a few.

PART 1

History

The Founding Period

Jan Lewis

CHAPTER 2

Representation of Women in the Constitution

It is axiomatic among scholars of the Constitution that women are nowhere mentioned in that document. What to make of that omission, however, has been a matter of debate. Some have read the Constitution's silence as implied inclusiveness. Just think of the contortions through which we put ourselves when we try to write in gender-neutral language. Surely, the Constitution's avoidance of "he" and "him," "male" and "man" must have been intentional. Just look at the Fourteenth Amendment, which for the first time introduced the word "male" into the Constitution: It was easy enough to make the Constitution an explicitly gendered document when that was the intention.[1]

At the same time, others have argued that the Constitution's failure to mention women was no mistake. At best, the framers of the Constitution were not thinking of women. At worst, they intended to exclude them. After all, republican political thought was misogynist, and the compact theory of government imagined that compact as a deal cut among men. If the political theories upon which the Constitution was based did not designate a role for women in the state, then neither could the Constitution.[2]

Some years ago, the historian Richard Morris bemoaned the Constitution's ambiguous silence on gender, saying "it would have been very helpful" if that document's authors "had given us a hint."[3] In fact, the framers of the Constitution did leave us a hint, and a very helpful one at that. It is to be found in James Madison's notes on the Federal Convention, which, although they were

I would like to express my thanks to Norma Basch and James Oakes.

not published until 1840, have been available to students of the Constitution ever since. I do not believe, however, that this passage has until now attracted the attention of scholars.

The place: Philadelphia. The date: Monday, June 11, 1787. The delegates are discussing the thorny topic of representation in the new national legislature that the delegates are proposing. James Wilson, delegate from Pennsylvania, suggests that representation in the lower house should be "in proportion to the whole number of white & other free Citizens & inhabitants of every age sex & condition including those bound to servitude for a term of years and three fifths of all other persons not comprehended in the foregoing description, except Indians not paying taxes, in each state."[4] Edited down into a more concise form, this formulation became the infamous Three Fifths Clause.

Significantly, the words that are of interest to us here — "of every age sex & condition" — attracted no attention whatsoever. It's not that the general issue, representation, was uncontroversial. After all, it was this very issue that would hold the delegates up most of that long summer. Nor was it that the states explicitly included women when they were apportioning representatives. In fact, none of the state constitutions then in effect explicitly included women (or children), and two states that wrote their constitutions in the 1790s allocated representatives on the basis of the number of free adult white males (Kentucky) and taxpayers (Tennessee).[5] Including women, then, was an innovation and, in terms of the state constitutions, not to mention the Northwest Ordinance, an anomaly as well. Yet in the four volumes of the Records of the Federal Convention there is not a single comment upon the inclusion of women.

The delegates accepted Wilson's language and sent it off for editing to the Committee of Style (the Convention's copy editors, who were charged with improving the document's rhetoric without changing its substance).[6] What came back became, after one subsequent minor amendment, the language that we recognize from Article I, Section 2 of the Constitution: "whole number of free persons, including those bound to service for a terms of years and excluding Indians not taxed, three fifths of all other persons." All free men, women, and children were now comprised in the more succinct term free "persons." The term "women" ended up on the cutting room floor, but we can, and should, understand that women were indeed included in the term "free persons," and, hence, that every place that the Constitution uses the term "person" or "persons" and probably every other place that it uses gender-neutral language as well, women were implicitly included.

Elsewhere I have explored this chapter in the history of the "founding."[7] My objective has, in part, been to demonstrate that the canonical texts of American politics and political thought are not, as is sometimes thought, irrelevant to women and their history. Instead, they are deeply relevant, not only because, as we historians of gender are always insisting, gender is every-where[8] but because those texts did, in fact, concern themselves with women. My larger project is to ask where women fit into the doctrines of American liberalism. Was the American republic constructed, as Joan Landes has argued for the French one, "against women, not just without them"?[9] Are women permanently and necessarily outside the state? Or are women inside it, and if they are, on what terms?

In a brief article, I cannot answer these questions, ones that have kept political theorists busy for several centuries now. But I do hope to suggest what it might mean for women's history, for political theory, and for constitutional thought that women were, in fact, included in the Constitution.[10]

We might begin by examining the context in which Wilson offered his language about "every age sex & condition." The practical issue was apportionment of representatives in Congress. Should representation be based upon some measure of population? Some states gave representatives, after all, to counties or districts of unequal sizes. And if representation were to be based upon population, what about the slaves? Counting them obviously enhanced the power of the slave states. Counting women and children, on the other hand, had virtually no practical effect. With sex and age ratios almost the same, including women in the basis for apportionment neither gave some states more representation nor others less.[11]

The theoretical issue, particularly as it applied to women, was more complex. The critical issue here, and it is one that the delegates discussed at some length, albeit without mentioning women, was who was to be represented in the new nation. The preamble to the Constitution, of course, begins "We the People," yet, as Edmund S. Morgan has noted, "the people" was a fiction.[12] The compact theory of government held that, as Massachusetts's James Sullivan put it in the spring of 1776, when Massachusetts was writing its first state constitution, "Laws and Government are founded on the Consent of the people, and that consent should by each member of Society be given in proportion to his Right. Every member of Society has a Right to give his Consent to the Laws of the Community or he owes no Obedience to them." But who were the people? As Sullivan acknowledged—indeed, this was his point—"a very great number of the people of this Colony have at all times been bound by Laws to which" they had never consented, not meeting the property requirement for voting. "[Y]et by Fiction of Law"—sometimes the documents that we historians work with are so good that it almost seems as if we made them up—"every Man is supposed to consent."

Sullivan did not mention women, but it seems pretty clear that he had women in mind and wondered by what logic—or illogic—they were excluded from the imaginary social compact that created the state. Several years later, while serving as Massachusetts attorney general, he defended the state from James Martin's suit to reclaim the property that the state had seized from his Loyalist mother, who had fled the state with her Loyalist husband. Part of the case turned on whether women were among the "every *inhabitant* and *member*" covered by the Massachusetts confiscation statute. Martin's attorney asserted that as a *feme covert*, a married woman whose legal capacity was absorbed by her husband, Anna Martin was "not a member" and had "no *political relation* to the *state* any more than an alien." She had no choice but to abandon her property and to follow her Loyalist husband when he left the country. In response, Sullivan insisted that "surely a *feme-covert* can be an inhabitant in every sense of the word. Who are the members of the body-politic? are not all the *citizens*, members: infants, idiots, insane, or whatever may be their *relative* situations in society?" Women, then were inhabitants, members, and citizens; the state constitution secured them their rights and privileges, and entailed upon them responsibilities. They were part of the social compact.[13]

Martin won his case, and Sullivan lost his argument. The justices adhered to an older, more patriarchal notion of the family and the state both: A woman's first obligation was to her husband; she related to the state only through him, and consequently, as far as the state was concerned, she was not a member of it.[14]

It is in the context of this case, and the majority opinion upholding coverture as a political principal, that the Constitution's doctrine of representation appears so radical. With nothing practical to be gained by it, James Wilson proposed and his fellow delegates accepted the principle that women—and children, and every inhabitant of the nation except for 2/5 of the slaves and all the untaxed Indians—were part of the body politic, to be represented by the elected officials of the new nation.

From our perspective, two centuries later, knowing how arduous the struggle for women's rights has been and still is, it is easy for us to overlook the radicalism of this doctrine of representation. Yet it is only by recovering this moment that we can understand the subsequent history of the women's rights struggle. James Wilson, James Sullivan, and other liberals developed a radical doctrine of representation, one that said that women were part of the body politic, among those whom the new nation was supposed to serve,[15] but its promise—of inclusion and protection for women—has still not yet been realized. Why not?

If we want to discover what became of the liberal doctrine of representation, we might begin by considering—and acknowledging—what it was able to accomplish. When men such as Wilson and Sullivan asserted that women were members of the body politic and entitled to representation, they thought of women as rights-bearing individuals.[16] In their simplest terms, the rights guaranteed by the Bill of Rights were guaranteed to women, as well as to men, whether they were married or single, propertied or not. Moreover, these rights—of speech, of religion, of assembly, of trial by jury—are by no means trivial.[17] Coverture—and republican theories of dependency—have had their limits.[18]

To say that women did not, at the time of the writing and ratification of the Constitution, enjoy all the rights, let alone exercise all the obligations, of citizenship is to state the obvious.[19] But the compact theory of government, which made women rights-bearing members of the body politic, necessarily presented a challenge to those exclusions and denials. It meant, at the very least, that the bases for exclusion and the denial of rights would have to be crafted anew, in a new language compatible with the compact theory. That is what John Adams realized when he and James Sullivan discussed the state constitution that Massachusetts was writing in 1776. Sullivan's letter to Adams has been lost, but a letter he wrote Elbridge Gerry that Gerry forwarded to Adams makes it clear that Sullivan accepted the Lockean premises of the compact theory. Adams accepted them too. "It is certain in Theory, that the only moral Foundation of Government is the Consent of the People." What Adams gave with one hand, however, he took away with the other: "But to what an Extent Shall We carry this Principle?" This was the problem that compact theory—that is, liberalism—presented: Accept its premises, and where do you stop?

Adams saw the problem immediately. "Shall We Say, that every Individual of the Community, old and young, male and female, as well as rich and poor [and note that he's anticipating perfectly Wilson's formulation of age, sex, and condition], must consent, expressly to every Act of Legislation?" This horrible question was, for Adams, rhetorical. "This is impossible." But it was also a problem. "Whence arises the Right of the Men to govern the Women, without their Consent?" Adams's real fear was that men without property, who, according to republican theory were dependents, lacking in virtue, and too easily bent to the will of the powerful, would be allowed to vote. His big concern was the "condition" part of the phrase "age sex & condition." But he understood that to some extent, the elements were interchangeable: Recognize one group as citizens whose consent was required, and what was the logic of excluding others? As Adams asked rhetorically, "Why exclude women?" And he warned Sullivan: "Depend upon it, sir, it is dangerous to open So fruitfull a Source of Controversy and Altercation. . . . There would be no End of it."[20] Those like Adams who feared the destabilizing effects of making women full beneficiaries of democracy would have to craft new bases of exclusion, ones at least nominally consistent with liberal principles. In due course opponents of women's rights would come to assert that women were by nature different from men and hence disqualified for government by their very nature, but we should understand that this way of thinking was not intrinsic to liberalism; instead, it was an attempt to thwart its potential.

If the question of women's rights has remained controversial and called forth a powerful opposition, another facet of the representation of women has not. At its simplest, most literal level, the representation of women in the Constitution means that women are among those whom the new government—now an old government—was supposed to serve. Sometimes we lose sight of this aspect of political thought and structure. Most of our focus, as women's historians, has been on rights, and in particular, the right to vote.[21] If we have not thought much about the meaning of representation, perhaps that is because American national government in the nineteenth century, and especially before the Civil War, was so weak. What, substantively, would it mean to represent the interests of women in government?

And so we return, once again, to the compact theory of government. We begin with Locke, and his observation that the purpose of government was to protect "Life, Liberty, and Estate."[22] Then we filter Locke through the philosophers of the Scottish Enlightenment, men such as Thomas Reid and Francis Hutcheson who developed the notion of *society*. Locke used the terms "community" and "government" almost interchangeably.[23] By the time that the Scots had elaborated the concept of society, Thomas Paine would be able to draw a sharp distinction between society and government. In the second paragraph of *Common Sense*, Paine proclaimed as if it were conventional wisdom that "society is in every state a blessing, but government even in its best state is but a necessary evil."[24] It was this notion of society that James Wilson, himself a Scot by birth, had in mind when he said that women should be counted in apportioning representatives.

Lecturing on the law several years later to an audience of both men and women in Philadelphia, Wilson built upon Paine: "By some politicians, society has been considered as only the scaffolding of government; very improperly, in my judgment. In the just order of things, government is the scaffolding of society: and if society could be built and kept entire without government, the scaffolding might be thrown down." Or, to put it more succinctly, "Government was instituted for the happiness of society."[25] And by society, he meant what Jürgen Habermas has called the "bourgeois public sphere"—all those places where men and women came together to create a public, for example, the hall at the University of Pennsylvania where Wilson was lecturing on the law.[26]

Again borrowing from the Scots, Wilson explained that women made a particular contribution to society. Women trained men in the ways of affection, and affection was the glue that held society together. It was the basis for humanitarianism—"we feel delight in the agreeable conception of the improvement and happiness of mankind"—and patriotism—"we entertain for our country an animated and vigorous zeal"—both.[27] This notion of affection made its way into the *Federalist Papers*, too. In No. 14, for example, in one of the most lyrical passages in the *Papers*, Madison urged ratification of the Constitution by telling the "people of America" that they were "knit together . . . by so many chords of affection," living "together as members of the same family."[28]

In liberal thought, the purpose of government was to protect society. It was to protect property as well, but liberals such as Madison, Sullivan, and Wilson did not see any conflict or contradiction here. For all of them, as for Paine, the family, society, and private enterprise were all on one—on the better—side of the sharp line that divided government from that which had to be protected from government. And if government was, almost by definition, suspect, then the family and private enterprise were imagined as unproblematic realms.[29] The exclusion of women from government should be read in the context of early American liberals' profound suspiciousness of government—and their concomitant idealization of the private sphere.[30]

Women were members of society, and government was supposed to protect society. The purpose of government, in Lockean terms, was to protect those who could not protect themselves. To some extent, the measure of any particular government was how well it protected those who could not protect themselves—the weak, the infirm, the aged, the young, the women. To make such a statement is not simply to make a logical inference from the liberalism of the Founding Fathers; it is to hit upon its bedrock.

But it is also to come up against its greatest obstacle, that is, the obstacle that it presented and continues to present to women—and to the weak, the poor, the infirm, the helpless. Yes, the Constitution included women. Yes, it represented them. Yes, it implicitly offered them protection. But it did not allow them to represent themselves. Instead, it entrusted their care to the men in their families, just as it entrusted the care of slaves to their owners. This comparison is not a mere figure of speech, an inflammatory analogy equating the position of women to the position of slaves. Rather, it is a precise description of the way in which women and slaves were represented in and by the Constitution. The Constitution made women rights-bearing citizens and represented them as members of the body politic, but it gave them no means of securing their rights. American feminists pointed out this discrepancy almost a century and a half ago,[31] and like them, we are still working and waiting for the promise of liberalism to be fulfilled.

NOTES

1. Among those who argue that the Constitution is gender neutral are Herman Belz, "Liberty and Equality for Whom? How to Think Inclusively About the Constitution and the Bill of Rights," *The History Teacher*, 25 (1992): 263–77; and Robert A. Goldwin, *Why Blacks, Women, and Jews Are Not Mentioned in the Constitution* (Washington, D.C., 1990). See similarly Thomas G. West, *Vindicating the Founders: Race, Sex, Class, and Justice in the Origins of America* (Lanham, Md., 1997). The Constitution uses the pronoun "he" most often when referring to the president and on occasion, to senators and representatives. Fleeing criminals are also called "he," though in this case, we must assume that the authors of the Constitution meant it generically; they could not have intended to protect fugitive female felons from extradition. On this point see Rogers M. Smith, *Civic Ideals: Conflicting Visions of Citizenship in U.S. History* (New Haven, 1997), 131. For the Fourteenth Amendment, see Alexander Keyssar, *The Right to Vote: The Contested History of Democracy in the United States* (New York: Basic Books, 2000), 176. Apparently Charles Sumner tried to make the Fourteenth Amendment gender-neutral, but as he later explained, "he wrote over nineteen pages of foolscap to get rid of the word 'male" and yet keep 'negro suffrage' as a party measure intact; but it could not be done." Quoted in Reva B. Siegel, "She the People: The Nineteenth Amendment, Sex Equality, Federalism, and the Family," *Harvard Law Review*, 115 (2002): 947–1045, n. 58

2. For various aspects of this argument, see Joan Hoff, *Law, Gender, and Injustice: A Legal History of U.S. Women* (New York, 1991), esp. 117–18; Joan R. Gundersen, "Independence, Citizenship, and the American Revolution, *Signs*, 13 (1987): 59–77; Carroll Smith-Rosenberg, "Dis-covering the Subject of the 'Great Constitutional Discussion,' 1786–1789," *Journal of American History*, 79 (1992): 841–73; Smith, *Civic Ideals*, 130–1; Sandra E. Van Burkleo, *"Belonging to the World": Women's Rights and American Constitutional Culture* (New York, 2001), 48–51; and Carole Pateman, *The Sexual Contract* (Stanford, 1988), whose critique of the compact theory of government has been deeply influential.

3. Richard B. Morris, *The Forging of the Union, 1781–1789* (New York, 1987), 190.

4. *The Records of the Federal Convention of 1787*, ed. Max Farrand (1911; repr., 4 vols, New Haven, 1966), I, 201.

5. Jan Lewis, " 'Of every age sex & condition': The Representation of Women in the Constitution," *Journal of the Early Republic*, 15 (1995): 364. This portion of my paper is drawn from this article.

6. In her comments, Carol Berkin asks whe ther the "Committee of Style" might have intentionally changed Wilson's wording, thinking it too radical. She asks whether further research might substantiate my claim that the Constitution indeed incorporates Wilson's inclusive construction of representation. Yet, as scholars in the field know, there are no minutes from the Committee of Style. The Convention met in secret, and its Journal, originally published in 1819, and later incorporated into Max Farrand's *Records of the Federal Convention*, is rudimentary. Several delegates kept notes on the debates (also incorporated into Farrand), but none of them

reports on the proceedings of the Committee. Berkin also asks for research into the private correspondence of the delegates. But these sources have been conveniently collected in Farrand's Appendix (Volume III of the *Records*) and James H. Hutson's 1987 *Supplement* to Farrand. They confirm that the Committee's alterations were stylistic, rather than substantive. (See, for example, III, 499). Finally, since the edited version of the Constitution came back to the delegates for their approval, had the Committee altered their meaning, they could have objected; the notes record no such objection. All the available evidence leads to the conclusion that Wilson's understanding of representation is incorporated in the Constitution. We may debate the implications of this conclusion but not the conclusion itself.

7. Ibid., 359–387; "Why the Constitution Includes Women," *Common-Place*, 2 (July 2002), http: //www.common-place.org/vol-02/no-04/roundtable/lewis.shtml.

8. Joan Wallach Scott, "Gender: A Useful Category of Analysis," in *Gender and the Politics of History* (New York, 1988), 28–50.

9. Joan B. Landes, *Women and the Public Sphere in the Age of the French Revolution* (Ithaca, N.Y., 1988), 171.

10. Let me note that I am not advocating an "originalist" approach to constitutional interpretation. That is, I do not believe that historians can recover perfectly the original intent of the framers of the Constitution, or that even if they could, constitutional interpretation should be based upon it. Assuming even that the original intent of the Founders could be discovered, subsequent constitutional interpretation and legislative action, not to mention more than two centuries of history, have (or should have) rendered the question of the Founders' intent largely moot for purposes of contemporary constitutional interpretation. For a cogent critique of originalism, see Jack N. Rakove, *Original Meanings: Politics and Ideas in the Making of the Constitution* (New York, 1996). Yet the underlying beliefs and assumptions of the men who wrote the Constitution remain of great interest to political theorists and historians, for they go to the heart of our questions about the nature of democracy.

11. Wilson took the language (including the three-fifths formula) from a Continental Congress resolution for apportioning expenses among the states. In 1775 John Dickinson proposed basing each state's levy on the total "Number of Inhabitants of every Age, Sex and Quality, except Indians not paying Taxes." Over the next several years, the delegates wrestled with the precise formula, in 1783 finally agreeing upon the three-fifths formula and substituting the phrase "age, sex and condition" for Dickinson's "Age, Sex and Quality." *Journals of the Continental Congress, 1774–1789*, ed. Worthington C. Ford, et al. (Washington, D.C., 1904–37), 5: 548, and 24: 223. In this context, the inclusion of the term "sex" was part of an elaborate dance between slave and nonslave states about whether slaves were to be taxed, and if so, how many of them; typically, slave women but not free women were taxed in slave states. Once Wilson imported this language into the Constitutional Convention's discussion about representation, the context changed the meaning significantly. Now the South would be rewarded, rather than penalized, for having slaves. And, in this new context, the inclusion of women served no practical purpose at all. The delegates recognized the implications for slavery—that implicitly, slaves were now

to be represented, by their owners, no less—but they did not mention at all the implications for women.

12. Edmund S. Morgan, *Inventing the People: The Rise of Popular Sovereignty in England and America* (New York, 1988), 13–14.

13. James Sullivan to Elbridge Gerry, May 6, 1776, *The Papers of John Adams*, ed. Robert J. Taylor, et. al. (Cambridge, MA: 1977–), 4: 212, n. 2.

14. Linda K. Kerber, "The Paradox of Women's Citizenship in the Early Republic: The Case of Martin vs. Massachusetts, 1805," *American Historical Review* 97 (1992): 349–78, quotations from 369, 371; see also her *No Constitutional Right to Be Ladies: Women and the Obligations of Citizenship* (Chapel Hill, N.C., 1998), 3–46.

15. Kerber, "Paradox of Women's Citizenship."

16. For similar arguments about the implicit radicalism of the Three Fifths Clause, see Jack N. Rakove, *Original Meanings: Politics and Ideas in the Making of the Constitution* (New York, 1996), 74; and Jan Lewis, "Rethinking the Three-Fifths Clause," Organization of American Historians, San Francisco, April 1997. As odious as this clause was, and as odious the purposes to which it was put, it rests on a radical notion of representation.

17. Rosemarie Zagarri, "The Rights of Man and Woman in Post-Revolutionary America," *William and Mary Quarterly*, 3d. Ser., no. 55 (1998): 203–30.

18. Freedom of religion, speech, the press, assembly, and petition all applied to women, as did the freedom from unreasonable search and seizure, the right to trial by jury, the right not to incriminate herself, and so on. The well-recognized but not constitutionally enumerated right of husbands and wives not to testify against each other provides an interesting exception or, to be more precise, amplification. Of course, constitutional interpretation has never been simple, and hence, the question of what "due process" means, or whether, as Justice Douglas wrote, there is a "penumbra" of rights, is quite complex. As Linda K. Kerber has noted, it is not so much the rights of citizenship that have been denied to women as the obligations, such as serving on juries and in the military. She has argued that it is the exemption of women from these obligations that has rendered them second-class citizens. See Kerber, *No Constitutional Right*.

19. Speaking in the most general terms, the concept of women's rights has appeared most threatening when it has been imagined to endanger the family. Consider, for example, Zagarri, 217–26. See also Kerber, "A Constitutional Right to be Treated Like Ladies: Women and the Obligations of Citizenship," in Linda K. Kerber, et. al., eds., *U.S. History as Women's History: New Feminist Essays* (Chapel Hill, N.C., 1995), 17–35; Kerber, "The Asymmetries of Citizenship," *Common-place* 2 (July 2002), http: //www.common-place.org/vol-02/no-04/roundtable/kerber.shtml; Siegel, "She the People," and Judith Resnik, " 'Naturally' Without Gender: Women, Jurisdiction, and the Federal Courts," *New York University Law Review* 66 (1991): 1682–1767. As both Siegel and Resnik point out, domestic relations law—which, obviously, governs women within the family—has historically been considered the province of the states, rather than the federal government, effectively preventing women from claiming the protection of the federal government. Moreover, federal

courts continue to assert as "natural" the differences between women and men and use those supposed differences to perpetuate what Kerber has recently called "the asymmetries of citizenship." For women as dependents, see Gundersen, "Independence, Citizenship, and the American Revolution."

20. John Adams to James Sullivan, May 26, 1776, in *Papers of John Adams*, L. H. Butterfield, et al., eds., *Adams Family Correspondence* (Cambridge, MA, 1963–), 4: 208–13.

21. Women's historians frequently conflate women's rights with the right to vote.

22. John Locke, *Two Treatises of Government* (1690), Peter Laslett, ed. (Cambridge, England, 1988), vol. 2, para. 87, p. 323. The literature on the Scottish Enlightenment is extensive. For its influence in America, begin with Morton White, *The Philosophy of the American Revolution* (New York, 1978); Garry Wills, *Inventing America: Jefferson's Declaration of Independence* (New York, 1978); and Henry S. May, *The Enlightenment in America* (New York, 1976).

23. See, for example, Locke, *Two Treatises*, para. 95, II: 330–1.

24. Thomas Paine, *Common Sense*, Isaac Kramnick, ed. (1776; London, 1976), 65.

25. James Wilson, *Lectures on Law*, in *The Works of James Wilson*, ed. Robert Green McCloskey, 2 vols. (Cambridge, MA, 1967), I: 86–7, 239.

26. Jürgen Habermas, *The Structural Transformation of the Public Sphere: An Inquiry into a Category of Bourgeois Society*, trans. Thomas Burger (Cambridge, MA, 1991. I have developed these ideas at greater length in "Of every age sex & condition."

27. Wilson, *Lectures on Law*, 1: 233. For humanitarianism, see Thomas L. Haskell, "Capitalism and the Origins of the Humanitarian Sensibility," parts 1 and 2, *The American Historical Review* 90 (1985): 339–61, 547–66.

28. *The Federalist*, ed. Jacob E. Cooke (Middletown, Conn., 1961), 88.

29. I have developed these ideas in "Politics and the Ambivalence of the Private Sphere: Women in Early Washington, D.C.," in Donald Kennon, ed., *A Republic for the Ages* (Charlottesville, Va., 122–51).

30. The point, it should be added, is not to exonerate liberals for barring women from government, but to recognize that, unlike classical republicans, they believed that human beings found their fulfillment and realized their potential in private life and the public sphere, rather than in government.

31. In 1866, when Elizabeth Cady Stanton, Susan B. Anthony, Antoinette Brown Blackwell, Lucy Stone, and a handful of other feminists petitioned Congress for universal suffrage, they noted that the Constitution "classes us as 'free people,' and counts us as *whole* persons in the basis for representation. " "A Petition for Universal Suffrage," National Archives, RG 233, copy at http: //ecssba.rutgers.edu/studies/petuniv.jpg.

CHAPTER 3

Declarations of Independence

Women and Divorce in the Early Republic

When Thomas Jefferson assessed the pros and cons of legitimating divorce shortly before the American Revolution, he came out firmly on the side of divorce. There could be problems, he conceded, with dividing marital assets, and although he assumed a man of any age could remarry with ease, he was concerned that a woman beyond a certain age might have difficulty finding a new partner. Still, he was convinced that the right of divorce would improve the status of women. In a world where the repudiation of a spouse had been a husband's prerogative, access to divorce, he asserted, would restore "to women their natural right of equality." That Jefferson envisioned divorce as a woman's remedy while representing a husband bent on blocking his wife's separate maintenance is not without some irony. Yet the natural rights language he used to support a woman's freedom to sever the bonds of matrimony presaged the rationale he would use for severing the bonds of empire. "No partnership," he declared in an argument that anticipated the Declaration of Independence, "can oblige continuance in contradiction to its end and design."[1]

The parallels between marriage and government in Jefferson's thinking are instructive in considering the legal status of women during the founding period. The sweeping legitimation of divorce in the wake of the Revolution presents a provocative alternative to the Constitution's silences on women. That is not to say that women were written out of the Constitution. As Jan Lewis has noted, white women were regarded by the founders not only as citizens who were fully entitled to representation but also as valued members of civil society. To include female inhabitants in apportioning representatives, she observes, constituted a significant departure from older formulas for representation. Slaves, by contrast, were encompassed in the three-fifths clause, and black men and women, both slave and free, enjoyed no comparable acceptance in civil society.[2]

Lewis's distinctions between gender and race, two categories often collapsed in discussions of the persons excluded from "We the people," are important. But although women were not excluded from the Constitution, they were clearly differentiated in it from men. The shifts in language from the gender-neutral "persons" to the distinctly masculine "he" indicate that the Constitution did not permit women to *be* representatives, and state constitutions with one brief exception did not permit women to *choose* representatives because women's relationship to the state was customarily mediated by their husbands. The marriage contract, then, with its provisions for coverture, which folded the wife's legal personality into that of her husband, was an integral part of the founders' conceptualization of white women's constitutional status. As Carole Pateman has argued, the story of the social contract, which is a story of freedom, represses the story of the marriage contract, or what she calls "the sexual contract," which is a story of subjection.[3]

Pateman's dazzling assault on liberal political theory has been at the forefront of a trend in feminist scholarship devoted to exposing the concealed subordination of women to the political fraternity of men. Such an approach to the early republic suggests that the men who wrote the words "We the people" into the nation's foundational text could create the illusion they were entering into a social contract that included women because they understood the degree to which the marriage contract would continue to empower them as men. Feminist critics of the Enlightenment, moreover, have marked out the late eighteenth century as a period in which sharp gender differentiation emerged, flourished, and laid the foundation for relegating women to the domestic sphere where they remained under the authority of husbands. Beneath the liberal rhetoric of individualism and contractualism, of freedom and consent, patriarchy, they argue, was in the process of being updated and hidden by becoming privatized.[4]

Divorce, however, provides a focal point for reconsidering the gendered implications of liberal values during the late eighteenth century. If the marriage contract that underpinned the social contract sustained conceptions of women's subordinate political status, how are we to read women's access to divorce? And how are we to understand the relationship between divorce and eighteenth-century political theory? Not without some qualifications in the story of women's concealed disempowerment. This essay aims to complicate sweeping feminist critiques of the social contract by assessing social contract theory in the context of the Revolution and the subsequent legitimation of divorce. I argue that in late-eighteenth-century America, the marriage contract instead of being concealed was openly present in political discourse, and I suggest that in providing for divorce in the wake of revolution, legislators were tentatively extending liberal political theory to the institution of marriage itself.

The legalization of divorce in the new nation was swift and widespread. There had been little interest in divorce before independence, and apart from in Puritan jurisdictions such as Connecticut, formal divorces were rare. In the United States, as in France, revolution was the handmaid of divorce. Concern with providing for divorce arose with the political turmoil of the 1770s and a Privy Council ruling against Pennsylvania in 1773 that designated "Acts of Divorce in the Plantations" as "either Improper or Unconstitutional." When divorce bills from New Hampshire and New Jersey were also disallowed, the Privy Council instructed colonial governors to void all future provincial divorces.[5] With independence those colonies that had been overruled by the Privy Council provided for divorce in new states statutes. Other states followed suit. By 1795 a disaffected spouse could put an end to a marriage in a local circuit court in the Northwest Territory.[6] By 1799 twelve states in addition to the Northwest Territory had recognized the right of divorce.[7]

The stunning nature of this transformation is best appreciated when balanced against late-eighteenth-century English practices. Fault divorce as we have come to call it in the age of no-fault was a legal option that departed significantly from the English parliamentary and ecclesiastical precedents on which it was based. In its gender-neutral approach to the fault, in the completeness of its dissolutions, and in the access it afforded litigants, American divorce diverged dramatically from its English roots. Indeed, from both a substantive and procedural perspective, divorce law in the early republic was light years beyond its English equivalent.

Clearly the Revolution played a role in reshaping the law of husband and wife. The right to end an adverse marital partnership was a direct byproduct of the frustration experienced under an adverse political partnership. At a tangible political level, then, it was independence that freed state legislatures to depart from English law. At a symbolic level, moreover, it was independence that provided them with a prototype for divorce and nowhere more than in its most celebrated text. Consider that in letting the facts be submitted to a candid world, the Declaration of Independence at once explained, decreed, and sanctified a divorce from the bonds of empire—and from the bonds of empire to the bonds of matrimony it was a short conceptual step. As Rousseau asserted in *The Social Contract*, families are the first models of political societies.[8] That common maxim of Western political theory acquired a new and expansive meaning in the American setting. The words "brethren," "consanguinity," and "kindred" in the Declaration not only exemplify the easy interchangeability of family and state in Enlightenment thinking but also mark their transfiguration. Severing the bonds of empire entailed the radical separation of two peoples who were as intimately related as the members of one family. That family, to paraphrase the end of the Declaration, was no more, and the two peoples, once knitted together as one, were to regard each other now as enemies in the war that was already under way. As this imagery suggests, the Revolution predisposed Americans to think of themselves in declaring independence as dissolving one family and, at the same time, as constituting another. The significance of that image is even greater than has been generally recognized. The Revolution not only killed the king, metaphorically speaking; it separated the family.

Although the Declaration conjures up a schism between male kinfolk, the image of the severed family could extend beyond filial and fraternal bonds. Like the Sons of Liberty, the warring brethren, and the founding fathers, husbands, and wives were prominent figures in the contemporary political imagination. Scholars exploring the centrality of consent in antipatriarchal representations of government have found that allusions to marriage only increased in the early republic as conjugal ties came to supplant filial ties in popular images of the state.[9] Of course the limits of consent in Anglo-American marriage law enabled marriage to serve as a conservative and stabilizing model for the new republic. Marriage, after all, was a public, prepackaged contract that was impervious to the wills of the contracting parties. To put it in political terms, you could say that a wife, having contracted for her ruler, was consigned to his rule for life. Americans of the post-Revolutionary era were not altogether comfortable with such an image, but neither were they prepared to abandon it completely. Both their discomfort with the traditional legal model of marriage and their reluctance to adopt a thoroughly contractual alternative illuminate the degree to which social contract theory intertwined with their perceptions of marriage and divorce.

In popular periodicals of the late eighteenth century the problem of defining the limits of consent pervaded analogies of state and familial power. Was consent a one-time thing to be given upon entering into the social contract and the marriage contract or could it be renegotiated? Tom Paine's construction of marriage as a loving and egalitarian partnership whose success hinged on the right to reject an unloving partner seemed to require perpetual consent. In his campaign for divorce in the *Pennsylvania Magazine*, Paine alleged that not one in a hundred unions bore any relationship "to happiness or common sense," and that without the freedom to end them, spouses simply doubled each other's misery "by way of revenge." Supporting his position with an innovative gloss on the union of Adam and Eve, the traditional source for the one-flesh doctrine and the indissolubility of marriage, Paine claimed that since God made us all in perfectly matched pairs, it was our duty to find the partner we were destined to have and to consummate the perfect partnership.[10]

Although few of Paine's contemporaries would advocate such an open-ended quest for Edenic happiness in which the sons of Adam and the daughters of Eve were perennially free to seek out the perfect partner, the theme of the perfect partnership was a popular one. As one writer noted in a neoclassical variation of the theme, Jupiter broke Androgyne, the perfect whole person, into two incomplete and unsatisfactory halves, leaving every man and woman thereafter with the need to find their other half. To be sure, this bifurcated, essentialist vision of marriage that rendered men and women so different from one another as to be tragically incomplete on their own illustrates that gender differentiation was a hallmark of the period. But in projecting a full complementarity between the sexes and investing women as well as men with the need to search for the perfect partner, the writer was framing marriage in intimate and egalitarian terms.[11]

Intimate and egalitarian constructions of the perfect partnership were countered by writers who framed marriage in the language of order and subordination. Marital advice was often rendered in a political idiom that imbued men with a potential for tyranny and women with a penchant for rebellion. Men, declared an essayist for the *Boston Magazine*, should not be tyrants to women, because tyrants produce rebels, and rebels when they prevail become tyrants themselves.[12] Contract was the basis for obedience as well as dissent, and according to popular columnists and essayists, men remained the rulers in the marriage contract, albeit with some modifications. Men should rule women, advised another essayist, but not "with a rod of iron."[13]

It is precisely because marriage in its consensual-but-indissoluble form stood as a far-reaching metaphor for the existing political order that it could serve as a convenient hedge against incipient political upheaval. A common analogy for the relationship between rulers and the ruled, it had been exploited by royalist defenders of Charles I to equate Parliament's rebellion with the ludicrous prospect of a wife divorcing her husband.[14] Gender was central to the effectiveness of the analogy. The figurative use of a divorce by a woman to signify the anarchic breaking of a sacred contract, thereby subjecting the action to ridicule, intimates that domestic rebellion enjoyed less credibility than political rebellion. But it also reveals parallels between the two rebellions in the grain of Anglo-American political thinking. The advent of the American Revolution turned the thrust of the analogy on its head, for just as divorce could serve to discountenance revolution, revolution, especially a successful one, could serve to legitimate divorce. Independence made the principle of indissoluble marriage more problematic.

The Declaration of Independence endowed the women and men of the Revolutionary era with an elegant and eloquent example of how to dissolve a sacred contract. Resting as it did on its purported proof of English despotism counterpoised against colonial innocence, its argument unfolded very much like that of a petitioner in a divorce suit who piled up and compounded the alleged causes regardless of the statutory grounds. Sacred contracts are not dissolved casually, and the long and arduous route to the decisive stage of separation, ran the argument in the Declaration, was determined by the respondent's cumulative and unremitting guilt. In unmistakably Lockean language, the Declaration averred that severing the bonds of empire was not undertaken for light and transient causes, but only in the wake of a long train of abuses and usurpations to which the petitioner had submitted patiently. So intense and sustained were these abuses—or so flagrant was the defendant's breach of contract—that it was not just the right but the duty of the petitioner to seek a formal dissolution of the union.[15] The juristic language, the familiar truths, the judicious caveats, the assembled facts—none of these could obviate the unbounded possibilities that lay at the heart of the Declaration, which was shaped so as to justify the right to begin all over again. What was written unequivocally into this other foundational text for the new nation was the principle of the second chance.

If fear of endless dissolutions and reconstitutions ran barely below the surface of post-Revolutionary culture, it was assuaged by a measure of faith in the justness of the Revolution. The connections between the political ideology of a just revolution and the liberating potential of a just divorce code were strong, durable, and rooted in the seventeenth century; the Revolution only served to strengthen them. It is no accident that John Milton wrote his divorce tracts in the midst of the English Civil War, tying the freedom to divorce to "all hope of true Reformation of the state."[16] Reference to the incompatibility between a contractarian theory of government and the principle of indissoluble marriage can be found also in John Locke's *Second Treatise of Government*.[17] In the wake of American independence, moreover, at least one wife expressed the belief that the Revolution had empowered her to reject a despotic husband. When Abigail Strong petitioned for a divorce in 1788, she reasoned that she was no longer under any obligation to submit to her husband's authority, since "even Kings may forfeit or discharge the allegiance of their Subjects."[18]

Despite Abigail Strong's ringing declaration of individual independence from the authority of her husband, it would be tendentious to argue that eighteenth-century legislators instituted divorce in order to liberate either women or men. Conservative impulses were at work here. Evidence suggests the immediate problem they were addressing was self-divorce. Couples were ending their unions anyway, and it remained for legislators to devise ways to end them legally. "Among the lowest ranks," complained a critic of self-divorce, "men part with their wives, and wives with their husbands, with as little delay or remorse as they would move from one boarding house to another."[19] A concern for marital legitimacy was undoubtedly a catalyst in legalizing divorce. Fear of unleashing a rash of casual dissolutions, moreover, was evident in both the wording of the statutes and the narrowness of the grounds. The preamble to the Pennsylvania divorce statute of 1785, for example, was a testament to the ideal of lifelong monogamy. It was "the design of marriage," declared the statute, "and the wish of the parties entering into that state that it should continue during their joint lives."[20] The preamble to the New York statute of 1787, which recognized the single ground of adultery, read more like a criminal statute on adultery than a civil statute on divorce. In accounting for the need for a divorce statute, it announced that "the laws at present in being within this state respecting adultery are very defective."[21]

Yet no matter how cautious or conservative the legislative impulse to institute divorce was, legislators were applying liberal political theory to the institution of marriage. It is precisely because they grasped the radical possibility of extending notions of consent beyond the initiation of the marriage contract that they were reluctant to call divorce what it was without exhortations and evasions. It is precisely because they sensed the liberating and even anarchic potential in the notion of the second chance that they could inscribe lifelong monogamy into the preamble of a state divorce statute. Breach of contract, after all, was a pliant idea, and fault could edge into no-fault if grounds were too casual or too numerous.

At issue, of course, is what effect did applying liberal political theory to the institution of marriage have on the status of women. Are we to read the suits women initiated against their husbands as acts of liberation? In most cases, the answer is probably no. We need to balance Jefferson's sanguine prediction about the effect of divorce on women's "natural right of equality" against the inequities of marriage and the legal system. Whatever the protections lifelong monogamy may have offered women, they were weakened with advent of divorce. As economic dependents confronting an all-male legal system that embraced the double standard, women suffered structural disadvantages at the hands of divorce law that are only too apparent. But we should not reject the liberation paradigm altogether. To the extent that suing for divorce was a legal option that depended on the voluntary, active, and even tenacious participation of female plaintiffs, it represented a reconfiguration of the marriage contract. The old common law legal fiction that husband and wife were one and the husband was the one could no longer hold quite the same authority once divorce challenged the male-dominated corporatism of marriage. In a world where the repudiation of a spouse had been a husband's prerogative, we should not dismiss the import of a woman's right to repudiate her husband in a court of law. One thing is certain: divorce by a woman no longer represented the anarchic breaking of a sacred contract.

The slender thread of autonomy embodied in a woman's right to divorce was not without political implications. As Lynn Hunt has argued with regard to the French Revolution, the liberal concepts animating a family law reform such as divorce made the political subjection of women more problematic.[22] Because liberalism and the political subjection of women did not go neatly together, maintaining them in tandem took an enormous amount of cultural work that often involved obscuring the ties between the social contract and the marriage contract. Much of that work took place in the nineteenth century when motherhood came to define the role of white, middle-class women, when the doctrine of separate spheres deterred women from the political arena, and when divorce came under serious moral attack. The Revolutionary generation, however, regularly connected the marriage contract and the social contract and exhibited a degree of consensus on the acceptance of divorce. That pattern may reflect a confidence in the stability of the gender system that was not possible by the Victorian era.

But even in the Victorian era, the ties between the social contract and the marriage contract were never fully obscured, especially by opponents of divorce. After the Civil War, when the Declaration of Independence had lost much of its authority as a foundational text, evangelical critics likened divorce to political rebellion, attributing its spread to "the infidel theory of the state" so popular at the time of the Revolution. [23] The so-called sexual contract whereby men, as Pateman has described it, arranged orderly access to women's bodies was never far from the surface of such critiques. If marriage is like other contracts, cautioned a California legislator opposing divorce, "so is the chastity of woman; so is her modesty, her delicacy, and her refinement." His warning against "relaxing rules which have fixed a high standard of female excellence"—a standard of excellence synonymous with female chastity—suggests the political challenge implicit in giving women the right of divorce.[24]

It remained for a prodivorce feminist such as Elizabeth Cady Stanton to render the challenge explicit by celebrating divorce for negating a husband's right of ownership in his wife's body. So much for patriarchal notions of chastity. It was logically consistent for a liberal of Stanton's stamp who could compare marriage to slavery to equate divorce with liberation.[25] Indeed, Stanton read divorce as a powerful challenge to the political subjection of women. When we consider the political implications of giving women access to divorce in the late eighteenth century and the controversy it sparked in the nineteenth century, the gendered implications of contract theory seem more complicated and less uniformly repressive than feminist critics have alleged. Killing the king was an idea that may have done little to enhance the political status of American women, but what both the opponents of divorce and Stanton understood was that once the family was separated, the world would never be the same.

NOTES

1. Jefferson's notes supporting divorce were developed in conjunction with the possible legislative divorce of Dr. James Blair of Williamsburg, who retained him as a lawyer-legislator in the event that Blair's wife, from whom he was separated, should insist on a separate maintenance. Blair died in December 1772 before Jefferson had an opportunity to try out his arguments. See Frank L. Dewey, "Thomas Jefferson's Notes on Divorce," *William and Mary Quarterly* 39 (1982): 212–23; citations on 218–219. On divorce and the status of women, see also Nancy F. Cott, "Divorce and the Changing Status of Women in Eighteenth-Century Massachusetts, *William and Mary Quarterly* 33 (1976): 586–614.

2. Jan Lewis, " 'Of Every Age Sex & Condition': The Representation of Women in the Constitution," *Journal of the Early Republic* 15 (1995): 359–87.

3. Carole Pateman, *The Sexual Contract* (Stanford: Stanford University Press, 1988), 1–18. On the links between marriage and political theory, see also Nancy Cott, *Public Vows: A History of Marriage and the Nation* (Cambridge: Harvard University Press, 2000).

4. On feminist critiques of the French Enlightenment, see especially Joan Landes, *Women and the Public Sphere in the Age of the French Revolution* (Ithaca, N.Y.: Cornell University Press, 1988) and Lieselotte Steinbrugge, *The Moral Sex: Women's Nature in the French Enlightenment*, trans. Pamela E. Selwyn (New York: Oxford University Press, 1995). On the United States, see Carroll Smith-Rosenberg, "Discovering the Subject of 'The Great Constitutional Discussion,' 1786–1789," *Journal of American History* 79 (1992): 349–78.

5. William Renwick Riddell, "Legislative Divorce in Colonial Pennsylvania," *Pennsylvania Magazine of History and Biography* 57 (1933): 175–80; Roderick Phillips, *Putting Asunder: A History of Divorce in Western Society* (New York: Cambridge University Press, 1988), 149–50.

6. *Laws of the Northwest Territory, 1788–1800*, ed. Theodore Calvin Pease (Springfield, Ill.: Trustees of the Illinois State Historical Library, 1925), 258–59.

7. On the acceptance and legalization of divorce in the early republic, see Norma Basch, *Framing American Divorce: From the Revolutionary Generation to the Victorians* (Berkeley: University of California Press, 1999), 19–42.

8. Jean Jaques Rousseau, *The Social Contract* (1762), trans. and ed. D. G. H. Cole (New York: E. P. Dutton, 1950), 4–5.

9. See especially Jan Lewis, "The Republican Wife: Virtue and Seduction in the Early Republic," *William and Mary Quarterly* 44 (1987): 689–721, and Jay Fliegelman, *Prodigals and Pilgrims: The American Revolution Against Patriarchal Authority* (New York: Cambridge University Press, 1982). Other explorations of the familial paradigm include Winthrop D. Jordan, "Familial Politics: Thomas Paine and the Killing of the King, 1776," *Journal of American* History 60 (1973): 294–308; Melvin Yazawa, *From Colonies to Commonwealth: Familial Ideology and the Beginnings of the American Republic* (Baltimore: Johns Hopkins University Press, 1985); and Cynthia S. Jordan, "Old Words in New Circumstances: Language and Leadership in Post-Revolutionary America," *American Quarterly* 40 (1988): 491–521.

10. [Thomas Paine], "Reflection on Unhappy Marriages," *Pennsylvania Magazine* (June 1775): 264–65.

11. "On Marriage," *The General Magazine and Impartial Review of Knowledge and Entertainment* (July 1778): 41–45.

12. "Essay on Love and Marriage," *Boston Magazine* (November 1783): 15–17.

13. "The Unreasonableness of the Law in Regard to Wives," *Columbian Magazine* (May 1788): 243–46.

14. Henry Ferne, *Conscience Satisfied that there is No Warrant for the Armes Taken up by Subjects* (Oxford, 1643), 12, cited in Phillips, *Putting Asunder*, 117. See also Mary Lyndon Shanley, "Marriage Contract and Social Contract in Seventeenth-Century English Thought," *Western Political Quarterly* 32 (1979): 79–81; and Gordon Schocket, *Patriarchalism in Political Thought* (New York: Basic Books, 1975).

15. Breach of contract is not the only legal construction that suggests parallels between declaring independence and justifying divorce. Equity was another, and it depicts the relationship between the governed and their governors as a trusteeship that has been violated. For emphasis on the protective, discretionary type of justice meted out by a court of chancery, see John W. Gough, *The Social Contract: A Critical Study of Its Development* (Oxford: Clarendon Press, 1957); and Peter Charles Hoffer, *The Law's Conscience: Equitable Constitutionalism in America* (Chapel Hill: University of North Carolina Press, 1990), 72.

16. John Milton, *Doctrine and Discipline of Divorce*, 2d. ed. (London, 1644), 3–4.

17. John Locke, *Two Treatises of Government* (1690), ed. Peter Laslett (Cambridge: Cambridge University Press, 1963), 339.

18. Cited in Sheldon B. Cohen, "To Part of the Word Unknown: The Circumstances of Divorce in Connecticut, 1750–1787," *Canadian Review of American Studies* 11 (1980): 289.

19. "Selling of Wives," *Mirror of Taste* 2 (1810): 432–34.

20. Cited in Thomas Meehan, "Not Made out of Levity," *Pennsylvania Magazine of History and Biography* 92 (1968): 442.

21. *Laws of New York* 1787, chap. 69.

22. Lynn Hunt, *The Family Romance of the French Revolution* (Berkeley: University of California Press, 1992), 201–4.

23. On the "infidel theory of the state," see Rev. Henry Loomis Jr., "Divorce Legislation in Connecticut," *New Englander* 25 (1866): 436.

24. Elcan Heydenfeldt, *California Senate and Assembly Journals, 1851*, doc. [M], 656–57.

25. See especially Stanton, "Speech to the McFarland-Richardson Protest Meeting," in *Elizabeth Cady Stanton, Susan B. Anthony: Correspondence, Writings, Speeches*, ed. Ellen Carol DuBois (New York: Schocken Books, 1981), 127–28; and Elizabeth Clark, "Matrimonial Bonds: Slavery and Divorce in Nineteenth-Century America," *Law and History Review* 8 (1990): 30–54.

CHAPTER 4

The Explanation Lies in Property

Gender and Its Connection to Economic Considerations

In two previous essays in this volume, Norma Basch and Jan Lewis remind us that there are still rich veins to be mined in the field of early American women's history—and scores of questions to be asked about America's "sacred texts" that scholars blind to gender have failed to ask.

Basch, in her chapter "Declarations of Independence: Women and Divorce in the Early Republic," clarifies for the reader why virtually every minority or marginalized group in America has turned to the Declaration of Independence, rather than to the Constitution, for the vocabulary of promise and the commitment to egalitarian principles upon which to build their case for inclusion. Although the primary purpose of the Declaration was to justify revolution by chronicling longstanding, persistent abuses of power and attacks on natural rights, Basch notes that the Declaration's subtext, if you will, is this: people can have a second chance, they can begin again, mistakes can be corrected, things can be put right—and indeed *must* be put right. In this positive assertion lies an implicit call for action—steps taken to restore the rights that have been eroded or to secure rights that have been denied. In this sense, while the Declaration does not compel social reforms, it provides reform a language of legitimation.

As Basch shows, the reform of the divorce laws drew upon this language— and upon the analogy between the colonists' right to end an adverse political partnership and a woman's right to end an adverse marital partnership. In other words, Basch argues, the colonial divorce from England became the prototype for the divorce of wife from husband. Even in the marriage contract, reformers argued, there must be "limits of consent"—although, as in the relationship of mother country and colonies, there must be irrefutable evidence of abuse before those limits were met. Women such as Abigail Strong grasped the power of the analogy when in 1788 she compared her release from obedience to her husband to the release of subjects when a king forfeited his right to their allegiance.[1]

Basch is not arguing, of course, that courts and legislatures were eager to liberate women from subordination in marriage or to create autonomous citizens where once there were *femes covert*. In fact, she acknowledges that divorce reform was largely an effort by legislators to bring under their control an alarming trend toward self-divorce spreading through postwar society. She is suggesting, however, that the way in which the discussion of divorce was framed owed much to this analogy to the "limits of consent" articulated in the Declaration of Independence, as well as to the reality of the revolution in asserting those limits.

This is an important point. But I think that it begs for a closer look at context. I raise the following questions not so much to challenge Basch's ultimate position but to suggest how many related research projects such a position might spark. First, there is the matter of the several colonial laws reforming divorce that *precede* the Revolution [and the Declaration] and that were disallowed by the British government.[2] What motivated these efforts to address divorce? How was the discussion framed? What justifications did these colonial legislators offer? And what problems were they attempting to deal with? Colonial society, it is true, rarely allowed absolute divorce, but separation of bed and board was commonly granted in most colonies. What would call this solution into question in the prerevolutionary years?

Secondly, how did the self-divorce of the postwar period differ from the common colonial practice of simple desertion? Colonial governments did not take the desertion problem lightly, for in a society where a man or woman could effectively end a marriage simply by moving to another colony, the fallout of desertion included bigamy and the burden of public assistance to abandoned wives and children. If the problems were as pressing in, for example, the 1680s as they were in the 1790s—why was absolute divorce not considered by seventeenth-century legislators?

I suspect the problems or consequences that troubled postrevolutionary legislators were different. And this leads me to ask: Do we know who stood to benefit from absolute divorce in American society after, say, the 1760s? That is, are there parties *outside* the marriage contract who might press for divorce reform by the 1770s? To answer this question, we might want to consider the alleged reform of dower rights in states such as Pennsylvania, where creditors pressed for the right to draw on a man's full estate after his death instead of exempting the widow's third.[3] The sacred nature of the marriage contract may have been weakened by more than the ideology of the Declaration; it was being eroded by an increase in borrowing, in risky investments, in shifts to business rather than land ownership—and in the growing power of creditors to demand marital inheritance reforms. Creditors wanted to be certain they could recoup what was owed to them; dower stood in the way. Certainly an ambiguous divorce, that is, a self-divorce, would stand in the way as well. What would happen if a woman who did not live with the deceased suddenly appeared to claim her dower? If she was not legally separated, if she was not legally *divorced*—wasn't her claim valid? Creditors, business partners—men of the rapidly expanding market economy—had some stake in clarifying, codifying, and regularizing the dissolution of a marriage. In short, I wonder if, although marriage may have been becoming more privatized, the end of marriage was becoming a more public concern.

Jan Lewis, in her chapter "Representation of Women in the Constitution," turns our attention to the Constitution—and to the alleged silence of that document on women. Whether scholars hold that this silence was accidental or intentional, they have been in general agreement as to its existence. Lewis challenges this notion—and draws our attention to a passage in the Constitution that few of us have noted before. Setting the scene artfully, she gives us the Pennsylvania conservative James Wilson, who rises to suggest that representation in the national legislature be "in proportion to the whole number of white & other free Citizens & inhabitants of every age sex & condition including those bound to servitude for a term of years and three fifths of all other persons not comprehended in the foregoing description, except Indians not paying taxes, in each state."[4] In essence: the three-fifths compromise is born as a formula for representation.

The Committee on Style altered—perhaps simply condensed—Wilson's phrasing. Gone was the delineation, "white & other free . . . of every age sex & condition"; instead, they wrote into Article I, section 2 "in proportion to the whole number of free persons, including those bound to service." But Lewis argues that if the term "women" wound up on the cutting room floor, the group "women" is definitely incorporated into the category "free persons." If this is so, she continues, then in every place that the Constitution uses the term "person" or "persons" women must be considered implicitly included. If Lewis is correct, we must discard our older assumptions that the Constitution does not concern itself with women. We must stop citing it as an example of a sacred text "silent" on gender and instead analyze it as a revolutionary text that deals with both women and men as "persons."

Lewis builds an argument for the comparative radicalism of the U.S. Constitution in this regard, citing one state's conservatism in a related case to make her point. James Sullivan did not attend the Constitutional Convention but, while serving as Massachusetts attorney general, he articulated liberal views on the relationship of women to the state consonant with those of James Wilson.[5] The circumstances are these: an heir to a Loyalist matron sues the state for restitution of his mother's property, confiscated during the Revolution. As a *feme covert*, argues the heir, his mother owed her loyalty to her husband not to any government—she had to leave the country and abandon her property if her husband demanded it. Sullivan defends the seizure, arguing that a Loyalist matron—and we assume any married woman—had her own political relationship to the state as a *citizen*. He concedes a hierarchy among citizens, but insists that women, infants, and even the insane are members of the body politic. Loyalism was treason. A traitor's land could be confiscated. The seizure was legal. The Massachusetts courts disagreed, and they ordered the restoration of the confiscated lands to the heirs. Thus, argues Lewis, an older patriarchal notion was upheld in Massachusetts, but the more radical inclusion of women as citizens—or at least as "persons" to be counted in representation—is victorious in the U.S. Constitution.

Lewis is not arguing that this inclusion insured women the privileges of full political citizenship in 1787. She is arguing that the compact theory of government—essentially Locke's theory that legitimate government ultimately rests on individual consent— no longer allowed for a clear-cut exclusion of women from the body politic. Wilson appears to recognize this when he lists women—white women—among those to be numbered as citizens. Sullivan seems to realize the complicated nature of women's inclusion when he observes that they are citizens, even if their citizenship is inferior or incomplete *relative to others.*

Much hinges, it seems to me, on whether Wilson's understanding of the implications of the compact theory of government was sustained in the Constitution. Did the Committee on Style assume this incorporation of women and simply employ an economy of language when they wrote "persons" rather than "inhabitants of every age sex & condition," or, did the alteration in the text reflect a judgment that Wilson had been too generous or too radical in his inclusion of women—much as the courts rejected Sullivan's argument in the confiscation case? Lewis does not address this question in her essay, but clearly the next step is to ask: Is there documentation from the committee discussions themselves that might shed light on this question? Perhaps there were no records kept. Will the private correspondence of the committee members confirm that they were incorporating women into "persons"? Until research is done to test the theory that Wilson's intent remained though his words were changed, Lewis's provocative assumption that the committee *did* incorporate women into the category "persons" remains only an assumption.

Finally, even if such further intentions in the founding debates can be un-covered, and women were being considered "free persons" and even "citi-zens" in some sense, Lewis does not directly address the issue that since an-cient times citizenship has been divided into "active" (full) and "passive" (incomplete) categories. Whereas slaves were for the most part considered "outside" the body politic, as far back as Aristotle (and throughout the me-dieval and the early modern period) women were characteristically viewed as members of the political state in a *passive* sense—as part of the free popula-tion.[6] Women were, after all, considered a part of the Greek, German, Dutch, etc., nations. This was particularly so when a body count was need-ed, or when the issue was heirs, or, again, when weighty property ownership issues were at stake. But this is not full citizenship in the active sense, which (at least in a democracy or republic) takes place between political equals. The full citizen alone—from Aristotle until Madison—was considered he who was capable of deliberating about his own, as well as the public, good, whether directly (by his own vote) in a democracy or indirectly (via the choice of representatives) in a republic. Thus the full citizen alone was ca-pable of a *genuine* representation—a point Lewis herself concedes by the end of her paper.

This suggests, however, that for the most part, not just Lewis, but the whole tradition equivocates between different senses of the terms "person," "citizen," and "representation." Nothing in the original constitutional debates—or even in Wilson's unabridged words—indicate that women were intended to be rep-resented in the U.S. Constitution as individuals *in their own right*—inde-pendently of their husbands or fathers, as beings capable of interpreting and representing their own or the public good, or (in the words of John Rawls) as self-interpreting sources of claims—in short, as full "citizens" worthy of self-representation. Even today, we might note, over two hundred years later, women in the United States have still not attained to the position whereby they genuinely *represent themselves*. That is, the demand gaining momentum in many other advanced industrial countries—the demand that at least 50 percent of the seats in congress be held by women—seems to hold little per-suasive force on this side of the ocean.[7]

The essays by Basch and Lewis are important contributions to women's his-tory and political theory. Together, they open up new paths of inquiry, new re-search trajectories. By their insistence that gender issues must be addressed even in arenas once considered bastions of male exclusivity, they do more than add to the growing body of historical scholarship on women. They add depth and dimension to traditional topics and they complicate stories we once thought had been fully told.

NOTES

1. As discussed in Basch (chapter. 3, this volume).

2. For example, the Pennsylvania assembly attempted to grant divorces by private bill, a reform that was disallowed by the British Parliament in 1773; see the discussion in Marylynn Salmon's *"Women and the Law of Property in Early America* (Chapel Hill: University of North Carolina Press, 1986).

3. See the discussion of dower rights in chapter 7, Salmon, *Women and the Law of Property,* 141–84.

4. *The Records of the Federal Convention of 1787,* ed. Max Farrand (1911; repr., 4 vols., New Haven: Yale University Press, 1967), 1:201. See also Lewis's discussion (chapter 2, this volume).

5. As discussed in Lewis, ibid.

6. See, for instance, Aristotle's *Politics,* 1260b, 22 where women are mentioned as comprising half the *polis.* This and the following point are due to discussion with Sibyl Schwarzenbach.

7. In many of the Nordic countries (led by Sweden), for instance, the percentage of legislative seats won by women hovers around 36–43 percent, and France has recently passed a law whereby at least 50 percent of candidates for public office by the various parties must be women. Indeed, when one looks at the statistics, the U.S. fairs among *the worst* of all advanced nations in terms of the self-representation of women. In 2002, for instance, out of the top twenty-six democratic countries, and in terms of the percentage of legislative seats won by women, Britain and the United States ranked only seventeenth and eighteenth, respectively (just above Portugal and Ireland). One of the most interesting examples in this respect is Switzerland where women only received the vote in 1971, yet by now hold 21 percent of the legislative seats (compared to only 13 percent in the U.S. after more than eighty years!). Many scholars account for this American backwardness—not merely by reference to the recent American aversion to "affirmative action"—but by reference to the European systems of proportional representation that, unlike our (and Britain's) winner-take-all systems, are evincing themselves as far more women (as well as minority) friendly. See, for example, the discussion in Douglas J. Amy, *Real Choices/New Voices: The Case for Proportional Representation Elections in the United States* (New York: Columbia University Press, 1993), 99ff. For the most recent statistics on the self-representation of women, see http://accuratedemocracy.com/d_dataw.htm.

Reconstruction

Peggy Cooper Davis

CHAPTER 5

Women, Bondage, and the Reconstructed Constitution

I have been working for more than ten years to promote the idea of a Reconstructed Constitution: an Antislavery Constitution.

It is odd that the idea of a reconstructed, antislavery constitution needs a promoter. We all know that the Constitution of the United States was amended during Reconstruction and amended in transformative ways. Universal citizenship was established; the federal government became guarantor of fundamental civil rights; slavery was forbidden; and the rights of free people were specified. It is a short step from these truths to say that the constitution was reconstructed according to the values of antislavery: Every human being on United States soil was recognized as holding the rights—always tempered by social duties—to be self-defining, morally autonomous, and active in the construction of social meaning.

Still, the late-nineteenth-century repudiation of Reconstruction took in its wake respect for the values upon which this nation was rebuilt after the Civil War. The people—most of whom were African American or female (or both)—who struggled successfully to constitutionalize antislavery interpretations of citizenship and human rights were erased from constitutional history, and the idea—and the ideals—of a reconstructed, antislavery constitution were lost to our national consciousness. If we value the idea—and the ideals—we must revive them.

My project here is an aspect of my broader project. It is to recall, and perhaps to revive, an African American feminist coalition that was vibrant during the antislavery years. It was a coalition grounded in a common respect for human dignity and human rights. It consisted of antislavery activists working to draw out, and enact in their own lives, the principles that underlay their opposition to enslavement. I refer to these principles as antislavery principles, but the phrase should be understood to encompass opposition to subordination in many forms and on many grounds. Especially on grounds of race and gender.

I have said that antislavery principles were both drawn out and enacted in the lives of antislavery people. It is important that they were acted out and not simply thought, written, or spoken. We have a tendency to separate thought and action. The people I want to recall and celebrate were admirable for many reasons and especially admirable for their ability to test thoughts in action and to put their principles into practice. When we examine these principles, we will always see, as Frederick Douglass saw, that antislavery meetings were the best schools in our nation. Then and thereafter. They taught a conception of human dignity and citizenship that informed the drafting of the Reconstruction Amendments and drew a blueprint for constitutional democracy in a diverse and freedom-loving society.

We can see in microcosm the principles of human entitlement and mutual respect that were nurtured—and lived out—in the antislavery and feminist movements if we consider the stances these movements took with respect to marriage. Moreover, looking separately at feminist and antislavery responses to nineteenth-century marriage laws, we can see how the effort to protect rights of self-determination played out differently in the face of different forms of subordination, in each case enriching the antislavery movement's fundamental human rights tenets. For feminists, respect for human dignity and self-determination were equally incompatible with slavery and with patriarchal marriage. For antislavery advocates—a phrase that includes, of course, virtually all enslaved people as well as free people seeking slavery's end—respect for human dignity and self-determination required that people be entitled to enter chosen marriages that the state would honor and protect. For many feminists and antislavery advocates, respect for human dignity and self-determination required that state-sanctioned marriage be critiqued, and abandoned or remade on more egalitarian and less statist terms.

The following section describes the feminist critique of marriage that emerged as women and men put their antislavery beliefs to practice in their daily lives. The next section describes the antislavery understanding of marriage that emerged as African Americans enacted freedom during and immediately after the Civil War. The final section asks what lessons this history holds for our times.

"The First Step from Slavery": Patriarchal Marriage as the Antithesis of Freedom

The antislavery movement was galvanized by a collective sense of outrage at slavery's denial of the marriage bond. The forced separation of spouses, the denial of marriage choice, the failure to recognize marriage among the enslaved, and slaveholders' sexual exploitation of enslaved people for pleasure and profit drew in sharp relief the implications of human bondage. If, as antislavery advocates believed, every human being had a right to make life-defining moral and affiliational choices and to count as a member of the body politic, then it was wrong for a community to dictate, force, or deny human partnerships or to fail to recognize human families. Slavery was wrong for many reasons, but its wrongs were aptly symbolized by the single wrong of denying enslaved people the right to form partnerships and families that the community would honor. The right to marry was therefore a principal tenet of the antislavery movement.

But the right to marry in nineteenth-century America was not an unqualified benefit. Marriage laws in the United States imposed patriarchal norms on human partnerships as a condition of legal recognition. By giving men control of most of the couple's property, authority as their wives' legal representatives, freedom to discipline their wives, effective control of both partners' domicile, more secure custodial rights in the couple's children, and a variety of other presumed advantages, the law recognized and honored marriage, not as an attribute of full citizenship and membership in the human family but as an instantiation of the social power of men and the subordination of women.

At the intersection of the feminist and antislavery movements, a courageous, influential initiative directly challenged the subordinating principles that defined nineteenth century marriage. In a deep sense, the initiative grew out of the abolitionist idea that human beings must have a significant measure of freedom in making life-defining choices. But it responded more conspicuously to the abolitionist and feminist idea that human beings should not be subordinated on the basis of race or gender. In a wave of Antislavery marriages, women and men claimed legal recognition as partners while declaring their defiance of the laws and norms that had made customary marriage an enslavement rather than a partnership.

To my knowledge, the first of these marriages in defiance of patriarchal marriage norms occurred in 1832 when the son and daughter-in-law of Robert Owen, founder of the utopian community of New Harmony, were wed in a service that included a denunciation of marriage laws of the day. Six years later the practice of beginning a marriage while expressly rejecting many of the legal definitions of marriage was given prominence as Angelina Grimké and Theodore Weld took vows in a ceremony witnessed by many of the most outstanding antislavery activists in the United States. Grimké, an indefatigable antislavery and feminist organizer, writer, and lecturer, was among the best-known women in America. Weld was also a well-known activist. He believed strongly in women's rights, but he thought the causes of abolition and women's rights were secondary to and derivative of a commitment to "the grand principle for which we struggle . . . HUMAN RIGHTS."[1]

Both Grimké and Weld were "identified with powerful moral movements: abolition, temperance, woman's rights, the whole great battle with 'factitious life.' "[2] Keenly aware of the ridicule and hostility with which activist women were regarded, the couple were determined to set an example by proving that strong and independent minds could find harmony in marriage. The abolitionist community was thrilled by the prospect, and the Philadelphia wedding was timed to fall between the annual convention of the American Antislavery Society and the annual convention of Antislavery Women. It was an orthodox abolitionist gathering with an integrated guest list including antislavery leaders William Lloyd Garrison, Maria Weston Chapman, Abby Kelley, Henry C. Wright, Henry B. Stanton, and Gerrit Smith. A wedding cake was baked "by a colored baker who used nothing but 'free sugar' " ; and black and white clergy offered prayers.[3] In a letter to a friend Maria Chapman described the occasion as "an abolitionist wedding."[4] The couple rejected traditional vows, uttering "such [words] as the Lord gave them at the moment."[5] Weld gave voice to his human rights commitments as well as to his love of Grimké as he condemned the "unrighteous power vested in a husband by the laws of the United States [and] abjured all authority save the influence which love would give to them over each other." Grimké promised to love and honor her spouse, carefully omitting the word "obey."[6]

"Abolitionist weddings" proliferated. When Abby Kelley and Stephen Foster married in 1845, they followed Quaker tradition and drew up their own wedding certificate, documenting "a matrimonial connection in accordance with the divine law of Marriage" and omitting any reference to the laws of the state (Massachusetts) in which they were wed.[7] To the fifty guests Foster "gave . . . his views relating to marriage" and Kelley spoke, not of a duty of obedience and domestic concern but "of her anti-slavery life, its toil and sacrifice."[8] Harriet Taylor, who followed developments in the American women's movement, and John Stuart Mill, who worked with her in formulating *The Subjection of Women*, included a denunciation of governing marriage laws when they married in England in 1851. And it is likely that abolitionist activists Lizzy Hitchcock and Ben Jones, who attended the Kelley-Foster wedding, spoke at their own wedding shortly thereafter to the dedicated and egalitarian life they intended to lead.

The most detailed surviving account of a marriage in defiance of sovereign authority is that of the courtship and marriage of Henry Blackwell and Lucy Stone. When their courtship began in 1853, Stone was a thirty-four-year-old feminist and antislavery activist, the first Massachusetts woman to have received a Bachelor of Arts degree. Although she regarded single life as "unnatural," she had vowed "not to be married ever." "I have not yet seen the person whom I have the slightest wish to marry," she wrote to a friend, "and if I had, it will take longer than my lifetime for the obstacles to be removed which are in the way of a married woman having any being of her own."[9] We do not know Stone's views with respect to same-sex partnership. Blackwell was an entrepreneur in his late twenties, ideologically committed to feminist and abolitionist causes but principally, although somewhat ambivalently, engaged in a quest for financial security. Stone's doubts about marrying Blackwell were overcome between the spring of 1853 and the spring of 1855, largely through the couple's correspondence, for she, based in Massachusetts, traveled so much as an antislavery lecturer that Blackwell imagined she was "born a locomotive,"[10] and he, based in Ohio, also traveled often, both for antislavery causes and in connection with land speculation and other business ventures.

Although Stone consistently discouraged talk of marriage, Blackwell regularly returned to the subject in his letters. He set forth his ideals and aspirations:

> My idea of the relation involves no sacrifice of individuality but its perfection—no limitation of the career of one, or both but its extension. . . . Perfect *equality* in this relationship . . . I would have—but it should be the equality of Progress, of Development, not of Decay. If both parties cannot study more, think more, feel more, talk more & work more than they could alone, I will remain an old bachelor & adopt a Newfoundland dog or a terrier as an object of affection.[11]

He announced himself liberated from prevailing sexist opinions:

> [A male friend and I] often talk on this question of marriage—he differs from me. He thinks it is dangerous for two persons of strong mind to marry. . . . He laughs at me for my too high ideal [of equality in marriage]. . . . Now I have felt for years the most imperious necessity for marriage. . . . But when it comes to the point, I find that I *cannot* forgo my ideal. Equality with me is a passion. I dislike equally to assume, or to endure authority.[12]

Blackwell then proposed a defiant stance against the laws and customs that enforced female subordination in marriage. Tellingly, his proposal was couched as a stance against *slavery*. He believed that no person should abide, at the hands of a master or of a government—subordination that precludes autonomous moral functioning or inhibits life's central affiliative choices. He therefore equated the slave system, under which life partnerships were subject to the will and economic interests of masters, and patriarchal marriage laws, under which life partnerships were constrained to take traditional, but morally unacceptable, forms. People must form families, he argued, in defiance of both. Stone resisted forming a marriage in accordance with patriarchal laws, but Blackwell wrote:

> Give me a *free* man—he can never be made a slave. Give me a free woman—she never can be made one either. Surely you enormously exaggerate the scope & force of *external* laws at the expense of *internal* power when you lay such frightful & hopeless stress upon a few paltry enactments. The great evil I think, in our institutions lies *here*—that they so crush the spirit out of people that they do *not make themselves free* . . . The first step from slavery is to seek freedom for *ourselves* . . . the next is to seek it for others & for all.[13]

And he promised a life of mutual encouragement in noble causes:

> I do not want you to forego *one sentiment* of independence, nor one attribute of *personality*. I want only to help you, as best I can, in achieving a really noble & *symmetrical* Life. I want you also to *help me* to do the same. We *can help* each other I am sure not merely as friends—not as lovers, but as husband & wife.[14]

Nonetheless, Stone reported that she experienced pain "at the idea of being placed in the *legal* position of wife."[15] Blackwell persisted, making specific proposals to circumvent laws by which the husband controlled marital property and family domicile, had no obligation to seek consent for sexual intimacy, and was the presumptive custodian of the children:

> "As to your property dear—it will be necessary . . . to settle all your *personal* property on yourself. . . . [T]he best way will be to put it into the hands of trustees for your benefit. . . . Then we will engage to *share earnings* on both sides—you to get half of mine & I half of yours, so long as we live together. If we ever separate, each to relinquish all claim to the others subsequent earnings & each to take half the children, you having the choice. If separation is from wrong conduct—the right to control chil-

dren to be decided by arbitrators—one each selected by you & me & one more selected by them. In case of death either party may will his or her property to whomsoever he pleases unless there are children, in which case enough to support & educate them, shall be reserved.

In case of death after separation, unless gross misconduct on either part has been the cause—the survivor takes the children previously held by the other partner & becomes their guardian—otherwise—the deceased partner shall have a guardian nominated by him or her in the will. Neither partner shall be liable for any debts contracted & liabilities incurred by the other partner previous to marriage—nor (except for maintenance if necessary) shall have any claim to property acquired by the other partner previous to marriage, nor shall the private property of either partner be liable for debts of the other. You shall choose when, where & how often you shall become a mother. Neither partner shall attempt to fix the residence, employment or habits of the other—nor shall either partner feel bound to live together any longer than is agreeable to both. All earnings *subsequent* to marriage during its harmonious continuance to be liable for family expenses equally, but all *surplus* of joint earnings to be annually divided & placed to the credit of each.[16]

When Stone eventually agreed to marry, the couple negotiated the terms of the "protest" that they would announce at their wedding. She admitted, "I shall rejoice as much as you, dearest, when we can fully share our life," but insisted that "[t]he promise to love, honor &c &c, I shall never make. Those things are dependent upon the qualities that can inspire them, and if they cease[,] all promises are vain."[17]

The wedding was intended as a public, political act. It featured a protest, conceived as a statement that the couple would not "endorse the present unjust laws, but by making our public & outside *contract*, enter a practical & efficient protest against them, the only protest which can be understood & *imitated*."[18] They drafted their words with care and in consultation with abolitionist colleagues, and published them in *The Worcester Spy* and *The Liberator*. This is what Blackwell read as the couple stood together before their vows:

While acknowledging our mutual affection by publicly assuming the relationship of husband and wife, yet in justice to ourselves and a great principle, we deem it a duty to declare that this act on our part implies no sanction of, nor promise of voluntary obedience to such of the present laws of marriage, as refuse to recognize the wife as an independent,

rational being, while they confer upon the husband an injurious and unnatural superiority, investing him with legal powers which no honorable
man would exercise, and which no man should possess. We protest especially against the laws which give to the husband:

1. The custody of the wife's person.

2. The exclusive control and guardianship of their children.

3. The sole ownership of her personal property, and use of her real estate, unless previously settled upon her, or placed in the hands of trustees
as in the case of minors, lunatics, and idiots.

4. The absolute right to the product of her industry.

5. Also against laws which give to the widower so much larger and
more permanent an interest in the property of his deceased wife, than
they give to the widow in that of the deceased husband.

6. Finally, against the whole system by which "the legal existence of
the wife is suspended during marriage," so that in most States, she neither
has a legal part in the choice of her residence, nor can she make a will,
nor sue or be sued in her own name, nor inherit property.

We believe that personal independence and equal human rights can
never be forfeited, except for crime; that marriage should be an equal and
permanent partnership, and so recognized by law; that until it is so recognized, married partners should provide against the radical injustice of
present laws, by every means within their power.

We believe that where domestic difficulties arise, no appeal should be
made to legal tribunals under existing laws, but that all difficulties should
be submitted to the equitable adjustment of arbitrators mutually chosen.

Thus reverencing law, we enter our protest against rules and customs
which are unworthy of the name, since they violate justice, the essence
of law.

The Stone-Blackwell protest was a model for antislavery couples, as was
Stone's decision to retain her name: for years after the marriage, women who
retained their surnames after marriage were known as "Lucy Stoners."[19]

Enacting norms of equality and human freedom within nineteenth-century
marriages proved difficult, of course. For all his eloquence, Henry Blackwell
had to confess after Lucy Stone's death that he had not lived up to his rebellious marriage vows.[20] Ideologies of motherhood and domesticity made consistent activism wrenching or impossible for some abolitionist wives, and some
abolitionist husbands insisted on or accepted their wives' radically disproportionate service in domestic spheres. Still, historian Chris Dixon's comprehensive review of abolitionist marriages concludes that they were stable, loving,
and liberating in important respects. Moreover, each of the protest marriages

reinforced commitment to abolitionist principles of equality and fundamental human freedom.[21]

"We Shall Be Established as a People": Marriage as an Incident of Freedom

When African Americans were enslaved, they responded, as did the celebrants in abolitionist marriages, to a human need to repudiate slavery and to partner in chosen, rather than dictated, ways. De facto marriages were unstoppable despite slave laws. Partnerships and families were formed despite the lack of legal recognition and despite the risk of forced separation.

When the institution of slavery began to crumble, former slaves enthusiastically seized the right to marry, not only for its private but also for its social meaning. By formalizing family relationships, African Americans consciously claimed the status and responsibilities of spouse, of parent, *and* of citizen. The formation of legally recognized marriage bonds signified treatment as a human being rather than as chattel—acceptance as people and as members of the political community.

The rush to take a place in the American political community by forming marriages under American law began as soon as the bonds of ownership were escaped. For many, it began on Civil War battlefields. In what W. E. B. DuBois described as a labor strike against the slave system, blacks abandoned Confederate plantations and swarmed to Union camps.[22] Many of these would-be soldiers traveled with their chosen families, for, if they did not, the family members left behind were at risk of retaliatory abuse and eviction. After some consternation, the Union Army put the labor of these people to the service of the Union cause, on the theory that they were "contraband." Fifteen months after the start of the war, black enlistment was finally permitted, and large numbers of escaped slaves and free blacks rushed to full military service. As "contrabands" and free blacks became soldiers, they moved to claim universal rights of family. A black soldier in Tennessee wrote to his division commander to complain that men in his regiment were being kept in handcuffs and denied the right to see their wives:

> mens wifes comes here to see them and he will not alow them to come in to they lines uur the men to go out to see them after the comg over hundred miles but evver offiscer here that has a wife is got her here in camps & one mans wif feel jest as near to him as anurther a colard man think jest as much of his wife as a white man dus of his . . . we volenterd and come in to the servest to portec this govverment and also to be portected our

selves at the same time but the way colonel luster is treating us it dont seem like to me that he thinks we are human.[23]

When military chaplains were authorized to solemnize marriages between African Americans, they were inundated with requests. A Freedman's Bureau agent, who reported legalizing seventy-nine marriages in a single day, described the scene as the opportunity was announced and quoted the response of a black soldier whose character was such "that every word had power":

"Fellow Soldiers:-

I praise God for this day! I have long been praying for it. The Marriage Covenant is at the foundation of all our rights. In slavery we could not have *legalised* marriage: *now* we have it. Let us conduct ourselves worthy of such a blessing—and all the people will respect us—God will bless us, and we shall be established as a people."[24]

The chaplain of a Mississippi black regiment reported the legalization of forty-three marriages, saying, "I think I witness a very decided improvement in the social and domestic feelings of those married by the authority and protection of Law. It causes them to feel that they are beginning to be regarded and treated as human beings."[25] The chaplain of an Arkansas black regiment reported twenty-five marriages registered during January 1865, "mostly, those, who have families; & have been living together for years." He added, "The Colord People here, generally consider, this war not only; their *exodus*, from bondage; but the road, to Responsibility; Competency; and an honorable Citizenship."

Enslaved peoples' commitment to family as a foundation of honorable citizenship did not spring full-blown on the eve of war. The effect of slavery on the family and the aspirations of African Americans for family integrity had long been paramount concerns of abolitionists. Goodell's treatise, published by the American and Foreign Anti-Slavery Society to "test the moral character of American slaveholding" by exhibiting the American Slave Code,[26] made the provisions of that code vivid with anecdotal accounts of slave families separated by sale and distanced by the demands of servitude. Accounts of family separations were buttressed by advertisements from Southern newspapers offering rewards for the capture or killing of slaves reported to have run away in order to join family members. Harriet Beecher Stowe had written in 1853 that "the worst abuse of the system of slavery is its outrage upon the family and . . . it is one which is more notorious and undeniable than any other."[27] An 1837 essay on the family in *The Liberator* declared that "the most appalling feature of our slave system is, the annihilation of the family institution."[28] Samuel Ward, antislavery activist and former slave, embedded a condemnation of the slave system's treatment of the fundamental human right to marry in a bitterly ironic account of the flogging of his father and the response, and subsequent punishment, of his mother. His story captures nicely how denial of family was central to the subordination of human will that slavery required:

> [My father] received a severe flogging, which left his back in . . . [a] wretched . . . state. . . . This sort of treatment of her husband not being relished by my mother, who felt about the maltreatment of her husband as any Christian woman ought to feel, she put forth her sentiments, in pretty strong language. This was insolent. Insolence in a negress could not be endured, it would breed more and greater mischief of a like kind; then what would become of wholesome discipline? Besides, if so trifling a thing as the *mere marriage relation* were to interfere with the supreme proprietor's right of a master over his slave, next we should hear that slavery must give way before marriage! Moreover, if a negress may be allowed free speech, touching the flogging of a negro, simply because that negro happened to be her husband, how long would it be before some such claim would be urged in behalf of some other member of a negro family, in unpleasant circumstances? Would this be endurable, in a republican civilized community, A.D. 1819? By no means. It would sap the very foundation of slavery—it would be like "the letting out of water": for let the principle be once established that the negress Anne Ward may speak as she pleases about the flagellation of her husband, the negro William Ward, as a matter of right, and like some alarming and death-dealing infection it would spread from plantation to plantation, until property in husbands and wives would not be worth the having. No, no: marriage must succumb to slavery, slavery must reign supreme over every right and every institution however venerable or sacred; ergo, this free-speaking Anne Ward must be made to feel the greater rigours of the domestic institution. Should she be flogged? that was questionable. . . . Well, then, . . . they could sell her, and sell her they would.[29]

The antislavery critique was more than a sentimental reaction to the drama of frustrated love and family separation. It was grounded in an analysis of the human condition as a moral quest for affiliation and self-assertion, an analysis that led to the conclusion that slavery was wrong because it unacceptably frustrated moral and affiliational behavior. Abolitionists undergirded their position with the natural law argument that rights of marriage and family were necessary to the fulfillment of religious and moral duty and therefore inalienable. To be recognized as human was to be recognized as morally autonomous, and moral as well as religious autonomy required *family* autonomy. Antislavery rhetoric reflected as much, demanding human rights and recognition of marriage in the same breath: "The slaves must be immediately recognized as human beings by the laws, their persons and their rights must be protected. Provisions must be made to establish marriage between them."[30]

The widespread commitment among antislavery Americans to protect rights to marry and to form and maintain families was sufficiently deep and appropriately placed to affect the meaning of the Reconstruction Amendments. Indeed it was expressed in Congress as a motivating factor in crafting the Thirteenth and Fourteenth Amendments. The inability of slaves to form and maintain marital bonds and the inalienability of their right to do so were recurring topics in the debates of the Reconstruction Congress. Speaker after speaker pronounced marriage rights fundamental and resolved that freedom in the United States would entail the right to marry. As one congressman put it, slave law could deny the fundamental right to partner only because it regarded enslaved people as chattel;[31] the right is, as another congressman said, "inalienable;"[32] a third Congressman drew the inescapable conclusion that enforcing universal freedom necessarily entailed guaranteeing rights of home and family.[33]

The Common Threads

These two forms of abolitionist marriage have a common animating principle: Free couples marrying in defiance of patriarchal laws and emancipated people marrying to establish their freedom all acted in response to an antislavery belief that to be human was to be entitled inalienably to function as autonomous agents rather than as subordinates to a master. This entitlement was embodied in the antislavery understanding of freedom and citizenship as they were guaranteed by the Fourteenth Amendment. One cannot function as a citizen of a free republic without moral agency and affiliational rights of choice. This principle underlies the Fourteenth Amendment's guarantee of citizenship, with all its privileges, as well as its safeguards against official denials of liberty or of equal protection of the laws.

I like to think that Congress acted with a renewed sense of the relationship between moral agency and citizenship when, in 1994, it enacted the Violence Against Women Act (VAWA) and included among its provisions a federal right of action for sexually motivated violence. The legislative record on which Congress grounded VAWA established that systematic, "private" violence against women impedes our functioning in political, social, and economic spheres and therefore constricts the citizenship guaranteed us by the

Fourteenth Amendment. For many of us, this was self-evident. Nonetheless, in *United States v. Morrison,* the Supreme Court held that creation of a federal right of action against "private," gender-motivated violence was beyond the authority conferred on the federal government by the Second Reconstruction Amendment when, in Section 5, it gave Congress the power to enforce the amendment "by appropriate legislation."[34]

The circumstances that led to the Morrison litigation are instructive. Antonio Morrison and James Crawford had an encounter with Christy Brzonkala, a fellow student at Virginia Polytechnic Institute. Brzonkala brought a civil action under VAWA, alleging that:

> [thirty] minutes after she met Morrison and Crawford in the dormitory where she resided, the two men pinned her down on a bed and took turns forcibly raping her. . . . Subsequently, Morrison allegedly announced publicly in the dormitory's dining hall that "I like to get girls drunk and f*** the s*** out of them."[35]

Brzonkala also alleged that after the rapes she became depressed and ultimately withdrew from school.[36] Her action was dismissed in response to Morrison's and Crawford's arguments that Congress could not give her a remedy against their "private" acts.[37] In Brzonkala's ultimate appeal to the Supreme Court, she (and the United States, which supported Congress's decision to give women in her situation a right to seek redress under federal law) argued that both the commerce clause and the Fourteenth Amendment are broad enough to authorize VAWA's response to private violence that perpetuates the social subordination of women. A majority of the Court disagreed. The justices thought violence against women too tangentially related to interstate commerce to justify VAWA as an exercise of federal power conferred by the Commerce Clause.[38] More significantly to the history recounted here, the Court also held that in enacting VAWA, Congress exceeded the power conferred by the Fourteenth Amendment's Section 5, giving Congress power to enforce the amendment by appropriate means. This was so, by the Court's reasoning, because the Fourteenth Amendment was less a guarantee of full citizenship than a set of narrow prohibitions against the states, and VAWA was a measure taken against private, rather than state action. As the majority saw it, violence against women was neither so tolerated by the states nor so intertwined with state actions as to justify the use of Section 5 Congressional authority.[39]

In its Fourteenth Amendment analysis, the *Morrison* majority embraced the niggardly interpretation that it had elaborated in the late nineteenth century when the nation turned from Reconstruction's egalitarian norms to accommodate the South's investment in racial hierarchy. It gave new life to *United*

States v. Harris,[40] in which the justices decided, in 1882, that the Fourteenth Amendment left Congress without power to forbid the terrorism of the Klan — systematic but "private" (in the sense that it was not enacted by government agents acting in their official capacity) violence that restored and perpetuated the antebellum subordination of African Americans.[41] And it gave new life to the *Civil Rights Cases*,[42] in which the justices decided in 1883, that the Fourteenth Amendment left Congress helpless to forbid discrimination against African Americans in the management of public accommodations.[43] The key to the Court's reasoning in both contexts was (1) to ignore the possibility that the Fourteenth Amendment language conferring citizenship on all persons born or naturalized in the United States guarantees a robust conception of citizenship, and (2) to emphasize the fact that the text of the Amendment goes on to prohibit explicitly only a state's (not a private individual's) denials of citizen rights of liberty and equality. Following this interpretive path, the Morrison justices agreed with the justices who participated in the dismantling of Reconstruction that the Fourteenth Amendment left Congress helpless should Klan or misogynist brutality still the exercise of freedom by targeted classes.

The antislavery coalition that laid the ground for Reconstruction is betrayed by this turn of events. A brief story will give you a sense of the reasons. Alonzo J. Ransier was an African American abolitionist. A free born clerk and editor of the South Carolina *Leader*, he was elected to the South Carolina delegation of the House of Representatives in 1872. He was a veteran of the South Carolina Constitutional Convention, which is to say that he cast one of the votes to ratify the Fourteenth Amendment. Speaking on the floor of Congress to the constitutionality of the 1875 Civil Rights Bill, he quoted Trumbull to remind his colleagues that the central goal of the Fourteenth Amendment was " *to secure all persons in the United States practical freedom.*"[44] He then made clear, quoting Blackstone, what practical freedom is: "that state in which each individual has the power to pursue his own happiness according to his own views of his interest and the dictates of his conscience, unrestrained, except by equal, just, and impartial laws".[45] After making the incontrovertible observation that black people in the United States did not enjoy practical freedom in 1871, he made his case for Congressional power:

> The fourteenth amendment expressly provides that all persons born or naturalized in the United States, and subject to the jurisdiction thereof, are citizens of the United States and of the States wherein they reside; that "no State shall make or enforce any law which shall abridge the privileges or immunities of citizens of the United States," &c.; and each of these amendments concludes with a proviso, that "Congress shall have power to enforce this article by appropriate legislation."

First, sir, there can be no doubt, as we have seen, that these people are citizens of the United States; secondly, that they labor under civil disabilities; thirdly, that they do not enjoy, practical freedom, not having "the power to pursue their own happiness," because of these disabilities; and fourthly, that not only has Congress the power, but it is made its solemn duty, in the exercise of its constitutional control over the entire subject, to provide, by "appropriate legislation," such a full and complete remedy as is demanded by the situation.[46]

As we think of the link between *Morrison* and *The Civil Rights Cases*, we would do well to heed Alonzo Ransier's definition of practical freedom. We would do well to think hard about the link between the pervasive effects of antiblack violence on the exercise of African American citizenship and the pervasive effects of gender-based violence on the exercise of women's citizenship. If we do so, it will come as no surprise that after declaring in debate on the 1875 Civil Rights Act that his race would be satisfied with nothing short of "equal civil rights, such as are enjoyed by other citizens," Ransier added:

And may the day be not far distant when American citizenship in civil and political rights and public privileges shall cover not only those of our sex, but those of the opposite one also; until which time the Government of the United States cannot be said to rest upon the "consent of the governed," or to adequately protect them in "life, liberty, and the pursuit of happiness."[47]

NOTES

1. Benjamin Platt Thomas, *Theodore Weld: Crusader for Freedom* (New Brunswick, N.J.: Rutgers University Press, 1950), 149.

2. Id. at 149.

3. Id. at 162–64; Dorothy Sterling, *Ahead of Her Time: Abby Kelley and the Politics of Antislavery* (New York: Norton, 1991), 60–62.

4. Sterling at 62.

5. Thomas at 164.

6. Sterling at 62.

7. Id. at 220–21.

8. Id. at 221. Although we do not know what words Foster spoke on that day, his marriage was regarded as a demonstration of "the possibility of a partnership of equals, neither affirming mastership, never a thought of superiority or dictation or control." Id. at 376, quoting Lucy Stone's remarks at Foster's memorial.

9. *Loving Warriors: Selected Letters of Lucy Stone and Henry B. Blackwell, 1853–1893*, Leslie Wheeler, ed. (New York: Dial Press, 1981), 114.

10. Id. at 54.

11. Id. at 45.

12. Id. at 55.

13. Id. at 76.

14. Id. at 85.

15. Id. at 108.

16. Id. at 109–10.

17. Id. at 123. A guest at the wedding wrote that although Stone omitted the word "obey," she did, in the event, promise to "love and honor" her spouse.

18. Id. at 85.

19. Id. at 3; Sterling at 301.

20. See Andrea Moore Kerr, *Lucy Stone: Speaking Out for Equality* (New Brunswick, N.J.:Rutgers University Press, 1992), 246.

21. For a comprehensive and critical account of the marriages of prominent abolitionists, see Chris Dixon, *Perfecting the Family: Antislavery Marriages in Nineteenth-Century America* (Amherst, MA: University of Massachusetts Press, 1997).

22. W. E. B. Du Bois, *Black Reconstruction: An Essay Toward a History of the Part Which Black Folk Played in the Attempt to Reconstruct Democracy in America, 1860–1880* (New York: Harcourt Brace, 1935), 57.

23. James A. McPherson, *The Negro's Civil War: How American Negroes Felt and Acted During the War for the Union* (Urbana: University of Illinois Press, 1991), 713.

24. Id. at 672.

25. Id. at 604.

26. William Goodell, *The American Slave Code in Theory and Practice* (New York: American and Foreign Anti-Slavery Society, 1853), 17.

27. Harriet Beecher Stowe, *The Key to Uncle Tom's Cabin* (New York: Arno Press, 1968), 133. Stowe writes in response to charges that family separations depicted in Uncle Tom's Cabin were unrealistic or atypical. Her evidence of the prevalence of slave family disruption includes eyewitness accounts of family separations resulting from slave auctions, id. at 137, and advertisements for the sale of slaves in South Carolina, id. at 134–36 and 138–42.

28. William Wells, "Family Government," *The Liberator* (December 1, 1837): 192.

29. Samuel Ward, *Autobiography of a Fugitive Negro* (1855; reprint, New York: Arno Press, 1968), 15–17.

30. S. F. D., "People of Color," *New York's Freedom Journal* 1, no. 7, (April 27, 1827): 1.

31. Cong. Globe, 38th Cong., 2d sess. (1865) (Representative Creswell).

32. Cong. Globe, 38th Cong., 2d sess. 200 (1865) (Representative Farnsworth).

33. Cong. Globe, 39th Cong., 1st sess. 2778 (1866) (Senator Eliot, speaking with respect to the homestead provisions of the Freedmen's Bureau Bill).

34. *United States v. Morrison*, 120 S.Ct. 1740, 1752 (2000).

35. Brief for the United States at 11–12, *Morrison* (nos. 99–5, 99–29).

36. Id. at 12.

37. *Morrison*, 120 S. Ct. at 1746, 1756–57.

38. Id. at 1748–54.

39. Id. at 1754–59.

40. 106 U.S. 629 (1882).

41. Id. at 637–40; see also *United States v. Cruikshank*, 92 U.S. 542, 554 (1875) (holding that the Fourteenth Amendment only prohibits state action and "adds nothing to the rights of one citizen against another").

42. 109 U.S. 3 (1883).

43. Id. at 8–19.

44. 2 Cong. Rec. 383 (1874) (emphasis added).

45. Id.

46. Id.

47. Id. at 382.

Adjoa A. Aiyetoro

CHAPTER 6

The Unkept Promise of the Thirteenth Amendment

A Call for Reparations

—*Dedicated to the memory of my great-great-grandmother Belle Jones who suffered the brutalities and indignities of chattel slavery.*[1]

From 1619 to this day, African peoples and their allies have fought in any number of ways to end their enslavement and the conditions of life attendant to such enslavement. One's sanity would be suspect if it were not acknowledged that the conditions of African peoples in the United States have changed somewhat for the better since 1865, when the Thirteenth Amendment ostensibly freed them from chattel slavery and the vestiges of that slavery. The very essence of chattel slavery, however—the badge of inferiority—remains.[2] The myth of inferiority of African peoples was created to maintain white supremacy and to enhance the ability, both physical and spiritual, of white people to sustain an institution that required the brutal subjugation of a race of people and their treatment as mere property to be dealt with as white people willed. This myth denuded African peoples of any claim to respect and humane treatment, allowing them to be subjected to the most bestial of treatment. For both African men and women, it included the right to control and direct their most intimate of relationships. For the African woman, it meant giving birth to children fathered by force by a white man who respected neither her nor the children.

Yet as can be gleaned from a review of the legislative history, the Thirteenth Amendment, with all its promise, has fallen far short of erasing the badge of inferiority—the linchpin of slavery. It suffers from the disease that created and sustained chattel slavery in what is now the United States, the disease that overthrew Reconstruction and designed, supported, and maintained Jim Crow and what is now commonly known as institutional racism: political expediency to feed the greed for money and power that required the maintenance of fictitious images of the inferiority of African peoples and other peoples of color, as well as of the superiority of white people.

The current demand for reparations is organically connected to the history of slavery and its abolition, as well as to the failure of the Thirteenth Amendment to eradicate the badges and indicia of slavery stamped on African descendants. The current-day badges and indicia of slavery are apparent in virtually every aspect of life for African peoples. Reparations is a demand that is linked to the failure of the Congress that passed the Thirteenth Amendment to pass legislation that would have served to place the newly emancipated Africans in a material posture to overcome the material deprivations born of their enslavement. It is a demand that is linked to the failure of the United States, in both its public and private institutions, to eradicate the fiction of inferiority that served to continue to expose African peoples to the brutalities of the predominant white society in health, education, political participation, employment and wealth-building activities, and the criminal punishment system—to name a few.

If the promise of the Thirteenth Amendment is finally to be kept, the United States government, state governments, and the private sector must come to the table and develop a reparations package with African descendants in the United States that publicly acknowledges the former's participation and complicity in the institution of slavery and in the continuing vestiges of slavery. This reparations package must be one that includes resources and programs that are designed to *eradicate the vestiges of slavery*; reparations for African descendants, therefore, is necessarily more than a check. This reparations package must make real the promise of the Thirteenth Amendment by putting into place and sustaining policies and programs that will end the badges and indicia of chattel slavery to which our forbearers were so brutally subjected.

The Thirteenth Amendment as Reparations

President Lincoln issued the Emancipation Proclamation, effective January 1, 1864, that freed those Africans enslaved in the Confederacy or those states engaged in rebellion against the United States.[3] During the latter stages of the Civil War and immediately following the war President Lincoln, the United States Congress, and some Union Army generals, such as General William Sherman, recognized that the "freedmen" and their families needed places to live, supplies, and protection from prior "owners" and their allies. A number of measures were passed to provide for the "freedmen" from what could be termed spoils of war as well as from the United States Treasury.[4]

The popularized notion that Congress had granted the newly freed Africans "forty acres and a mule" and that President Andrew Johnson vetoed this bill emanates from the somewhat complicated history of field orders and legislative enactments of this period. Indeed, much like the creation of the myth that in some sense elevated President Lincoln to sainthood in many African descendant communities, the Johnson veto of the proposed amendments to the Freedmen's Bureau Act has perhaps placed too much of the blame in his lap for the failure to provide the newly freed Africans with a reparations package or "forty acres and a mule."

In truth, except for General Sherman's Field Order Number 15, there was never a *grant* of land to newly freed Africans.[5] What the Freedmen's Bureau Act[6] and its subsequent amendment in 1866 did was grant the right to freedmen to rent or purchase confiscated Confederate land. In the original act freedmen were allowed to rent up to forty acres with the right to purchase this rented land for its value, after a period of three years.[7] In the subsequent amendment the freedmen were given the right to purchase up to twenty acres of land for $1.50 per acre. Those who were initially given land pursuant to General Sherman's field order were also allowed to purchase up to twenty acres for $1.50.[8]

Indeed, the Freedmen's Bureau Act and its amendment gave no material reparations to the freedmen, although they did provide protections for the freedmen in the exercise of legal rights. In the material sense, these bills were similar to discretionary and arbitrarily enforced welfare acts by giving the Commissioner of the Freedmen's Bureau the authority to provide assistance to "destitute, suffering or dependent" freedmen, unless they could work and thereby avoid destitution.[9] There was no recognition that there was a debt owed for almost 250 years of forced, unpaid labor, brutalization, and control, regardless of state of destitution, suffering, or dependence.

A review of the legislative history and other legislation passed by Congress during the Civil War and immediately after it, suggests that the Thirteenth Amendment, along with the Freedmen's Bureau Act, the Civil Rights Act of 1866, and other legislation passed to effectuate the Thirteenth Amendment, was viewed in some sense as just compensation for enslaved Africans—or in current-day parlance—reparations. "While some suggested providing economic reparations to accompany the constitutional guarantee, a strong consensus developed among moderates and conservatives favoring equal protection of the law for all men."[10]

Indeed, with perhaps a few exceptions, the Congress of the United States was composed of white men who, although committed to ending the enslavement of Africans for various and sundry reasons, were likewise committed to the myth of the superiority of whites over those of African descent.[11] This sense of superiority colored their view of even the abolition of slavery, casting it in the mold of a beneficent act and avoiding for the most part a recognition in word *and* deed of the tremendous material, physical, social, spiritual, as well as legal wrong that they and their forbearers had committed against African peoples.

The Promise of the Thirteenth Amendment

After much debate Congress passed the Thirteenth Amendment with the necessary two-thirds majority on January 28, 1865.[12] The requisite number of states ratified it in December 1865. The amendment was passed because its proponents wanted to capture the moment in law and assure that the enslavement of African peoples would not be repeated.[13] That enslavement, in addition to being viewed by some, although not necessarily all of the proponents of the amendment as being inhumane treatment, was also seen to have marginalized the white laborers and impacted their ability to work and make a living wage.[14]

There appear to have been three purposes for the Thirteenth Amendment: First, it was intended to strike "the shackle . . . from the limbs of the hapless bondsman;" next, to extend liberty rights for African Americans, slave and free; and finally, to broaden constitutional rights for white citizens.[15] The abolition of slavery was viewed as a duty by some of those who supported it, and the Thirteenth Amendment was the fulfillment of that duty by purportedly being the vehicle by which enslaved Africans could obtain the same rights as white men and women.[16] These supporters were essentially speaking about removing the badge of inferiority that had been forcibly and fraudulently placed on African peoples in order to sustain the institution of slavery. Indeed, some jurists and legal scholars have distilled the legislative history of the amendment into the concept of removing this stamp of inferiority.[17] It was placed on African peoples from the start of chattel slavery in the colonies in 1619, and from 1619 to 1865 this presumed status gained legal definition and enforcement.[18] This badge of inferiority had many faces, from the manner in which Africans were stolen from the shores of Africa and torn from their land and families to the manner in which they were debased and treated as mere property, without any rights to own their labor, sustain their families, educate themselves, and defend themselves and their loved ones. In descriptions of their experiences, the badge of inferiority comes to life and is palpable.

During the Middle Passage

Few can imagine the horrors that awaited my people aboard the slave vessels. The filth, the stench, the loss of life, the disease, the packing of men [and women] in spaces so tight that they could neither turn, nor stand, nor squat, nor sit, is beyond human comprehension . . . the journey known as the Middle Passage or Maafa ("the massive disaster").[19]

Crammed in suffocating heat, held fast by chains bolted to the floor, forced to lie in their own waste, breathing air rancid with vomit, disease, and sickness—my people suffered unimaginable horrors. There, amid huge rats that gnawed through wood and flesh, men went mad. There on floors covered with blood and excrement, pregnant women gave birth. There the living awoke, chained to the dead.[20]

At the Auction

He took me by the hand and led me out to the middle of the street, and turning me slowly around, exposed me to the view of those who attended the venue. I was soon surrounded by strange men who examined me and handled me in the same manner that a butcher would a calf or lamb he was about to purchase, and who talked about my shape and size in like words. . . . I was then put up to sale. . . . The people who stood by said that I had fetched a great sum for one so young a slave. I then saw my sisters led forth and sold to different owners. . . . When the sale was over, my mother hugged and kissed us and mourned over us, begging us to keep up a good heart. . . . It was a sad parting, one went one way, one another, and our poor mammy went home with nothing.[21]

The Work of the Enslaved African

For my ancestors who toiled on plantations, work began at sunrise and ended late at night. Picking cotton and working in the sugar and rice fields were just a few of the grueling tasks given to them. . . . Slaves [on what appeared to be a more "lenient" slaveholder's plantation] were given four days off for Christmas and three other days off during the year.[22]

The life of house slaves was little better. But whatever perks they received—castoff clothing from the slaveholding family, first choice of food left from the master's meals—surely paled next to the labor they performed and the indignities they suffered. They cooked the meals, nursed the children, fanned the flies, were used as foot warmers, spun the yarn, milked the cows, swept the floors, served as butlers and maids, and hauled the water. Unlike their brothers and sisters who worked in the fields, house servants' work lasted beyond sunset. When the evening guests came, house servants were required to work as long as visitors stayed. They were the ones who served the food, poured the tea, cleared the table, and stood awaiting every beck and call. They had to stand unflinchingly as slaveholders made cruel remarks, lashed out in rage, or hurled insults, suffering silently the abuse.[23]

THE MAKING OF A SLAVE

The plantation was a closed system, the overseer and master the ultimate authority. If a slave denied this, the overseer could withhold food. If the slave fought back, the slaveholder could sell the slave or a loved one. For refusing an order, the rebellious slave could be hung by the thumbs, beaten with a paddle, or left to blister in the burning sun. . . . [They] were whipped for leaving the plantation without a pass, shut up in a "nigger box" for lying or stealing, castrated if accused of violating a white woman, mutilated and chained for running away, hung for killing a white man, even if it was in self defense.[24]

Those who pressed for the passage of the Thirteenth Amendment, both legislator and activist, were aware at some level of the degradation, brutality, and horrors of the lives of enslaved Africans. The Thirteenth Amendment was a constitutional attempt to eliminate the badge of inferiority that created and sprang from the status conferred by chattel slavery on the enslaved African, with the anticipation that the conditions of slavery, the badges and indicia of slavery would be eliminated.[25] Although the debates chronicled in the *Congressional Globe* of the Thirty-eighth Congress, touched on the breadth of the invasion, loss, and inhumaneness of chattel slavery, the response in terms of the actual amendment was couched in sterile words that only a review of the legislative history, and the recorded historical accounts of nearly 250 years of forced bondage and brutalization of African peoples, could bring to life.

Section 1. Neither slavery nor involuntary servitude, except as a punishment for crime whereof the party shall have been duly convicted, shall exist within the United States, or any place subject to their jurisdiction.

Section 2. Congress shall have power to enforce this article by appropriate legislation.

Thus, after its passage, the battle to establish the breadth and scope of its application was begun. As Frederick Douglass prophesied at the time of its passage "the work does not end with the abolition of slavery, but only begins."[26]

The Jockeying for Control of the Thirteenth Amendment's Application

The history of the application of the Thirteenth Amendment is the history of the political jockeying for power in the United States. It is reminiscent of the jockeying for power over the language of the Constitution of the United States that allowed importation of enslaved Africans until 1808.[27] Although clearly there were well-meaning white men who truly believed that the enslavement of Africans was wrong, that it should be ended and their rights established, this premise never became fixed in the law and the fabric of this country. It therefore led to the content of legal and human rights of African descendants being determined in the political game played by those in power in the United States, whether of the executive, judicial or legislative branches. African descendants became the ball, passed among those who defined and led the game.

The Legislative Interpretive Response

The lead proponents of the Thirteenth Amendment in the 38th Congress soon learned that the passage of the Thirteenth Amendment was insufficient to guarantee the newly emancipated Africans their human and civil rights, although that was their intent. Violence erupted in the South shortly after the amendment was ratified by the states, the Black Codes were created, and wholesale violations of the Africans' rights were the rule of the day.[28] The sterile, uninstructive language of the amendment gave little direction to what was meant by abolishing slavery and involuntary servitude, and the laws that were passed in the South, such as the Black Codes, acted to reenslave the Africans.[29] The lead advocates for the Thirteenth Amendment, therefore, developed and passed the Civil Rights Act of 1866, successfully overcoming President Johnson's veto.[30] The Civil Rights Act served to put in succinct language the intent of the primary supporters of the Thirteenth Amendment. The substance of the rights secured and protected by this act is contained in the first section:

> *Be it enacted by the Senate and House of Representatives of the United States of America in Congress assembled,* That all persons born in the United States and not subject to any foreign power, excluding Indians not taxed, are hereby declared to be citizens of the United States; and such citizens, of every race and color, without regard to any previous condition of slavery or involuntary servitude, except as a punishment for crime whereof the party shall have been duly convicted, shall have the same

right, in every State and Territory in the United States, to make and enforce contracts, to sue, be parties, and give evidence, to inherit, purchase,
lease, sell, hold, and convey real and personal property, and to full and
equal benefit of all laws and proceedings for the security of person and
property, as is enjoyed by white citizens, and shall be subject to like punishment, pains, and penalties, and to none other, any law, statute, ordinance, regulation, or custom, to the contrary notwithstanding.[31]

The United States Congress had done its job. It was now the responsibility
of the judicial branch of government to assure that the promise of the Thirteenth Amendment, as articulated in the Civil Rights Act of 1866, was kept. The
history of the judicial response to attempts to enforce the Thirteenth Amendment mirrors the all too ready willingness to sacrifice the humane and fair treatment of Africans for the interest of whites, most frequently of white men.

Judicial Interpretation and Application

The judicial decisions start off strong, with Supreme Court justices sitting
as designated circuit court justices and ruling in a manner that upholds the
integrity of the Thirteenth Amendment and the Civil Rights Act of 1866. In
United States v. Rhodes,[32] Supreme Court Justice Noah Swayne upheld a federal removal prosecution made pursuant to the 1866 act. The removal was
done to avoid the application of Kentucky state law that barred African people from testifying against whites in a case where three white men were
charged with burglarizing the home of an African family in Kentucky. If the
removal had not been upheld, "crimes of the deepest dye [could continue to
be] committed by white men with impunity."[33]

Chief Justice Chase upheld both the Thirteenth Amendment prohibition
against involuntary servitude and the equal protection rights of the 1866 Act,
by invalidating an apprenticeship contract that required the petitioner to work
until she was eighteen years old for the man who had previously enslaved her
and provided fewer financial and educational benefits than white apprentices
were entitled to under Maryland law.[34] Between 1866 and 1871 several other
federal courts and a few state courts upheld the constitutionality of the Civil
Rights Act of 1866.[35] Yet, serving as a preview of the end of Reconstruction,
the Supreme Court of the United States began to gut the promise of the Thirteenth Amendment in 1872.

The gutting of the promise of the Thirteenth Amendment and the Civil
Rights Act of 1866 took approximately thirty-four years. During this period
the tortured reasoning of the majority of the Supreme Court indicates a
commitment to uphold the myth of white supremacy and the fiction of

African descendants' inferiority, regardless of the legislative history of the Thirteenth Amendment and the clear language of the Civil Rights Act of 1866.[36] The majority of the Court decided to use the black robes of the highest judicial authority in the land to support a political agenda of returning African peoples to their purported rightful place: subservient and inferior to white people.[37]

The evisceration of the promise of the Thirteenth Amendment began with the decision in 1872 that the removal clause of the Civil Rights Act of 1866 to allow African people to testify in court against white people did not apply to family members who witnessed the murder of an African couple, their son, and his grandmother.[38] *Blyew* is a precursor of the post–Thirteenth Amendment cases that support the view that white people can commit acts of violence against African peoples with federal government impunity—continuing the devaluation of the lives of those of African descent that began with the enslavement of Africans. The Court held that the removal applied to "persons in existence" and that the only persons in existence as it related to this crime were the two white defendants.[39]

The Court in *United States v. Cruikshank*[40] continued this license to commit violence against African peoples with federal impunity by dismissing the federal indictments of three members of the Ku Klux Klan, indictments that were based on the mutilation and murder of sixty soldiers in the Black Republican militia by white supremacists attempting to install the Democratic nominee for governor of Louisiana in a disputed election. The Court failed to discuss the Thirteenth Amendment; rather, it gave complete authority to the states criminally to charge and prosecute cases of this nature.[41] Finally, the Court reached the low point of this refusal to protect the rights of Africans to be free of racial violence when it decided *Hodges v. United States*.[42] The Court overturned a federal conviction of several white defendants who used violence and threats to force African descendant workers to surrender their jobs. The Court ignored the legislative history of the Thirteenth Amendment and the Civil Rights Act of 1866 and instead relied on the definition of slavery in Webster's dictionary.[43] These cases gave clear notice to whites that acts of violence against African peoples would go unpunished by the federal courts—exacerbating the climate of racial violence that began with the institution of slavery and continued, if not worsened, after the passage of the Thirteenth Amendment.

Likewise, the right to equality of treatment in civil matters that the legislative history of the Thirteenth Amendment supports as the purpose of that amendment, and the clear language of the Civil Rights Act of 1866, was made meaningless by the Supreme Court in two major cases.[44] In the *Civil Rights Cases*, a consolidation of five lower court decisions, the Supreme Court refused to extend the coverage of the Thirteenth Amendment to public accommodations, construing the limits of the Thirteenth Amendment to be those vestiges of slavery specifically identified in the Civil Rights Act of 1866.[45] Of particular note, the *Civil Rights Cases* included one case that addressed the status of African women as "ladies."[46] In *Robinson* the Tennessee jury, based on the judge's instruction, determined that it was appropriate for Mrs. Sallie Robinson and her nephew to be excluded from the "ladies' car" (first-class train accommodations) because the conductor assumed that Mrs. Robinson was a prostitute traveling with a white man. The conductor's testimony was that in his experience when a white man is traveling with an African descendant woman this is usually the case.[47] The Supreme Court's decision in the *Civil Rights Cases* keeps intact this stereotypical view of African women, ignoring the fact that this very assumption is an exemplar of the badges and indicia of slavery borne by African descendant women, who during slavery were identified by the "master" as his personal sexual property to have whenever and however he willed. Courts during slavery upheld this view. In Missouri the Supreme Court in *State of Missouri v. Celia*, upheld a conviction for first-degree murder of an enslaved African woman who fatally struck her "master" when he came to once again force his sexual attentions on her.[48]

The majority opinion in the *Civil Rights Cases* reveals that the justices engaged in political partisanship rather than judicial objectivity. For example, they found that so-called free Africans were not discriminated against in the exercise of their legal rights and that therefore racial discrimination was not a badge or incident of slavery.[49] The Court, however, in restricting the scope of the Thirteenth Amendment embraced the view that the amendment "establish[ed] and decree[d] universal civil and political freedom"[50] and endorsed the conclusion that the amendment gave Congress the power "to pass all laws necessary and proper for abolishing all badges and incidents of slavery in the United States."[51]

Following the *Civil Rights Cases* the Supreme Court rendered an opinion in *Plessy v. Ferguson*[52] that, according to Higginbotham, "was one of the two most venal decisions ever handed down by the United States Supreme Court."[53] The Court continued its derogation of duty by basing its white supremacist decision on cases decided prior to the passage of the Thirteenth Amendment; in fact, some were even rendered prior to the Civil War.[54] In *Plessy* the Supreme Court continued to uphold the view, put forth in the *Civil Rights Cases*, that discrimination in public accommodations was not violative of the Thirteenth Amendment. However, the Court went one big step further than it did in the *Civil Rights Cases*, finding that racial segregation does not place a badge of inferiority on "the colored race" and that if it does, "it is . . . solely because the colored race chooses to put that construction upon it."[55]

The Supreme Court, therefore, legitimizes segregation by convoluted reasoning that says just because we exclude you from accommodations in a status other than that of a total dependant (a nurse caring for a white child in the white train compartment) and can punish you for sitting in that compartment, it's really all in your mind if you view this as a badge of inferiority. Justice Harlan in his dissent countered this faulty reasoning: "Every one knows that the statute in question had its origin in the purpose, not so much to exclude white persons from railroad cars occupied by blacks, as to exclude colored people from coaches occupied by or assigned to white persons."[56]

The Thirteenth Amendment became moribund after these litany of cases, and African descendants continued to be subjected to the vestiges of slavery; when a remedy was obtained, it was most often cast in an ahistorical context—tying it largely to present-day violations that frequently seemed to spring historically from nowhere.[57] The disconnect that the Supreme Court created in these cases between racial segregation and badges and incidents of slavery went far deeper—it became a disconnect between *all* discriminatory and racially motivated conduct, even that explicitly identified by the Civil Rights Act of 1866, from the historical context for that conduct in the enslavement of African people. Indeed, it was not until 1968 that the Supreme Court put life back into the Thirteenth Amendment in *Jones v. Alfred H. Mayer Company*.[58]

In *Jones* the Court held that the refusal to sell a house in a so-called white community to an African descendant couple violated the Thirteenth Amendment and the Civil Rights Act of 1866. The Court resurrected the Thirteenth Amendment and the Civil Rights Act and gave them the meaning that a review of the legislative history revealed the creators intended them to have. It did not have to reverse previous decisions of the Court, since even the most horrific cases, such as *Plessy*, had not held the Civil Rights Act of 1866 unconstitutional. Indeed, the Supreme Court specifically affirmed its constitutionality in *Blyew*.[59] What it did was decide the case based on the facts of the case and the purpose of the Thirteenth Amendment and the Civil Rights Act of 1866 as found in the legislative history. Indeed, the refusal to sell property to the Joneses was specifically addressed in the 1866 Act provision of the right of African peoples "to . . . purchase . . . real . . . property," and the Court, by connecting the refusal to sell the home to them because of their race to the segregated housing conditions during slavery, breathed life into the Thirteenth Amendment. It acted with judicial integrity, yet even in this instance the political climate is important since the case was decided at the height of the modern day Civil Rights movement and during the year of the murder of Dr. Martin Luther King Jr. The *Jones* Court, nonetheless, left certain important questions unanswered, including whether the Thirteenth Amendment was self-executing and therefore could be the basis of litigation, absent the use of a statute passed pursuant to it, and whether the Thirteenth Amendment placed an affirmative duty on public and private institutions.

Holding the Line Post-Jones

Pro-civil-rights legal scholars and activists such as Arthur Kinoy were ecstatic about the Court's decision in *Jones* and viewed the decision as indicative of a reassertion of the rights of African descendant people to be free from the vestiges of slavery.

> The profound understanding reflected in the *Jones* decision—that the vast disturbing problems which are erupting from the black ghettos of America, urban and rural, are a direct consequence of white America's failure to uproot the vestiges and remains of the barbaric system of human slavery—places these questions in the only perspective which will allow of their solution short of an expanding series of catastrophes and cataclysms which could well destroy the nation.[60]

Indeed, Justice Douglas in his concurring opinion gave strong voice to the view that the vestiges of slavery went beyond the purchase of property by African descendants, listing a litany of cases that had come before the Supreme Court that, in his view, represented vestiges of slavery, including interferences with the right to vote, exclusion from juries, provision of inferior and segregated schools and other segregated facilities.[61] Subsequent Supreme Court decisions have continued to uphold the interpretation of the Thirteenth Amendment that it abolished slavery and its badges and incidents;[62] however, the decisions have been narrow in scope, reminiscent of the *Civil Rights Cases* where the Court refused to find a badge or indicia of slavery that had not clearly been articulated in the Civil Rights Act of 1866.[63]

Reclaiming the Promise of the Thirteenth Amendment

The retention of the interpretation of the Thirteenth Amendment that it abolished the badges and indicia of slavery is the good news for those who support public policy initiatives for reparations[64] or seek to litigate issues of present-day rights to reparations pursuant to the Thirteenth Amendment. Although the courts have been reticent to give this interpretation its full and rightful meaning, as I have already described, retention keeps the door open for advocates of the broader meaning of the amendment's protections. Indeed, the history of the reparations movement is a history of African peoples and their allies seeking, implicitly and explicitly, to make real the promise of the Thirteenth Amendment.

The U.S. Reparations Movement's Demands are for the Fulfillment of the Promise

The proponents of the Thirteenth Amendment and the Civil Rights Act of 1866, urged that the freed Africans have equality before the law. Justice Harlan's statement in *Plessy*, that indeed whites were superior,[65] had some basis in the material reality that African descendants had little material wealth as compared to whites at that time. The congressional proponents of the Thirteenth Amendment and the subsequent supporters of equal legal rights such as Justice Harlan, with a few exceptions, failed to acknowledge that this inequality was itself a vestige of slavery that required a remedy.

Even rough equality in material resources requires some affirmative response to the stolen labor of African peoples that left most African peoples without financial resources when slavery was abolished. This need was discussed by some senators in the debates over the Thirteenth Amendment[66] and addressed woefully inadequately in the Freedmen's Bureau Act for those who were "destitute." In the 1890s, some twenty-five years after the failure of the Freedmen's Bureau Act to provide material reparations for the newly freed African, the Ex-Slave Mutual Relief, Bounty & Pension Association was founded. One of its primary leaders was an African woman, Mrs. Callie House. The purpose of this organization was to obtain pensions for those formerly held as slaves, their surviving spouses, or their descendants. One of the bills that this association supported was Senate Bill 4718, which was introduced on June 6, 1898. Mrs. House, national promoter, and Rev. Isaiah Dickerson, general manager, along with others, organized hundreds of thousands of African descendants to support this and other initiatives.[67] Congress failed to pass Senate Bill 4718 or other legislative initiatives to address the debt the country owed previously enslaved Africans and their families, once again firmly entrenching the myths of the inferiority of African peoples and the superiority of white peoples.

Badges and indicia of slavery exist today, as during the time of slavery, in every sphere of life. These reflect the failure to end the racially demeaning and life-devaluing treatment in health, education, employment, and wealth development, as well as in the imposition of punishments, to name a few.[68] The movement for reparations today is one that must cut through this deeply entrenched myth of inferiority that has taken on forms that are at times difficult to identify. Many African descendant leaders and organizations have been the voice for ending the unequal treatment to which African descendants have been subjected after the promise of equality that was made by the Thirteenth Amendment. One of the foremost proponents of reparations for slavery and its aftermath was Queen Mother Audley Moore, the mother of the modern-day reparations movement, who cofounded in the 1960s the Reparations Committee of Descendants of U.S. Slaves, Inc. This organization was formed to obtain reparations for the "gross exploitations of slavery and its aftermath." Queen Mother Moore was also a leading spirit and voice in the formation and work of the National Coalition of Blacks for Reparations in America (N'COBRA) until her death, at 100 years old, in 1998.[69]

Some have suggested that Malcolm X (El Hajj Malik Shabazz) provided a context for the modern-day reparations movement:

> [Malcolm X] changed the way black people thought about themselves. Malcolm moved us from being the footnotes in someone else's history, to becoming the key actors in the making of new history. Instead of singing someone else's song, we discovered the beauty in our own voices. Reparations thus becomes a way for us to challenge and to subvert the master narrative of white capitalist America, and to testify to the truth of our own history.[70]

The National Coalition of Blacks for Reparations in America, a coalition of organizations and individuals organized in 1987, has developed its work around the economic value of the stolen labor that was a hallmark of slavery and the brutality and human deprivations of slavery that affected Africans in every sphere of their lives including health, education, the ability to be self-determining, and the spiritual, as well as subjecting them to arbitrary and capricious punishment. [71] N'COBRA's demand for reparations is not simply a demand regarding the violations of fundamental rights of humanity that were the daily experience of Africans for 250 years, it is a demand with respect to the failure of the government to eliminate the badges and indicia of slavery. In this vein N'COBRA embraces the analysis of Arthur Kinoy that the Thirteenth Amendment places an affirmative duty on all branches of government to eliminate all badges and indicia of slavery.[72]

Keeping the Promise by Unraveling the Myth

The myth of inferiority of African peoples has become so much a part of the fabric of the United States that it continues through the actions or inactions of people implementing institutional policies in often unconscious ways.[73] If the promise of the Thirteenth Amendment is to be kept, this myth, in all its many institutionalized forms, must be debunked. A number of scholars have analyzed the continuation of this myth in the various aspects of life of African descendants in the United States.[74] For instance, particular attention has been

paid in recent years to the birth of gynecology in the United States in the un-
anesthetized wombs of enslaved African women, and connections are being
made between this barbaric, brutal treatment and the at best frequently marginalized health care African descendant women continue to receive.[75] Given
the exclusion of conviction for crimes from the coverage of the Thirteenth
Amendment prohibition against involuntary servitude, yet the explicit inclusion in the Civil Rights Act of 1866 of the requirement for equal punishments,
the continuation of the badges and indicia of slavery in the criminal punishment system requires special mention.

The failure to eradicate the badge of inferiority, that is the insignia of slavery, has maintained and strengthened the myth that African descendants have
a propensity to violence and are by nature more criminal than white people.[76]
This myth has led to the disproportionate use of severe punishments on
African descendants, including long terms of incarceration and the death
penalty. African descendant women—the fastest growing prison population—
in addition to being subjected to the unfair punishment schemes in general
for crack and powder cocaine, have been subjected disproportionately to the
imposition of criminal charges for endangering their unborn child when
found to be addicted to drugs while pregnant.[77] The Fourteenth Amendment
has been largely unsuccessful in addressing the issue of disproportionate sentencing, since the trappings of this amendment have included the need to
prove that the individuals before the court have themselves been specifically
discriminated against in the applications of the criminal statutes.[78] Although
scholars have documented the arbitrary and cruel imposition of punishment
on both "free" and enslaved Africans during the period of slavery, statistics reveal the continuation of this disproportionality in the imposition of punishments, and some studies have indicated that race is the most significant factor
in explaining this disproportionality,[79] no branch of the federal government
has acted to institute measures to eliminate this badge and indicia of slavery.[80]

To implicate the Thirteenth Amendment in public policy arguments as
well as in litigation, the relationship between the disproportionate imposition
of punishments on African descendants and the badges and indicia of slavery
must be examined. This disproportionality is in direct violation of the Thirteenth Amendment and the Civil Rights Act of 1866. The prison industrial
complex that is incarcerating for longer times a rising number of people, most
of whom are people of color, and disproportionately African descendants,
cannot be allowed to continue and expand in direct violation of the precepts
of equality that the Thirteenth Amendment instituted. Those who seek reparations must include in their demands the elimination of the prison industrial complex, the elimination of sentencing schemes such as the federal sentencing guidelines that provide higher punishments for conduct that

predominantly African descendants are accused of, when similar conduct predominantly committed by whites carries a much lesser punishment, as well as the adoption of a racial justice act that would place an affirmative duty on governments to address the imposition of disparate punishments.[81]

To paraphrase Dr. Martin Luther King Jr., the Thirteenth Amendment was a promissory note given to African descendant peoples as they were being freed from chattel slavery. To date, this promissory note has been returned, marked "insufficient funds." Those who were responsible for the passage of the Thirteenth Amendment in Congress and its ratification by more than the requisite number of states, promised that the amendment would result in the legal equality of African descendants and the removal of the badges and indicia of slavery. Rather than keeping this promise, all branches of government have participated in the continuation of the badges and indicia of slavery by, among other things, supporting political agendas that decry the elimination of the myth of white superiority and African descendant inferiority despite the clear requirements of the Thirteenth Amendment and the Civil Rights Act of 1866, now codified as 42 U.S.C. sec. 198.

African descendant women and men have been subjected to the demeaning and brutal continuation of these badges and indicia of slavery. For African descendant women, there is a continuing struggle to own their own bodies and overcome the sexual stigmas that were created to justify their rape by white men and subjection to other forms of sexual abuse by these same men. For African descendant women, who are the fastest growing population in our prisons, and for African descendant men, it is a continuing struggle to obtain equal treatment under the law and to be viewed with the humanness with which whites are viewed—thus avoiding the imposition of overly harsh and brutal punishments. For African descendant peoples it is the right to equal and humane treatment in all aspects of their lives—health, education, political participation, employment, and wealth development, as well as in the criminal punishment system—that is the promise of the Thirteenth Amendment. It is a promise that must be kept if this nation is to heal the wounds of the crimes committed against African peoples during slavery, the badges and indicia of which continue to this day.

NOTES

1. Belle Jones was born in Missouri, the child of Paul and Maria Jones, also enslaved Africans. She was "given" to a visiting Navy officer, and the product of that encounter was my great-grandfather and the first African man to vote in St. Louis,

Missouri, Antonio Haskell. Belle had vowed that one thing she would never accept was physical force from the "slave owner." On one occasion, after the birth of Antonio, her so-called master struck her, and she struck him back. She was sold by this master and sent to Louisiana.

2. Slavery has existed for thousands of years; however, records of the form of slavery prior to the institution of chattel slavery in the colonies and the United States indicate that the stripping of the enslaved person's humanity was unique to chattel slavery. See e.g., Velma Maia Thomas, *Lest We Forget* (New York: Crown, 1997), 5.

3. The popular story around the Emancipation Proclamation is another fiction that serves to uphold the underlying fiction of white superiority. In recognizing the importance of President Lincoln to the ending of slavery, we have been taught that Abraham Lincoln freed the slaves, pointing to the Emancipation Proclamation. A reading of the Emancipation Proclamation reveals otherwise. It freed "all persons held as slaves within any state or designated part of the state" where people were *"in rebellion against the United States."* Emancipation Proclamation, 12 Stat. 1268 (1863).

4. See *The Forty Acres Documents: What Did the United States Really Promise the People Freed from Slavery?*, introduction, Amilcar Shabazz (Baton Rouge, La.: The Malcolm Generation, Inc., 1994); *General Sherman's Field Order No. 15* (Baton Rouge, La: The House of Songhay, 1994); the first Freedmen's Bureau Act, Ch. 90, 13 Stat. 507 (1865); the second Freedmen's Bureau Act, Ch. 200, 14 Stat. 173 (1866).

5. On January 16, 1865, General Sherman issued Field Order Number 15, which among other things provided land in the islands from Charleston, South Carolina, south to the county bordering St. Johns' River, Florida, to three "respectable negroes, heads of families." These three "respectable negroes" were given the right to subdivide this land into plots not to exceed forty acres of "tillable ground" for each individual family.

6. Ch. 90, 13 Stat. 507.

7. Id. sec. 4.

8. Ch. 200, 14 Stat. 173, sec. 7.

9. Supra note 6, sec. 3 and supra note 8, sec. 5.

10. Douglas L. Colbert, "Liberating the Thirteenth Amendment," *Harvard Civil Rights-Civil Liberties Law Review* 30 (1995): 1, 12.

11. Justice Harlan, one of the strongest judicial advocates for the protection of the legal rights of African descendants in the late 1800s, embraced the concept of white superiority: "The white race deems itself to be the dominant race in this country. And so it is, in prestige, in achievement, in education, in wealth and in power. So, I doubt not, it will continue to be for all time, if it remains true to its great heritage and holds fast to the principles of constitutional liberty." *Plessy v. Ferguson*, 163 U.S. 537, 559(1896) (Harlan, J., dissenting).

12. Cong. Globe, 38th Cong., 2nd sess. 216 at 531.

13. Colbert, supra note 9 at 9.

14. See id. at 9.

15. Id. at 10.

16. Neal Kumar Katyal, Notes, "Men Who Own Women: A Thirteenth Amendment Critique of Forced Prostitution," *The Yale Law Journal* (103): 791, 820; see also, Senator Trumbull's statement, "It is ideal to say that a man is free who cannot go and come at pleasure, who cannot buy and sell, who cannot enforce his rights. These are rights which the first clause of the constitutional amendment meant to secure to all . . . " Cong. Globe, 39th Congress, 1st sess. 323 (1866)

17. *Jones v. Alfred H. Mayer Co.*, 392 U.S. 409, 445 (1968) (Justice Douglas concurring); see also, Arthur Kinoy, *"Jones v. Alfred H. Mayer Co.*: An Historic Step Forward, *Vanderbilt Law Review* 22 (1969): 475, 480–81.

18. See A. Leon Higginbotham Jr. *Shades of Freedom* (New York: Oxford University Press, 1996), pp. 15–16.

19. Velma Maia Thomas, *Lest We Forget* (New York: Crown, 1997), p. 6.

20. Id. at 7.

21. Id. at 10, quoting from Henry Louis Gates Jr., ed., *The Classic Slave Narratives* (New York: Mentor, 1987), p. 191.

22. Id. at 13.

23. Id. at 12–13.

24. Id. at 17.

25. See Colbert, supra note 10 at 9.

26. Eric Foner, *Reconstruction: America's Unfinished Revolution 1863–1877* (New York: Harper and Row, 1988), p. 76.

27. Article I, Section [1].

28. See Colbert, supra note 10 at 11.

29. Id. at 12; see also Higginbotham, *Shades of Freedom*, supra note 18 at 75.

30. Colbert, supra note 10 at 14.

31. Civil Rights Act of 1866, ch. 31, sec. 1, 14 Stat. 27 (current version at 42 U.S.C. sec. 1981 [a]).

32. 27 F. Cas. 785 (C.C.D. Ky. 1866).

33. Id. at 787.

34. In re Turner, 24 F. Cas. 337 (C.C.D. Md. 1867).

35. See Colbert, supra note 10 at 16, fn. 97.

36. For a summary discussion of these cases see Higginbotham, supra note 18 at 79–80, 87–91; Colbert, supra note 10 at 17–28.

37. Cf. A. Leon Higginbotham's assessment that the Supreme Court engaged in political machinations rather than principled adjudication in the majority's opinion in *Plessy v. Ferguson*, 163 U.S. 537 (1896), supra note 18 at 117; cf. also, Bruce Wright, *Black Robes, White Justice*, (Secaucus, N.J.: Lyle Stuart, 1987).

38. *Blyew v. United States*, 80 U.S. (13 Wall.) 581 (1872).

39. Id. at 581.

40. 92 U.S. 542 (1875).

41. Id. at 553–54.

42. 203 U.S. 1 (1906).

43. Id. at 16.

44. *Civil Rights Cases*, 109 U.S. 3 (1883) and *Plessy v. Ferguson*, 163 U.S. 537 (1896)

45. *Civil Rights Cases,* 109 U.S. at 22. The Court found that the Civil Rights Act of 1875, prohibiting race discrimination in public accommodations, was unconstitutional. Id. at 24.

46. *Robinson v. Memphis & Charleston Railroad Company* (C.C.W.D. Tenn. 1880) (No. 2611, United States Supreme Court) (reported as Transcript Record in the United States Supreme Court) (hereinafter *Robinson*).

47. See Higginbotham, supra note 18 at 103.

48. *State of Missouri v. Celia,* 2 Index to Court Cases of Callaway County, File No. 4,496 at 13 (1855).

49. *Civil Rights Cases* supra note 44.

50. Id. at 20.

51. Id.

52. 163 U.S. 537 (1896)

53. Higginbotham, supra note 18 at 117.

54. Id. at 113.

55. Plessy, supra note 52 at 551.

56. Id. at 557 (Harlan dissenting).

57. See Colbert, supra note 10 at 41–42 (discussing limits of cases decided pursuant to the Fourteenth Amendment).

58. 392 U.S. 409 (1968).

59. 806 U.S. (13 Wall.) 581 (1872)

60. See Kinoy, supra note 17 at 479.

61. 392 U.S. at 445–46 (Douglas concurring opinion).

62. See *Runyon v. McCrary,* 427 U.S. 160 (1976) and *Patterson v. McLean Credit Union,* 401 U.S. 164 (1989).

63. See e.g., *Palmer v. Thompson,* 403 U.S. 217 (1971) (holding that the closing of swimming pools rather than desegregating them did not constitute a badge or incident of slavery); *City of Memphis v. Greene,* 101 S.Ct. 1584 (1981) (refusing to find that a street closing violated 42 U.S.C. sec. 198 (a) because the plaintiffs failed to show that it prevented them from exercising the same property rights as whites).

64. Congressman John Conyers Jr. (D MI) has introduced legislation each year since 1989, which would create a commission to study the need for reparations for slavery and the vestiges of slavery. The bill is currently numbered H.R. 40.

65. Supra note 10.

66. See Colbert, supra note 10 at 12, fn 65.

67. See generally, Mary Berry, "Reparations for Freedmen, 1890–1916" 57 *The Journal of Negro History* 219, (1972); Linda Allen Eustace and Imari A. Obadele, *Eight Women Leaders of the Reparations Movement USA,* (Baton Rouge, LA: The Malcolm Generation, Inc., 2000).

68. Adjoa A. Aiyetoro, "The Development of the Movement for Reparations," *Journal of Law and Society* 3 (2002): 133.

69. See Eustace and Obadele, supra note 68 at 22–25.

70. Manning Marable, *Reparations and Our Rendezvous with History,* BRC-reparations-owners@egroups.com, February 2, 2002.

71. See generally,. Aiyetoro, supra note 68.

72. Kinoy, supra note 60 at 481–82 and footnote 29 in which Kinoy quotes Justice Harlan in his dissent in the *Civil Rights Cases*: "the Wartime Amendments created an affirmative duty that the States eradicate all relics, 'badges and indicia of slavery' lest Negroes as a race sink back into 'second-class' citizenship."

73. See Charles Lawrence III, "The Id, the Ego, and Equal Protection: Reckoning with Unconscious Racism," *Stanford Law Review* 39 (1987): 317.

74. See e.g., Clarence J. Munford, *Race and Reparations: A Black Perspective for the 21st Century*, (Trenton, N.J.: Africa World Press, 1996).

75. See Deborah Kuhn McGregor, *From Midwives to Medicine: The Birth Gynecology* (Rutgers University Press, 1998); *An American Health Dilemma: A Medical History of African Americans and the Problem of Race, Beginnings to 1900* (New York: Routledge, 2000); *An American Health Dilemma*, vol. 2, *Race, Medicine, and Healthcare in the United States*, (New York: Routledge, 2002).

76. See generally, Charshee McIntyre, *Criminalizing a Race: Free Blacks During Slavery* (New York: Kayode, 1984); A. Leon Higginbotham, *In the Matter of Color: Race and the American Legal Process—The Colonial Period* (New York and London: Oxford University Press, 1978).

77. See Dorothy Roberts, *Killing the Black Body: Race, Reproduction, and the Meaning of Liberty* (New York: Pantheon, 1999).

78. See *McClesky v. Kemp*, 481 U.S. 279 (1987); Jason Gillmer, "*United States v. Clary*: Equal Protection and the 'Crack Statute,' " *American University Law Review* 44 (1995): 497.

79. See e.g., *McCleskey* at 286–87.

80. The disproportionate application of the death penalty has led two states, Illinois in 2000 and Maryland in 2002, to place a moratorium on its implementation until the racial disparity and other fairness factors in its imposition can be analyzed and the apparent arbitrariness eliminated.

81. See Nkechi Taifa, "Beyond Institutionalized Racism," *National Bar Association Journal* 13 (Sept/Oct 1996); Colbert, supra note 10 at 4, fn. 14 indicating that Professor Laurence Tribe testified before the United States Senate that the Thirteenth Amendment provides constitutional support for the passage of a proposed Racial Justice Act that would have placed an affirmative duty on states to explain disparate sentencing patterns.

Women and the Welfare State

Frances Fox Piven

CHAPTER 7

The Culture of Work Enforcement

Race, Gender, and U.S. Welfare Policy

The passage of the 1996 welfare law was a milestone in the continuing campaign to "reform" welfare by making cash assistance for impoverished mother-headed families hard to get and hard to keep. The campaign reflects a number of different currents in contemporary American politics. It is one manifestation of a broader effort to reorient social policy generally so as to increase labor discipline. It is an instance of the recurrent use of racism by politicians to mobilize support among the white majority. It is an expression of America's enduring sexual obsessions. And it is no doubt much else besides. This complexity notwithstanding, I think much about the politics of welfare reform is illuminated by considering the role of welfare in shoring up class, race, and gender inequalities in labor markets. Most important, the dramatic change in policy that the 1996 law effected reflects the ongoing transformation of gender roles as women's traditional caretaking work in the home is downgraded in favor of "real" work for wages.

Historical Background

To appreciate the relationship of this shift in gender roles to welfare policy, we have first to recognize that programs to provide material assistance to the poor have always also been labor policies. From the invention of relief systems across Europe in the late middle ages, relief policies were molded by the dual preoccupations with maintaining civil order when economic calamity made the poor desperate and doing so in a way that did not allow the poor to evade work on whatever terms were offered by local employers. Thus when the crops failed or local markets collapsed and the poor took to the streets, provision might be made to aid them. But little was given, and that only on the strictest conditions. By the nineteenth century, as manufacturing grew, relief was frequently conditional on the pauper entering the workhouse. This policy heritage was imported into the United States. Here, however, relief programs remained strictly local until the Great Depression, a reflection of the great variations in labor requirements in a huge and diversified economy. America also imported a sexual theme in welfare talk, the Malthusian conviction that it was dangerous to provide the poor with even the barest means of survival, for then they would reproduce without limit.

Our first national welfare program was initiated in 1935 in the wake of a series of abrupt shifts in relief policy. Early in 1933 the new Roosevelt administration had pushed emergency relief legislation through Congress in an effort to quell insurgency that economic depression had spurred among the poor and the unemployed. The spirit of crisis led to relatively generous relief payments to millions of people, without much regard for whether they were "employable" or "unemployable," men or women. But as in the past, liberal relief proffered in response to the threat power of the poor did not last.

In 1935, as part of the Social Security Act, Aid to Dependent Children (ADC), later renamed Aid to Families of Dependent Children (AFDC), was enacted to replace emergency relief. The new program restricted assistance to poor children and their mothers, depicted as dutiful—and white—widows, much as recipients of the earlier local "widow's pension" programs had been depicted. Men, who were considered workers or potential workers, were usually not eligible for welfare.[1] Nevertheless, in principle the creation of this federal program might have been a large step forward. Even the restriction of the program to fatherless children and their mothers might have seemed to protect the program from the punitive forms of relief administration that work enforcement had always encouraged. Also, for the first time, there was a federal role in relief, and federal grants-in-aid paid much of the cost, although the members of Congress who shaped the legislation insisted on a good deal of state (and local) autonomy, in setting grant levels, in specifying conditions for eligibility, and, most important, in administering the program. Later, as a result of amendments in 1939, social security coverage was extended to include the dependents of retired or deceased workers covered by social security. Most of the white widows who had given some legitimacy to the principle of government support for mothering were now covered by another program. As a consequence, ADC and then AFDC came in practice to resemble the old poor relief programs.

It was the states that set formal benefit levels and elaborated eligibility criteria, and the counties that determined how these would be applied, when they were applied. The Social Security Act delimited the categories of people whose benefits would be eligible for federal cost sharing—only impoverished orphans in the case of ADC—but the states were free to set additional limits on who could be aided and how much they could be aided.

The states in turn typically turned the administration of the program over to the counties, and the counties were generally allowed to introduce further restrictions in their interpretation of state law. Such monitoring as was done by either the federal or state governments was aimed at discovering excessive generosity in the form of ineligibles on the rolls, or overpayments. And to cope with employer pressures and popular animosities, county governments elaborated the distinctive combination of regulatory complexity, intensive bureaucratic oversight, and wide caseworker discretion that characterized the U.S. welfare system created in 1935 and has now been resurrected under Temporary Assistance to Needy Families (TANF). The maze of detailed rules, compiled in voluminous and usually secret procedural manuals, in practice gave line workers great discretion in determining eligibility and benefits. At the same time close bureaucratic supervision of these workers was directed exclusively to scrutiny of decisions to give aid and not to decisions to withhold aid, inevitably tilting the uses of discretion toward restrictiveness. The vigorous efforts of the states under the current TANF regime to change the "culture" of the welfare office so that aid is withheld whenever possible, by withholding information about benefits, by requiring numerous trips to ascertain eligibility, by subjecting potential applicants to legal and illegal strategies of diversion, or by simply rejecting applicants, is in fact a reconstruction of the welfare "culture" that originally prevailed under AFDC. In the 1960s the New York City welfare manual moralized that "the withholding of assistance can be as important as the giving of assistance,"[2] and this is now the main message of the new TANF regime.

Why were the reform hopes of 1935 so badly disappointed? One reason was simply that the legislative segregation of women and children from "employables" was necessarily difficult to implement. Human relationships are not easily restricted by legislative categories, so state and local administrators remained preoccupied with the possibility that the grants made to mothers and their children would find their way to the men with whom those women and children associated. Hence the notorious "man-in-the-house" rules, which barred women from welfare if a man was present in the home, as well as the practices of midnight searches by welfare department investigators determined to uncover these informal relationships.

Another reason was that policy talk notwithstanding, many women, especially poor women, were in fact part of the labor force. Most obviously, black women in the rural south were workers. The overwhelming majority of American blacks lived in the South until well after World War II, so it was therefore the welfare programs of southern states and counties that bore on the life circumstances of blacks. Southern congressmen had pressed hard and successfully for the elimination from the Social Security Act of any wording that might have been construed as constraining the states from racial discrimination in the administration of welfare. And they used the latitude they had won to run the welfare program in ways consistent with the racial order of their region. This meant that southern welfare laws and practices were designed to shore up a rigid caste labor system. Blacks were less likely to get aid,[3] and when they did, their benefits were lower than those of whites, meaning that their welfare checks would compare unfavorably with even the miserable earnings of field hands.[4] The average relief payment per person in the southern region was about half the average elsewhere, and black families received less than white families. In rural areas they received much less.[5] And while welfare benefits might be used to sustain some black families at bare subsistence levels when they were not needed in the fields, such families were either cut off when seasonal employment became available or their benefits were reduced. In 1943 Louisiana was the first state to adopt an "employable mothers" rule, which instructed local officials to refuse assistance to mothers of school-age children when employment was deemed to be available. Georgia soon followed suit, with a rule that permitted local officials to deny aid to mothers of children over three years of age whenever employment was deemed to be available, prohibited county departments from supplementing wages even when they fell below welfare grant levels, and directed welfare officials to deny all applications and to close all cases of mothers deemed able to work when employment was considered to be available.[6]

The South also outdid other regions in inventing moral criteria for welfare eligibility. By 1942 most southern states had enacted "suitable home" laws, under which black mothers who violated sexual norms were denied aid. Myrdal observed that, "since all Negroes are believed to be 'immoral,' almost any discrimination can be motivated on such grounds."[7] The preoccupation of southern welfare departments with the sexual morality of their cases meshed nicely with their preoccupation with enforcing work on even the harshest terms. When the implementation of Florida's "suitable home" law drove seven thousand families with children born out of wedlock from the rolls in 1959, most of them black, the mothers had no choice but to take whatever work they could get, even work that paid less than Florida's benefit of $15 per month per person.[8] Long before the contemporary campaign against welfare, the practices of the South vividly illustrated the intertwining of labor exploitation, racial animosities, and the peculiar sexual obsessions that bedevil American culture.

The culture of the white South was, of course, also deeply racist, so that popular attitudes supported degraded labor arrangements and restrictive welfare laws and practices. But cause and effect are difficult to disentangle here. When a racial group is kept at the bottom of a labor system and excluded from its social and political institutions, the result may be to create, or at least to nourish, the racist popular culture that is then said to be the cause of labor market and political discrimination.

So long as they remained in the rural South, there was little blacks could do to change the racial social order. For one thing, rural blacks were in the grip of the planters on whom they depended for work, welfare, and credit, as well as for some protection from the official and unofficial terror that undergirded southern race politics. Moreover, they were without even the recourse of the vote and without whatever influence could be wielded by organized voters, for southern electoral systems meshed with southern labor systems by effectively disenfranchising most blacks. The labor system and the political system worked together to sustain the racial order. Under these conditions, a state- and county-run welfare system, and the skewed discretion it allowed line workers, produced a deeply racist system of welfare.

The post–WWII massive migration of blacks from the rural South to the urban North by itself changed little. The welfare regimes of northern states and counties were not exempt from the American racial order, and in any case used their discretion in ways that were extremely restrictive to poor whites as well as blacks. Indeed, jurisdictions in the North responded to the influx of impoverished black migrants from the South by becoming more restrictive in an effort to ward off the newcomers. A series of political dramas resulted, as politicians fomented scandal after scandal over local welfare liberality. In 1961 and 1962, Senator Harry Byrd, Democrat from West Virginia launched an investigation of the Washington D.C. welfare department. His spectacular exposés, well covered by the press, resulted in a sharp drop in the approval of welfare applications and a sharp rise in terminations. Subsequently, the welfare department's fraud investigators put hundreds of AFDC mothers under parked car surveillance and concluded that 60 percent of recipients were ineligible, mainly because they appeared to have male visitors. Not surprisingly, in the wake of the exposés, welfare applications fell sharply.

Meanwhile, in Newburgh, New York, local officials similarly stirred up welfare scandal, charging massive fraud and illegitimacy. This sort of political theater inevitably affected the exercise of line worker discretion. Even a New York legislative commission commented on the vague reasons for which families were denied aid. And a national study of terminations conducted in 1961 reported that far more blacks than whites were terminated from the rolls for what were recorded as "other reasons."[9] A few years later New York City officials explored the options available to them for lowering the welfare rolls and (premonitions of TANF) suggested longer waiting periods, an intake procedure that would send applicants to an employment agency before they were allowed to complete their application, and the elimination of at least seven offices so that the system would become less physically accessible and backlogs would build up.[10]

The 1960s Struggle for "Welfare Rights"

In the course of the 1960s the welfare system changed dramatically. The federal role enlarged, local discretion was curbed, and something like the rule of law was brought to the system. The agents of this transformation were the protest movements of the period, including protests over civil rights, poverty rights, and welfare rights. Blacks, and especially black women, were major participants in all of these movements. And in welfare rights, black—and Hispanic—women were the main participants.

The process through which the movements changed welfare policy was not simple and direct. Underlying the rise of protest and government responses to it were the large-scale changes in American politics spurred by the mechanization of southern agriculture and the ensuing migration of blacks from the rural south to the cities of the South and North. Migration freed blacks from the feudal domination of the rural South, and concentration in the cities lent them at least some resources for collective action. The chain of disturbances that ensued rocked American politics. First, the eruption of civil rights protests and the efforts of national political leaders to appease them helped to precipitate white southern voter defections in Democratic presidential contests, beginning as early 1948. As traditional southern support of the Democrats became more uncertain, the big-city base of the Democratic Party became more important, especially because urban voters were sometimes able to throw the electoral votes of the big industrial states into one party column or another. Thus, as black numbers, now voting numbers, in the cities grew, they became a critical factor in Democratic presidential calculations. And there was growing evidence that all was not well, as the election of 1956 when the black Democratic vote plummeted by 20 percentage points showed. Stimulated by the civil rights movement, urban blacks who had been loyal Democrats since 1936 were beginning to defect, a pattern that the spread of protest to the cities was likely to worsen.[11]

National Democratic leaders responded with a series of federal programs targeted to the inner cities where black newcomers were concentrated. The programs, first launched under John F. Kennedy's "New Frontier" and then continued and expanded under Lyndon Baines Johnson's "Great Society," brought rhetorical encouragement and some resources, including legal resources, to impoverished black communities. And as black discontent escalated, the new federal programs themselves became agents of movement demands, for jobs or housing or education or civilian control of the police or welfare. At least in the short run, the resistance of organized whites whose stakes were being challenged was intense. There was less resistance in welfare. The rolls rose steadily throughout the 1960s and early 1970s, and spiraled as protests in the cities escalated after 1965.

The expansion of the welfare rolls in the 1960s has received a good deal of attention. But another aspect of the 1960s transformation was also important and contributed to the expansion. The developments of the 1960s curbed the license of local administrators and staff, and even brought something like the rule of law to welfare. With protestors in the streets and sometimes in the welfare offices, staff discretion was limited for fear of escalating the disorder, and more people received aid. The protests, in turn, owed something to the new federally funded poverty services, which provided resources and legitimation to poor minority communities. Just as important, advocacy services and the litigation that the federal legal services program spearheaded, had the effect not only of curbing line worker discretion but of striking down some of the most egregious rules of the AFDC system in the courts. These several developments were cumulative, each lending momentum to the other. For example, both the new federal programs and the movement organizations set about making information about welfare entitlements available, preparing handbooks and flyers on welfare entitlements and regulations, and distributing these materials widely. Nothing quite like this had ever happened, and information about "welfare rights" helped spur protests by local groups. At the same time, the federally funded neighborhood offices in the inner cities helped people cope with the welfare system. After all, what people typically needed was money, whether to pay the rent or buy food or shoes so the children could go to school, and the better informed and more confident service center workers could help them get it. Meanwhile, restrictive welfare laws were challenged in suit after suit, with the consequence that the federal courts struck down state residence laws, man-in-the-house rules, "substitute father" rules,[12] and employable-mother rules. In *Goldberg v. Kelly*, the Supreme Court even required that recipients be allowed to challenge welfare decisions through quasi-judicial administrative proceedings.[13] The federal Department of Health, Education and Welfare (later renamed

Health and Human Services) also cooperated, issuing new federal regulations that constrained local welfare administration, including a regulation requiring that oral requests for aid be considered formal applications.

The development of a federally influenced rule-bound regime was an achievement. For one thing, it meant that money flowed to the poorest people in the country, households headed by women, many of them minorities. For another, it meant that a new set of rights was in the process of being established. The protestors had called these welfare rights. But if welfare rights meant that poor women raising children on their own were entitled to support from government and that procedures were in place that would ensure that those entitlements were delivered, then welfare rights meant the rights of poor women, especially minority poor women, to be protected from a work-enforcing penury and to be *mothers*. In other words, poor women now had the right to conform to traditional gender roles. Nearly forty years later it is hard to reconstruct the heady sense of liberation that women expressed when they asserted that because they were mothers, they deserved welfare.

The Work-Enforcement Crackdown

Even as poor women reached for the respect and resources presumably accorded other women as mothers, American understandings of motherhood were changing. One reason was that families were changing, as rates of divorce and separation rose and more women who bore children did not marry. Fewer and fewer women were in situations that resembled the traditional family to which ideas about motherhood were linked. Another reason was that more and more women were leaving the home for wage work, some pushed by declining male earnings, some eager to take advantage of new opportunities to participate in the work world. The images associated with this transformation were often images of suited women swinging attaché cases. Most women, however, entered the expanding low-wage service sector as fast-food workers, or clerks, or office cleaners. While this shift from domestic work to market work did not of itself cause the turn to a work-enforcing welfare policy, it undermined those groups—including not only welfare recipients themselves but feminist and social welfare organizations as well—that might otherwise have resisted that turn more forcefully.

In fact, efforts to restore work enforcement to welfare policy began even as liberalization was occurring in the late 1960s. Over the course of the next three decades a variety of measures were enacted by Congress to encourage work by providing recipients with welfare supplements, or to require work as a condition for receiving grants, or to require recipients to search for work. However, not many women were placed in jobs as a result of these programs, partly because there were not many jobs for unskilled women, especially mothers whose childcare responsibilities might make them unreliable workers,[14] and partly because division and ambivalence among congressional Democrats led to measures hemmed in by exceptions and procedural protections.

Meanwhile, another sort of work-enforcing solution was unfolding. Once the movements of the 1960s subsided, the states allowed the real value of welfare grants to fall steadily, simply by not adjusting them to keep pace with inflation. Had wages held firm, the steady deterioration of welfare benefits would probably have driven many women from the welfare rolls into the market. But wages did not hold firm. In fact, for two decades from the mid-1970s to the mid-1990s, the real value of welfare benefits fell in lockstep with the falling minimum wage. Of course, one solution to the work-enforcing quandary would have been to raise the minimum wage. The other solution, however, was to slash welfare, along with other means-tested programs. This was the solution for which the increasingly well-funded right wing think tanks campaigned, sponsoring the public intellectuals, the books, articles, conferences, and reports that kept welfare in the news.[15] As the campaign continued, welfare retrenchment became more and more politically acceptable.

The campaign received an extraordinary boost when Bill Clinton introduced the slogans "End Welfare As We Know It" and "Two Years and Off to Work" into the presidential campaign of 1992. When a Republican majority took control of the House of Representatives in 1994, they upped the ante on President Clinton's rhetoric and promised to enact a "Personal Responsibility Act." Welfare reform moved to center stage, and the propaganda campaign about the perverse effects of welfare was in full swing. A too liberal welfare, it was claimed on all sides, was the reason slothful women, widely understood to be black women, did not take jobs. Democrats and Republicans were now competing for the political support that could be gained by tapping the deep antipathies in American culture toward the poor and toward black and Latina minorities who were thought to be the main beneficiaries of welfare, and also tapping the energy and excitement evoked by talk of women and sex and sin, the women who wanted to have babies without husbands and live on the dole. By the summer of 1996 Clinton was ready to sign the Personal Responsibility and Work Opportunity Reconciliation Act. With that stroke, all of the painfully won "welfare rights" protections won in the 1960s, already eroded, were wiped away and AFDC was replaced by Temporary Assistance to Needy Families (TANF).

TANF imposes a five-year lifetime limit on eligibility for assistance. Even shorter time limits are imposed on cash assistance as opposed to one or another form of workfare. Unless a state opts out of this requirement, women are required to work at "community service" after two months in exchange for whatever benefits they get. In any case, 50 percent of the women on the roles must work at least thirty hours a week for their benefits after two years. The work requirements under the old AFDC law were far less stringent. Moreover, and this is important in assessing the impact of work requirements on labor markets, the old law included elaborate provisions to prevent the use of welfare recipients to displace existing workers. Most of those provisions have been eliminated or weakened.[16] Aside from these restrictions on generosity, the new legislation gives the states wide latitude in designing their welfare programs. Some states are using that latitude to reduce benefits, impose shorter time limits on assistance, or introduce sanctions that penalize families with benefit cuts for a variety of undesirable behaviors, such as the birth of an additional child, the failure to get children immunized, the truancy of a child,[17] or even minor rule transgressions. In March 1998 a federal study showed that in one three-month period the previous year, 38 percent of the recipients who were dropped from welfare nationally were dropped because they were sanctioned. Georgia families who received two sanctions were banned from assistance for life. The *Washington Post* of March 23, 1998, reported that in Alabama, recipients could lose benefits for failing to show up for an appointment. Mississippi succeeded in slashing the number of families receiving assistance by more than half between 1993 and 1997, and the ready use of sanctions for rule infractions appears to have been the main method for reducing the rolls.[18]

At the same time elaborate hurdles have been introduced into the application process, including extended waits, multiple investigations, fingerprinting and drug tests, and participation in "job search" classes, all justified by argument that the "culture" of the welfare office has to be transformed into a job culture. The inevitable consequence has been to ward off the needy poor, as evidenced by the Urban Institute's finding that the proportion of the eligible actually receiving cash assistance fell from 79 percent in 1996 to 52 percent in 1999.[19]

Or consider the new restrictions on social supports for immigrants that were also incorporated in welfare reform. Most legal immigrants are no longer entitled to Medicaid, food stamps, or cash assistance. If the public appears to go along with these exclusions, it is probably because they think immigrants should not enter the country unless they can support themselves. But the idea that benefit cutoffs will deter immigration finds little confirmation in data or experience.[20] More likely, the exclusions simply ensure that the immigrants who do come here remain without any public protections to tide them over periods of unemployment or low wages. This may indeed be just what was intended, since the business think tanks and congressional bloc that fought strenuously against tighter controls on immigration also fought to slash the benefits for which immigrants would be eligible. During 1996, the year that cutbacks on aid to legal immigrants were made law, almost a million legal immigrants were admitted to the U.S., the largest number since 1914.[21]

During the turbulent 1960s income support programs expanded in all rich countries. Some social scientists applauded this expansion and the "decommodification" of labor that resulted when workers were shielded from the market by welfare state income protections.[22] Others bemoaned the expansion, pointing to the same relationship to draw a very different moral—that the terms of labor had become unresponsive to the market, or "inflexible," because income support programs were too generous. Either way, the "law" holds: income protection programs come to constitute a floor under the terms of the labor market. The broad comparative evidence is compelling, and it has become more compelling in the last two decades, as income programs have been rolled back. Haveman points out that in countries where income support programs, such as unemployment benefits or assistance for poor families, provide only low benefits, particularly the U.S., the United Kingdom, and Japan, wages for the low-skilled fell sharply during the 1980s, by between 10 and 25 percent. But in countries with generous programs, the wages of the less skilled did not fall, and measures of income inequality did not rise as they did in the United States, a development often labeled "wage inflexibility."[23]

A similar relationship between welfare benefit levels and the wages of poor women eligible for welfare has been shown in the United States. Even under the old AFDC program, it was the states that set benefit levels, which varied widely. Elaine McCrate shows that these state-to-state variations in benefit levels were correlated with variations in the earnings of less-educated women. With each $100 drop in the benefit package, the wages of women with a high school degree or less fell by 3 percent.[24] Similarly, Michael Hout shows that cuts in the real value of AFDC benefits in the 1980s combined with the erosion of the real value of the legal minimum wage to depress the earnings of less-educated women.[25]

In a word, because welfare cutbacks force mothers to work, they exert downward pressure on the labor market, especially low-wage sectors of the labor market. During the closing years of the 1990s a booming economy concealed this effect, as overall unemployment fell to the historically remarkable level of 4.2 percent and wages rose. But without welfare reform, wages would have risen far more than they did at the end of the boom. Now, as the economy falters and unemployment rises, the effects of welfare reform will become more apparent. As hundreds of thousands of women lose welfare benefits, whether because of time limits or sanctions or bureaucratic snafus, they will stream into the labor market to compete with other women (and men) for less-skilled and low-paying jobs.

The Culture of Work Enforcement

The bearing of welfare on labor markets is not only the result of the interplay between the material incentives of wage work and welfare. Welfare programs and the discourse that surrounds them also help to define the identities of those who participate in the labor market and those who don't. The campaign to reform welfare was itself a powerful intervention in American culture, one that argued the worthlessness of poor women raising children on the dole. And the new punitive practices ushered in by the legislation—sometimes called "tough love"—reinforce those denigrating meanings.

The cultural campaign against welfare and welfare recipients has also been going on for decades, if not centuries. In the late middle ages paupers in England were tied to carts and paraded around the market place to publicly degrade them. American politicians have been figuratively doing much the same. Barry Goldwater charged that welfare "transforms the individual being into a dependent animal creature." Richard Nixon campaigned against George McGovern with an ad that claimed McGovern wanted to put half the country "on welfare," and later Ronald Reagan used the bully pulpit of the presidency to popularize the image of the "welfare queen," rightly perceiving that the association of the Democrats with welfare was a vulnerability for the Democrats and an opportunity for the Republicans. Kevin Phillips, for example, lists welfare with rising crime, judicial permissiveness, riots, and the death penalty in accounting for "much of the critical GOP momentum in the Nixon and Reagan years."[26]

None of this talk was about labor markets. Rather, everyone focused relentlessly on the ostensibly perverse effects of welfare on the creatures who received it. In fact, it had a good deal to do with labor markets, for it created a national drama that heaped insult on women who were poor if they were presumed not to work. The politics of the 1960s had reduced the stigma of being on the dole, and as a consequence more people in need applied for welfare and the rolls rose; the politics of the 1990s increased stigma, and beginning in 1993 the rolls began to fall rapidly and more and more impoverished mothers worked, and worked more and more hours in the effort to stay afloat without welfare.

The point I want to make about these new practices is that they are simultaneously material and cultural in their effects. Grants are reduced, or terminated, which is obviously a very material change. But material practices, especially material practices with such awesome consequences as the loss of a welfare grant, are also cultural because they help to shape the way people think about themselves and their world. Conversely, cultural practices are also material, because by helping to shape the way people think about themselves and their world, they change the way they respond to material conditions. The years-long campaign against welfare was a kind of theater, one that changed the way many Americans thought about welfare and even changed the way recipients thought about welfare, making it less likely that women would apply for aid if they could somehow survive without it. In the same vein, welfare practices that require finger printing and intrusive investigations as a condition of aid heighten the stigma of welfare receipt, which leads many women to shun the dole for whatever work they can get. In fact, many women have always chosen to work rather than be exposed to the shame of welfare, even when the wages they earned did not make up for their added costs in day care and transportation, leaving them worse off than welfare recipients.[27] Inevitably, as stigmatizing rituals proliferate, the shame of welfare increases, and more women will work.

Taken together, these several policy developments are having a large impact both on poor, mother-headed families and on the contemporary American labor market. The reason is simple and can be stated as a kind of policy law. Public programs, which provide people with income that is not conditional on work, create a floor under wages. In nineteenth-century England the law was recognized as the principle of "less eligibility," a principle that meant no one receiving poor relief should be as well off as the meanest independent laborer. Of course, people take jobs for many reasons beyond material incentives. Nevertheless, if people can survive without wage work in a manner judged reasonable by the standards of their community, many will, at least if the only work available to them entails dreary toil at low wages with little reason for pride. It follows that when these public supports are slashed, and when the stigma or harassment associated with receiving them is increased, more people will be willing to search for work, they will search more intensely, and more of them will take whatever job they can find.

The focus on work that characterizes the new welfare regime is not new. Relief or welfare policy has always been shaped by the twin concerns of maintaining civil order and enforcing work. Over the course of the twentieth century, however, some programs were introduced to make allowance for the responsibilities of women as mothers, an acknowledgement first evident in the state widow's pensions programs earlier in the century and reiterated in the provisions of the early AFDC program. But images of worthy widows that adorned these programs notwithstanding, the preoccupation with work enforcement remained dominant, and few poor women got aid. That changed in the 1960s when welfare became less restrictive, partly in response to a movement of women who asserted their right to state support because they performed traditional gender roles. They were mothers.

Liberal welfare did not last. The main reasons were the demise of the 1960s movements on the one hand and the subsequent rise of business power in American politics, along with the neoliberal celebration of markets unfettered from government intervention, on the other. Meanwhile, and partly as a result of the decline in male breadwinner earnings that followed the rise of neoliberalism, more and more women entered the labor force. For many women, this was a liberating experience. It meant the right to participate in the more public world of work, and for some it even meant entry into the professions and management positions from which women had previously been largely barred. For many others, however, it meant that the drudgery of low-wage work was added to the unpaid domestic work they had always done. But either way, women were now viewed as workers. For impoverished women raising children on their own, the moment when they had almost won the right to be mothers had passed.

NOTES

1. Other income programs created under the Social Security Act were directed to men, or at least to white men in the primary labor market. These programs were, in contrast to ADC, strongly work-conditioned. For a discussion of the "two-channel" welfare state, see Barbara Nelson, "The Origins of the Two-Channel Welfare State: Workmen's Compensation and Mothers' Aid," in Linda Gordon, ed., *Women, the State, and Welfare* (Madison: University of Wisconsin Press, 1990).

2. See the discussion in Frances Fox Piven and Richard A. Cloward, *Regulating the Poor* (New York: Pantheon, 1993), 151–56.

3. See Gunnar Myrdal, *An American Dilemma: The Negro Problem and Modern Democracy* (New York: Harper & Row, 1962), 359, who documents this discrimination. The most extreme case he found was Georgia where, in 1940, 38 percent of all children under fifteen were black, but blacks accounted for only 11 to 12 percent of those on ADC in 1937 to 1940.

4. The techniques for underbudgeting included assigning high income values to rent-free shacks in cotton plantations, counting contributions from relatives who were not contributing, assuming utilities were free when they were not, and so on. See Piven and Cloward, supra, note 2, 163–64.

5. Ibid., 131.

6. Ibid.,: 134–35,

7. Myrdal, supra, note 3, 360.

8. Piven and Cloward, supra, note 2, 140.

9. Elaine M. Burgess and Daniel O. Price, *An American Dependency Challenge: A Study by the Institute for Research in Social Science of the University of North Carolina* (Chicago: American Public Welfare Association, 1963), 55 (table 3.8) and 163.

10. Piven and Cloward, supra, note 2, 150, 157–58, 160–61, 174,

11. See Frances Fox Piven, "The Great Society as a Political Strategy," in Richard A. Cloward and Frances Fox Piven, *The Politics of Turmoil* (New York: Pantheon, 1974), 271–83.

12. In effect these rules made families ineligible when the mother was known to have a relationship with a man.

13. *Goldberg v. Kelly* 397 U.S. 254 (1970).

14. For a discussion, see Piven and Cloward, *Regulating the Poor*, chap. 11.

15. See Lucy A. Williams, "The Right's Attack on Aid to Families with Dependent Children," *The Public Eye* 10, nos. 3–4 (fall/winter 1996).

16. See Sharon Dietrich, Maurice Emsellen, and Jim Williams, "Comments of the National Employment Law Project to the Proposed TANF Regulations" (New York: National Employment Law Project, February 18, 1998); Mathew Diller, "Dismantling the Welfare State: Welfare Reform and Beyond," *Stanford Law and Policy Review* (winter 1998): 19–43.

17. See Center on Hunger and Poverty, "Are States Improving the Lives of Poor Families? A Scale Measure of State Welfare Policies?" (Medford, MA: Tufts University, February 1998), 1–13.

18. Bill M. Brister, Jesse D. Beeler, and Sharon Chambry, "Implementation Process Study: Mississippi's Temporary Assistance for Needy Families Program (Jackson, Mississippi: Center for Applied Research, Millsaps College, December 1997).

19. See U.S. Department of Health and Human Services, Indicators of Welfare Dependence: Annual Report to Congress 2002 (www.dhhs.gov).

20. See Douglas Massey, "March of Folly: U.S. Immigration Policy After Nafta," *The American Prospect* (March/April 1998): 22–23.

21. Peter H. Schuck, "The Open Society," *New Republic*, April 13, 1998, pp. 16–18.

22. For a good discussion, see Gosta Esping-Andersen, *Politics Against Markets: The Social Democratic Road to Power* (Princeton, N.J.: Princeton University Press, 1985), 31–36.

23. See Robert Haveman, "Equity with Employment," *Boston Review* (summer 1997): 3–8. See also Organization for Economic Cooperation and Development, *The OECD Jobs Study: Evidence and Explanations* (Paris: OECD, 1994); and see Gosta Esping-Andersen, *The Three Worlds of Welfare Capitalism* (Princeton, N.J.: Princeton University Press, 1990).

24. See Elaine McCrate, " Welfare and Women's Earnings," *Politics and Society* 25, no. 4 (December 1997): 417–42.

25. See Michael Hout, "The Effects of Welfare, the Minimum Wage, and Tax Credits on Low Wage Labor Markets," *Politics and Society* 25, no.4 (December 1997): 513–24. See also Robert Moffitt, "Incentive Effects of the U.S. Welfare System," *Journal of Economic Literature* 30, no. 1 (March 1992).

26. Kevin Phillips, *Boiling Point* (New York: Random House, 1993), 248.

27. See Kathryn Edin and Laura Lein, *Making Ends Meet: How Single Mothers Survive Welfare and Low-Wage Work* (New York: Russell Sage Foundation, 1997).

Patricia Smith

CHAPTER 8

The Silent Constitution

Affirmative Obligation and the Feminization of Poverty

A constitution reflects and reinforces a political consensus or ideology, at least among those in power, who establish and interpret it. Ideally, it is intended to represent a political consensus of the population at large—the will of the people, as it is often put. This ideal is never realized in fact, since there never is a political consensus of the population at large, especially in diverse societies, and often the interests of entire groups are ignored or subordinated to the good of others. Furthermore, it is possible for a constitution (or more often, for parts of it) to become obsolete or ineffective; provisions and protections may be ignored or interpreted into vacuity.

Yet, despite these qualifications, a constitution ordinarily tells us something about the society it represents. It lays out the structure: democratic or dictatorial, secular or religious, acknowledging civil rights and protecting material security or not, and so on. In this respect a constitution articulates the "official view," even if that official view may be undermined or diverted in practice to some extent, even to a great extent. The constitution is what we declare to the world. It is what we say we stand for.

The U.S. Constitution provides clear protections of civil liberties (we stand for freedom) but no guarantee of material security to anyone. At the time it was written no constitution did so, but since then many have been established that include protections and guarantees of positive benefits, such as rights to employment or income security, medical care, education, and retirement pensions. While the eighteenth and nineteenth centuries saw the proliferation of civil liberties, during the twentieth century a greater recognition of positive rights to material security emerged in many nations.[1] Yet no constitutional amendment in that direction has had any show of solid support in the U.S.

Perhaps that indicates what we stand for. We won't bother you, but you are on your own here. Commentators have often described this as a policy of benign neglect or a commitment to small government. The clear implication is that government should stay out of people's lives as much as possible and simply allow individuals to work out their common interests and conflicts for themselves. It is quite clear that this restrictive view (of government) was the overriding presumption of constitutional thought—the political consensus—in the U.S. through the nineteenth century.[2]

On the other hand, a great deal of legislative activity creating positive benefits occurred during the twentieth century.[3] Many programs were established. Education, at least at the primary and secondary level, is now guaranteed (and required) by the individual states for all children (not equally, but minimally). Retirement and disability pensions became available through Social Security. Public housing, cash assistance, food stamps, medical care, and so on are now provided for certain populations, at least on a temporary basis. No constitutional amendment was needed for any of these reforms to take place. And in certain cases, such as the public school system, or the Social Security, Unemployment, and Worker's Compensation programs, the results have been rather good, critical commentary to the contrary not withstanding.[4] That is, the results are good in that they indicate a positive effect on the material condition of the vast majority of the population and provide a positive indication of an informal political consensus that approximates a constitutional commitment.[5] Most of these programs have done little for the most needy or vulnerable in our society. Still, the legislative activity complicates the picture of the political consensus in America by the twentieth century. Do we still stand for the policy of benign neglect? Not exactly, since all children are required to be educated and all workers are required to participate in the Social Security program, and so on. But we are far from a European model of social welfare, especially for the poor.

How well we have done in solving (or even addressing) the problem of poverty in America depends on the particular problem or population viewed and to what it is compared. If we compare our comprehensive social welfare program (such as it is) to that of Sweden, Germany, or France, we will not fare well.[6] But if we look at our elderly population, we will see that the poverty rate has dropped from over 20 percent in the 1920s to less than 10 percent since Social Security pensions were fully implemented. If we compare our overall level of poverty today with our level of poverty during the 1930s, we can note that we have taken our country from a 50 or 60 percent poverty rate to about a 15 or 20 percent rate.[7] That sounds like real progress until it is acknowledged that the poverty rate has hovered at around 20 percent since 1965 when Michael Harrington announced the discovery of the "new poor"—the "Other America" that was being left out of the affluent economy.[8] President Johnson's "war on poverty" was intended to address this population with retraining, rehabilitation, housing, and job programs.[9]

By the mid-90s, however, poverty was still a problem and welfare (AFDC) was a political target. Politicians, smelling the blood of the vulnerable, vowed to end welfare as we knew it, and did so.[10] The welfare rolls (not to be confused with the poverty rate) plunged; the American public now has a whopping 1 percent of its national budget to spend on something else; the poverty rate, of course, is no better than it was; and business at the soup kitchens is up.[11] Indeed, it is worth noting that 80 percent of the poor today are women and children, a direct reflection of the fact that the number of female-headed households has gone up considerably since the 1970s. These are the (so-called) new poor of the new millennium. In fact, however, women and children have always been especially susceptible to the problem of poverty.[12]

But some populations have done better, notably the elderly and the temporarily unemployed. In contrast to the welfare program, the Social Security Program is considered a political untouchable.[13] In this regard it is basically a constitutional feature of American political life at this point, in the sense I have outlined above. That is to say, it is fully accepted as an entitlement by the population at large. Similarly, worker's compensation and unemployment compensation have become unquestioned guarantees of income security and medical coverage for certain populations.[14] These represent clear advances in the socialization of certain burdens or risks that exhibit none of the instability of welfare and related "entitlement" programs. Thus, unlike the prevention of poverty itself, protections of material security for certain groups have in effect become constitutional features of American political life. They are guarantees that are part of what America stands for—part of our expectations and rights of citizenship.

Yet these programs are generally conditioned on full-time long-term employment. Hence they do little to help the poor, particularly the most vulnerable populations, including women and those they care for—the sick and disabled, the old and the young. Indeed, as I have just noted, the percentage of women and children in poverty has gone up in America, a trend that is often labeled the "feminization of poverty." This statistical trend betrays a harsh and hypocritical attitude that claims respect for women and reverence for motherhood, while penalizing both at every turn.

In what follows I would like to compare the relative success story of Social Security to the American treatment of poverty and to poverty programs often termed "entitlement programs," such as AFDC (welfare), food stamps, housing subsidies, and TANF (Temporary Assistance to Needy Families). In the process I will consider the attitudes or presumptions implied in the American treatment of poverty, and its special effect on women and children. I argue here that the ambivalent attitude of Americans toward the vulnerable, our refusal to socialize these responsibilities, and our delegation of them to women without compensation accounts for much of the feminization of poverty.

Policies and Presumptions on Pooling and Poverty

Our silent constitution reflects American ambivalence about poverty, pooling resources, and the place of women in public life. The demographics of poverty change over time, but until recently the material well-being of women has always been tied to and evaluated as part of the wealth of the men who were their breadwinners. Even when nineteenth-century legal reforms made it possible for women to own property or sign contracts, they were not expected (or encouraged) to lead a separate existence. Women were part of families. During the eighteenth and nineteenth centuries family income in America depended largely on the success of the family farm or on providing services to it. Thus, the U.S. Constitution was written against the backdrop of an agricultural nation organized around the economy of the small town and the family farm. It was individualistic only in the sense that it relied on private enterprise rather than governmental direction. This organization presumed that women and children, as well as the sick, disabled, and elderly, were maintained by and contributed to the overall family economy. The state cared little for the vulnerable.

By the twentieth century, however, America was becoming predominantly urban, and the family was becoming "nuclear." Factory work replaced farming, and unemployment became a major source of poverty. The situation of women and children during the late-nineteenth and early-twentieth centuries was precarious. Child labor laws and safety regulations were slow to be enacted, while wage and hour laws were even slower to come. Women and children worked in the lowest-level, lowest-paid jobs with no possibility of advancement. The very idea of advancement for women was tied to the idea of marrying well. Among the most vulnerable populations of the time were the sick, disabled, and old. These people were completely dependent on the good will of their families or on private charity. And even many of those who were able to earn a decent living while they were young and productive were unable to save for old age or disability. Still, at this point there was little distinction between the poverty of men and women, except that women were not in a position to be independent. The family income set the level of material security for both sexes.[15]

Although reformers and special interest organizations (such as the American Association for Labor Legislation or the American Association for Old Age Security) as well as fledgling labor unions lobbied for worker's accident insurance, unemployment insurance, and old age pensions, as of 1930 no state had enacted an unemployment compensation program and poverty in old age was mostly handled by family charity or by almshouses.[16] State laws, dating from the nineteenth-century poor laws, authorized towns to make contracts with private citizens to care for the indigent, to prosecute people who refused to support poor relatives, and to "warn out" newcomers who seemed likely to become public wards. The treatment of many destitute elderly people under these conditions was truly deplorable, and virtually no oversight or quality control was exercised on their behalf.[17]

The sick, the disabled, and the elderly; female-headed households; disadvantaged minorities; and residents of depressed areas formed a persistent core of poverty-stricken populations during the entire twentieth century, joined intermittently by unemployed men in bad times. Despite the diversity of this group, the attention of reformers was sharply focused on employment. Thus the American attitude toward poverty was that it could largely be prevented with good values, a strong work ethic, and a growing economy.[18] Unlike the social welfare movements in Europe during the early twentieth century, Americans continued to be suspicious of governmental solutions to social problems and to rely heavily on their faith in the free market to provide the good life for those who were strong enough and motivated enough to secure it.[19] Thus vulnerable populations were considered private (largely family) problems, if they were considered at all. Americans did not want to think about the vulnerable as a political matter. America is about strength, not weakness. One estimate indicated a rise in total welfare spending from $180 million in 1913 to $750 million in 1929. This represents an increase from .45 percent to .73 percent of the GNP, a miniscule amount by European standards.[20]

What this shows is that before the 1930s Americans did not distinguish among different types of social assistance, basically resisting all types of governmental control or aid, especially that of centralized or federal government. Aid for the destitute was strictly a local matter. A distinction was always drawn between the "deserving" poor, such as the blind or widows (who got a little help if they were of high moral character) and the "undeserving" poor, such as vagrants, migrants, or illegitimate children (who got nothing); but no one was helped much by public assistance, whatever the source of the poverty. The general view was that family members were responsible for their own. Failing that, private charities should help the poor. Affirmative obligations of the community or state to provide for the material security of its members simply were not recognized. The idea of a welfare state was basically unthinkable in America at this time.[21]

It took the disaster of the Great Depression to jolt Americans into turning to the federal government for solutions. Again, the focus was sharply on employment. Yet the Depression, at least temporarily, instilled a new attitude about governmental obligations to insure a decent economic environment for its people, and the extent of the crisis made federal intervention both natural and necessary. It has been suggested that nothing affected the future of welfare in America so much as the emergency circumstances under which its initial programs were created. During the mid thirties the four parts of the American welfare state established the following categories of aid.[22]

First, "general relief" was to be a local responsibility to address the needs of individuals often called "unemployables." These were the long-term unemployed, the emotionally disturbed, the vagrants, the alcoholics, the disabled without families, as well as recent migrants and orphans. Generally speaking, these were the outcasts. Allocating responsibility for them to the discretion of local officials was no departure from traditional policy. It insured that little would be done for this category. These people would be the last on the list to be helped (but at least they were on the list in some sense.)[23]

The second category was "work relief," a federal responsibility to create work for those thrown into the unemployment lines by the crisis. These are the programs most people associate most directly with the New Deal and the Depression. They were all temporary, emergency measures, such as the WPA and CCC, which had varying levels of success and a relatively short duration—about two or three years at most. They were never intended to solve the problem (of unemployment) but only to alleviate the most severe effects. That is, no one thought that the solution to an unemployment crisis was to put everyone to work for the government, except as a temporary emergency measure. The solution to the problem was to restore a robust economy, which no one actually knew how to do but which many believed could be done by governmental stimulation. This was a significant change of attitude. Furthermore, many people did go to work for the government (both state and federal) as bureaucrats, in numbers greatly exceeding any considered reasonable before that time. Thus was governmental bureaucracy begun.[24]

The third part of the new welfare state was "categorical aid" for particular groups of needy people: primarily those over 65, the blind, and mothers of dependent children. Established by the Social Security Act of 1935, this program supplied matching federal dollars for local expenditures, with local administration. This was the beginning of welfare as we know it. It was a very modest program from the start and was obviously dependent on local attitudes and expenditures. Hence it was unlikely to be generous. The focus of local administration was always on cost saving, so many devices were used to declare otherwise eligible needy people to be "undeserving," especially mothers of dependent children.[25] The result was that welfare was a matter of total discretion by officials, so many eligible people were turned away, and given the stigma attached to receiving this aid many more never applied. Thus, as always, the most vulnerable people were not helped much by public assistance.

But at least it was a start, in several respects. First, it took a tiny step toward federalizing and professionalizing (or at least bureaurocratizing) the service. Second, it officially acknowledged the existence of certain vulnerable groups that are basically excluded from the economy. Certain groups are not helped by a good economy. These are the young, old, and disabled or those who care for them. Their problems will not go away if the economy corrects itself. As obvious as it is, this has been a reality that seems difficult for Americans to face. Third, it implicitly acknowledged that not all needy people have relatives who can support them. This means that some other solution to their problem is necessary. Indeed, it could be interpreted as creating a claim against government on behalf of the needy whatever the status or ability of their relatives to help them. (It was not, in fact, interpreted or administered this way until the 1960s, but the implication was always there.) It could be viewed as the beginning of an acknowledged affirmative obligation of the society at large to insure the basic material security of its most vulnerable members. Americans in fact are highly ambivalent about this idea to this day, but a seed is planted here.

Finally, the fourth part of the welfare package of the 1930s was not really welfare (i.e., not public assistance) at all but social insurance—an idea toward which Americans are much more positively inclined. It is the program now called Social Security, the greatest success story of the Social Security Act of 1935. It includes retirement pensions, and unemployment and accident compensation for qualified workers. The pension program did (eventually) reduce the number of elderly poor, not as much as it should, but at least from about 25 percent to about 10 percent. Furthermore, a great many people have been helped to some degree, and there is no stigma attached to it.

The program has some serious flaws, however. The taxes that fund it are highly regressive; the funds are not necessarily well managed; it badly underfunds those who need it most; and it pays benefits to those who do not need it at all. Those helped most are middle-class and working-class men (i.e., full-time workers), not the poor and not women. This, of course, is because in this program the less you pay in the less you get out, and given the structure of family and work responsibilities plus traditional discrimination, women typically earn much less than men. Married women have a choice to claim benefits based on their own earnings or on 50 percent of their husband's earnings. This provision was specifically enacted to discourage wives from working at a time of massive unemployment. It has never been revised. Even today a majority of women do better by basing their benefits on 50 percent of their husband's lifetime earnings than on 100 percent of their own. This, of course, does not show that women do not work. It shows that they are not paid—that is, they often receive no formal wage for their work. And since they receive no formal wage, they are not eligible for benefits based on or deducted from wages. Thus disadvantage perpetuates disadvantage, and dependency reproduces itself.

Overall, the reforms of the 1930s introduced two basic ideas that produced a limited change of political consensus in America. The first was the idea of social insurance. There is now a widespread acceptance of the idea that federal solutions to some problems—such as the risk of poverty or disability in old age—are appropriate. Few Americans today think that elderly people should be entirely dependent on their families. People do not expect or want to be supported by their children when they are old or disabled. Social Security is not a complete answer (since it is rather minimal), and private pension plans are pervasive. Yet the basic point here is that the very idea of a federal pension plan (an idea further extended by Medicare) represents a change of political consensus. Social insurance is now accepted.

Yet this idea is sharply limited through private employment. The American version of federalizing pensions (and medical insurance) is not much of an equalizing force. It is not universal. It is not a solution to poverty, especially for groups that are vulnerable before they are old. And it discriminates against women who care for the vulnerable. Nevertheless, it is a form of pooling resources for the common benefit for a certain (large) population, and it is widely accepted.

The second idea was the recognition of categorical aid—that is, aid to particular categories of people who need aid precisely because they are excluded from economic participation for one reason or another. The primary categories are age, disability, and dependent children lacking a breadwinner. By comparison to the idea of social insurance (which is that we all pay in and we all get back, but only if we paid in), the idea of categorical aid does in fact recognize social obligations to provide for vulnerable groups who cannot participate in the ordinary economic arrangements. Thus it is potentially equalizing. It does (or could potentially) address the problem of poverty. And it does (or could potentially) alleviate the unfair and uncompensated burden of caregiving for women. Unfortunately, this idea has not been widely accepted or acknowledged in America, especially as applied to caregivers and dependent children. The result has been the feminization of poverty.

One Woman's Story

Aid to Families with Dependent Children (welfare) was a failure in this country. Before the 1960s it was available to very few and was denied to many who were eligible. It could not be accepted without stigma, and its benefits provided subsistence at best. It lifted no one out of hardship. Even in the 1960s and 1970s, when welfare rights gained prominence, it was only a little better than it had been before. Welfare was always administered by local officials, who always needed to save money. The program itself was irrational and demoralizing. I know this from personal experience.

Let me tell you just one story of the many I know from the 1970s and 1980s. This is the story of a woman I will call Sherry. I expect her story was common. In 1973 I was a Head Start teacher living in a small town in Florida. Sherry had a daughter in my class of four-year-olds, a beautiful child, very neat, a little quiet. Sherry walked her daughter to class every day and met her afterward, carrying her two-year-old with her. She was very involved with her children. She wanted them to do well, especially in school.

I became involved with Sherry because of the way other people treated her—namely, as if she wasn't there. She was what might be called a town reject because of how she lived. She lived with her five children in a shack on the edge of an orange grove, which was provided to her rent free, so to speak, because she had a special relationship with the grove owner, a prominent married man in town. She was a diabetic and had no dependable income. I told her that she was entitled to aid—cash, housing, medicine. All she had to do was apply, I said, although I did not really know much about it at that time. I found the number and gave it to her. She was thrilled. It turned out that she had to call from a pay phone, finding quarters and balancing her baby in the phone booth, since she didn't have a phone of her own. Then she came to me in tears. They told her she couldn't apply by phone. They wouldn't mail her an application. She had to apply in person. (That was illegal in 1973, but they still did it, and I didn't know it was illegal then.) So Sherry got her things together, everything she needed for the baby for the day, and she and the baby took the bus (no regular bus service, as you might imagine, and she had no car and no license) downtown to the welfare office. They told her she was too late. You had to be there by 9:30 to get on the list. (After that you just sat there until they called your name sometime that day if you were lucky. If you were unlucky you had to come back the next day.) Getting there by 9:30 meant that she had to leave home before her children left for school in the morning in order to get there early enough to get on the list. She was very reluctant to do that. The Head Start Center was in a church. I found someone in the church who agreed to drive her downtown and drop her off at the welfare office by

9:30 (a fairly simple thing if you didn't have to take the bus.) The welfare evaluators turned her down. They told her she was not qualified, she said. But that is impossible, I said. You are a diabetic, with five children and no income, I said. She cried. She said she didn't take the right papers. She couldn't prove anything. She said she could never qualify because she wasn't smart enough. She couldn't remember what papers she needed. I asked her if they gave her a list or an application form. She said no. I asked her if they told her what she needed. She said yes but she couldn't remember what they had told her. I asked her why she didn't write it down. She cried. I said let's get some coffee. She said she had to get home before her kids came home from school. I had the same problem. I drove (with her and her two youngest) to her house. We picked up her other three kids and took them all to my house. There over coffee I finally found out that she was illiterate. She couldn't read the form well enough to fill it out. She was very ashamed of this, but it shouldn't have been hard for a trained welfare worker to figure it out. Yet no one had helped her. They just turned her down. I was furious.

I called a friend who was on welfare. She told us what Sherry needed—basically, proof of family composition, income, and expenses: last month's bills, the children's birth certificates, divorce decree, etc. Not an unreasonable list but not necessarily easy to assemble if you were not a good record keeper or you didn't know what you needed. It turned out that Sherry was careful with her important papers, but she didn't have last month's paid bills. Why would she? It took a month to assemble her papers. My friend (the savvy welfare mother) gave Sherry a mock interview. "Here's what they will ask you. Here's what you tell them." One would think it would be easy in Sherry's case: just tell the truth. But then there was the "free rent" situation that she was trying to get out of. If you wanted welfare to cover your rent, you were supposed to show that you already paid it. Your allotment was based on your expenses (minus your income.) If you raised your income, you got less from welfare. If you reduced your expenses, same result. If you didn't pay for rent, they didn't either. So, if you ever did manage to get on welfare, the most important lesson most people learned quickly was not to change anything. Not that they gave you enough to live on. They didn't. But it took real ingenuity to figure out what (if anything) to do about that. Most potential improvements (such as, say, babysitting in your home to earn money) were either subtracted (if you reported it) or illegal (if you didn't). Most people just learned to get by and settle for less. Still wondering why this system didn't work?

The end of the story is that Sherry finally did get on welfare and out of the orange grove. She even got a job eventually—bagging groceries. I will never forget how excited she was over that pitiful little job. (I should talk. With tips she probably made as much as I did.) They subtracted it from her welfare allotment, of course, so financially she was no better off than if she did nothing. The last time I remember seeing her, she and her kids were all huddled in the kitchen trying to keep warm by using the oven as a heater, since her spiffy new place had no heat. This is not a crisis in Florida, but it can get pretty chilly, and it was an indication as she warmed her hands by the oven that she hadn't really made it out of the hole yet. Nor would she ever, if she just stayed on welfare. No matter what you have heard, most welfare mothers do not live well.

I have told this story for several reasons. First, many people do not understand how eligible individuals get turned down for public assistance. I hope this story illustrates how. Just like this. Applicants generally have few resources and face many hurdles. Many give up. The system is purposely set up to produce that result. Second, I hope to have illustrated why it is so difficult for people without resources to meet ordinary requirements that many of us would not think twice about. It is much harder to make a phone call if you don't have a phone, or to go downtown or out on the edge of town (or wherever) if you don't have transportation. Most places in the country do not have reliable public transportation, so you will probably be walking a long way and waiting a long time for a bus, and you will be trying to amuse and feed and carry your preschoolers while you do all this. Most people do not even know, let alone remember how hard this is. And how many of us understand what it is like, terrifying perhaps, or demoralizing, to apply for anything when you are illiterate? Thus the fewer resources a person has the more everything is a barrier. Consequently the most vulnerable, those who need it most (like Sherry) are the most likely not to apply, the most likely to be denied and the most likely to give up. Third, there is nothing unusual about this story. I could tell twenty others that would vary only in detail over the particular hardships and the particular hurdles. It is just an anecdote. I could tell a different anecdote about a "queen" who milked the system, too. But the difference is that queens are rare. Sherry's case may not be universal, but trust me, you can generalize from it. In recent years I have been collecting *New York Times* articles outlining Mayor Giuliani's ingenious "new" devices for reducing the welfare roles.[26] It is nothing new; just more of the same. Fourth, this story took place in 1973. That was supposed to be a good year. That was after welfare was liberalized and before it was retracted again. Can you imagine what the bad years must be like?

Poverty and Social Obligation

We should not mourn the passing of AFDC (except to contemplate what might replace it). It was ineffective, irrational, demoralizing, and stigmatizing. It never pulled any mother or her dependent children out of poverty (which is not to say that no mother ever did that, but only that welfare was not set up to help her do it. Only the WIN program did that, and it was of very short duration). It only enabled them to subsist, to survive in hardship. The feminization of poverty coincided with the rise in the welfare rolls. Many women living below the poverty line were living on welfare. Obviously, then, welfare did not prevent poverty. It could have, if the benefits had been more generous. But they weren't. They never were, and they still are not. So one question that could be asked is: Why? Why, in a country that says it reveres motherhood, is a mother not deemed to be worthy of or entitled to a standard of living higher than poverty, merely by virtue of taking care of her children? Why in addition are dependent children not thought entitled to a standard of living any higher than poverty, unless their parents can provide it? These are the implications of the benefit levels of AFDC. Furthermore, the implications of TANF, the program that replaced AFDC, are even more stringent. Not only are the benefits no higher than poverty level, mothers are entitled to them for no more than two years at a time, five years in a lifetime, and only if they are willing to work, even if their wages will be below the poverty line. That is what American mothers are entitled to today. It does not matter if they live in poverty all their lives. They are entitled at most to temporary emergency assistance. The question, again, is: Why?

The answers are many, complex, and varied, but I will presume to over-simplify them for the present purpose. In the most general terms we Americans do not acknowledge any right to a minimum standard of living above subsistence, because Americans do not recognize any affirmative obligations to provide for their fellow members. Nor do we view the American economy as a pool of common resources in which all members deserve some share. We don't want people to starve, but not because we think we are *obligated* to feed them. We just think we should be charitable. We do not think people are *entitled* to a minimum income or standard of living. And we certainly do not think they should get it because it is their *share of the pie*. There is no share of the pie here. You are on your own. That is what we stand for. We will be charitable (we won't let you die) if you fail, but you are entitled to nothing.[27]

Ironically, AFDC, food stamps, public housing, and the like were referred to as "entitlement programs," but no one ever acted as though anyone was entitled to the benefits. Well, perhaps that is an overstatement. Perhaps, the blind and the disabled are considered entitled to a decent living at this point, but certainly not dependent children and their mothers. Welfare mothers themselves (unsurprisingly) do not act as though they are entitled to a decent living or a share of the pie for taking care of the children (or the sick, disabled, or elderly, for that matter). That is a labor of love. You do not get money for that, even if you need it to live. You are not entitled to it. Caregiving, for your own family, no matter how much work it is, for some reason (custom, I suppose) is not considered gainful employment.[28]

For a very short while (possibly ten years) there was a fledgling welfare rights movement concentrated in the biggest cities. For that short time and space some women came to believe and behave as though they were actually entitled as mothers (or caregivers) to a decent standard of living. But it didn't stick and it didn't spread. No one else was convinced. Too radical for America. And the timing was off. By a quirk of fate the welfare rights movement of the late 1960s coincided with the great movement of women into the workforce. Just as poor women won the right to stay home with their children, as middle-class women had long done, middle-class women left the home for the work place. By the 1980s both middle- and working-class women were criticized for selfishly going to work, while poor women were condemned for staying home with the children. Furthermore, as working-class wages stagnated for three decades, working-class women found that they were unable to stay home, since it took two incomes to support a family. The result was enormous resentment of the welfare system without much understanding of it. And eventually that system was ended.

Would a constitutional basis (say, a right to a minimum income) have made a difference? Obviously, it could do so, but only in the following limited respect. The details of any given program cannot be constitutionally set, so any particular program can be dissolved when it is deemed unworkable or becomes obsolete. This is as it should be.

But a basic right (and correlative duty) could be guaranteed constitutionally. In that case any given program could be cancelled, but measures would have to be taken to meet the duty in some other way. And not just anything would qualify. What the demise of AFDC demonstrates clearly is that what the legislature gives, it can also take away. A constitutional right would limit that capacity. All this is obvious and well known.

But establishing a constitutional right requires an even greater level of consensus than a legislative action would. It would seem that if you have the consensus necessary for the latter, you don't much need the former. Consequently, in this context it seems to me that the notion of constitution as political consensus is more helpful. One-fifth of our nation's children live in poverty today because Americans do not recognize an obligation to prevent it. Eighty percent of our poor are women and children because we allow it to be that way. We certainly have the resources to prevent it, but we choose to expend them in other ways. And we do not think we are violating anyone's right thereby. Women and children have no right to any particular standard of living.

Compare this with our attitude about education. Children have a right to an education. It is violated if they are not provided with an education. They are entitled to this benefit, and the American people would be remiss if we did not provide it. We do not leave it up to individual parents (although parents can certainly provide more if they wish). The public is responsible for providing the basic benefit. It is recognized as a common obligation.[29]

This is the attitude that needs to be developed toward a decent standard of living. We are moving toward acknowledging a right to a share of our economic resources or an obligation to guarantee a decent standard of living to the elderly and to some disabled populations.[30] But any such general right clearly is not thought to apply to the population at large, including to women and children. America is not ready for that. Furthermore, there is little recognition of the unfairness of the economic system itself, which makes more subsidies needed. It is not the lack of welfare that causes poverty. Welfare is simply one potential solution to poverty that Americans do not use. Yet there is virtually no acceptance of the idea that America owes those on the bottom a subsidy, because the American economy puts them there by insuring that a certain percentage of the population must occupy that position.[31]

On the other hand, Americans do accept the idea of a negative income tax. One of the worst features of AFDC was that it alienated the poor from mainstream society and created resentment among the working classes. A negative income tax has no such effect. And this should be a clue. Programs to eliminate (or alleviate) poverty should be integrative rather than divisive. In this regard TANF, for all its shortcomings, could potentially become a genuinely helpful program. It is intended to integrate women into the workforce rather than separating them from it. As currently structured, it is uncertain, radically varied from state to state, mostly underfunded, and stingy. It doesn't help women out of poverty; it just moves them off public assistance into low-level jobs. But suppose it were combined with real training programs, good day care, and a negative income tax to supplement poverty-level wages. These are possibilities Americans might accept. Perhaps we could even come to view them as common rights and obligations. This is what every American is entitled to: a fair chance to participate and a decent standard of living.[32]

If programs like these come to be instituted as part of the political consensus in the way Social Security has come to be viewed, everyone will be better off, including women and children. To make it happen we must cultivate a stronger notion of common obligations to provide a fair chance for

a decent life to all members of our community. We don't need special provisions for women, except insofar as we impose special burdens upon them.
And even the traditional burdens of caretaking could be broken into pieces
that are more acceptable and less isolating (such as providing day care and
elder care, socializing medical care, and ending discrimination against part-
time workers). None of these benefits are restricted to women, but instituting them would do much to reduce the feminization of poverty. Establishing them requires not so much a change of the Constitution as a change of
heart.

NOTES

1. Germany, France, Sweden, Denmark, Russia, and China are major and well-
known examples.

2. See e.g,. L. Tribe, *Constitutional Law* (Boston: Little, Brown, 1979).

3. And even some constitutional modification, such as the establishment of the
federal income tax power and the right of women to vote.

4. For example, American education is harshly (and rightly) criticized as ineffective and unfairly distributed, but it should also be recognized that there is a public school system, and it is available (in some form) to all. As a result illiteracy in
America is low. That is not true in some countries today, and was not true in the
U.S. in the nineteenth century.

5. What I am suggesting is that, for example, a right to a basic education has become a constitutional feature of American political life, even though it is not a formally accepted (federal) constitutional right. Indeed, such a right was formally rejected by the Supreme Court in *San Antonio Public School District v. Rodriguez*
(409 U.S. 434,1973). But the political consensus is nevertheless that every child is entitled to an education. So one question of interest here is what is the relation between a constitutional political consensus and a constitutional right?

6. See note 1. One problem is that the U.S. has no comprehensive social welfare
program. We even lack a comprehensive medical program.

7. See e.g., J. Patterson, *America's Struggle Against Poverty 1900–1985* (Cambridge: Harvard University Press, 1986). The specific figures depends on the year
and the source. There is considerable variation in such statistics.

8. M. Harrington, *The Other America: Poverty in the United States* (New York:
Random House, 1962).

9. For interesting discussion that took place at the time see e.g., B. Weisbrod, *The
Economics of Poverty* (Englewood Cliffs, N.J.: Prentice-Hall, 1965).

10. For discussion, see Fox Piven (chapter 7, this volume).

11. This is not hyperbole. The *New York Times* and other news sources documented the clear correlation between the rise in demands on private charities (including soup kitchens) and the reduction in the welfare rolls. Of course, someone

could claim that it is a coincidence. See e.g., *New York Times*, 26 February, 1999, 1A; or 12 December, 1999, 1A.

12. See e.g., J. Williams, *Unbending Gender* (New York: Oxford University Press, 2000), 63.

13. This is not to say that it is never criticized or that no one argues for its abolition. Still, the common view is that attacking Social Security is political suicide.

14. Specifically those that are regularly employed full-time with an earning level that meets the bottom line requirements.

15. Women, of course, were much more vulnerable than men in nearly all respects. Job and wage discrimination were overt, and single "working girls" were both sexually and monetarily vulnerable. O.Henry told many poignant stories about them.

16. See Patterson, n. 7, pp. 26–29.

17. Id.; see also L. Friedman, *A History of American Law* (New York: Simon & Schuster, 1973).

18. Patterson, n. 7, ch. 4.

19. Id. at p. 38.

20. Id at p. 28.

21. Id.

22. Id. at ch. 4.

23. Id. at 60–63.

24. See Patterson, n., 7 at 63–68. The Works Progress Administration and the Civilian Conservation Corps were two of the better-known programs intended both to provide relief to the unemployed and to stimulate the economy, all with very limited success. In fact it took the massive infusion of funds needed for the war effort to actually turn the economy around.

25. For example, a mother had to be of "high moral character," have no illegitimate children, have no man in the house, and not employable. Some states required mothers to sign affidavits swearing not to "have any male callers coming to my home nor meeting me elsewhere under improper conditions," and not to do anything that would "cause my children to be shamed by my conduct." See Patterson, n. 7 at 88.

26. See e.g., J. DeParle, "What Welfare-to-Work Really Means," *New York Times Magazine*, December20, , 1998, at 5off.

27. Many public opinion polls bear out these generalizations of predominant American attitudes. They are not universal, of course. See e.g., Patterson, n. 7 at 109, 110, or 196.

28. On this common attitude see e.g., Martha Fineman, *The Neutered Mother, the Sexual Family, and Other 20th Century Tragedies* (New York: Routledge, 1995); or Williams, n. 12.

29. Of course, this right is also formally recognized in every state in the union. But is it the legal recognition that makes the social commitment so solid? It could as easily be the other way around. There was some talk of abolishing public schools in certain states to avoid integration orders after *Brown v. Board of Education* (1954).

This would have provided an interesting test case, but it didn't happen. Why didn't it? I think because public recognition of the general obligation to provide education was too strong.

30. Attitudes toward the disabled are varied and complex in fascinating ways. There has long been a recognized obligation to help the blind expressed in public policy, for example, whereas hypertension and back trouble have always been suspect. Attitudes (and public policies) toward the mentally ill have always been erratic at best, and addiction is not really recognized as a disability at all.

31. For further discussion and support see P. Smith, *Liberalism and Affirmative Obligation* (New York: Oxford University Press, 1998), chapter 9.

32. Id.

PART 2

Interpretation

*The U.S. Constitution
in Comparative Context*

Judith Resnik

CHAPTER 9

Federalism(s), Feminism, Families, and the Constitution

Categorical Federalism

The United States Constitution creates a federal structure, outlines with broad strokes the powers provided to the national government, provides mechanisms for interstate coordination, and in a general fashion reserves powers to the people. The Constitution itself, however, has no textual definition of the word "federalism." Rather, the question of how to share power in a federation has been an arena of contest since the country's inception.

Repeatedly, efforts to address women's inequality have been met with arguments that something within United States federalism prohibits national action.[1] That approach governed in 2000, when a five-person majority of the Supreme Court ruled in *United States v. Morrison* that the civil rights remedy in the 1994 Violence Against Women Act (VAWA) was unconstitutional.[2] According to Chief Justice Rehnquist's opinion for that majority, Congress had exceeded its constitutional powers when authorizing victims of violence, animated by gender bias, to bring civil damage lawsuits against assailants in federal courts. In his view, such issues were for the states because the "Constitution requires a distinction between what is truly national and what is truly local."[3]

This chapter builds on my related essay, "Categorical Feminism: Jurisdiction, Gender, and the Globe," *Yale Law Journal* 111 (2001): 619–80. Thanks to Sarah Russell, Vicki Jackson, Dennis Curtis, and Cori Van Noy for thoughtful advice.

"Truly local." "Truly national." The use of the modifier "truly" indicates that calling something local or national does not suffice to capture a categorical constitutional distinction. With the modifier, the stress is placed on identifying an activity as somehow inside of, and definitional to, a level of governance.

"The local" is, however, an idea as well as a place. How do we come to understand some forms of human endeavors as suitably governed only by local authorities and others not appropriate for local governance? Why assume these two categories to be exclusive and oppositional? Why, as the new century begins with pronouncements on the import of globalization, do we find renewed insistence on the categories "local" and "national" in interpreting the constitutional import of federalism? And what do those boundaries have to do with gender and families?

These questions are the subject of this chapter, and the litigation about one aspect of VAWA offers a means by which to explore them. Enacted in 1994, VAWA authorized millions of dollars for programs to train police and to provide shelters for victims of violence and created new civil and criminal provisions to ease interstate enforcement of protection orders.[4] At issue in and held unconstitutional by *Morrison* was only one provision, termed by Congress a "civil rights remedy" and designed "to protect the civil rights of victims of gender motivated violence" by permitting them to bring damage actions in federal courts.[5] When striking the civil rights remedy of VAWA, the Supreme Court majority discussed family and criminal law, as if violence against women necessarily folded into those categories and as if, by invocation of family and criminal law, the "non-national" character of the claims covered by VAWA would be transparent.

"Categorical federalism" is the term I offer for this form of reasoning. Categorical federalism's method first assumes that a particular rule of law regulates a single aspect of human action: a law is described as about the family, crime, or civil rights, as if a law was univocal and human interaction similarly one-dimensional. Second, categorical federalism relies on such identification to locate authority in state or national governments, and then uses that identification as if to explain *why* power to regulate resides within one or another governmental structure. Third, categorical federalism has a presumption of exclusive control—to wit, if it is family law, it belongs *only* to the states. Categories are thus constructed around two sets of human activities, the subject matter of regulation and the locus of governance, with each assumed to have intelligible boundaries and autonomous spheres.

Categorical federalism has appeal, particularly in a world as full of vivid changes as the one we inhabit. Categorical federalism posits and promises clearly delineated allocations of power and suggests, comfortingly, that these delineations flow "naturally" through United States history from a topic to a geographically located government. As federal judges distinguish the "truly local" from the "truly national," they abjure their own responsibility by casting their project as empirical rather than interpretive, as a historical exercise aimed at describing and implementing agreements forged in 1789. Further, proponents of categorical federalism argue that its virtue lies in its democracy-enhancing features. The Court's interventions in the name of federalism are supposed to promote transparent lines of accountability.

But categorical federalism fails—because category errors are common and because reliance on enduring categories is itself misguided. That which is national and that which is local result not from natural forces but from human agency. The claim that definitions derive from the Constitution of 1789 cannot work because "the federal" had yet to be made. The issue then, as now, was what content and purposes to give to federal and state governments.

Today, debates about the "local" effects of transnational laws are also before us. Technology permits easy transgeographic exchanges that diminish the significance of physical boundaries. Transnational organizations promulgate worldwide legal norms, affecting practices within the nation-states. In international parlance, local law refers to what in the United States is termed national law.

Moreover, national borders are not the only lines that are blurring. Boundaries of gender roles are also shifting as women and men explore the possibility that their gender offers less instruction on their life opportunities than has been assumed for thousands of years. Gender systems work through assumptions that the categories of "women" and "men" mark important differences. Historically, those demarcations were maintained by walling off "the family" from "the market" and "the private" from "the public." Currently, violence and money continue to distinguish the lives of women and men. Women live with threats to their physical safety from men within and outside their households; women's unpaid household labors facilitate men's market capacities.

But equality movements aim at breaking down those distinctions to diminish the categorical coherence of gender. Efforts to extricate women from the dominion, both physical and economic, of male-headed households are underway worldwide as longstanding rules of politics (such as who can vote), of entrenched legal and social practices (such as who controls access to women's bodies), of markets (such as what work is remunerated), and even of war (such as whether victors may exercise sexual dominion over enemy civilian women) are all being revisited.

Given this context, return then to the Chief Justice's locution—"truly national," "truly local"—and reread it to betray anxiety as well as insistence, as an effort *to make* meaningful a division that is not only elusive but increasingly inaccurate. Categorical federalism ought to be understood as a political claim, advancing an argument that certain forms of human interactions should be governed by a particular locality, be it a nation-state or its subdivisions. But this political stance, attempting to buffer the states from the nation, and this nation from the globe, is faulty as a method and wrong as an aspiration.

Below, I first sketch the empirical case against categorical federalism by showing that an area characterized in the VAWA litigation as "local"—family life—has long been subjected to federal lawmaking. Decades of federal constitutional family law create substantive rights anchored in the Fourteenth Amendment for parents and children, just as decades of federal legislation—addressing welfare, pension, tax, bankruptcy, and immigration have defined membership in and relationships in groupings denominated "families" by the national government. Second, I provide a normative critique of categorical federalism, for it is not only fictive but harmful. By deflecting attention from the many political and legal judgments made by the nation's judiciary, Executive, and Congress as they regulate the lives of current and former householders, categorical federalism wrongly shelters federal actors from responsibility for shaping the gendered meaning of family roles.

Moreover, categorical federalism provides a false sense of security from transnational lawmaking. United States laws of all kinds are increasingly altered, if not trumped, by practices stemming from quarters physically distant from Washington but not far in forms of space that globalization has come to represent. The United States government needs to develop means of interacting with these laws rather than assuming its ability to remain insular. In the twenty-first century, believing one can mandate one's own boundaries is seductive but wrong (a lesson all too powerfully plain since September 11, 2001).

Thereafter, I suggest reframing the issue of violence against women by looking at it from different angles. If a man raped a woman and proclaims he did so because he likes to inflict such pain on women, what should law call that action? Should the description vary if the man and woman have been (or are) married instead of strangers? If they were employer and employee? Opponents in a war? Should the legal import vary if the man assaults the woman as she is about to leave the house on her way to school, work, or another shelter? Do understandings of the relevant legal norms shift upon concluding that many men rape women, many husbands beat wives, many employers sexually assault certain kinds of employees, and many soldiers rape women in countries at war? As these questions illustrate, in law, decisions to categorize are purposeful, consequentialist, and situational. Moreover, more than one legal regime may address any given interaction.

My goal is not to refuse categorization but to introduce other presumptions into federalism discourse—that many categories are intertwined in lawmaking enterprises and that more than one source of legal regulation is likely to apply to any set of behaviors. To underscore the many layers of governance and the political choices endemic therein, I suggest revising the terms in which we discuss these issues. The words "multifaceted federalism" help legal theory mirror contemporary research about categorization in cognitive psychology, now demonstrating that, when humans characterize, what features count as relevant varies with context.[6] Multifaceted federalism brings those insights into legal discourse by providing better descriptions of contemporary practices and more desirable goals for federations functioning within a wealth of transnational and local activities. The term underscores that any assignment of dominion can be transitory, and that the assignment of regulatory authority is itself a self-conscious act of power, exercised with an awareness that a sequence of interpretive judgments, made in real time and revisable in the future, undergirds any current designation of *where* power to regulate *what* activities rests.

I also commend a revision of the term "federalism" by pluralizing it. If we said "federalisms," we would be constantly reminded that United States constitutional history is filled with conflicts about how to allocate power in this polity and that competing theories of what is comprehended by a constitutional federation abound. We would also be reminded that it is not the level of government but the decision-makers who promote greater equality. As we seek to entrench norms of equality, we must not valorize any level of governance as intrinsically more or less committed to equality but understand that, to redress inequality, interactions among all levels of government are required.

Violence Against Women, National Lawmaking Powers, and Federal Laws of the Family

Supporters of national efforts against violence targeted at women understood that women's capacity as equal economic actors was at stake. In the legislative record about VAWA, witnesses testified not just that violence in general had an effect on the national economy but specifically that, because of violence, women workers chose certain jobs and avoided others, such as those that entailed late night use of public transportation. Further, Congress received some twenty reports, commissioned by state judiciaries, detailing the problems faced by women seeking protection from and redress for violence. These state reports repeatedly detailed evidence of discrimination by police, prosecutors, jurors, and judges against women victims of violence. Attorneys General from about forty states added their voices in support of providing a supplemental remedy for victims of such violence by giving them access to civil damage suits in federal courts. Congress responded, relying on its powers under both its Article I powers under the Commerce Clause and its Fourteenth Amendment authority to ensure equal protection of the laws, by enacting VAWA.

In contrast, a majority of the Supreme Court rejected the categorization of the problem as one of equality and economic capacity and insisted that it fell within the rubric of local crime and the family, subject to state, not national, governance. Even if one were to assume that VAWA was aimed at regulating families (or more aptly, dissolving disabled families), that categorization does not preclude federal regulation. In fact, upon entering the categorical box of the family, one finds a great deal of federal law inside.

Federal Family Law

That federal law should speak substantively about, impose requirements upon, and offer protection to family life is an artifact of this country's founding, expressed periodically during the nineteenth century through federal legislation using marriage policy to limit polygamy, to establish rights of freed slaves, and to distance Indian tribal members from their communities.[7] During the twentieth century, action on this federal front (like many others) expanded. Interest in developing federal family law stemmed from several factors, including an increasingly mobile population, economic crises clarifying the relationship between individual circumstances of poverty and national markets, waves of immigration, and comparative data that the United States lagged behind other nations in addressing infant mortality and children's health.[8] As a consequence, contemporary federal family law is a mélange of national norms aimed at affirming certain conceptions about how families are constituted, the relationships within families that have primacy, and the material consequences of family life.

The legal routes to federal family lawmaking are—like federalist theories themselves—premised on a range of constitutional provisions including the Commerce and Spending Clauses, the Full Faith and Credit Clauses, and the Fourteenth Amendment. A brief sketch of some statutes and constitutional law that create substantive federal family law policies exemplify the breadth. Federal tax law defines family units and creates economic incentives for members.[9] Social security law endows wage-work with the power of producing retirement benefits but treats unpaid household labor differently.[10] Although state law initially organizes assets between divorcing couples, "federal bankruptcy law radically alters all the financial obligations created by state law."[11] Immigration law gives meaning to the act of marriage,[12] and the Defense of Marriage Act defines marriage for purposes of federal law and interstate obligations.[13] The Employ-

ment Retirement Income Security Act (ERISA) creates federal marital property law in pensions that trumps state property laws.[14] In short, a variety of familiar areas of federal law intersect with and regulate aspects of family life.

Federal Child Support Laws

Categoricalists define the care and economic support of children as a core
aspect of family law. Governments can facilitate parental provision of care by
a variety of methods, such as paying parents to provide care to children, sub-
sidizing care outside of homes, supplying food and health benefits, and requiring employers to provide release time from work. The choice of policy
sustains or alters assumptions about the parental roles and earning potential
of women and men. Further, given cultural, religious, and ethnic variations
in family patterns, governments also have decisions to make about which individuals to recognize as constituting a family. Thus, when governments impose obligations of child support, their rules either reaffirm or disrupt extant
understandings of family constellations and gendered allocations of labor.

That state laws make such decisions is common ground. What the *Morrison* majority ignored is that federal law also makes such decisions. Federal social welfare legislation, sometimes assumed to have begun through the 1935
Social Security Act, was launched decades earlier.[15] Prompted by women's organizations seeking to reduce infant mortality rates, the federal government
created the Home Education Division of the U.S. Bureau of Education in
1911, the Children's Bureau in 1912, and the Women's Bureau in 1918. By 1921,
through the Federal Act for the Promotion of the Welfare and Hygiene of Maternity and Infancy (the "Sheppard-Towner Act," in force until 1929), federal
funding provided more than a million dollars to the Children's Bureau to dis-
perse to cooperating states for family care.

During the following seventy years of federal lawmaking, substantive policies reflected and reinforced gendered assumptions about parental responsibilities. Aid to (Families with) Dependent Children, a program begun during
the first half of the twentieth century, represented a federal policy that mothers who lacked their own income or that of spouses should be able to stay at
home to care for children. Welfare legislation in 1996 illustrates a different federal policy: that such women should be prepared to entrust their children to
others and demonstrate their commitment to gaining market employment.[16]

Attitudes toward the role fathers should play also shifted over the century.
As Linda Gordon explains, in 1900 and in 1960, more than 85 percent of children lived with two parents.[17] Further, "from the late nineteenth century until
the 1930s, in all classes, races, and ethnic groups, most single mothers were
widows" — 77 percent; by the 1930s, however, the number of single widowed

mothers had fallen to under 55 percent.[18] Men had left households but, with divorce generally uncommon, desertion was the description.

The issue was what obligations these men had to those left behind. In the 1930s and 1940s, state laws did not offer uniform answers on which adult members of families were obligated to support children of what ages[19] and whether to pursue violators civilly or sanction them criminally. The variation became a subject of discussion among state leaders, who attempted to create uniform laws[20] but found themselves unable to lower the costs of pursuit or to sustain interest in pursuit from prosecutors in states distant from the particular families in need.

With the creation in the 1930s of federal welfare benefits for needy children came federal interest in ensuring that adult family members who had the resources to pay child support did so. The development of federal policy stemmed from substantive visions about who constituted families, about which adults had obligations to children, and about how to spend tax dollars wisely. Federal family policy proscribed gender-conventional roles rather than altering norms of masculinity by promoting fathers as care providers. Fathers were identified as the primary wage earners; mothers were situated as caregivers.[21]

Federal involvement in child support increased as federal dollars went toward support of children and as state actors sought help in enforcement of their collection laws. Initially, federal statutes focused on encouraging and assisting state collection of child support from wayward fathers. Subsequent federal regulation sought to take direct action against adults liable for support, resulting in what some have termed "the federalization" of child support enforcement. Through laws passed in 1968, 1974, 1984, 1988, and 1996, Congress created a federal locator system and imposed federal standards on how to search for absent fathers, how to recoup funds from them, and how to assess how much to recoup from them. The 1996 act mandated adoption of uniform state laws on child support as a condition of federal funds, resulting in state enactments that march to a federal drum.

Federal criminal law also serves as a vehicle for national norms. During and after World War II, federal legislators began to consider what became known as the "Runaway Pappy Act."[22] Proponents sought to craft a federal crime based upon a father's willful departure from a state to avoid child support obligations. They argued for federal lawmaking because: (a) during World War II, the federal government had contributed to the problem by encouraging fathers to leave their households to work in factories or to go to war; (b) state laws varied, and interstate enforcement was expensive and sometimes unavailing; and (c) by moving from state to state, fathers could avoid obligations of support.[23] Some of the proposals permitted direct prosecution and imposed criminal penalties, while others wanted to deploy the federal courts as a registry for interstate support orders and therefore as a means of enforcement of moneys due. Members of Congress assumed that obligations for child support had a sufficient nexus to the economy to support federal legislation, which was welcomed by state officials seeking federal assistance.

As is familiar to those who focus on either family law or federal jurisdiction, the criminal legislation (the Child Support Recovery Act, or "CSRA")[24] became law decades later (in 1992), by which time "runaway pappys" had become "deadbeat dads." Today, whether wisely or not, both civil and criminal federal statutes focus on collecting child support payments from fathers. Less familiar is that major opposition to the deployment of federal legal resources for these efforts came from the federal judiciary itself.[25] At first, objections came through commentary from the official voice of the Article III judiciary. Between 1958 and 1992, the policymaking body of the federal judiciary opposed all of the many proposals for the use of federal courts to register support orders or to enforce criminal sanctions.[26] Subsequently, the Supreme Court limited federal involvement in family life in other forms, such as by declining to interpret legislation to endow individuals with rights of enforcement[27] and by imposing restrictions on jurisdictional provisions that could have enabled litigants to file family-related claims in federal court.[28] And, vividly, in *Morrison*, the Court held that Congress has no power to vest certain matters in federal courts.

These exchanges represent a long history of the judiciary and Congress debating—and disagreeing about—the shape of federal family law policies and, particularly, about whether Congress could or should enlist the federal courts in implementing its family-related laws.[29] Such debates are themselves further testament that federal statutory family policies are plentiful. Through a range of civil and criminal statutes, Congress has developed a regulatory regime reflecting substantive decisions about family policy. Within the category of the family can be found federal regulation, and within the category of the federal can be found rules of family life.

Constitutional Family Law

Congress is not the only source of federal law relating to family life. When one turns from statutes to the Constitution, one finds that the federal judiciary is itself a font of federal family lawmaking. The word "family" does not itself appear in the Constitution. The concept is only mentioned by way of prohibitions on forms of intergenerational inheritance: no titles of nobility may be passed from parent to child, nor shall the treasonous acts of ancestors result in penalties to children by way of "corruption of blood."[30] Yet United States Supreme Court justices have regularly understood that they have the power to speak about families. For example, in 2000, the Court construed the Constitution in *Troxel v. Granville*[31] (popularly styled the "grandparents' visiting rights" case), to prohibit the State of Washington from conferring on judges the ability to require parents to make possible visits between their children and a range of other adults. Only Justice Scalia's dissent claimed that federal law had no role in correcting what he saw as a misguided state provision.[32] In contrast, his eight colleagues (through five opinions) all agreed that the United States Constitution applied, although they disagreed about what flowed from its deployment.

Troxel does not stand alone. From the 1920s forward, justices have articulated federal constitutional norms regarding families—including that legal parents are protected from state intervention absent compelling evidence,[33] and that they have various forms of control over their children, such as direction of their education.[34] Similarly, federal constitutional law has bounded state rules on marriage and sexuality (by banning race-based marriage barriers, prohibiting polygamy, and permitting contraception[35]) and on child custody,[36] as well as prohibited discrimination based on whether parents were married at the time of a child's birth.[37] Given the many cases that address the parental status of men,[38] the Court could even be understood as specializing in the law of fatherhood.

My claim is not that federal law, statutory or constitutional, specifically regulates all aspects of family life but rather that denominating an issue as about family life has not precluded federal legal regimes from imposing obligations, structuring sanctions, and creating incentives among individuals designated as family members. Even in areas such as marriage, divorce, alimony, and child custody, often listed as the set of "domestic relations" especially under the aegis of state law, federal law plays an important role. When couples with certain forms of income divorce, the federal rule on spousal pension rights is central to the division of assets. For couples at lower income brackets, federal welfare laws structure economic options, and, as federal funding diminishes, federal child support obligations become all the more central. Moreover, international law is playing a growing role in family life as nations join conventions on children and as parents in conflict transport children across national boundaries.

In the areas of both family life and crime, state systems currently bear the brunt of dealing with the volume of disputes. But state courts do more of the work for all forms of disputes; federal filings (of some 350,000 civil and criminal cases annually) are a small fraction of the thirty million disputes brought annually to state courts. To use (or to fear) quantities of work stemming from legal regulation as the basis for reading into the Constitution a prohibition on federal lawmaking gives judges arbitrary and unaccountable power. Calling

VAWA a family and criminal law statute does not provide an argument about *why* Congress could not act. Rather, the interacting legal regimes in these arenas demonstrate the prevalence, in practice, of multifaceted federalism. Overlapping layers of law are the norm.

Conceptualizing the Injuries of Violence: Global Counterpoints and "Local" Anxiety

Such layers of lawmaking—related to violence, families, and equality—go beyond state and federal law within the United States. Beginning in the late 1940s with the Universal Declaration of Human Rights, international treaties recognized women's equality. More recent laws (such as the Convention on the Elimination of All Forms of Discrimination Against Women, the Declaration on the Elimination of Violence Against Women, and regional agreements[39]) expressly address women's right to physical safety. Indeed, in the VAWA litigation, a group of human rights scholars argued that Congress had the power to enact VAWA as part of its obligation to implement the International Covenant on Civil and Political Rights (which the United States has ratified) and to enforce customary international law.

Also beginning in the 1940s, politicians in the United States opposed such transnational lawmaking as a threat to this nation. They relied specifically on states' rights as an argument against participation in the new human rights laws.[40] Transnational efforts to define equality are therefore relevant in two respects to the contemporary invocation of categorical federalism. First, an overview on gender equality elsewhere makes plain how much at odds the response of the *Morrison* majority is with lawmaking in other countries that acknowledges the links among women's safety, equality, family roles, and economic capacity. Second, the existence of these new definitions of women's rights reveals yet another function of categorical federalism—its role in attempting to buffer the United States from the effects of lawmaking beyond its borders.

Developing Human Capabilities and Creating Legal Innovation

The harms suffered by women have become a subject of study around the world. Illustrative is an international survey, *Domestic Violence Against Women and Girls*,[41] issued by UNICEF in 2000. This report concludes that violence against women is "one of the most pervasive of human rights violations, denying women and girls equality, security, dignity, self-worth, and their right to enjoy fundamental freedoms."[42] While noting that most countries prohibit such violence, the report finds that violations are common and are often sanctioned under the garb of cultural practices or norms or through misinterpretation of religious tenets. Moreover, when the violation takes place within the home, as is very often the case, the abuse is effectively condoned by the tacit silence and passivity displayed by the state and law-enforcing machinery.[43]

Indeed, although the "family is often equated with sanctuary . . . for many it is a place that imperils lives, and breeds some of the most drastic forms of violence perpetrated on women and girls."[44] In contrast to the jurisdictional lines drawn by the *Morrison* majority, the UNICEF report refuses to bound its inquiry into the family, culture, and religion. Rather, the report identifies the systemic and widespread practices of violence against women as predicated upon economic dependency, acculturation to sex roles, and legal and political inequality. Poignantly, "women's increasing economic activity and independence is viewed as a threat which leads to increased male violence," particularly in economies that are themselves in transition.[45]

International analyses also address "human capability," a term used to denote a range of activities including but not limited to economic activity. Since the early 1990s, the United Nations has provided an annual *Human Development Report* with "balance sheets," listing a rise of women's economic activity in the progress column and the high incidence of physical violence against women by their intimate partners on the debit side.[46] The variable of gender correlates with educational and poverty levels. As Ruth Bader Ginsburg and Deborah Jones Merritt explain, for every one man who is illiterate around the world, two women are,[47] and 70 percent of world's poor are women. Women's risk of violence, their poverty, and the high illiteracy rates relate to women's roles within families. The job of being a parent limits market options, as does the danger of violence. Martha Nussbaum relies on such research for what she terms a feminist argument that attends specifically to women's status as "less nourished than men, less healthy, more vulnerable to physical violence and sexual abuse."[48]

The economic and sociological work is both a product and a source of international efforts to obtain recognition of women's equality.[49] A series of constitutional documents recognize women as rights-holders. Some instruments make more wide-ranging commitments to action for achieving equality than does contemporary equality law in the United States. For example, in 1979, the United Nations' General Assembly promulgated the Convention on the Elimination of All Forms of Discrimination against Women (CEDAW).[50] Although signed by then-President Jimmy Carter in 1980 and adopted by more than 165 countries, the United States Senate has not (yet) ratified CEDAW. That convention defines prohibited gender-based discrimination to include "any distinction, exclusion or restriction [that] has the effect or purpose of impairing women and men's equality and exercises of human rights and fundamental freedoms." Further, CEDAW requires that "State parties shall take in all fields, in particular in the political, social, economic, and cultural fields, all appropriate measures, including legislation, to ensure the full development and advance of women, for the purpose of guaranteeing them the exercise and enjoyment of human rights and fundamental freedoms on a basis of equality with men."[51]

The "appropriate measures to eliminate discrimination" may include "temporary special measures aimed at accelerating de facto equality between men and women"[52]—in United States parlance "affirmative action." In the early 1990s, the expert committee superintending the convention concluded that its provisions prohibit violence against women, whether occurring in the family, the community, or other institutions. A year thereafter, the U.N. adopted a resolution addressing violence against women.[53]

In addition to such transnational efforts, many countries have created new laws and institutions aimed at undermining gender inequality. Political governance is one arena of concern. Despite women's access to the vote, women remain markedly underrepresented in most democracies. In response, the European Union (EU) supports "parity democracy," by which is meant the "balanced participation" of women and men at all levels of government and in all commissions, committees, and councils.[54] Concern that only small numbers of women served in elected positions prompted France to enact legislation requiring that equal numbers of women and men candidates, with equal placement on lists of candidates, be put forth for most elections.[55] Some two dozen countries, including some beyond Europe such as Argentina and South Africa, have variations on this approach. Governments have also forged new positions, such as the Ministry for Women established in Great Britain. That work is part of the effort to implement what both the EU and the United Nations describe as "mainstreaming,"[56] bringing questions of women's equality into all policy areas and ensuring that all policies be made with an awareness of their effects on women.

If one axis is political governance and participation, another is the workforce and households. As Norwegian sociologist Arnlaug Leira comments, "Mothers have changed the gender balance in breadwinning. Changing the gender balance in caring may prove even more difficult."[57] In Denmark, Norway, and Sweden, a portion of all parental leave is reserved to each parent as a "non-transferable right" to prompt both mothers and fathers to take paid time (including in some instances, part-time) away from their workplaces.[58] Further, in Sweden and Norway, benefits provided upon the birth of a child are reduced if both spouses do not participate by taking time off from work. Parental leave is thus an element of efforts to promote gender equality. Such provisions point to an appreciation that "[i]ncreasingly . . . what differentiates gender roles is not *whether* individuals have a job, but the *amount of time* spent in paid employment."[59]

A third focus is on women's lack of physical security. Although VAWA's attempt to make certain assaults a breach of national norms did not succeed in the United States, that approach is being adopted internationally, as rape is comprehended—for the first time—to be a crime against humanity, a war crime.[60] In the winter of 2001, an international tribunal dealing with war crimes in the former territories of Yugoslavia convicted perpetrators of such crimes.[61] This premise has also been codified in the Treaty of Rome,[62] "the first international treaty to recognize a range of acts of sexual and gender violence as among the most serious crimes under international law"[63] to be redressed in the International Criminal Court.

This brief sketch highlights the degree to which male prerogatives to run or to dominate governments, workplaces, households, international relations, and war are being challenged through both texts and practices. Globalism has helped to make plain the patterns of inequality. Technology has enabled individuals, nongovernmental organizations (NGOs), and countries committed to diminishing such inequality to communicate with each other. As a result, transnational understandings are developing that achieving equality for women and men requires reorganization of all aspects of daily life, from homes to streets, markets, and politics. Many of these remedial efforts are not continuous with the political cultures in which they are placed but interrupt prior patterns. Illustrative is the change to democratic parity in France; the "citizen" (unmodified) had been the only category in French law until the recent enactments aimed at achieving parity for women and men.

One cannot therefore dismiss cross-cultural comparisons as evidence that some innovation, "natural to them," cannot provide insight "here." Categories such as the family or war, previously used to preclude gender equality norms from operating, are no longer understood as prior to and thereby exempt from new rules and practices. Returning to the United States, *Morrison* becomes remarkable not just as a "local" example of a Supreme Court override but as parochial refusal to permit innovations aimed at altering gender roles in the face of a national and growing worldwide consensus that all social institutions require reconsideration in light of knowledge of gender subordination.

Fears of "the Foreign" Within

These developments "abroad" illuminate another aspect of the appeal of categorical federalism in the United States. Insistence on the "truly local" as a jurisdictional limit underscores territorial boundaries in an effort to defend against waves of transnational laws and increasingly homogenized cultures. Categorical federalism therefore promises (or threatens, depending on one's view) not only to limit (or undo) the New Deal but also to reinscribe isolationist foreign affairs policies aimed at returning the globe to a description of the planet rather than a powerful presence within the physical boundaries of the United States. Categorical federalism deploys the local as if it is inevitably a site of participatory democracy that protects some categories of human enterprise from distant power by safely ensconcing them in decisional processes controlled by one's friends, one's neighbors, and oneself.

Categorical federalism is thus especially responsive to the history of this nation's birth in rebellion from a distant and centralized power. The central gesture of the American Revolution—separation from King George—is reenacted by claiming that the "Constitution requires a distinction between what is truly national and what is truly local,"[64] thereby limiting Washington's power. Moreover, a central tenet of constitutional faith, that the Constitution defines and confines all power, is invoked to justify the Court's exercise of its own power. In addition, categorical federalism has psychological appeal. People "often believe that there is an underlying essence of reason for categories to be the way that they are."[65] Categorical federalism thus helps to cushion anxiety occasioned by dissolving boundaries.

Working in conjunction with other precepts of current federalism jurisprudence about the relationship between "the local" and "the international," the boxes constructed through categorical federalism become fortresses designed to ward off incursions not only from the national government but also from abroad. The claim that states' rights ought to preclude the application of international human rights law was raised in the early 1950s, when, after the creation of the United Nations and the promulgation of the Universal Declaration of Human Rights, Senator John Bricker proposed a constitutional amendment that would have limited federal treaty power if deployed to undercut states' rights.[66] Bricker "wanted to insure that international agreements would not lead to United Nations interference on moral, liberal, social, and economic policies and legislation in the United States."[67]

Although the Bricker Amendment did not become law, some believe it has become fact through practices of the Senate that consistently limit the application of international laws by reference to federalism.[68] For example, when the Clinton administration proposed that the Senate ratify CEDAW, it also submitted "reservations, understandings, and declarations" (RUDs)—caveats used in international treaty-making to enable selective adherence to treaty provisions. The CEDAW RUDs specified that the convention's provisions would not be enforceable domestically, that ratification would not result in "changing U.S. law in any respect."[69] Further, in what is termed a "federalism understanding," the RUDs specify that the allocation of power between state and national governments would be unaffected. Parallel reservations accompanied the United States' joining of the Convention on the Elimination of All Forms of Racial Discrimination, and of the International Covenant on Civil and Political Rights.

States' rights are one set of prerogatives to be protected; gender roles are another. Since the 1940s, the fear of international law undoing gendered relationships in the United States has been expressed. The theme emerged in hearings on the Bricker Amendment and has now been put forth vividly through a 2001 Heritage Foundation publication entitled *How U.N. Conventions on Women's and Children's Rights Undermine Family, Religion, and Sovereignty.*[70] That monograph argues that the implementation of CEDAW undervalues the nuclear family and marriage by encouraging mothers to "leave their children in the care of strangers" and to enter "the workforce." Complaining that the 'United Nations has become the tool of a powerful feminist-socialist alliance that has worked deliberately to promote a radical restructuring of society," the monograph calls on Congress to devote time and resources to protect against the dangers the UN poses to sovereignty.[71]

These concerns about the influence of "foreign" ideas are based on *accurate* appraisals of the capacity for ideas and practices to transcend boundaries. But an assumption that bolstering states' and nations' sovereignty could achieve safety from such influences is ill-founded. The relationships among the local, the national, and the international are yet more complex. Within the United States, localities are turning to international law as a model for their own lawmaking. For example, although the United States Senate has yet to ratify CEDAW, the City of San Francisco has—making it a part of its local law in 1998.[72] (Since then, the City's Departments of Juvenile Services and of Public Works have filed reports, as CEDAW requires on an international level, detailing the results of "gender analyses" to understand the role of gender in their processes, structures, and decisions.[73]) And, as of 2000, nine states, the Territory of Guam, sixteen counties, and thirty-eight cities have enacted ordinances calling on the United States to ratify CEDAW.[74]

The legality of local lawmakers engaging with international human rights was also the subject of decision-making in 2000 by the United States Supreme Court. In *Crosby v. National Foreign Trade Council,*[75] the Court imposed some limits by relying on the category of the international to preclude certain forms of local innovation. In *Crosby,* commercial litigants challenged a Massachusetts boycott on goods from Burma. Massachusetts defended that its police powers supported its refusal to spend state dollars on goods produced in violation of its local standards. The Supreme Court held, however, that Massachusetts could not refuse Burmese goods because federal statutory provisions and Executive actions addressed the issue, preempting the state's rules. The Burma boycott case is thus an example of "the local" (Massachusetts) voluntarily allying itself with "the international" (human rights law) and defining local obligations in reference to international standards.

But the idea of boycotting goods made through forced labor was not unique to Massachusetts. That state's human rights ordinance was achieved through a mixture of local, national, and transnational organizing efforts, which Harold Koh terms "issue networks."[76] Such practices are not new. Voluntary associations are often organized in layers (national, state, and local) to link activists in this country and abroad. In the early part of the twentieth century, for example, women's clubs in the United States coordinated to help create "mothers' pensions."[77] More recently, a wave of local ordinances objected to apartheid in South Africa, as others have sought a ban on land mines and to enhance women's rights. This list does not cover the spectrum of local ordinances, which range from expressive efforts to seek social and political change at a national level (such as cities calling for the ratification of CEDAW) to reliance on a locality's economic or political power to produce immediate changes in practices abroad (such as the provision at stake in *Crosby*) to the use of international exchange to enhance a municipality's economy.

These enactments might be read as demonstrating the utility of rigorous enforcement of federalism boundaries, enabling experimentation generated by varying legal regimes. But such an interpretation misses the political purposes that are the predicates of localities' involvement with labor standards and with CEDAW. Proponents' goals are to change local, national, and international laws; their means deploy local actors working in concert with outsiders. To conceive of local action as rooted in specific conditions and indigenous to a particular place is to miss how often that work is a product of broad efforts to shift social policy. New technologies facilitate national and international campaigns by repeat players, who organize campaigns for issues as seemingly parochial as elections of local judges to those evidently transnational, sometimes in an effort to generate universal human rights and other times horrifyingly to destroy them. In short, not only does categorical federalism fail as a description; it is unattainable as an aspiration.

The Many Federalisms

A multifaceted approach to federalism makes more difficult the valorization of certain levels of government as especially able to get any particular social policy "right." Take the claim that the national is a venue committed to civil rights and that the federal courts are especially able to implement such commitments. Relying on the symbolic capital of a link between national law-making and civil rights, VAWA proponents argued that it was a traditional function of the national government to protect equality and to do so by vesting federal judges with jurisdiction.

But that tradition was painfully incomplete at the founding, invigorated after the Civil War, then dismantled, then renewed, and now called again into question. The identity of the federal courts has shifted during the twentieth century—at times seen as institutions of oppression (by labor and other populists) and at other moments as institutions of salvation (by civil rights claimants). Both state and national constitutions speak of their commitments to equality, as do many other countries' constitutions and many international declarations. But to embody equality requires recommitment of national law in that direction, not simply the invocation of the nation as if it has intrinsically and inevitably allied itself with practices of equality.

To equate the local with progressive human rights movements would also be erroneous. I have discussed a series of local innovations—focused on forced labor, land mines, apartheid, and women's rights—cheerfully allied with transnational human rights movements. But another group of local activities in the United States stand in opposition to such efforts and have been the brunt of targeted criticism from abroad. For example, localities in the United States have insisted on their right to execute individuals, juveniles included, despite transnational efforts to ban capital punishment.[78] The phrase "states' rights" has been shorthand for hostility to African Americans. Localities have also enacted ordinances aimed at limiting rights of lesbians and gays and of immigrants. In short, federalism is not a singular set of arrangements enduring over time. Using the term "federalisms" and adding adjectives such as "multifaceted" undermine assumptions that either the national or the local is intrinsically a font of equality.

In parallel fashion, while CEDAW has been discussed as a powerful example of the possibilities of transnationalism to improve gender relations, neither transnational lawmaking nor globalism are necessarily engines of equality. Indeed, some current expressions of globalization do significant harm to women. An oft-cited example is that offshore manufacturing is made attractive by the unending supply of impoverished female workforces, seeking to survive through a range of underpaid jobs. I claim no essence for globalization but only its existence, in that physical distances that had previously precluded certain forms of interactions no longer serve that function. What globalization—under current market and political conditions—has done is to promote interest in forms of governance that regulate transactions outside and beyond the nation-state. That interest, in turn, has generated new opportunities for women to advance. Equality is not a necessary outcome of federating, but with the formulation of new governance structures comes opportunities for alternative allocation of power. Gaps in governance are spaces in which all power-seekers, be they entrenched or newly fabricated, try to gain toe-holds. And in this era, women's rights and human rights advocates have prompted governance institutions to make statements of commitment to equal treatment.[79]

That women have windows of opportunity to participate in generating laws does not necessarily result in laws good for all women. Serious questions, constant within feminism, remain about how to shape such equality demands and about which women will benefit. The category "women"—like the others discussed herein—is neither unitary nor necessarily permanent. Indeed, proponents of many forms of affirmative action deploy categories of identity in the hopes of their future incoherence. Further, provisions that may benefit one group of women may not serve others of differing classes and races. The debates about the enactment of VAWA addressed such concerns. Transnational rights advanced in the name of women must also be interrogated to understand how their applications vary.

Moreover, words about equality committed on paper in transnational documents such as CEDAW do not necessarily translate into conditions of equality in the lives of women and men. For example, some of the 165 countries that have ratified CEDAW have conditions oppressive to women more detrimental than those in the United States, a country that has not ratified CEDAW. Further, even when countries ratified CEDAW, they did so with usually high numbers of reservations. In addition, CEDAW has limited means of implementation.[80] CEDAW constitutes an achievement of significant legal and political proportions, but its translation into practice has not fully materialized. Similarly, I make no claim that international organizations are particularly receptive to women's rights; indeed, some are notoriously poor places for women to work. Nor are NGOs a glorious alternative, as they often not only reflect gendered allocations of work and authority but risk reinscribing them.

Rather, globalism offers a contested political space—an interesting, additional place of potential power, of shifting categories and of new organizations. Proponents of women's rights have had the occasion to use those venues to bring attention to injuries that had not been of much interest to international institutions. A contemporary account can properly point to the correlation between expressions of human rights and certain transnational efforts but ought not lapse into essentializing any level of governance as intrinsically a source of equality norms.

Moving toward a multifaceted approach thus requires a willingness to face such complexities. The nation-state has been the means of governance for some three centuries, and for each harm that form of government has generated, a benefit can also be detailed. If the nation no longer serves as a unit of accountability, if (for example) within the United States the "one voice" doctrine of international law relaxes, will a larger role for regions and localities do harm to the political stability of the United States and whatever human rights agendas that it espouses? Might categorical federalism be a better route to import evolving equality norms into United States jurisprudence, based on an understanding that international law is itself a part of national law and therefore could preempt divergent state practices? Are international human rights obligations assigned at the national level at risk if localities gain prominence and the saliency of national borders diminishes?

These questions are not, of course, novel or unique to the United States. Every federation is an ongoing experiment in how to maintain accountability and distinctive agendas concurrent with the reduction of the saliency of borders. While at one time physical power and physical space provided at least temporizing answers that made plausible that unity of power (democratic or not), those boundaries no longer have the capacity to contain.[81]

The argument is not that place is irrelevant. The local is very much present in each person's life, manifested by the persons with whom one forms families and communities, by the weather systems that shape daily routines, and by the regimes that are proximate and offer either friendship or hostility. But the boundaries of a given nation no longer control markets and can no longer promise physical security. In a parallel fashion, the family unit (predicated on very undemocratic power) once controlled goods, services, and people. The revolt against patriarchal families also ruptures the ability to confine familiar relationships to only certain kinds of pairings and offspring. The litigation about the civil remedy in VAWA raised an enduring problem of United States constitutional law about how to divide the power of judgment between courts and legislatures and, to a lesser extent, between states and Congress. The majority sought to answer by turning back to old images of state boundaries and to worn equations of jurisdiction and gender. The assumptions that located certain forms of action in the nation and other forms of action in local institutions have been overtaken by the permeability of institutions, both large-scale political and small-scale familial. Therefore, a retreat to those categories becomes a willed but unsuccessful effort to buffer oneself and one's country from the transformations with which we have to live.

One cannot essentialize particular forms of federated governance as guarantees of certain outcomes or particular kinds of family relationships as generative of human growth. In the end, neither categorical nor multifaceted federalism provide solutions to the problem of democratic organization and accountability. These are but the forms that may, depending on the content and meaning humans import to them, serve such ends.

NOTES

1. See, e.g., Reva B. Siegel, "She, the People: The Nineteenth Amendment, Sex Equality, Federalism, and the Family," *Harvard Law Review* 115 (2002): 947–1046; Judith Resnik, " 'Naturally' Without Gender: Women, Jurisdiction, and the Federal Courts," *New York University Law Review* 66 (1991): 1682–1772.

2. *United States v. Morrison*, 529 U.S. 598 (2000).

3. Id. at 617–18.

4. See 18 U.S.C. §§ 2262, 2265 (1994); 42 U.S.C. §§ 3796gg, 10416 (1994).

5. 42 U.S.C. § 13981.

6. See generally Linda B. Smith and Larissa K. Samuelson, "Perceiving and Remembering: Category Stability, Variability, and Development," in *Knowledge, Concepts and Categories*, ed. Koen Lamberts and David Shanks (Cambridge: MIT Press, 1997), 161, 170; Audrey S. Kaplan and Gregory L. Murphy, "The Acquisition of Category Structure in Unsupervised Learning," *Memory and Cognition* 27 (1999): 699, 856.

7. See Nancy Cott, *Public Vows: A History of Marriage and the Nation* (Cambridge: Harvard University Press, 2000), 9–23, 115–31; Peggy Cooper Davis, *Neglected Stories: The Constitution and Family Values* (New York: Hill and Wang, 1997); Jill Elaine Hasday, "Federalism and the Family Reconstructed," *University of California Los Angeles Law Review* 45 (1998): 1297–1400; Judith Resnik, "Dependent Sovereigns: Indian Tribes, States, and the Federal Courts" *University of Chicago Law Review* 56 (1989): 671–759.

8. An increasingly rich literature analyzes the effects of social policy on gender and gender's role in shaping policy. See, e.g., Alice Kessler-Harris, *In Pursuit of Equity: Women, Men, and the Quest for Economic Citizenship in 20th-Century America* (Oxford; New York: Oxford University Press, 2001); Alisa C. Klaus, *Every Child a Lion: The Origins of Maternal and Infant Health Policy in the United States and France, 1890–1920* (Ithaca, N.Y.: Cornell University Press, 1993); Suzanne Mettler, *Dividing Citizens: Gender and Federalism in New Deal Public Policy* (Ithaca, N.Y.: Cornell University Press, 1998); Theda Skocpol, *Protecting Soldiers and Mothers: The Political Origins of Social Policy in the United States* (Cambridge: Belknap Press of Harvard University Press, 1992), 7–55.

9. See Boris Bittker, "Federal Income Taxation and the Family," *Stanford Law Review* 27 (1975): 1389–1463; Edward J. McCaffery, *Taxing Women* (Chicago and London: University of Chicago Press, 1997).

10. See Mary E. Becker, "Obscuring the Struggle: Sex Discrimination, Social Security, and Stone, Seidman, Sunstein & Tushnet's Constitutional Law," *Columbia Law Review* 89 (1989): 264–89.

11. Teresa A. Sullivan, Elizabeth Warren, and Jay Lawrence Westbrook, *The Fragile Middle Class: Americans In Debt* (New Haven: Yale University Press, 2000), 175.

12. *Nguyen v. INS*, 533 U.S. 53 (2001) (upholding the constitutionality of a statutory distinction drawn between fathers and mothers for how children of unmarried parents obtain citizenship).

13. See Defense of Marriage Act of 1996 (DOMA), Pub. L. No. 104–99, § 3, 110 Stat. 2419, 2419 (1996) (codified at 1 U.S.C. §7 (Supp iv. 1998) (defining marriage as between one "man" and one "woman" for federal statutes and regulations) and at 28 U.S.C. § 1738(c) (Supp. 1999) (eliminating from the requirements of full faith and credit the decisions of other states to treat same sex relationships as marriages).

14. 29 U.S.C. § 1055; § 1056(d)(3)(D) (1994); *Boggs v. Boggs*, 520 U.S. 833 (1997) (holding that the Employee Retirement Income Security Act of 1974 (ERISA) preempts state community property rules).

15. See Skocpol, supra note 8, at 525–39; Linda Gordon, *Pitied But Not Entitled: Single Mothers and the History of Welfare, 1890–1935* (New York: Free Press; Toronto: Maxwell Macmillan Canada; New York: Maxwell Macmillan International, 1994), 289–93.

16. See Personal Responsibility and Work Opportunity Reconciliation Act of 1996, which provides that recipients of Temporary Assistance for Needy Families (TANF) must partake in the paid labor force, with certain excerpts related to inability to secure child care. Pub. L. No. 104–193, § 407, 110 Stat. 2105, 2129 (1996); codified at 42 U.S.C. § 607(e)(2), (g); ("It is the sense of the Congress that . . . each State . . . assign the highest priority to requiring adults in 2-parent families and adults in single-parent families that include older preschool or school-age children to be engaged in work activities.").

17. Gordon, supra note 15, at 18.

18. Id. at 19–20.

19. For example, in some states mothers—who, if married, had no rights to property—did not have support obligations. See Harry D. Krause, *Child Support in America: The Legal Perspective* (Charlottesville, Va.: Michie, 1981), 4–5, 38–44.

20. See generally William J. Brockelbank, *Interstate Enforcement of Family Support: (The Runaway Pappy Act)* (Indiana: Bobbs-Merrill, 1960).

21. See Alice Kessler-Harris, *A Woman's Wage: Historical Meanings and Social Consequences* (Lexington: University Press of Kentucky, 1990).

22. H.R. 1538, 81st Cong. (1949).

23. See generally *Making Abandonment of Dependents a Federal Crime: Hearings before Subcommittee No. 2 of the Committee on the Judiciary*, U.S. House of Rep., 81st Cong. 1st & 2d Sess. on H.R. 1538, H.R. 2143, H.R. 3802, H.R. 4565, 4580, 7312, & 8051, and H.R. 5974 (Mar. 2, Apr. 4, 1949; May 12, 1950) (Serial No. 23, 1950).

24. 18 U.S.C. § 228 (1994), amended the Deadbeat Parents Punishment Act of 1998, Pub. L. No. 105–187, 112 Stat. 618.

25. See Judith Resnik, "The Programmatic Judiciary: Lobbying, Judging, and Invalidating the Violence Against Women Act," *Southern California Law Review* 74 (2000): 269–93.

26. For analysis of the history and propriety of the judiciary taking positions on pending legislation, see Judith Resnik, "Trial as Error, Jurisdiction as Injury: Transforming the Meaning of Article III," *Harvard Law Review* 113 (2000): 924, 961–67.

27. *Thompson v. Thompson*, 484 U.S. 174 (1988); *Blessing v. Firestone*, 520 U.S. 329 (1996); *Suter v. Artist*, 503 U.S. 347 (1981).

28. See, e.g., *Lehman v. Lycoming County Children's Services Agency*, 458 U.S. 502 (1982); *Moore v. Sims*, 442 U.S 415 (1978); *Ankenbrandt v. Richards*, 504 U.S. 689 (1991); See Martin Guggenheim, "State Intervention in the Family: Making a Federal Case Out of It," *Ohio State Law Journal* 45 (1984): 399.

29. On the legitimacy of the federal judiciary having any such collective view, see Resnik, "The Programmatic Judiciary," supra note 25, at 276–80. On the wisdom of the particular federal policies crafted, see, e.g., Sylvia Law, "Families and Federalism," *Washington University Journal of Law & Policy* 4 (2000): 175–238; Naomi R. Cahn, "Children's Interests in a Familial Context: Poverty, Foster Care, and Adoption," *Ohio State Law Journal* 60 (2000): 1189; David L. Chambers, "Fathers, the Welfare System, and the Virtues and Perils of Child-Support Enforcement," *Virginia Law Review* 81 (1995): 2575–2605.

30. U.S. Const. art. I, § 9, cl. 8; Art. I, § 3, cl. 2.

31. *Troxel v. Granville* 530 U.S. 57 (2000).

32. *Troxel*, 530 U.S. at 92 (Scalia, J., dissenting).

33. See *Santosky v. Kramer*, 455 U.S. 745 (1982).

34. See, e.g., *Meyer v. Nebraska*, 262 U.S. 390, 401 (1923); *Pierce v. Society of Sisters*, 268 U.S. 510, 534–35 (1925).

35. See *Loving v. Virginia*, 388 U.S. 1, 2 (1967); *Reynolds v. United States*, 98 U.S. 145 (1878); *Cleveland v. United States*, 329 U.S. 14 (1946); *Eisenstadt v. Baird*, 405 U.S. 438 (1972).

36. *Palmore v. Sidoti*, 466 U.S. 429, 433 (1984) (prohibiting reliance on a parent's interracial marriage as a grounds for assigning custody to the other parent).

37. *Levy v. Louisiana*, 391 U.S. 68 (1968); *New Jersey Welfare Rights Organization v. Cahill*, 411 U.S. 619 (1973).

38. See, e.g., *Michael H. v. Gerard D.*, 491 U.S. 110 (1989); *Little v. Streater*, 452 U.S. 1 (1981); *Caban v. Mohammed*, 441 U.S. 380 (1979); *Quilloin v. Walcott*, 434 U.S. 246 (1978); *Stanley v. Illinois*, 405 U.S. 645 (1972).

39. See, e.g., Inter-American Convention on the Prevention, Punishment and Eradication of Violence Against Women, June 9, 1994, art. 5 ("Every woman is entitled to the free and full exercise of her civil, political, economic, social and cultural rights . . . [and signatories] recognize that violence against women prevents and nullifies the exercise of these rights"), adopted by the General Assembly of Organization of American States, 33 I.L.M. 1534 (1994).

40. See Louis Henkin, *The Age of Rights* (New York: Columbia University Press, 1990), 76–77.

41. UNICEF, *Domestic Violence Against Women and Girls* (Florence, Italy: United Nations Children's Fund Innocenti Research Ctr., Innocenti Digest No. 6, 2000), http://www.icdc.org/publications/pdf/digest6e.pdf.

42. Id. at 2 (Overview).

43. Id.

44. Id. at 3. While violence against women crosses cultural lines, the grounds and sources of injury reflect cultural patterns. See Lama Abu-Odeh, "Comparatively Speaking: The 'Honor' of the 'East' and the 'Passion' of the 'West,' ' *Utah Law Review* 2 (1997): 287–307.

45. UNICEF, *Domestic Violence*, supra note 41, at 8.

46. *United Nations Development Programme, Human Development Report* (New York: Oxford University Press, 1999), 22.

47. Ruth Bader Ginsburg and Deborah Jones Merritt, "Affirmative Action: An International Human Rights Dialogue," *Cardozo Law Review* 21 (1999): 253, 257.

48. Martha C. Nussbaum, *Women and Human Development: The Capabilities Approach* (Cambridge and New York: Cambridge University Press, 2000), 1.

49. See Lelia J. Rupp, *Worlds of Women: The Making of the International Women's Movement* (Princeton, N.J.: Princeton University Press, 1997).

50. 1249 U.N.T.S. 20378 (entered into force, Sept. 3, 1981) [hereinafter *Convention for the Elimination of All Forms of Discrimination Against Women*]. "CEDAW," technically the name of the committee empowered with oversight of its deployment, is sometimes used as a shorthand for the convention.

51. See *Convention on the Elimination of All Forms of Discrimination Against Women*, supra note 50, at Article 3. Article 5(a) addresses the need "[t]o modify social and cultural patterns of conduct of men and women" to eliminate stereotypes; Article 6 calls on state parties to reduce trafficking in women; Article 7 seeks women's equal participation in formulation of government policy and for equal employment possibilities; and Article 16 seeks the elimination of discrimination against women in all matters relating to marriage and family relations.

52. Id., Article 2 (e), (f) & Article 4 (i). When equality is achieved, they are to be discontinued.

53. Id. CEDAW Committee, General Recommendation No. 19, Violence Against Women, U.N. Doc. A/14/38 at 1 (1992).

54. See Fiona Beveridge, Sue Nott, and Kylie Stephen eds., *Making Women Count: Integrating Gender into Law and Policy-Making* (Aldershot: Dartmouth Pub. Co.; Burlington, Vt.: Ashgate, 2000), 273–74.

55. Noelle Lenoir, "The Representation of Women in Politics: From Quotas to Parity in Elections," *The International and Comparative Law Quarterly* 50 (2001) 217, 242–43.

56. See *Making Women Count*, supra note 54 (analyzing efforts at integrating policymaking in five EU countries).

57. Arnlaug Leira, "Childcare as Social Right: Cash for Childcare and Daddy Leave," *Social Politics* 5 (1998): 362, 375. See generally Peter Moss and Fred Deven, eds., *Parental Leave: Progress or Pitfall? Research and Policy Issues in Europe* (Wellington, N.Z.: Ministry of Women's Affairs, 1999), x–xi.

58. Payment structures in countries vary, with some having flat-rate allowances and parental wages and others replacing earnings at the same levels as unemploy-

ment or illness. See Suzan Lewis, Janel Smithson, and Julia Brannen, "Young Europeans' Orientation to Families and Work," *The Annals of the American Academy of Political and Social Science* 562 (1999): 83, 85; Ministry of Children and Family Affairs, The Rights of Parents of Small Children in Norway (Oslo: National Insurance Administration, 2000). http://odin.dep.no/archive/bfdvedlegg/01/01/Smaab034.pdf.

59. Deborah M. Figart and Ellen Mutari, "Degendering Work Time in Comparative Perspective: Alternative Policy Frameworks," *Review of Social Economy* 56 (1998): 460, 465.

60. See Rhonda Copelon, "Gendered War Crimes: Reconceptualizing Rape in Time of War," in *Women's Rights, Human Rights*, ed. Julie Peters and Andrea Wolper (New York: Routledge, 1995), 197, 201; Catharine A. MacKinnon, "Rape, Genocide, and Women's Human Rights," in *Mass Rape: The War Against Women in Bosnia-Herzegovina*, ed. Alexandra Stiglmayer, trans. Marion Faber (Lincoln: University of Nebraska Press, 1994), 183.

61. *Prosecutor v. Kunarac*, Case Nos. IT-96-23-T, IT-96-23/1-T (Int'l Crim. Trib. For Former Yugoslavia Feb. 22, 2001), http://www.un.org/icty/ind-e.htm. See generally Judith Gardam and Michelle Jarvis, "Women and Armed Conflict: The International Response to the Beijing Platform for Action," *Columbia Human Rights Law Review* 32 (2000): 1–65; Patricia M. Wald, "Judging War Crimes," *Chicago Journal of International Law* 1 (2000): 189–96.

62. The Rome Treaty entered into force on July 1, 2002.The United States became a signatory at the end of President Clinton's term, but George W. Bush's administration opposed ratification and has sought to limit the ICC's jurisdiction over Americans.

63. See Cate Steains, "Gender Issues," in Roy S. Lee, ed., *The International Criminal Court: The Making of the Rome Statute* (The Hague; Boston: Kluwer Law International, 1999), 357.

64. *United States v. Morrison*, 529 U.S. 598 (2000) at 617–18.

65. Thomas L. Spalding and Gregory L. Murphy, "What Is Learned In Knowledge-Related Categories? Evidence from Typicality and Feature Frequency Judgments," *Memory and Cognition* 27 (1999): 856, 864.

66. S.J. Res. 130, 82d Cong., 98 Cong. Rec. 908 (1952) ("No treaty or executive agreement shall be made respecting the rights of citizens of the United States protected by this Constitution. . . . "), reprinted in Duane Tananbaum, *The Bricker Amendment Controversy: A Test of Eisenhower's Political Leadership* (Ithaca, N.Y.: Cornell University Press, 1988), 222.

67. Id. at 31.

68. See Louis Henkin, "U.S. Ratification of Human Rights Conventions: The Ghost of Senator Bricker," *American Journal of International Law* 89 (1995): 341–62.

69. Convention on the Elimination of all Forms of Discrimination Against Women: Hearing Before the S. Comm. on Foreign Relations, 103d Cong. 13 (2d Sess. 1994) (statement of Jamison S. Borek, Deputy Legal Advisor, Department of State).

70. Patrick F. Fagan, *How U.N. Conventions on Women's and Children's Rights Undermine Family, Religion, and Sovereignty*, The Heritage Foundation Backgrounder,

no. 1407 (Washington, D.C.: The Heritage Foundation, 2001), http://www.heritage.org/library/backgrounder/bg1407.html.

71. Id. at 21.

72. S.F., CA, Admin. Code ch. 12K.1 (2001) http;//www.amlegal.com/sanfran/.

73. See S.F. Commission on the Status of Women and CEDAW Task Force, A Gender Analysis: Implementing CEDAW: A Report (1999); S.F. CEDAW Task Force, Fourth Progress Report (2001), http://www.ci.sf.ca.us/cosw/cedaw/cedaw_5.htm.

74. Women's Institute for Leadership Development for Human Rights, CEDAW Around the U.S. at http://www.wildforhumanrights.org/cedaw_around_us.html. The texts of these resolutions vary; some seek national ratification while others also require local implementation.

75. *Crosby v. National Foreign Trade Council*, 530 U.S. 363 (2000).

76. Harold Hongju Koh, "Bringing International Law Home," *Houston Law Review* 35 (1998): 623, 649.

77. Skocpol, supra note 8, at 464–65.

78. See generally *Breard v. Green*, 523 U.S. 371 (1998).

79. See Helen Durham, "Women and Civil Society: NGOs and the International Criminal Law," in vol. 3 of *Women and International Human Rights Law*, eds. Kelly D. Askin and Doreen M. Koenig (Ardsley, N.Y.: Transnational, 1998), 819–43.

80. One mechanism is a state-to-state complaint, brought to the International Court of Justice. Another is a system of reports, in which member states take on the obligation to study and report on their own implementation efforts. A committee, comprised of twenty-three members, receives the reports and then engages in an exchange with the reporting state about the achievements and problems. In 2000, a third implementation mechanism came into play, when a sufficient number of countries had ratified an optional protocol that permits women, after exhausting available internal remedies, to bring complaints directly to the CEDAW committee. Optional Protocol to the Convention on the Elimination of All Forms of Discrimination Against Women, U.N. GAOR, 54th Sess., Agenda Item 109, U.N. Doc. A/RES/54/4 (1999).

81. Jean-Marie Guéhenno, *The End of the Nation-State*, trans. Victoria Elliott (Minnesota: University of Minnesota Press, 1995).

Martha C. Nussbaum

CHAPTER 10

What's Privacy Got to Do With It?

A Comparative Approach to the Feminist Critique

> *In a sensitive sphere which is at once intimate and delicate the introduction of the cold principles of Constitutional Law will have the effect of weakening the marriage bond.*
> —DELHI HIGH COURT, in *Harvinder Kaur v. Harmander Singh*, 1984

Privacy and Feminist Politics

The pursuit of sex equality through constitutional law has sometimes taken a detour through the disputed and murky concept of privacy. The United States, lacking an explicit provision of sex equality in its constitution, and having failed in the 1960s to amend the constitution to add one, revived the once-discredited tradition of substantive due process—that is, of reading substantive rights into the notions of "life and liberty" in the Due Process clauses of the Fifth and Fourteenth Amendments, closely analogous to Article 21 of the Indian Constitution. The tradition had gone into eclipse after a period early in the twentieth century, during which substantive due process was used by the Court to strike down a number of socially progressive laws protecting the rights of workers, including minimum wage and maximum hours laws. The Court had held that such laws violated rights of employers and that these rights derived constitutional status from the vague notion of "life and liberty." Criticism of these decisions mounted, inside and outside of the Court, until the key case, *Lochner v. New York*,[1] was finally overruled in 1934—after the Court had, in the interim, invalidated two hundred pieces of

This essay, is a revised and shortened version of my earlier "Sex Equality, Liberty, and Privacy: A Comparative Approach to the Feminist Critique" which appeared in E. Sridharan, Z. Hasan, and R. Sudarshan, eds., *India's Living Constitution: Ideas, Practices, Controversies* (New Delhi: Permanent Black, 2002).

progressive economic legislation.[2] After this, substantive due process was viewed for a long time as a retrogressive and discredited stratagem.

Thirty years after the overruling of *Lochner*, however, in a range of cases dealing with contraception and abortion, the U.S. Supreme Court again returned to the Due Process Clause and the allegedly substantive rights contained therein, recognizing "a right to privacy" that was admittedly nowhere explicit in the Constitution. In a famous and much-discussed opinion, Justice Douglas claimed that "specific guarantees in the Bill of Rights have penumbras, formed by emanations from those guarantees that help give them life and substance."[3] Declaring unconstitutional a Connecticut law that made the use of contraception by married couples illegal, Douglas argued that a right to privacy resides in the "penumbras" of several explicit provisions, including above all the Due Process clauses, but including, as well, the Fourth Amendment's strictures against unreasonable and unwarranted search and seizure, the First Amendment's guarantee of freedom of speech (which was interpreted to have freedom of association in its "penumbra"), the Third Amendment's prohibition of quartering of soldiers in people's houses in time of peace, and the Ninth Amendment's tantalizing remarks about other rights "retained by the people." Other cases soon followed, recognizing this right in areas highly relevant to women's equality—most notoriously, *Roe v. Wade*,[4] which recognized a woman's right to abortion.

Is privacy a useful concept, a concept that gives good guidance in law and public policy? And is it a concept that helps law advance the cause of sex equality? I shall answer "no" to both of these questions. A generally negative answer to the first question has been given before—most influentially by Judith Jarvis Thomson, in her path-breaking and deservedly much cited paper.[5] I shall be agreeing with Thomson that the interest in protecting privacy is really in protecting a cluster of distinct interests, but I shall go further and argue that the concept of privacy becomes useless for legal and political purposes. It is particularly ill-suited and even pernicious in advancing the interests of sex equality.

I shall not, however, agree with some very influential voices in the tradition of feminist criticism that links American and Indian feminists, voices that conclude that the notion we need to replace privacy is simply that of equality.[6] Instead, I shall argue that we articulate the issues in the most perspicuous way if we recognize, in addition to the interest in equality or nonsubordination, a plurality of distinct human liberties as all deserving state protection. Among such liberties are some that have been associated with the concept of privacy: for example, the freedom to be free from unreasonable and unwarranted search and seizure, the freedom of movement and travel, the freedom of association, the freedom to control in certain ways the public use of information about oneself. While these, I shall argue, should not be swept under the umbrella of privacy, they also should not be, and could not be, funneled into equality. Thus we are left with what we might have thought we had all along: a plurality of distinct vital human interests, all of which should be enumerated, and all of which need constitutional protection.

While many scholars have analyzed the role of privacy in constitutional law and related political and legal discourse simply by reference to the U.S. experience, focusing on India helps such an analysis move forward. The Indian constitutional tradition, during its fifty years of life, has committed itself firmly and explicitly to sex equality, unlike our American one. In recent years, however, Indian constitutional jurisprudence has borrowed wholesale the problematic privacy jurisprudence of the U.S. Supreme Court, using it to fill gaps in the understanding of protected liberties—in areas ranging from unwarranted search and seizure to informational privacy to bodily integrity and personal autonomy. By exploring the tensions that have arisen between privacy and equality in the Indian tradition, therefore, I believe we will see new and strong reasons to distrust the notion of privacy. Moreover, some promising paradigms emerge of how that concept may be replaced by the public recognition of both an interest in equality and a plurality of distinct interests in liberty, as all deserving state protection.

I begin with some preliminary discussions of cultural context and comparison and of some significant differences between the U.S. and Indian constitutional traditions. I shall then introduce the most important feminist objections that have been made to privacy as an organizing concept and sketch my own preferred approach—referring, as I do so, to important Indian cases. My treatment of the cases will focus on the long-contested issue of "restitution of conjugal rights," but I shall consider, as well, significant cases that deal, respectively, with issues of police surveillance and solitary confinement.

Privacy and Cultural Difference

Before the argument can even begin, we need to establish that we are entitled to speak of the concept of privacy when addressing Indian culture. There is a familiar canard about non-Western societies: that they don't ascribe the same value we do to privacy. This sentiment is vividly expressed by Paul Ehrlich in *The Population Bomb*, when he describes a taxi ride in Delhi:

> The streets seemed alive with people. People eating, people washing, people sleeping. People visiting, arguing, and screaming. . . . People, people, people, people. As we moved slowly through the mob, hand

horn squawking, the dust, noise, heat, and cooking fires gave the scene a hellish aspect. Would we ever get to our hotel?[7]

This extraordinarily chauvinistic description (which might suggest that Ehrlich has never visited New York) is nonetheless typical of a way in which many Americans react when they visit a strange culture. And indeed India does provide such particular experiences. Americans are likely to be surprised, for example, by a relative absence of regard for or interest in the personal solitude of the proverbial "room of one's own" in family customs across class and region. Personal solitude is at least one of the things that is not too misleadingly named by the term "privacy."

But of course these experiences show us nothing about whether there is a value of privacy in Indian culture; only that India draws certain concrete lines in different places from America. In fact, if we consider the general meanings of "privacy" typically acknowledged as most salient in American legal and philosophical discussions of these matters, Indians also mark each of the notions as salient, and ascribe some positive value to their protection.

One of the human interests most commonly associated with the term "privacy"—sometimes even said to be the primary such interest—is the interest in controlling the access to and dissemination of information about oneself. Not surprisingly, in India as in America—and probably every place in the world—people recognize that certain types of information about oneself are privileged, that one is entitled to conceal such information, and that it is bad for outsiders to publicize it without consent. Case law in India prominently recognizes the confidentiality of medical records,[8] and there are similar issues about other personal information, about libel and slander, about the entire range of so-called privacy concerns of an informational character.[9] People's preoccupations in these areas are not very different from the preoccupations of Americans—although concrete lines are drawn in different places. One doesn't need a "room of one's own" in order to want to keep a secret.

Another interest very commonly associated with the term "privacy" is the interest in controlling access to one's body—by touching, sight, and other forms of surveillance. Some would argue that this interest is reducible to the interest in control over personal information; but most theorists generally agree that there is a distinct further interest in protecting one's person from unwanted looking or touching.[10]

Here differences of class, sex, and region construct major internal differences within each nation, but again, we can say that in India as in the United States, there is a deep concern for keeping certain parts of the body, and certain bodily acts, hidden from the sight of others, and also a more general concern that, whatever one is doing, one should not be watched without one's consent. Again, Indian lines are drawn differently from American lines in some concrete cases, but here it is India, on the whole, that more jealously guards the relevant areas of privacy. For instance, there is no stratum of society in which people, no matter how poor, do not seek an unobserved place for urination and defecation.[11]

Lest someone suggest that this concern with privacy reflects a borrowing of Western values, let me quickly mention that it is among the most ancient and deeply traditional concerns of both Hindu and Muslim cultures. The Quran, famously, enjoins modesty for both men and women, and modesty on both sides entails not looking in lascivious ways at the bodies or activities of others.[12] There are times when the symmetry of these provisions is ignored and the protection of modesty is applied to women only, but Muslim writers frequently note that this is a distortion of the tradition.[13] As for ancient Hindu law, along with the elaborate focus on rules for bathing, tooth-brushing, etc., there is equally elaborate focus on strict rules for privacy in urination and defecation.

Of course, although Americans sometimes talk as if we value this sort of privacy highly, we actually do not have nearly as strong a sense of impropriety about public excretion. Men urinate more or less anywhere they need to, although occasionally this is punished by law.[14] Women are permitted the same courtesy in certain contexts, such as that of public long-distance running.[15] By contrast, in India it is utterly unacceptable for a woman to urinate in public, even when circumstances make this a highly desirable option.

Indian customs also prescribe an intense concern with modesty in personal dress: women still rarely wear shorts, and athletic clothes typically cover the legs and at least the shoulders. In the U.S., of course, one would not need to have any such thoughts about modesty, since the only clothing that would cause dismay would be an entirely topless outfit for a woman or total nudity for a man. Finally, privacy with regard to the dwelling place is also recognized in Hindu law from ancient times. Cases dealing with new windows or doors that enable someone to overlook another person's dwelling place allude to a customary "right of privacy" in this regard and cite ancient sources for it.[16]

As this observation already indicates, law in India reflects this anxious concern for privacy in the sense of modesty, protecting to almost absurd lengths a person's right to control the access of others to any sight of the person. Section 509 of the Indian Penal Code of 1860 makes it a crime to intrude upon the privacy of a woman intending to insult her modesty. (This is only one of the numerous laws dealing with issues of modesty, which have lately been used as a major resource in feminist struggles to get protection against sexual harassment.[17]) Furthermore, even though such laws are more likely to protect middle-class than working-class women, there is at least some legal recognition that the value of privacy extends to all: in a 1962 case involving a police raid on a brothel, the Court found it legally unacceptable that the police officer walked into a prostitute's bedroom "without even the civility of a knock or warning to her to prepare for the intrusion."[18]

But it is a third aspect of the concept of privacy (or an alleged such aspect) that is most at stake in our cases concerning sex equality: this is the interest in decisional autonomy or liberty in certain areas especially definitive of the self. It is this decisional type of privacy that is invoked in *Griswold* and *Roe*, and it is this aspect, too, that most centrally figures in Indian cases concerning the restitution of conjugal rights. I shall shortly be arguing that this is the aspect of "privacy" most misleadingly brought under that concept, but I need to discuss it at least briefly, since it has frequently been suggested by some American feminists that the interest in self-governed choice is an outgrowth of "Western individualism" and is foreign to non-Western cultures.

We might start with the Preamble to the Indian Constitution, which states in the most unequivocal terms that the liberty and dignity of the individual are central aims of the nation. But it seems to me important to state, as well, that Indian male traditions attach an extremely high value to decisional autonomy for males and that more recent feminist traditions insist on asserting this same value in the case of women. Rabindranath Tagore was among the leaders: his character Mrinal, in the 1914 short story "Letter From a Wife," writes to her husband, "I found myself beautiful as a free human mind" — and this conception of herself is what led her to leave a life in which she could have no decisional freedom. She invokes longstanding (if dissident) Hindu traditions of female liberty in her defense: the Rajput queen Meerabai, who left her own husband and became an itinerant singer, in service of her conception of god.[19] Today in women's organizations in India, the same idea is ubiquitous. Women strive for more control over finances, working conditions, literacy, and the daily conditions of existence.[20] Often the precedent of India's own independence struggle is invoked: just as India could only become independent of her colonial oppressor by pursuing economic and political self-sufficiency, so too women will only be free from their oppression at the hands of men when they achieve a measure of economic and political control and autonomy.

The U.S. and Indian Constitutions: Fundamental Rights, Equal Protection, Due Process

I shall now set the stage for discussion of the Indian cases by characterizing some of the central features of the Indian Constitution, and comparing it to the relevant features of the U.S. Constitution.[21] India, like the U.S., has a written constitution with an enumerated list of fundamental rights; it also has a Supreme Court that is the final interpreter of the Constitution and has increasingly seen its function as similar to that of the U.S. Supreme Court. Thus judicial review of statutes has become increasingly common in India, though it was not so at first; U.S. cases are frequently cited as precedents.

Several differences between the two documents are important for the tradition I am about to discuss. First, the Indian document is in many respects much more explicit than the U.S. document, concerning the rights and entitlements of citizens that enjoy constitutional protection. The Fundamental Rights are in some central cases described as positive entitlements, as that to which "All citizens shall have the right," rather than simply in terms of what legislators may not do. The U.S. document is typically negative in its expression and consequently vague about positive entitlements.[22]

Moreover, whether positively or negative described, the Indian rights are typically described in considerable detail. First, each particular right is discussed at greater length, with a clear intent to resolve certain disputes that have plagued the U.S. tradition. Thus, for example, Article 15, concerning nondiscrimination on grounds of religion, race, caste, sex, or place of birth, contains an explicit provision for affirmative action for both lower castes and women and children.[23] The endless debates and agonies of the U.S. context are thus avoided—unless opponents of affirmative action should prove able to amend the Constitution. Second, as in Article 19, there is simply a larger list of explicit entitlements, including equality of opportunity in public employment, freedom of association, the right to form labor unions, the right of travel and freedom of residence anywhere within the nation, the free choice of occupation, a prohibition of the traffic in human beings and of forced labor, and so forth. U.S. constitutional law has had to arrive at some of these liberties by a much more indirect route. The right to travel, for example, has been read into the meaning of the word "liberty," as it occurs in the Due Process clause of the Fifth Amendment.[24]

Although the Indian list of rights is on the whole more explicit than its U.S. analogue, at least two omissions from the U.S. list are striking, and will concern us in what follows. The Indian Constitution has no analogue of the U.S. Constitution's Eighth Amendment, forbidding "cruel and unusual punishments"—although there is an extensive guarantee of habeas corpus and a prohibition of certain types of arbitrary preventive detention. Nor is there an analogue of the U.S. Constitution's Fourth Amendment, prohibiting unreasonable and unwarranted searches and seizures.

The Indian Constitution contains analogues of both the Due Process clause of our Fifth and Fourteenth Amendments and of the Equal Protection clauses of our Fourteenth Amendment. Article 14 states: "The State shall not deny to any person equality before the law or the equal protection of the laws within the territory of India." Article 21 states: "No person shall be deprived of his life or personal liberty except according to procedure established by law." As we shall see, these provisions, and especially Article 21, have been the primary avenues through which our privacy jurisprudence has made its way into Indian law—although Article 19's list of concretely enumerated rights has also played an important role.

Notice that the Indian document contains a number of resources for the empowerment of women that the U.S. document lacks. First, it contains an explicit provision of nondiscrimination on the basis of sex and an explicit interpretation that this is not to be taken to be incompatible with affirmative action programs aimed at improving women's lot.

Second, the explicit attention to freedom of assembly, freedom of travel, equality of opportunity, and labor rights sets up a favorable situation for women who may need to appeal for protection of just such rights in connection with their pursuit of social equality. These freedoms, of course, are among those that are most commonly infringed on grounds of sex.

Third, the understanding of equality in the Indian document is explicitly and from the start substantive, rather than abstract and formal, in that it is made clear that special protective legislation advancing the interests of a disadvantaged group should not be construed as impermissible discrimination. A primary complaint of the U.S. feminist tradition has been that the legal understanding of equality in the tradition is purely formal: thus so long as laws treat everyone the same, it doesn't matter if this sameness of treatment reinforces hierarchy.[25] Feminists have urged instead that equal treatment, and equal protection of the laws, be understood substantively, as requiring an end to systematic hierarchy and discrimination. But this idea is already well entrenched in Indian constitutional jurisprudence.

Against Privacy: Four Feminist Arguments

At this point we are ready to introduce the most common criticisms that feminists have made against the use of the concept of privacy in U.S. constitutional law. These criticisms, although initially articulated with reference to U.S. law, have become common currency in the international feminist movement. In each case, I shall introduce the argument and then turn to the Indian situation to see how that legal tradition helps us assess the feminist charge.

Privacy, it is claimed, is simply too diffuse and unclear a concept to serve any useful legal role.[26] This objection has been made by many scholars, not all of them feminists; but it is an important part of the feminist charge. The claim is not just that the concept is a cluster concept, nor that it is simply in need of further specification; many core concepts of constitutional law are like this. The claim is that the concept is so unclear and amorphous that judgments of what falls under it are highly likely to be arbitrary and willful. This is a feminist issue, because arbitrary judgments are especially likely to express the views of current convention or the current arrangement of male power (see the next section).

Indian legal thinkers have made precisely this point with regard to privacy, so we should not think that the concept has acquired a superior clarity of definition in the Indian legal or nonlegal tradition. The Press Commission of India in 1982 opined that "Privacy is a very nebulous concept and criteria which may constitute its violation cannot be drawn up," and Rajeev Dhavan, an eminent authority on the seclusion and information aspects of privacy, summarizing the situation writes, "Even in its constitutional context, it is not clear as to what "privacy" means and how far the right to privacy extends."[27]

One probably could map out a reasonably coherent cluster-concept of privacy that would cover the informational and seclusion-and-modesty related interests that I have already identified, especially if we leave off the area of personal liberty and autonomy, which is the most serious source of confusion. But the special problem that arises when we consider so proceeding is that privacy, even so delimited, covers a large number of distinct areas of law: the law of the press, the law of torts, laws related to housing, and, in the area of modesty, the criminal law. It seems far better to demarcate precisely what citizens have a right to, and a right to be free from, in each of these areas, rather than simply to assert that they have "a right to privacy." Or rather, the statement that they have "a right to privacy" does absolutely no work in indicating how to shape these diverse areas of law, until we enumerate the distinct privacy interests at a much more concrete level.

The central argument in Catharine MacKinnon's internationally influential critique of the privacy concept is that appeals to privacy have standardly functioned to insulate bad behavior—and behavior that is, in J. S. Mill's sense, "other-regarding" and affects the interests of others—from state scrutiny. "In this light," MacKinnon writes, "a right to privacy looks like an injury got up as a gift."[28] Thus, appeals to the alleged privacy of the home have characteristically accompanied defenses of the marital rape exemption, as well as of noninterference with domestic violence and with child abuse. As MacKinnon notes, it is not women's privacy that is being protected here, it is the male's privacy. Recognizing a sphere of seclusion into which the state shall not enter means, simply, that males may exercise unconstrained power. Such action is conceived as "self-regarding action"—an action that implicates no interests other than his own—because traditionally women and children were not considered, for either legal or ethical purposes, as separate individuals with separate interests.

More generally, MacKinnon, Carol Pateman, and other feminist critics look at the whole history of the public/private distinction and see in it a stratagem through which men have claimed for themselves an unlimited exercise of power, among whose primary uses has been to subordinate women. The Greek distinction between the *polis* and the *oikos*, one of the most foundational sources for our modern public/private distinction, functioned exactly this way. As Aristotle articulates it, it is the distinction between a sphere in which a man is an equal among equals, constrained by demanding norms of reciprocity and justice, and a sphere in which he rules as a king.[29] Similarly, John Locke's state of nature, yet another formative source of modern Western traditions of privacy, is a realm in which men need not "ask leave" of another: it is "a state of perfect freedom to order their actions, and dispose of their possessions and persons as they see fit, within the bounds of the Law of Nature."[30]

What this history tells us is that even when appeals to privacy appear to protect the interests of women (or children), we should be skeptical, asking whose interests really are advanced. Laws that protect the modesty of women from violation by the eyes or even touch of a stranger seem in one way protective of women; and they have been used by feminists who hope to squeeze progressive results out of antiquated codes. But the concept of womanly modesty is inextricable from the history of patriarchy, and it subjects women to asymmetrical limitations on their freedom. The prohibition on outraging womanly modesty is just the flip side of the prohibition of immodest behavior on the part of a woman who might want to wear clothing of her choice or to walk with freedom in the world.

Another related way in which the appeal to privacy does harm is that it shores up traditional hierarchies surrounding marital heterosexuality. What gets protected is the privacy of the marital couple in the conjugal home. Same-sex couples and even unmarried heterosexual couples are less likely to achieve the same protection.[31] Thus *Griswold v. Connecticut* defended the right to contraception as a right of married couples, and it was only later, in *Eisenstadt v. Baird*,[32] and on grounds of equal protection, not privacy, that the same protection was extended to unmarried individuals.

For such reasons, feminists have thought it unwise of American jurists to seek protection for certain key liberty rights of women by sliding them into the all-too-capacious envelope of privacy. The right to contraception and the right to abortion are not naturally linked with the notion of privacy in the sense of either confidentiality/secrecy or modesty/seclusion. People can take birth control pills when all the world is watching, and many people make no secret of the fact. Legal abortion by its very nature is always done with others present and is no more secluded than any other medical procedure; if it is right now more confidential than some procedures, this is largely because of the climate of hostility surrounding it. What is at stake in contraception and abortion is decisional autonomy or liberty. The issue is whether a certain life-defining choice will or will not be open to women (or, in other cases, men).

Because I have referred to the Western tradition of the private/public divide as the source of my problem, I have raised again the question: Do Indian traditions contain the basis for a comparable worry? Most emphatically, they do. Traditional Hindu law gives the household considerable autonomy. At the same time, one of the central prerogatives, and indeed duties, of the householder is strict control over the women of the house: chapter 9 of the Laws of Manu states that women are by nature untruthful, lustful, and in need of constant supervision. Here too, the idea of the household as a protected sphere of male authority is established.

In keeping with this general picture, marriage is thought to imply consent to sexual intercourse, so there is no traditional concept of rape in marriage. Certainly traditional sources are quite critical of cruelty and violence in the home (unless there has been adultery). But even violence of a quite remarkable type has at times been countenanced under the doctrine of implied consent. The issue is compounded by the traditionally low age of marriage. Can a girl of ten or eleven by any stretch of the imagination be presumed to consent to sexual intercourse? And yet, as we shall see, that proposition has been energetically defended.

An especially pernicious development of the idea of male rule over the household took over during the time of British domination, with British connivance, resulting in a keen interest in justifying even extremely cruel conduct as simply within the husband's husbandly prerogative. In an impressive article, historian Tanika Sarkar has investigated the rhetoric surrounding the tragic death of Phulmonee, a girl of ten or eleven, who was raped by her husband, Hari Mati, a man of thirty-five, and died of the resulting injuries.[33] Sarkar convincingly shows that in reaction to British domination of external political life, nationalists turned inward, boosting the idea of male autonomy in the home as the one cherished zone of self-rule, "the last pure space left to a conquered people"; this autonomy was understood to be built around the submission, and indeed the much-praised and allegedly voluntary suffering, of women. Nationalists of this stripe resisted internal demands for reform of child marriage, painting them as subversions of their cherished (but really constructed) traditions.[34] The British were complicit in this development: they understood that leaving the subject a sphere of self-rule was to their advantage, and thus they actively assisted in the codification of personal law and the privatization of marriage and family. In short, anyone who takes up the weapon of privacy in the cause of women's equality must be aware that it is a double-edged weapon, long used to defend the killers of women.

Let us now turn to recent cases on the question of "restitution of conjugal rights"—where we shall see, I believe, that the appeal to privacy muddies the waters, setting women up for a most unfortunate reversal. The remedy of forcible restitution to the conjugal home is not originally Hindu in origin; it derives from British ecclesiastical law. As articulated in the Hindu Law of Marriage, it can be claimed by either husband or wife, and it frequently operates as a prelude to divorce in the modern era, in that a person who obtains an order of restitution that is not obeyed can use this fact as a ground of divorce.

The idea of forcible restitution has an infamous history, going back to the time of Phulmonee's death.[35] A young woman named Rakhmabai, from a rich family, was given a good education by her reformist stepfather, a prominent Bombay doctor. At age eleven she was married to one Dadaji Bhikaji Thakur, but she continued to live with her parents because her stepfather opposed early consummation of marriage. As the years passed, Dadaji proved idle and ignorant; he also contracted tuberculosis. He kept trying to persuade Rakhmabai to come live with him, but he was unsuccessful. Eventually, he filed a lawsuit (in 1884, when she was twenty) for restitution of conjugal rights. Rakhmabai went public, writing an anonymous letter to the *Times of India* complaining that women "are treated worse than beasts" and ending with a plea for higher female education and for the abolition of child marriage.

The case became a rallying point for reformers on the one side, traditional guardians of male authority on the other. Rakhmabai disobeyed the order of restitution and was about to be sentenced to six months in jail when a committee of reformers intervened on her behalf. Because the court was unwilling to enforce the decree, Dadaji eventually accepted a property settlement. Although the marriage was never legally dissolved, Dadji remarried, while Rakhmabai got a medical degree in England and worked as a doctor in Bombay until her retirement in 1917.

Another famous case begins the recent uproar over restitution. A well-known movie actress from Madras, Sareetha, was sued for restitution of conjugal rights by her husband, Venkata Subbaiah.[36] She had married him while still an unknown high-school girl, and the two had separated before her career began, largely as a result of quarrels over her desire to be an actress. Seeing that she was rich and famous, her husband apparently wanted either to get her back or to get a substantial financial settlement. In a much heralded and dramatic opinion, Justice Choudary of the Andhra Pradesh High Court declared the relevant section of the Hindu Marriage Act unconstitutional, on grounds that it violated Article 21's guarantee of "life and liberty." Drawing on the U.S. tradition of privacy-right jurisprudence and explicitly citing Griswold and Roe as precedents, he declared that Article 21 implies a right to privacy, which must be understood to be implicit in the meaning of human "life and liberty." The remedy of restitution is "a savage and barbarous remedy, violating the right to privacy and human dignity guaranteed by Art. 21 of the Constitution." Justice Choudary also held, in a separate argument, that the remedy was unconstitutional on equal protection grounds as well, thus violating Article 14.

The privacy arm of the argument was not entirely unprecedented: as we shall see below, such a right had been recognized in the area of search and seizure. But the application to women's liberty interests, following the U.S. line, was entirely new—and, I shall argue, somewhat unfortunate. It is not that the opinion does not make a compelling feminist argument. Indeed, its eloquence is most impressive:

> The purpose of a decree for restitution of conjugal rights . . . is to coerce through judicial process the unwilling party to have sex against that person's consent and freewill. . . . It cannot be denied that among the few points that distinguish human existence from that of animals, sexual autonomy an individual enjoys to choose his or her partner to a sexual act is of primary importance . . . a decree for restitution of conjugal rights constitutes the grossest form of violation of an individual's right to privacy."

Nor is Justice Choudary unaware of the concept of privacy's slippery multiplicity; he is just satisfied that "any plausible definition of right to privacy is bound . . . to include body's inviolability and integrity and intimacy of personal identity, including marital privacy." And it was enough for him if he could show that on all the major understandings of the right to privacy that focus on the body and its integrity (he mentions the definitions of Tribe, Parker, Gaiety, and Bostwick), that right was violated by the law in question.

The question is, however, why one should have brought the issue of bodily integrity and liberty under privacy in the first place. Surely it does not naturally belong there. Justice Choudary's reference to "marital privacy" betrays the difficulty: the traditional concept of "marital privacy" tells precisely *against* women's liberty and bodily integrity. It is that very concept that makes it so difficult, even today, to get marital rape criminalized and domestic violence prosecuted. Surely if what was wanted was a right of control over one's body, that right would much more naturally have been read out of Article 19's guarantee of freedom of movement, travel, and residence (as the surveillance cases suggest) or out of various aspects of the Criminal Code forbidding assault and rape. If it was felt that a separate right had to be recognized to give this area sufficient protection, why not say directly that Article 21's guarantee

of life and liberty involves protection of the very basic right of sexual autonomy—the right to refuse sex one does not want—without which, as the Judge
eloquently states, human life is more bestial than human. Why bring privacy
into it?

I believe I have said enough to indicate why privacy is a dangerous way of
proceeding. Mention the traditional idea of marital privacy and people will
immediately start thinking of the traditional patriarchal household, where
women's sexual autonomy is absent. And indeed, it was with reference to the
traditional ideal of the household that Justice Choudary was eventually overruled. At approximately the same time, a restitution case was heard in the
Delhi High Court. The Court argued directly against the Choudary opinion,
which had created a stir, holding that the remedy of restitution was not unconstitutional under either Article 14 or Article 21.[37] The essence of the Delhi
argument, as can be seen from my epigraph, is that the intimate nature of
marriage makes the application of constitutional principles inappropriate.
Similarly, in 1984, in a different case, the Supreme Court sided with the Delhi
Court and again against Justice Choudary.[38] Conjugal rights, held the Justices, are "inherent in the very institution of marriage itself." Quoting from
the Law Commission's 1955 report on the Hindu Marriage Act, the Justices
concluded restitution "serves a social purpose as an aid to the prevention of
break-up of marriage."

Now we can see that what happened, on the face of things, was that the
whole strategy of appeal to Article 21 was denied. But I would argue that it was
easy to deny it because of the way in which the alleged right was framed, as a
right of privacy. Perhaps the Supreme Court would have refused to recognize
any liberty-right for women here, no matter how framed. But surely the appeal to a concept deeply identified with the allegedly seamless unity of the patriarchal family, and with the presumption of consent to sex in marriage, did
no good in staving off this result.

I have so far only mentioned another especially interesting aspect of Justice
Choudary's opinion, his appeal to equal protection. He acknowledges that formally the law is neutral: either husband or wife can petition for a decree of
restitution. But then, in keeping with the less formalistic and more substantive understanding of equality in Indian constitutional traditions, he says that
the reality is otherwise. The enforcement of such a decree, especially given
that it may result in the conception of a child, will alter and may even "crip-
ple" the wife's future in a way that it could not possibly alter the husband's.

As a result this remedy works in practice only as an engine of oppression
to be operated by the husband for the benefit of the husband against the
wife. By treating the wife and the husband who are inherently unequal as
equals, Section 9 of the act offends the rule of equal protection of laws. For

that reason [it] should therefore be struck down as violative of Article 14 of the Constitution.

One could not have a more succinct statement of MacKinnon's feminist position on equality—although, as I have noted, this understanding is traditional in Indian law and radical only in the U.S. context.[39] Choudary recognizes that formal equality does not guarantee substantive equality: we must look at social context and history. But then he goes further: when we so look, we find that formal equality is actually incompatible with substantive equality. This is the line of reasoning used in some U.S. cases involving race (separate-but-equal schools, formally neutral bans on interracial marriage[40]); but U.S. courts have never stated the principle so clearly in the context of sex equality. This extremely progressive aspect of the case was, unfortunately, briefly stated and far less emphasized than the privacy argument. It was denied by the Delhi Court and overruled by the Supreme Court, but with no comment. The critique, like Justice Choudary's argument, focused on the privacy issue. I believe that here, as in the U.S. cases involving race, the equality line is ultimately the more productive and progressive one.

These cases dramatically illustrate the dangers for women of jumping on the privacy bandwagon. Privacy is inherently a retrograde value, linked with the idea of a protected patriarchal sphere of authority. What, then, should be the feminist approach?

I believe that we cannot make much progress for women without rejecting utterly the idea of a protected private sphere within which the law does not meddle. The privacy tradition typically conflates two ideas of the protected sphere: a spatial idea (the home, as privileged place), and an institutional idea (marriage, as a privileged relation). It seems to me very clear that the protection of an institution under cover of the notion of privacy is simply mistaken: the fact that people are linked as husband and wife does not entail that the law has no business in protecting members of that relationship. As for the appeal to a special place, or sanctuary, this seems more plausible, and in some areas (for example, that of unwanted surveillance) it may seem appealing. Typically, however, such an idea of home as protected place has served to *insulate* family relationships from legal scrutiny. Even the liberties that we most closely associate with the idea of home as protected place (for example, the right to be free from unreasonable and unwarranted search and seizure) would be better understood to protect persons and their property whether or not they are at home and whether or not they have a home.

It seems to me that we should begin, on the one hand, by adopting Mill's distinction between self-regarding and other-regarding acts. If an act is other-regarding (with impact for the interests of nonconsenting others), it gets no special protection by being placed in a home rather than elsewhere.

If harm is done to a person, that harm is the business of law, no matter where harm occurs. Bad behavior gets no more sanction by being in the bosom of the family.

On the other hand, MacKinnon's suggestion that we can do all we need to do by appealing to equal protection and an end to hierarchy and domination seems to me insufficient. Such an appeal succeeded in overturning U.S. antimiscegenation laws—because they really did shore up an existing "White Supremacy." It shows some signs of making progress in the contested terrain of abortion, where it was at least recognized in *Planned Parenthood v. Casey*[41] that the denial of abortion rights to women does have a serious equality aspect: women, and not men, are being forced against their will to support fetal life.[42] And in the Indian cases it seems sufficient to show the unconstitutionality of the remedy of restitution.

But there may come a time when the races in the U.S. are equal, and even when the sexes are equal—and yet we would still want to overturn, or so I think, laws that forbade a person to marry the person of her choice and laws that gave one person the right to bring back an unwilling partner to the conjugal home. Some feminists may say that there would be no such laws in a regime of sex equality, but I think that we cannot be so certain, and we don't want to stake our liberty on that guess. In a regime of sex equality, a law denying women access to abortion would still be objectionable on grounds of liberty, even if the equality issue no longer existed. Which is just to say that there are certain cherished areas of human freedom that need protection. Among these are the freedom to leave a marriage when one wishes and the free choice of a marital partner. Those liberty interests need express protection, and they do not get that protection from equality alone.

One can see that the U.S. Justices were in a bind: the U.S. Constitution is so relatively thin on enumerated liberties that they had to grasp for something, and privacy looked like one way of plugging an egregious gap. And yet it was, nonetheless, a defective way. Whether or not the political difficulty we have had with this issue would have been in any sense mitigated by starting from a different analysis, a different analysis seems required, for the reasons given: it is always dangerous to use opportunistically a set of concepts implicated in such a shady history. As the Indian example shows, such a tactic can all too easily backfire. The Indian Constitution offers more appealing options, among them the freedoms of movement, assembly, and travel. And, as I have suggested, if those were found lacking one could have argued directly from the concept of "life and liberty" itself—as Justice Choudary in effect did.

As for acts that do no harm to others, and that are in Mill's sense self-regarding, it seems unclear, again, that the concept of privacy does useful work in helping us see when and how these acts should be protected. Does something harmless become less worthy of protection because it occurs in what is defined as "public space"? Of course, when an act moves out of the home into the "public space," new questions need to be raised, such as the effects of the act on nonconsenting onlookers. But frequently there are no such issues—and yet acts are given less protection anyhow, simply because they are not in someone's home. At first, contraception was protected only in the marital home, and the actions of activist Bill Baird, in giving out contraceptives publicly to unmarried undergraduates, were not protected—until the equal protection-based decision intervened. This was wrong: contraception is a pure self-regarding act, and the state has no business meddling with it, no matter where the relevant transactions take place. Similarly, the recent tendency, in European law, to protect homosexual sodomy on grounds of the privacy of the home suggests a pernicious distinction: if men have sex in their own dwelling place, it is legally protected. But if they frequent a gay bathhouse—even if all the people there are consenting and nonoffended—the act no longer enjoys the same protection. Here again we see how privacy works to shore up traditional heterosexual hierarchies.

Again, public nude dancing before a consenting and eager audience is likely to be unprotected, whereas the same dance performed in the home will be protected. [43] The use of pornography was protected in *Stanley v. Georgia*, [44] on grounds of the privacy of the home; this precedent would not give protection to the use of pornography—equally noninvolving of children or noconsenting parties—in an adult store.

These examples require us to note that the public/private distinction, as it is standardly used in such cases, is not the same as a distinction between places where there are nonconsenting parties around and places where there are no such parties (Mill's distinction). Outside the home there are many spaces and places where there are only consenting parties—sex clubs, bathhouses, dance clubs, sex stores (assuming that they bar entry to minors below some reasonable age of consent)—and it is only in *a portion* of that space denominated "public" that Milleans need to worry about effects on the non-consenting. A Millean self-regarding act does not deserve less protection—if it really remains self-regarding—by being in some space denominated "public."

Various Indian cases once again show the wisdom of bewaring of such a use of the "private" to defend harmless acts only when they take place in a protected sphere. The first cases to recognize a right to privacy in connection with Article 21 were cases involving police surveillance. In the first of these, *Kharak Singh v. State of Uttar Pradesh*, [45] the dissenters recognized such a right, and in the second, *Govind v. State of Madhya Pradesh*, [46] the majority recognized the right, citing American privacy cases from a variety of distinct areas, including search and seizure, but also including the Fourteenth Amendment privacy-right cases *Griswold* and *Roe*. As I have mentioned, the right to privacy is invoked in these cases because the Indian Constitution has no analogue of our Fourth Amendment prohibiting unreasonable and unwarranted searches and seizures.

At issue was a state police regulation, framed in accordance with directives provided by a national Police Act, according to which people who had a criminal record or were in other ways suspected of "a determination to lead a life of crime" could be subject to unannounced domiciliary visits, often in the middle of the night, and could also be followed and spied on when outside the house. Justices Mathew, Lyer, and Goswami, referring to the 1877 U.S. case *Munn v. Illinois*, and citing the dissent in *Kharak Singh*, opine that "in the last resort a person's house, where he lives with his family, is his 'castle,' that nothing is more deleterious to a man's physical happiness and health than a calculated interference with his privacy. " Once again, the sacred privacy of the householder in his dwelling place is invoked.

Significantly enough, the Justices do understand that the actions of the police threaten important human liberties even when they are not directed at the "sanctity of the home." And they do mean to call into constitutional question not only the domiciliary visits but the whole pattern of police spying.[47] At this point, however, they turn to the enumerated liberties of Article 19 and argue that freedom of movement must be given an expansive interpretation, holding that "movement under the scrutinizing gaze of the policeman cannot be free movement." They even write that "individual autonomy is perhaps the central concern of any system of limited government." But the question then is, why all the fuss about privacy, if the key issue in the case is understood to be one of personal liberty and autonomy?

I do not mean to object to the general line of the Court's impressive argument. I believe that *Govind* is an important opinion and one that, in its basic holding, strikes a delicate balance between the State's interest in surveillance and the individual's liberty rights. I intend only to question the detour through the concept of privacy.

Privacy has functioned—in both U.S. and Indian law—as a rubric under which to introduce into the Constitution interests that are not explicitly otherwise recognized therein. It is a gap-filler, and as such, easier than the process of constitutional amendment. And yet, it is conceded by most who survey the history of the cases that a good number of the interests that come in that way are oddly grouped under that rubric. As I have already noted, privacy is an odd way of protecting the right to obtain contraception (which is publicly sold and even used) or of protecting the right of abortion (which is no more private than other medical procedures).

We shall see that the Indian cases that use substantive due process to introduce previously unenumerated rights are similarly all over the map—although Indian jurisprudence is somewhat more self-aware in recognizing the limits of the privacy concept, which therefore is not introduced where its introduction would be most blatantly peculiar, as we shall see when we turn to prisoners' rights. But if we are going to recognize unenumerated rights under substantive due process without appeal to the concept of privacy, in even a small number of cases, then why should we rely on it at all, in cases that we must strain to squeeze under the concept?

There can be no clearer demonstration of this issue than one of India's most eloquent and vivid Article 21 cases, *Sunil Batra v. Delhi Administration*, discussing the extent of personal liberty possessed by prisoners on death row.[48] (India and the U.S. are alike in retaining capital punishment.) Mandatory solitary confinement for death-row prisoners is held unconstitutional on grounds of Article 21 and Article 14. Article 14 is used to attack the punishment as "arbitrary": "The treatment of a human being which offends human dignity, imposes avoidable torture and reduces the man to the level of a beast would certainly be arbitrary and can be questioned under Art. 14." Article 21 is violated because among the liberty rights guaranteed by that article is now held to be a "right to society." In the words of the opinion (ornate and rhetorical even by Indian standards):

> This segregation . . . is violation of the primordial gregariousness which, from the beginning of the species, has been man's social milieu and so constitutes a psychic trauma, when prolonged . . . , even in our ancient land of silent mystics and lonely cavemen. For the great few, solitude sometimes is best society but for the commonality the wages of awesome seclusion, if spread over long spells, is insanity.

The actual legal argument is a tangled one, since it attempts to bring the right to society under procedural rather than substantive due process. I shall not analyze that aspect of the opinion. What interests me is that the Justices plainly see the need here to recognize a dimension of human liberty previously unenumerated. It is a dimension that could not even by stretching be brought in under a right to privacy. So they don't try. They simply go directly to the concept of liberty, arguing that "liberty" itself in Article 21 implies the right to society in question.

This seems to me basically the correct strategy. Why use "privacy" as a gap-filler at all, given its other difficulties, when we see that one may perfectly straightforwardly, through an incremental process of judicial interpretation, get the rights from the place they really reside, the notion of liberty?

Constitutions and Capabilities

The moral of this investigation, it seems to me, is that constitutions protect a rich plurality of distinct human interests. One might do well, I suggest, to think of the goal as that of protecting a wide range of distinct human capabilities, meaning the ability of people to do and be certain things of central human importance. Each of the central human capabilities is distinct in quality from all of the others. Thus it is always dangerous to reduce one constitutional value to another one or to understand one constitutional value in terms of another one. One risks losing the distinctive nature of the vital human interest involved. Privacy has served too long as a catchall value, into which values of very different types (equality, freedom of movement, freedom of association) have been siphoned, without adequate thought about their distinctive nature. If this process has seemed inevitable in the U.S. context, where the Constitution does relatively little to enumerate a wide range of liberties and equality interests that deserve protection, it is surely far from inevitable, and indeed most unwise, in the Indian context, where the Constitution supplies ample resources for the protection of distinct liberty and equality interests as the very human capabilities they are.

Each constitutional tradition must draw on its own resources of text and history. I therefore make no concrete suggestions for either legal tradition; I confine myself to a general philosophical recommendation. What I would favor, to sort our way out of this mess, is a three-pronged approach:

1. A reliance on equality and equal protection where the relevant issue involves systematic hierarchy and subordination. Often, in cases involving sex, this will be the most relevant line and may prove sufficient to protect the interests that need protecting.
2. A general presumption of a Millean kind against the prohibition of self-regarding acts, whether in public or in private: the state will have to make a strong showing (for public safety or for other reasons) if it is to defend the prohibition of such acts.
3. The enumeration of specific human liberty interests that are of especially central importance for protection from interference: as India has done with the right to travel, the free choice of occupation, the right of prisoners to human society, etc., and as the U.S. has done with the right to be free from unwarranted search and seizure and from cruel and unusual punishments.[49] Control over information about oneself—the aspect of a constitutional right to privacy most reasonably denominated "privacy"—can be recognized through a plurality of distinct stratagems in the various areas of law (torts, press,

constitutional law) in which informational issues arise. These may be called "privacy rights" if one wishes, though, as I have said, the plurality of different areas of law in which they arise makes it implausible to speak of a unitary "right to privacy."

Meanwhile, various liberty interests now covered under privacy, such as the right to marital choice, to contraception, and to abortion, need to be extricated from the privacy morass and introduced through a more straightforward route—although it is beyond my practical political expertise to state how, in the case of each constitutional tradition, this can best be done. The human capabilities at stake in this debate are too important to leave them in trust to privacy, that most untrustworthy and compromised of concepts. Certainly in matters of sex equality, to turn to privacy is indeed to dress up an injury and call it a gift.

NOTES

1. *Lochner v. New York*, 198 U.S. 45 (1905); the Court held unconstitutional a New York statute providing that no employee shall "work in a biscuit, bread or cake bakery or confectionary establishment more than sixty hours in any one week, or more than ten hours in any one day." This was held to violate the right to contract that was held to be part of "liberty" as protected by the Fourteenth Amendment.

2. The turning point came in *Nebbia v. New York*, 291 U.S. 502 (1934), when the Court upheld mandatory minimum prices for milk, holding that "neither property nor contract rights are absolute; for government cannot exist if the citizen may at will use his property to the detriment of his fellows, or exercise his freedom of contract to work them harm." This common-sense observation might seem in the India context too obvious to need stating; in the U.S. context, it was (and in some ways still is) a radical thought.

3. *Griswold v. Connecticut*, 381 U.S. 479 (1965).

4. 410 U.S. 133 (1975).

5. Judith Jarvis Thomson, "The Right to Privacy," *Philosophy and Public Affairs* 4 (1975): 295–314. Thomson's well-known article is cited in a number of Indian Supreme Court opinions.

6. On the American side, see, most famously, Catharine MacKinnon, "Privacy v. Equality: Beyond Roe v. Wade," in MacKinnon, *Feminism Unmodified* (Cambridge: Harvard University Press, 1987), 93–102. See also Cass Sunstein, "Pornography, Abortion, Surrogacy," in *The Partial Constitution* (Cambridge, : Harvard University Press, 1993), chapter 9. On the Indian side, a related approach is in Ratna Kapur and Brenda Cossman, *Subversive Sites: Feminist Engagements with Law in India* (New Delhi: Sage, 1996).

7. Paul R. Ehrlich, *The Population Bomb* (New York: Ballantine, 1968), 15.

8. See *Mr. X v. Hospital Z*, AIR 1999.

9. See Rajeev Bhavan, "Protecting Privacy," in *Only the Good News: On the Law of the Press in India* (Delhi: Manowar, 1987), chapter 8.

10. See, for example, Judith De Cew, *In Pursuit of Privacy: Law, Ethics, and the Rise of Technology* (Ithaca, N.Y.: Cornell University Press, 1997).

11. See Leela Gulati, *Profiles in Female Poverty: A Study of Poor Working Women in Kerala* (Delhi: Hindustan Publishing Company, 1981).

12. See *Quran* 24.30 and 24.31.

13. See other citations and discussion in my *Women and Human Development* (Cambridge: Cambridge University Press, 2000).

14. See Dan Kahan, "What Do Alternative Sanctions Mean?" *University of Chicago Law Review* 63 (1996): 591–653, discussing the penalty for public urination in Hoboken, N.J., where offenders had to scrub the streets with a toothbrush.

15. Semipublic defecation is even recommended in print. Typical is this pre-race advice from Bob Glover, Jack Shepherd, and Shelly-lynn Frances Glover, *The Runner's Handbook* (New York: Penguin, 1996), one of the most popular advice manuals for runners: "Make a final bowel movement and empty your bladder. Don't be modest. The bushes may be your only choice."

16. See P. V. Kane, *Hindu Customs and Modern Law* (Pune, India, 1944), pp. 99–100.

17. On some of the complexities of this feminist strategy, see my "The Modesty of Mrs. Bajaj: India's Problematic Route to Sexual Harassment Law," in *Directions in Sexual Harassment Law*, ed. Catharine MacKinnon and Reva Siegel (New Haven: Yale University Press, 2002).

18. *In re Ratnamala*, AIR 1962 (Mad. 31, 35).

19. See the discussion in my *Women and Human Development*, chapter 1.

20. For many examples, see Kalima Rose, *Where Women are Leaders: The SEWA Movement in India* (Delhi: Vistaar, 1992).

21. For more detail on all of this, see my "India, Sex Equality, and Constitutional Law," in *Constituting Women: The Gender of Constitutional Jurisprudence*, ed. B. Baines and R. R. Marin (Cambridge: Cambridge University Press, forthcoming 2003).

22. Thus the U.S. First Amendment: "Congress shall make no law respecting an establishment of religion" and The Fourth Amendment: "The right of the people to be secure in their persons, houses, papers, and effects, against unreasonable searches and seizures, shall not be violated" and so forth.

23. Article 15 contains the phrase "Nothing in this article . . . shall prevent the state from making any special provision for the advancement of any socially and educationally backward classes of citizens or for the Scheduled Castes and the Scheduled Tribes".

24. See *Rockwell Kent v. John Foster Dulles*, 357 U.S. 116: 2 L. Ed. 2d 1204 (1958). Thus India guaranteed its citizens freedom of travel before the U.S. did.

25. Most famously, MacKinnon (1987), *supra* note 6.

26. Thomson (1975).

27. *Report of the Second Press Commission* (1982), 77 pr. 43, cited in Rajeev Dhavan, *Only the Good News*, 341.

28. Catharine MacKinnon, "Privacy v. Equality," *Feminism Unmodified*, 100.

29. See Aristotle, *Politics*, I.1.

30. John Locke, *The Second Treatise on Government*, para. 4.

31. On this see Lauren Berlant and Michael Warner, "Sex in Public," *Critical Inquiry* 24 (1998): 547–66.

32. 405 U.S. 438 (1972); in a 6–1 decision, the Supreme Court declared unconstitutional a Massachusetts statute prohibiting the dispensing to unmarried persons of any contraceptive device. Significantly for my argument, the relevant acts were done in public: Bill Baird, a contraception advocate was dispensing contraceptives to undergraduates at Boston University.

33. Tanika Sarkar, "Rhetoric Against Age of Consent: Resisting Colonial Reason and Death of a Child-Wife," *Economic and Political Weekly*, September 4, 1993, 1869–1878.

34. Sarkar shows that consent-based alternatives, even in ancient India, were summarily dismissed as aberrations at this time. She notes that authority for child marriage comes only from Raghunandan, a late and local authority.

35. This famous case is discussed in many places, including Sarkar's article.

36. . *Sareetha v. T. Venkata Subbaiah*, AIR 1983 Andhra Pradesh 356.

37. *Harvinder Kaur v. Harmander Singh Choudhry*, AIR 1984 Delhi 667.

38. *Saroj Rani v. Sudarshan Kumar*, AIR 71 (1984) 1562 S. C.

39. Indeed, MacKinnon cites this case in her new casebook on sex equality, *Sex Equality* (New York: Foundation Press, 2001), as supportive of her general approach.

40. See *Brown v. Board of Education of Topeka* 347 U.S. 483 (1954), declaring that separate but equal schools violate equal protection; *Loving v. Virginia*, 388 U.S. 1 (1967), declaring unconstitutional, on equal-protection grounds, a Virginia law forbidding interracial marriage; the law, held the Court, was but a device to uphold "White Supremacy."

41. *Planned Parenthood of Southeastern Pennsylvania v. Casey*, 505 U.S. 833 (1992).

42. See references above to equality-based analyses of abortion, beginning with J. Thomson, who is cited in the Supreme Court's opinion.

43. See *Barnes v. Glen Theatre*, Inc, 501 U. S, 560 (1991).

44. 394 U.S. 557 (1969).

45. AIR 1963 SC 1295.

46. IR 1975 S.C. 1378

47. The actual holding is complex: they say that it is possible that the entire pattern is unconstitutional, but for now they will simply hold that the State needs to show a compelling interest in public safety if it is to apply these procedures to a particular individual.

48. AIR 1978 (SC 1675).

49. On the relationship between this recommendation and the "capabilities approach," see my "Capabilities as Fundamental Entitlements: Sen and Social Justice," forthcoming in *Feminist Economics*, 2003, special issue on Sen. I argue there that it is important to enumerate specific liberty interests, rather than, as Sen at times suggests, to make freedom a general all-purpose social good.

CHAPTER 11

Women's Human Rights and the U.S. Constitution

Initiating a Dialogue

Does the United States Constitution protect women's human rights? How, in fact, does it compare in its treatment of women's rights to the various international human rights instruments, both those United Nations documents of a general nature such as the Universal Declaration of Human Rights (1948), the International Covenant on Civil and Political Rights (1966), and the International Covenant on Economic, Social and Cultural Rights (1966), as well as those addressed more specifically to women's rights, especially the Convention on the Elimination of All Forms of Discrimination against Women (or, as it is commonly referred to, CEDAW, or the Woman's Convention, 1979)? Of course, we must here refer to the Constitution as it has been interpreted, not simply to the Constitution as it was written over two hundred years ago. Still, the answer to the question of how it compares to these other documents is, perhaps surprisingly, "Not very well at all." Indeed, discussions of the U.S. Constitution, as well as of women's rights protected by it, have until very recently proceeded in a rather insular fashion, without regard to the international context of human rights documents, despite the United States' having taken a leadership role in the promulgation and enforcement of human rights abroad.

This chapter intends to contribute to remedying that deficiency by considering the U.S. Constitution's treatment of women's rights in the context of

This paper was originally presented at the Conference on Women and the U.S. Constitution, Baruch College, C.U.N.Y., New York, NY, February 8, 2001, and in revised form at the European University Institute, Fiesole, Italy, April 6, 2001.

their somewhat richer treatment in the international human rights documents. Of course, this more extensive discussion at the international level does not necessarily translate into a more just practice elsewhere, that is, into a more genuine respect for, or implementation of, women's rights. But at the theoretical level, at least, there is much to be learned from that international framework, and I will consider some of the leading features of U.S. constitutional protections of women's rights—especially equal protection and privacy—in connection with the approaches in the international instruments. I will then take note of some respects in which the U.S. Constitution may afford fuller protection than these instruments and thus may provide some help in conceptualizing human rights internationally.

Through the course of this analysis, it will become clear that certain key problems arise for both frameworks to varying degrees, and I focus more directly on these in the final section of the paper. These difficulties may be listed provisionally here as follows: (1) how to draw the public/private divide, along with the closely related question of the applicability of the recognized rights not only for the actions of states (which was the original primary concern of the rights documents) but for the interactions of nonstate actors as well—including nongovernmental organizations as well as individuals in their relations with each other; (2) the old and persistent issue of "special" vs. "equal" treatment for women, that is, whether differential treatment of women in matters such as pregnancy necessarily constitutes discrimination against them; and (3) the relevance of care, as a mode of being and acting centrally associated with women's experience, in the context of human rights. Although a full analysis of these complex questions is beyond the scope of this chapter, my goal is to frame several of the core issues so as to contribute to a new public dialogue about the relations between the U.S. Constitution and the human rights of women. It should perhaps be added that my interest is not one of comparative law but, rather, lies in opening up the conceptualization of women's rights to more global and cosmopolitan considerations, albeit to ones that can remain sensitive to diversities of culture and history. Another important proviso is that it is not my view that a focus on rights is sufficient for improving the situation of women; nothing can replace social critique and political action. But rights have a role to play as well.

Before proceeding to consider the core rights for women that the Constitution protects, it is worth observing that the alienation of the constitutional discussion—including the discussion surrounding the Bill of Rights—from the various accounts of international human rights is not unique to women's issues. The separateness of United States discussions in this regard, and the deference shown uniquely to the Constitution, has been noted by Ann Elizabeth Mayer, who also criticizes the U.S. approach to CEDAW in this regard.[1]

In fact, the United States, though a signer of that convention, has not yet ratified it (although it has been ratified by 166 countries, needless to say with numerous official "reservations"). The U.S. did ratify the Convention on the Political Rights of Women, but did not ratify several of the other documents that have import for the human rights of women. The implicit (and indeed increasingly explicit) idea that these human rights covenants infringe on United States sovereignty raises some interesting general questions about the relation of human rights to the nation-state, particularly during this period of globalization, but I will not be able to develop that aspect of the issue in this chapter.

Women's Rights in the U.S. Constitution

In order to provide a basis for our comparison with the international treatments, let us turn first to the Constitution and briefly enumerate certain rights of women implied there and developed in subsequent constitutional interpretation. First, there are a set of rights and obligations that stem from general rights enumerated in the Bill of Rights, not only those that clearly apply to everyone but others that, though they may originally not have applied to women, have been extended to them over time. An example is the right to sit on a jury, which also permits women the opportunity to be tried by their peers, if the occasion requires it. (The exemption by local governments of women from service on juries was finally ruled unconstitutional in 1975 in *Taylor v. Louisiana*, citing the Sixth Amendment.)

In addition to such interpretations of the Bill of Rights, a second, and very central, support for women's rights has been the Equal Protection Clause of the Fourteenth Amendment (with support also from the Due Process protection in the Fifth Amendment) and its subsequent elaboration extended to women at work and in the family. As is well known, the Fourteenth Amendment states that "No State shall . . . deny to any person within its jurisdiction the equal protection of the laws." There has been extensive discussion of the interpretation of this clause in feminist legal theory, such as Deborah Rhode's helpful efforts to distinguish "difference" from "disadvantage." Rhodes argues that it is best to conceive of the equal protection of women under the law as requiring compensating for and eliminating any historical disadvantages that may be due to one's gender, rather than being a matter of treating women either identically the same or differently from men (men have tended to remain the standard of comparison, as MacKinnon pointed out some time ago).[2] Patricia Smith also gives a useful account of this issue in the introduction to her collection *Feminist Jurisprudence*, noting that the issue of equal protection is ill framed as one of equal treatment vs. special protection for women; the point is rather that differences should not be a basis for disadvantage.[3] Along these lines, as several contributors to that collection point out, we need to be concerned with eliminating institutional barriers to equality—and not only with compensating for disadvantages but, indeed, with empowering women (though the Supreme Court is rather far from adopting this interpretation).[4]

Finally, the judicial history of equal protection interpretation has involved a distinction between so-called strict scrutiny of any legislation that seeks to set up racial or religious classifications, where there is a presumption that such classifications are inherently suspect, and the somewhat reduced and less stringent standard of intermediate scrutiny that is held to be appropriate for gender classifications. Given that women (unlike race or religious affiliations) necessarily make up 50 percent of the voting population, gender-based distinctions *may* be acceptable if they can be shown to "serve important government objectives" and if they are "substantially related to achievement of those objectives."[5] (It is true that Ruth Bader Ginsburg has recently contributed to a certain strengthening of the intermediate scrutiny test.)[6] This judicial emphasis on types of scrutiny in the United States will be seen to contrast with the treatment of discrimination implied in a number of the international documents.

We might add that equal protection has in recent years also been proposed as a basis for countering domestic violence, a problem of grave concern for women in the United States and worldwide, on the grounds that dealing with it should be equal to other efforts to fight violent crime. Likewise, equal protection has been put forward as an alternative ground for protecting abortion rights, in that to do otherwise reinforces women's subordination and denies them the equal opportunity to lead a life of their own. It is even held to offer a ground for public funding of abortions, as a condition for all women's control of their own childbearing functions, thereby enabling women equal participation at work and in the home.[7]

As is well known, abortion rights have instead most often been grounded in the right to privacy, as was argued in the Supreme Court decision of *Roe v. Wade* (1973), and this idea of privacy constitutes a third significant feature of women's rights under our Constitution (at least as presently interpreted). This right to privacy is based in large part on the guarantee of due process of law as a protection for people's liberty and resonates with ideas of the freedom of the person implied in the First Amendment (as well as elsewhere). It assures a right, initially within the context of marriage, to be free from state interference in deciding matters concerning reproduction—a right subsequently extended to nonmarried individuals as well.[8] Whereas some feminist theorists have proposed jettisoning this right,[9] because of the problematic protection it seems to give to gender-based violence against women in the home (which I discuss further below), I believe instead that we need to clarify the concept and bring it back to its roots in the autonomy or freedom of the person, along with respect for the individual's bodily integrity. Other aspects of privacy, such as the right to control information about oneself, e.g., one's medical records, are also of obvious significance, though in this case to everyone equally and not especially to women.

A final right worth noting, this one explicitly mentioned in the Constitution, is women's right to vote (the Nineteenth Amendment), which is rather straightforward and now of limited interest in itself. But in connection with this political and democratic right, we are prompted to ask about its adequacy taken alone, without any consideration of the means to assure the representation of women. There has been considerable notice in the press of the French law mandating equal representation of women as candidates for many offices, and it is clear that our Constitution provides no comparable basis for assuring women's representation. Of course, this is much easier to accomplish in a parliamentary system than in a winner-take-all system of the U.S. variety. Although I cannot pursue this interesting issue here, we may nonetheless raise the question whether women's' democratic rights are in fact adequately protected by the right to vote alone.

The Relative Richness of Human Rights Instruments (Especially the CEDAW)

Let us now turn to the international documents that lay out, or at least pertain to, women's human rights and, in very schematic fashion, consider their strengths relative to the U.S. constitutional treatment. There has been a substantial elaboration of the human rights of women in recent decades, but before proceeding to the analysis of CEDAW, it is important to note a serious qualification at the outset, namely, that—as Anne Bayefsky has neatly put it— "Perhaps nowhere is the gulf between standards and enforcement more evident than in the context of women's rights."[10] She goes on to explain that while there are over twenty treaties devoted specifically to women and/or sexual discrimination, and whereas sex is explicitly listed as a ground for nondiscrimination in all the treaties that include equality or nondiscrimination among their enumerated rights (not to speak of CEDAW itself with its extensive provisions for nondiscrimination), it is nonetheless the case that women's rights remain marginalized in the implementation of international human rights law.[11] This is so in the case of CEDAW first because of the very large number of reservations that states have entered as a condition for ratification (noteworthy are those by the Islamic states—which in some cases directly contravene its provisions—though there are some significant reservations from other states as well). Additional factors that militate against implementation are the relative weakness of the CEDAW Committee that meets to implement the convention, the fact that many states fail to live up to their reporting obligations under it, and the lack of an individual petition mechanism associated with this convention.[12]

Beyond this weakness of CEDAW in the area of implementation, women's rights are marginalized in the body of human rights doctrine more generally because of the intended application of human rights almost exclusively to the public domain (to prevent harms that men fear, such as torture, as Hilary Charlesworth has pointed out[13]). Human rights doctrine has not often been interpreted in ways that derive from, and have direct import for, women's experiences in the more private realm, with the concern especially for gender-based violence and the prevention of such harms as domestic abuse, woman battering, or even wife murder. Still, considerable theoretical progress has recently been made in reinterpreting human rights to apply to these wrongs and to others such as sati, rape both within and outside marriage, female genital cutting, forced prostitution, and sexual harassment. Approaches have been devised for addressing these wrongs in principle, even though they may not be directly perpetrated by states but, rather, by private individuals, or in some cases by cultural or social institutions. Of course, the most extensive protection at the international level, though this too remains largely at the level of pronouncements, is given to equality itself and the prohibition of sex discrimination.

CEDAW (adopted in 1981) is at the forefront of these international documents on women's human rights, together with more recent statements such as the CEDAW Committee's General Recommendation No. 19 on Violence against Women, the 1993 General Assembly Declaration on the Elimination of Violence against Women, and the follow-up Inter-American Convention on the Prevention, Punishment, and Eradication of Violence against Women (1995). Without going into all of its details here, we can observe that CEDAW is strongly principled in calling on state parties to prohibit discrimination against women, which it defines broadly in Article 1 as,

> any distinction, exclusion or restriction made on the basis of sex which has the effect or purpose of impairing or nullifying the recognition, enjoyment or exercise by women, irrespective of their marital status, on a basis of equality of men and women, of human rights and fundamental freedoms in the political, economic, social, cultural, civil or any other field.

Noteworthy in this definition is its reference to the *effect* as well as the purpose of governmental measures and also to the fact that discrimination is not limited to that carried out through state action alone but extends more widely to all actors within society. Indeed, as noted in the final phrase "in any other field," discrimination as defined there extends to family life too (as is also evident elsewhere in the document, which somewhat blurs the old public-private line).

Article 2 of CEDAW further calls on states to "pursue by all appropriate means and without delay a policy of eliminating discrimination against women," including that states "embody the principle of the equality of men and women in their national constitutions or other appropriate legislation" (2a). Crucially, this article goes on to require them "to take all appropriate measures to eliminate discrimination against women *by any person, organization or enterprise*" (2e) (italics added) and "to take all appropriate measures, including legislation, to modify or abolish existing laws, regulations, customs and practices which constitute discrimination against women." Several authors have noted the importance of the phrase just cited in 2e concerning eliminating "discrimination against women by any person, organization, or enterprise" as supporting the application of the provision, and indeed the convention as a whole, to the private, nongovernmental sectors of society. It seems to require action *against* discrimination even among individuals.

Other noteworthy features of CEDAW are its grand goal (in Article 3) "to ensure the full development and advancement of women;" its endorsement, though somewhat limited, of affirmative action in Article 4; and its call on states in Article 5 "to modify the social and cultural patterns of conduct of men and women, with a view to achieving the elimination of prejudices and customary and all other practices which are based on the idea of the inferiority or the superiority of either of the sexes or on stereotyped roles for men and women."

Some feminist theorists have already taken note of the superiority of CEDAW's protections to those in the U.S. Constitution, with its rather scanty "Equal Protection" clause.[14] This fact, together with the requirement to change existing laws to bring them into compliance, may have led to some of the U.S. reservations against CEDAW. These reservations may also have been prompted simply by a desire to preserve the status quo, since, as Mayer points out, the Constitution does not provide a ceiling for rights but, rather, a floor, permitting the more extensive protections in international documents.[15] Indeed, as Rebecca Cook notes, CEDAW itself constitutes an advance over earlier human rights conventions "by addressing the pervasive and systemic nature of discrimination against women, and identifies the need to confront the social causes of women's inequality by addressing 'all forms' of discrimination that women suffer."[16] It thus to a degree speaks to the requirement posed by feminist theorists in the constitutional context of addressing the institutional framework for women's oppression and the empowerment of women. Clearly, its strong requirement of equal rights for women surpasses the U.S. Constitution. Indeed, CEDAW goes beyond requiring a sex neutral opposition to sex discrimination per se and toward requiring the elimination of discrimination against women specifically. As noted, it also opposes laws that are detrimental in effect, even if they are neutral on their face, as well as those specifically detrimental to women, such as nonprovision of obstetric services.[17] And, in contrast to the intermediate scrutiny standard, or even its recent strengthening in Ginsburg's 1996 decision, CEDAW and other human rights instruments require that distinctions based on sex are deserving of the highest degree of judicial scrutiny, as Anne Bayefsky has pointed out.[18] (We might note, however, that the somewhat medieval distinctions that have characterized Supreme Court interpretations of equal protection are becoming somewhat blurred, and may well deserve to disappear.) Yet, despite these strengths of CEDAW in comparison with the U.S. constitutional standard, it has been criticized by some for proposing a conception of equal treatment as simply extending to women those rights that men now enjoy and thus "serves only to reinforce existing norms and values without in any way subverting the inherently gendered nature of the existing rules."[19]

In discussing CEDAW's strengths, Cook has pointed out another of its advantages, namely, its import for state responsibility. She writes, "Although a state is not internationally responsible for a private act of sexual discrimination, it is bound to undertake means to eliminate or reduce and mitigate the incidence of private discrimination, and to achieve the result that such private discrimination should not recur."[20] Indeed, states are even supposed to act to prevent anticipated violation of human rights, including those initiated by private persons. CEDAW's General Recommendation 19 further specifies this as applying to harms to women in the so-called private sphere of family and personal relations by calling on states to take "appropriate and effective measures to overcome all forms of gender based violence, whether by private or public act." In holding states accountable for developing systems to prohibit discrimination by private persons, CEDAW (and certain other human rights instruments) are evidently far beyond the United States' constitutional approach.

Indeed, one comparative law theorist has suggested that "with the exception of the Thirteenth Amendment prohibiting slavery and involuntary servitude within the United States, the prohibition to interfere with rights and freedoms of individuals has not been declared directly applicable to private persons, but only to actions of either the federal or state governments."[21] Constitutional rights, at least in their conservative interpretation by the U.S. Supreme Court, remain largely "negative" protections against abuse by government rather than imposing affirmative obligations on it. As Rehnquist has written in his interpretation of the Fourteenth Amendment's due process clause in DeShaney, "its language cannot fairly be extended to impose an affirmative obligation on the State to ensure that those interests do not come to harm through other means."[22] This question of affirmative obligations certainly remains open to diverse interpretations, but the prevailing view appears to hold that American constitutional protections do not require government to guarantee to individuals any basic human needs.

This brings me to the final and perhaps most important aspect of the strength of international human rights documents relative to the Constitution (at least as currently interpreted), namely, their attempt to protect economic and social rights, in addition to the civil and political ones. I suggest that this is especially crucial for women, both nationally and internationally. It is well known that women make up the largest part of both the poor and the elderly in the United States. The unfortunate absence of any explicit protection for well-being in the Constitution thus impacts them differentially. In the international context as well, I would argue (as several women's NGOs have recently pointed out) that women's access to employment and their material level of well-being contribute directly to the protection of their rights to life and health and can meliorate such human rights abuses as wife battery and domestic violence. Well-being levels may be tied also to the diminution of forced prostitution (by reducing families' perceived need to sell their daughters into such a state) and even to female genital cutting (inasmuch as, by reducing economic dependence, genital cutting's perceived benefits for marriageability may be lessened; it might also bring with it access to health information and health care, which would likely be beneficial in this context). From a more general perspective, it can be argued that the diremption between the civil and political human rights, and the economic, social, and cultural ones—and the absence of explicit reference to the latter group in the U.S. Constitution—is unfortunate, inasmuch as the interests they protect are closely bound together in reality. This is especially the case for women, including in the U.S., where the lack of a welfare provision among the basic rights impacts differentially on women (and children). Of course, we must avoid glorifying the international human rights documents in this context, for they remain rather deficient in their treatment of the economic and social rights of women as well, particularly in regard to the lack of consideration given to women's work in households.

Strengths of the U.S. Constitution

Let us now take brief note of certain respects in which feminist theorists might prefer the formulations in the Constitution, inasmuch as they may be thought better to protect women's human rights. I see three areas where this may be the case, although all are controversial. They are: (1) the right to bodily integrity, and the related, though contested, right to privacy; (2) the treatment or lack of it of the family and marriage; and (3) the separation of religion and state. Although I cannot develop these in detail here, we may summarize the issues as follows:

1. As Helen Holmes pointed out in her prescient 1984 critique of the Universal Declaration of Human Rights, that document in fact lacks a right to bodily integrity, which she also takes to be a right to control one's body.[23] The Universal Declaration does, of course, contain a right to security of the person (article 3), against slavery (article 4), and against torture (article 5). Article 12 also protects privacy but not in a way that is tied to the body. (It reads, "No one shall be subjected to arbitrary interference with his privacy, family, home or correspondence.")[24] Likewise, if we look at the Covenant on Civil and Political Rights, we find liberty and security of the person but not bodily integrity. Moreover, as Hilary Charlesworth has pointed out, this protection of the person "operates only in the context of direct action by the state. It does not address the fear of sexual violence, which is a defining feature of women's lives."[25] Indeed, CEDAW also lacks any explicit recognition of this right, seemingly central for protecting against sexual assault and violence directed toward women *as* women.

To the degree that a right of privacy in U.S. constitutional interpretation strengthens the commitment to bodily integrity, afforded also by the Constitution's protection of the security of the person and certain other of its clauses, it is an important development in the protection of women's rights. Privacy tied to bodily integrity in this way lends support to abortion rights and reproductive freedom more generally, as Ronald Dworkin argues. Thus, in addition to other constitutional considerations that he cites in favor of abortion rights, Dworkin notes that the abortion decision is more private than others that the court has protected, "because the decision involves a woman's control not just of her own connections to others, but of the use of her own body, and the Constitution recognizes in a variety of ways the special intimacy of a person's connection to her own physical integrity."[26] It is interesting to observe in this connection that abortion rights are nowhere mentioned in CEDAW (is its antidiscrimination emphasis sufficient to explain this?), nor are reproductive rights given adequate attention in the other human rights instruments, with the Universal Declaration only speaking of a right to marry and found a family (article 16). And while we may suggest that abortion rights and reproductive rights generally are more securely based on a concept of freedom that is in fact included in the documents (though its import is not specified for this case), still such reproductive rights do gain support *also* from this aspect of the right to privacy, developed more fully in the United States context. Yet it is worth pointing out that the reproductive rights that need to be protected as human rights go beyond this right to choose abortion to include the right to be free from unwanted sterilization or abortions and from pressures for sex selection and female infanticide. These latter aspects of reproduction have tended to be recognized more fully in the global rather than the U.S. context.

2. The mention of the right to marry and found a family in the Universal Declaration is one of numerous pronouncements on families in the international human rights documents, including the idea there that "the family is the natural and fundamental group unit of society and entitled to protection by society and the state" (article 16). CEDAW, too, contains a rather extensive discussion of the family and marriage. While feminists usually have no objections to families—certainly they are important for child-raising, among other functions—still they have been concerned not to give protection to patriarchal and oppressive families, where women may be imprisoned within the home, or where women are raped or battered, or children abused, nor to give priority necessarily to heterosexual, nuclear families at the expense of other possible arrangements.

There are two directions we can go here, by way of an alternative course. One can follow the European Convention on Human Rights, which talks explicitly about families but gives them a progressive interpretation, such that the term can apply to de facto family units not necessarily married. Or, instead, one can talk about protecting families by protecting the individuals within them, including children. In some ways, the U.S. interpretations of privacy that see it in individualistic terms (cf. *Eisenstadt v. Baird*) move in this latter direction. This could be used to protect individual choice or autonomy without requiring a family context. Yet we might prefer a more relational approach that gives an important place to familial relations. Further, inasmuch as families are so important to cultures worldwide, an approach exclusively in terms of individualistic choices of interpersonal relations seems to have a limiting Western aspect to it, and in this sense the European direction would be more appealing. I would propose that an approach that protected families would have to see this protection as limited by respect for the human rights to life, liberty, equality, and bodily integrity of all the family's members.

3. A final respect in which the U.S. Constitution may offer the possibility of enlarging women's human rights is perhaps even more controversial and unfashionable than the preceding two but, in my view, it is worth considering. This concerns its First Amendment feature of prohibiting the establishment of religion by government and, to a degree also, the more generally accepted free exercise clause. Whereas the latter finds parallels in some of the human rights doctrines, the wall of separation of church and state does not.

Freedom of religion is enunciated in article 18 of the Covenant on Civil and Political Rights, which states that "Everyone shall have the right to freedom of thought, conscience and religion. This right shall include freedom to have or to adopt a religion or belief of his choice, and freedom, either individually or in community with others and in public or private, to manifest his religion or belief in worship, observance, practice and teaching." The Human Rights Committee's subsequent comment on this article specifies that this protects theistic, nontheistic, and atheistic beliefs, and also insists that where there is a state or official religion, there be no discrimination against other religions.

Yet there is a question, I think, as to whether this is possible in fact, and not enough attention has been given to this issue of separation in theorizing about human rights. For our purposes here, we may note only that many features of women's subordination worldwide have a religious dimension, and this becomes a particularly difficult problem in those cases in which religious law comes to dominate over secular law. Such religious law (Shari'a is only one example of this) may embody features that violate human rights, and this is especially apparent in regard to the treatment of women. Religious tenets concerning rights within families, particularly those pertaining to marriage and divorce, as well as inheritance and personal status, frequently violate the equality of women that CEDAW requires. Certainly if secular courts apply religious law in these cases, women's equality cannot be respected.[27] We have to question, then, whether sufficient progress can be made in this area so long as religions remain dominant in the public sphere. If they did not, there would still be their dominance in the private domain to contend with, but the problems would probably be less severe. Some have argued that in the Islamic case, the direction to take is instead that of reinterpreting Shari'a in a way compatible with human rights, while leaving Islamic domination of states uncontested.[28] But it is not clear to me that this direction will suffice to produce full equality for women.

Key Problems for the Theory of Women's Rights

In the final section of this paper, I would like to focus more directly on certain conceptual problems that remain in both the U.S. constitutional and international human rights framework for women's rights, and make a few suggestions concerning how they may be approached.

The first regards the private/public divide that characterizes both contexts. This vexing distinction that permeates Western legal thought has been especially troubling to feminists who hold, as Olsen succinctly puts it, that "Privacy doctrine tends to shield from public scrutiny the abuse of women that takes place within the 'private realm of family life.' "[29] In this way, a distinction between what is subject to law and what remains largely unregulated can condone sexual violence and perpetuate inequalities within the family. Likewise, Hilary Charlesworth, Celia Romany, and others have traced the impact of this distinction within human rights doctrine. As was suggested earlier, these human rights are regarded as holding against nation-states and have been developed in a way that primarily addresses the concerns and fears of men — those who have historically predominated in the public domain. Yet feminist theory has already made some progress in reinterpreting these rights to encompass more fully women's experiences — for example, in seeing the right to be free from torture to apply to rape as well as to the actions of states.[30] Further, as noted earlier, these rights are increasingly being extended to nonstate actors, not only as their beneficiaries but in terms of holding such actors responsible for respecting them — including corporations and even private individuals. Although at present states are only responsible for putting systems in place to prevent human rights violations and punish transgressions by these actors, this is itself a considerable improvement on earlier human rights law.

On the other side, the right of privacy has itself commended itself to feminists and others, both for its protection of abortion and reproductive rights and because all of us would like a "zone of privacy" with respect to our bodies and our intimate relations. I have suggested how reproductive rights actually appeal to our autonomy or freedom, as well as to bodily integrity. But this aspect of the idea of privacy is one that we would be loath to give up, along with its other aspects of control over information about ourselves and the more general protection of a personal and interpersonal space for our reflections and relationships. Our individual freedom, I would suggest, requires this sort of space, where this supports an expectation of nonintrusiveness by the state. Yet this expectation cannot be absolute, and I would propose that a step toward resolving this dilemma of the desirability and undesirability of privacy for feminists involves recognizing the increased scope of the human rights. That is, human rights need to be respected in *all* domains, including the family. Inasmuch as they can be interpreted as rights that hold by each on all the others globally (that is, they are claims on society at large), and not merely against states, they need to be respected and enforced in the private domain of families and interpersonal lives as elsewhere. My suggestion here thus proposes for human rights what Susan Okin has suggested for justice,[31] namely, that they apply not only to the so-called public domain but to family and personal life as well. Thus the respect for personal and interpersonal privacy has to be compatible with the human rights. And, of course, violence against women is a human rights issue.

Turning now to the remaining conceptual issues, we can note that the issue of special vs. equal treatment for men and women, or of sameness/difference, has been a problem both in U.S. law and in the human rights context. Numerous discriminatory sex-specific statutes in the U.S. have thankfully disappeared in recent decades, and those that remain, e.g., regarding differential liability or penalties in a few states for nonconsensual sex with teenagers depending on whether the perpetrator is male or female, will likely continue to be phased out.[32] Of course, laws that compensate for and attempt to rectify past discrimination, such as those regarding affirmative action, will, it is to be hoped, remain. In the human rights framework as well, while explicit references to pregnancy may be in order, we may wonder about the appropriateness of the emphasis on motherhood—without mention of fatherhood—in some of the international documents. More deeply, these human rights (like those in the U.S.) have correctly been criticized as simply extending to women the privileges of men. They have not yet been subjected to a thoroughgoing examination of the degree to which they might draw on women's experiences as well as those of men whose more public orientation tended to influence their formulation. This observation also raises the final issue of the role of care in the rights framework, and here I will make some brief comments on both of these conceptual issues.

On the question of the same or differential treatment of men and women, we need to appeal to a principle of equal freedom (in my view, equal positive freedom) for guidance. This very general idea, which is at the core of our intuitions here, is that people have equal rights to be agents and, I would say, to the conditions of their agency or freedom. Among these conditions are basic ones needed for any human action, and these give rise to certain basic rights, namely, life and liberty, as well as health care and a certain level of education and training. Beyond this, there are conditions that people need for the fuller expression of their freedom as self-development, where these conditions, like their freedom itself, are appropriately seen as differentiated among individuals. The nonbasic human rights speak to the conditions for this equal, but differentiated, self-development.

Unfortunately, the human rights documents lump all these basic and nonbasic rights together, regarding them as coequal, from the right to life to the right to a paid vacation. Yet in principle a distinction can be drawn, and this helps to make room for equal, in the sense of equivalent, treatment of people with respect to meeting their differentiated nonbasic needs, but more rigorously equal treatment in respect to basic rights. Even in regard to these basic rights, however, a certain differentiation is called for at the level of application, in the sense of accommodating physical differences (including pregnancy and childbirth) or various handicaps as a condition for meeting the basic needs of life and health. Such differentiation in these cases is a condition for full treatment *as an equal*. We might say that if differences were not used against people and were subject to their own self-interpretation and assent, then recognizing them for certain purposes would not necessarily be problematic. Further, where they have given rise to disadvantage, this needs to be compensated for and eliminated, as Rhode and others have argued.

Yet this still does not touch the issue of reconceiving the rights themselves not only to apply to women's experience in families, for example, but to open their corpus to being shaped by these experiences, including by the related ideas of nurturance, care, and concern. It is almost an open field to bring care theory, heretofore developed primarily within ethics, to the theory of human rights and women's rights more generally. Without going into this in any depth here, I would suggest that the antithesis that some theorists have drawn between rights and care is inaccurate and that in fact human rights draw strength from the care and the feelings of shared commonality that we have for all people, including those remote from us. Care thus does not have to remain narrowly confined to those whom I know personally, but, as a caring outlook—rooted in empathy—it can extend more widely to support the universalistic standpoint normally associated with a human rights perspective. Moreover, a care perspective is important to assure that the human rights are in fact applied in each particular case, not only enunciated in generalities. Another implication of care for human rights doctrine is the support this concept gives to rights to means of subsistence and health care, as well as to education, inasmuch as these are basic to life and the development of persons. Human rights instruments, not to speak of the U.S. Constitution, still tend to denigrate these economic and social rights in favor of the civil and political, where they include them at all.

An emphasis on the social and political importance of care and nurturance lends weight to a requirement for meeting people's basic needs if it can be shown that these are aspects of what people owe each other in societies, and not only characterize the particularistic obligations or responsibilities that they have to those close to them. Although it is certainly the case that as individuals we cannot fully care for all equally (and here care differs from the idea of respect, which is susceptible of this equality), nonetheless I would suggest that there is an extensibility of what we might call basic care that does apply universally. We cannot take care of all others, in the sense of directly being responsible for meeting their needs personally (in the way that we can, for example, for our children, or at least try to do so). Nonetheless, we can, I think, be jointly responsible for meeting the basic needs of all the others, and this imposes some fundamental human rights obligations on each of us. In this sense, it makes sense to speak of a human right to care, or to be cared for. This does not necessarily mean, however, that we have to add yet another right to the long list of recognized human rights (although there may be arguments for doing this). But it does entail that the caring rights mentioned earlier—e.g., those to means of subsistence or to health care—have a deep basis not only in the respect we have for others but in the basic care that we collectively must have for them.

By way of closing, I would like to return to the theme that I enunciated at the outset, namely, initiating a public dialogue between the U.S. Constitution and women's human rights. I would suggest that recognizing the validity of international human rights documents in the United States would be one important way to strengthen women's rights here. The United States is in this respect in a similar situation to other countries and their women's movements—whether it be Egypt, the United Kingdom, or elsewhere. International human rights laws have the potential to advance the treatment of women in domestic law. Of course, we cannot expect the U.S. Constitution to do everything for us; much needs to be left to legislation, not to speak of social action. But it is a conclusion of this chapter that a fuller range of human rights, especially those applying to women, should either be in the Constitution itself—whether by way of amendment or interpretation—or should be subscribed to independently, such that they are regarded as binding upon all of us.

NOTES

1. Ann Elizabeth Mayer, "Reflections on the Proposed United States Reservations to CEDAW: Should the Constitution Be an Obstacle to Human Rights?" *Hastings Constitutional Law Quarterly* 23 (spring 1996): 727–823.

2. Deborah Rhode, *Justice and Gender* (Cambridge: Harvard University Press, 1989), 111.

3. Patricia Smith, ed. *Feminist Jurisprudence* (New York: Oxford University Press, 1993).

4. See especially Ann Scales, "The Emergence of Feminist Jurisprudence: An Essay," in Patricia Smith, ed. *Feminist Jurisprudence*, 94–109.

5. *Caban v. Mohammed*, (1978); also see *Craig v. Boren* (1976).

6. In *United States v. Virginia* (1996), which requires "exceedingly persuasive justification" for a classification to be acceptable.

7. Deborah Rhode, "Reproductive Freedom," in Patricia Smith, *Feminist Jurisprudence*, 339–40.

8. In *Eisenstadt v. Baird*, 405 U.S. 438 (1972) concerning the distribution of birth control to a single woman, the Supreme Court held that "if the right to privacy means anything, it is the right of the *individual*, married or single, to be free from

unwarranted governmental intrusion into matters so fundamentally affecting a person as the decision whether to bear or beget a child."

9. An argument that seems to point in this direction can be found, for example, in Martha Nussbaum's contribution to this collection (chapter 10).

10. Anne Bayefsky, "General Approaches to the Domestic Application of Women's International Human Rights Law," in Rebecca J. Cook, ed., *The Human Rights of Women* (Philadelphia: University of Pennsylvania Press, 1994), 351.

11. Bayefsky, "General Approaches," 351–52.

12. Ibid., 352–53.

13. Hilary Charlesworth, "What are 'Women's International Human Rights'?," in Cook, ed., *Human Rights of Women*, 71.

14. See especially the discussion in Mayer, "Reflections."

15. Mayer, "Reflections," 758.

16. Rebecca J. Cook, "State Responsibility for Violations of Women's Human Rights," *Harvard Human Rights Journal* 7 (1994): 125, 155, cited in Mayer, "Reflections," 735.

17. See Rebecca J. Cook, "State Accountability under the Convention on the Elimination of All Forms of Discrimination Against Women," in Cook, *The Human Rights of Women*, 236.

18. Bayefsky, "General Approaches," 357.

19. See, for example, F. Beveridge and S. Mullally, "International Human rRghts and Body Politics," in J. Bridgeman and S. Millns, *Law and Body Politics: Regulating the Female Body* (Aldershot, U.K.: Dartmouth, 1995), 257, fn. 18.

20. Cook, "State Accountability," 237.

21. Gerda A. Kleijkamp, *Family Life and Family Interests: A Comparative Study on the Influence of the European Convention of Human Rights on Dutch Family Law and the Influence of the United States Constitution on American Family Law* (London: Kluwer Law International, 1999), 75.

22. *DeShaney v. Winnebago County Dept. of Social Services*, 1989, cited in Kleijkamp, *Family Law and Family Interests*, 75. Kleijkamp notes, by contrast, that the European Court of Human Rights has interpreted aspects of its convention (in particular, article 8's "respect for family life") as imposing "a member state's affirmative obligations to facilitate the exercise of individual rights, even to the extent of requiring the government to protect individuals against interferences from other individuals (115)."

23. Helen Bequaert Holmes, "A Feminist Analysis of the United Nations Declaration of Human Rights," in Carol C. Gould, ed., *Beyond Domination: New Perspectives on Women and Philosophy* (Totowa, N.J.: Rowman & Littlefield, 1984), 256.

24. See the discussion in Holmes, "A Feminist," 257.

25. Hilary Charlesworth, "What are 'Women's International Human Rights'?" in Cook, *Human Rights of Women*, 73.

26. Ronald Dworkin, "The Great Abortion Case," *New York Review of Books*, June 29, 1989, 50–51, cited in Frances Olsen, "Unraveling Compromise," in Smith, *Feminist Jurisprudence*, 337.

27. See Donna Sullivan, "Advancing the Freedom of Religion or Belief through the UN Declaration on the Elimination of Religious Tolerance and Discrimination," in Henry J. Steiner and Philip Alston, *International Human Rights in Context,* 2d ed. (Oxford: Oxford University Press, 2000), 473.

28. See especially Abdullah Ahmed An-Naim, "Human Rights in the Muslim World, in *International Human Rights in Context*, pp. 393–95.

29. Frances Olsen, "Unraveling Compromise," in Smith, *Feminist Jurisprudence,* 337.

30. See Rhonda Copelon, "Intimate Terror: Understanding Domestic Violence as Torture," in Cook, *Human Rights of Women,* 116–52. Needless to say, this is not to imply that only women are raped nor that only men are subject to torture by states. Rather, it is a question of historical or social experiences, where this too does not reveal any absolute divide along these lines.

31. Susan Okin, *Justice, Gender, and the Family* (New York: Basic Books, 1989).

32. It is interesting to note, however, that in Deborah Rhode's critique of the decision in *Michael M. v. Superior Court* (a 1981 case that let stand California statutory rape legislation that differentiated in liability between a male or a female having sex with teenagers, imposing criminal penalties only on males having sex with underage females but not on females), she found the problem with the decision not to be primarily its lack of gender neutrality but with the court's emphasis on pregnancy and chastity rather than on the more important factor of consent. According to Rhodes, "gender neutrality may obscure factual asymmetries in sexual relationships. In this culture, men and women are not equally vulnerable to coercive sex (Rhode, *Justice and Gender,* 103).

Privacy and Family Law

Elizabeth M. Schneider

CHAPTER 12

Battered Women, Feminist Lawmaking, Privacy, and Equality

In the late 1960s a movement of feminist activists and lawyers began to bring the problem of woman abuse to public attention. At that time there was no legal recognition of a harm of violence against women by intimates—today known as domestic violence. It simply didn't exist in the legal vocabulary. In 1992 the United States Supreme Court recognized the pervasiveness and severity of intimate violence for the first time in *Planned Parenthood v. Casey*, and in 1994 Congress passed the Violence Against Women Act. This chapter, drawn from my work over many years and my recent book, *Battered Women and Feminist Lawmaking*,[1] describes the process of feminist legal advocacy and lawmaking on intimate violence that has led the Supreme Court, other courts, Congress, and state legislatures to recognize this harm, and focuses on issues of privacy.

Planned Parenthood v. Casey is widely known as the decision in which the Supreme Court narrowly upheld constitutional protection for women's right to reproductive choice, not as a case about intimate violence. But the restrictive Pennsylvania abortion statute challenged in *Casey* included a mandatory "spousal notification" provision. Battered women's advocacy organizations argued that enforcement of this provision would mean that women who faced intimate violence, and who could not tell their partner that they were pregnant without fear of harm, would be unable to freely exercise their reproductive choice. The Court struck down this provision as unconstitutional on these grounds.

In its decision, the Court described the problem of domestic violence, drawing on a startling statistical picture:

- In an average twelve-month period in this country, approximately two million women are the victims of severe assaults by their male partners. In a 1985 survey, women reported that nearly one of every eight husbands had assaulted their wives during the past year. The [American Medical Association] views these figures as "marked underestimates" because the nature of these incidents discourages women from reporting them and because surveys typically exclude the very poor, those who do not speak English well, and women who are homeless or in institutions or hospitals when the survey is conducted. According to the AMA, "researchers on family violence agree that the true incidence of partner violence is probably *double* the above estimates; or four million severely assaulted women per year."

- Studies on prevalence suggest that from one-fifth to one-third of all women will be physically assaulted by a partner or ex-partner during their lifetime. . . . Thus on an average day in the United States, nearly 11,000 women are severely assaulted by their male partners. Many of these incidents involve sexual assault. . . . In families where wife-beating takes place, moreover, child abuse is often present as well.

- Other studies fill in the rest of this troubling picture. Physical violence is only the most visible form of abuse. Psychological abuse, particularly forced social and economic isolation of women, is also common.

- Many victims of domestic violence, remain with their abusers, perhaps because they perceive no superior alternative. . . . Many abused women who find temporary refuge in shelters return to their husbands, in large part because they have no other source of income. . . . Returning to one's abuser can be dangerous. Recent Federal Bureau of Investigation statistics disclose that 8.8 percent of all homicide victims in the United States are killed by their spouses. . . . Thirty percent of female homicide victims are killed by their male partners.[2]

The statistics that the Court recited, though horrifying, were not news. Feminists in the United States had argued for more than two centuries that women's legally sanctioned subordination within the family denied them equality and citizenship. They saw intimate violence as an important vehicle of this subordination, for, as Wendy Williams put it, it involves the "ultimatum: do as I say, . . . subordinate yourself to me, or you will be injured."[3] Feminists claimed that domestic violence threatened not only women's right to physical integrity and perhaps even life itself, but also women's liberty, autonomy, and equality. Yet it was only in the late 1960s that any aspect of this link between violence and equality began to be reflected in law and culture.

Since then, the rebirth of a women's rights movement in the United States has had a substantial impact in shaping social attitudes and defining public issues. Law has been a critical component of this process of change, and feminist lawyers have played a central role in shaping it. Feminist activists and lawyers have challenged assumptions about gender roles, the family, and the workplace. Through a process of feminist lawmaking they have given name and visibility to harms experienced by women, such as intimate violence and sexual harassment, that were previously buried by cultural complicity.

The development of a battered women's movement has been one of the most important contributions of the women's rights struggle. This movement created the theoretical concept of battering, and the issue has now moved from social invisibility as a "private problem" to an important public concern. There is hardly a day when a story on some aspect of domestic violence does not appear in the media. The o. J. Simpson case, with its subtext of battering, held public attention for several years. There has been an explosion of innovative activist and advocacy efforts in both state and federal legislative arenas. Organizations have founded shelters or networks of "safe homes," set up telephone hotlines, challenged police practices that fail to intervene effectively to assist battered women, drafted legislation to protect women through civil orders of protection as well as criminal and tort remedies, and developed programs to work with battering men. Lawsuits and legislation have produced improved police and court practices. Activists have developed teen dating violence programs and special law school and medical school courses. Government reports, legal and social-science literature, and media coverage have proliferated. Advocates and scholars continue to formulate new legal approaches to violence against women. Work in the United States is linked to a feminist human rights campaign on gender violence around the world.

Nevertheless, this many faceted barrage of activity has not achieved linear, ascending progress; instead, the result has been complex change, partial inroads, and deep resistance. In this chapter I briefly examine both accomplishments and contradictions through the lens of feminist legal advocacy efforts on violence against women in the United States.

Feminist legal arguments about gender violence have developed from feminist insights about the way heterosexual intimate violence is part of a larger system of coercive control and subordination; a system that is based on structural gender inequality and has political roots. The source of insight about the connection between lived personal experience and structural power relations was the notion that "the personal is political." In the context of intimate violence, the impulse behind feminist legal arguments was to redefine the relationship between the personal and the political, to definitively link violence and gender.

Although there have been dramatic strides in the way the law on intimate violence has incorporated these insights, feminist ideas about the relationship between violence and gender have been simultaneously transformed, depoliticized, subverted, and contained in the process of lawmaking: the broader link between violence and gender inequality that animated those ideas has, to a large degree, been lost, or at least undermined. For example, widespread use of the term "battered woman syndrome" has reinscribed notions of female pathology, provocation, and victim blaming into legal discourse. In the very process of change, systemic analysis of gendered violence consistently meets with ambivalence and resistance. Each step forward provokes efforts to dilute and contain the original theoretical framework.

I have been deeply involved in the work of the movement that I describe. I first became concerned with the problem of violence against women through work as a lawyer on issues of legal treatment of battered women who, having defended themselves against their assailants, faced problems of gender bias in the criminal law. I have continued to work on these issues in a variety of capacities: in teaching, writing, legal advocacy, and public education; in preparing a report for the Ford Foundation on legal reform efforts for battered women; in training judges and lawyers about issues of gender and violence; and in working to integrate issues of gender generally, and gender violence in particular, into legal education. I teach courses on intimate violence in law school, and am the co-author of a law school casebook, *Battered Women and the Law*.[4] I have also done work internationally on these issues, most recently in South Africa and China. These experiences as activist, lawyer, and theorist have given me a wide vantage point to critically evaluate feminist lawmaking on domestic violence.

My work has explored the social and political meaning of legal claims in feminist struggle and particularly within the battered women's movement. This work on rights claims began with the development of a theoretical framework that I have called the "dialectical interrelationship between rights and politics." The assertion of legal claims and claims of rights has been shaped by political struggle. Legal argumentation and the articulation of rights reveal tensions and contradictions that sharpen political analysis and move it forward; these theoretical insights must be integrated into practice in order to reshape it. I emphasize the need for close attention to the interrelationship between theory and practice in our understanding of the complexity of women's lives and in the articulation of women's experiences into legal claims.

This theoretical perspective on the relationship between law and social movements shapes this chapter. I examine concrete ways in which this dialectical interrelationship operates in feminist lawmaking on battering. I analyze how the articulation of rights has exposed tensions and paradoxes in

feminist legal strategies and visions but has also clarified issues and sharp-
ened debate.

Now is a time of enormous challenge and opportunity for work on male
battering of women. The passage of the Violence Against Women Act of 1994
(VAWA I) and the recent passage of the Violence Against Women Act of 2000
(VAWA II)[5] have given broad national attention to this issue. Stories of
women murdered by battering men continue to receive widespread publicity.
Grants of clemency to battered women who killed their abusers have attracted much media attention. In states where restraining-order legislation or the
mandatory arrest of batterers has strengthened legal remedies, the percentage
of batterings that are reported has increased dramatically. Nevertheless,
women who seek help often face "mutual restraining orders" or arrest along
with their abusers. And at the same time that legal reform efforts have expanded, public response to clemency efforts has rekindled a national debate
on issues of violence against women and women's "retaliation." Anita Hill's
experience in alleging sexual harassment against Supreme Court nominee
Clarence Thomas, and other more recent, highly publicized sexual harassment cases have underscored the tenacity of views of women as unreasonable
and provocative. And in 2000, the United States Supreme Court held in
United States v. Morrison,[6] that the civil rights remedy of VAWA I was unconstitutional on the ground that it exceeded Congress's powers under the
Commerce Clause and the Fourteenth Amendment. The current right-wing
backlash on such issues as the Violence Against Women Act contests claims
of the seriousness of the problem.

The Violence of Privacy

Historically, male battering of women was untouched by law, protected as
part of the private sphere of family life. This rhetoric of privacy, the "veil of relationship," has been the most important ideological obstacle to legal change
and reform.[7] Since the battered women's movement in this country has made
issues of battering visible, battering is no longer perceived as a purely private
problem and has taken on the dimensions of a public issue. The explosion of
legal reform and social service efforts—the development of battered women's
shelters and hotlines, as well as new legal remedies developed for battered
women—has been premised on the idea of battering as a public harm. Nevertheless, widespread resistance to acknowledging battering as a public issue
continues.

Concepts of privacy permit, encourage, and reinforce violence against
women. The notion of marital privacy has been a source of oppression to

battered women and has helped to perpetuate women's subordination within the family. The idea of privacy continues to pose a challenge to theoretical and practical work on woman abuse. The ideological tenacity of conceptions of battering as "private" is revealed in the meanings of "public" and "private" in American family life; in the Supreme Court's decision in *De-shaney v. Winnebago County Department of Social Services*;[8] in the inadequacy of legal reform efforts to date; and in tensions that persist within the battered women's movement.

Meanings of Private and Public in the Family

The dichotomy of "public" and "private" has shaped our understandings of gender. The traditional notion of separate spheres is premised on a dichotomy between the private world of family and domestic life (the "women's sphere") and the public world of marketplace (the "men's sphere"). In 1982 Nadine Taub and I examined the difference between the role of law in the public sphere and its role in the private sphere.[9] In the public sphere, sex-based exclusionary laws join with other institutional and ideological constraints to limit women's participation directly. In the private sphere, the legal system operates more subtly: the law claims to be absent in the private sphere, and historically it has refused to intervene in ongoing family relations. We described the traditional role of privacy in family law in the following way:

> Tort law, which is generally concerned with injuries inflicted on individuals, has traditionally been held inapplicable to injuries inflicted by one family member on another. Under the doctrines of interspousal and parent-child immunity, courts have consistently denied recoveries for injuries that would be compensable but for the fact that they occurred in the private realm. In the same way, criminal law declined to punish intentional injuries to family members. Common law and statutory definitions of rape in many states continue to carve out a special exception for a husband's forced intercourse with his wife. Wife beating was initially omitted from the definition of criminal assault on the ground that a husband had the right to chastise his wife. Even today, after courts have explicitly rejected the definitional exception and its rationale, judges, prosecutors, and police officers decline to enforce assault laws in the family context.[10]

Some aspects of this legal system have changed today—there is no longer interspousal immunity, and marital rape has been recognized—but the vestiges of these rationales continue in the law. Although a dichotomous view of the public sphere and the private sphere has some heuristic value and considerable rhetorical appeal, the dichotomy is overdrawn. The notion of a sharp demarcation between public and private has been widely rejected by feminist and critical scholars.[11] In practice, no realm of personal and family life exists totally separate from the reach of the state. The state defines both the family, the so-called private sphere, and the market, the so-called public sphere; "private" and "public" exist on a continuum.

Consequently, in the sphere of domestic and family life, purportedly immune from law, the law is always being applied, though selectively. "Privacy" is selectively invoked as a rationale for immunity in order to protect male domination. For example, when the police do not respond to a battered woman's call for assistance, or when a civil court refuses to evict her assailant, the woman is relegated to self-help, while the man who beats her receives the law's tacit encouragement and support.[12] Legislative and prosecutorial efforts to control women's conduct during pregnancy in the form of "fetal" protection laws—premised on the notion that women's childbearing capacity, and pregnancy itself, subject them to public regulation and control—provide another example. A pregnant battered woman may face criminal prosecution for drinking liquor, but a man who batters her does so with impunity.[13]

The rhetoric of privacy that has isolated the female world from the legal order sends a message to the rest of society. It devalues women and their functions and says that women are not important enough to merit legal regulation:

> This message is clearly communicated when particular relief is withheld. By declining to punish a man for inflicting injuries on his wife, for example, the law implies she is his property and he is free to control her as he sees fit. Women's work is discredited when the law refuses to enforce the man's obligation to support his wife, since it implies she makes no contribution worthy of support. Similarly, when courts decline to enforce contracts that seek to limit or specify the extent of the wife's services, the law implies that household work is not real work in the way that the type of work subject to contract in the public sphere is real work. These are important messages, for denying woman's humanity and the value of her traditional work are key ideological components in maintaining women's subordinate status. The message of women's inferiority is compounded by the totality of the law's absence from the private realm. In our society, law is for business and other important things. The fact that the law in general claims to have so little bearing on women's day-to-day concerns reflects and underscores their insignificance. Thus the legal order's overall contribution to the devaluation of women is greater than the sum of the negative messages conveyed by individual legal doctrines.[14]

The concept of privacy has historically been viewed as problematic by feminist theorists. Privacy rests on a division of public and private that has been oppressive to women and has supported male dominance in the family. The concept reinforces the idea that the personal is separate from the political; privacy also implies a realm that should be kept secret. Privacy inures to the benefit of the individual, not the community. The right of privacy has been viewed as a passive right, one that says that the state cannot intervene.[15]

Nevertheless, privacy is important for all people—particularly women.[16] It provides an opportunity for individual self-development, for individual decision making, and for protection against endless caretaking. Rights to autonomy, equality, liberty, and freedom of bodily integrity are central to women's independence and well-being. For women who have been battered these aspects of privacy are particularly relevant. Remedies for intimate violence must preserve opportunities for safety, seclusion, intimacy, and individual decision making.

Definitions of "private" and "public" in any particular legal context can and do constantly shift. Their meanings are based on social and cultural assumptions of what is valued and important, and these assumptions are deeply gendered. Thus the interrelationship between what is understood and experienced as "private" and what is understood and experienced as "public" is particularly complex in the area of gender, where the rhetoric of privacy masks inequality and subordination. The decision about what we protect as private is a political decision that always has public ramifications.[17]

Privacy and Denial

Although battering has evolved from a private to a more public issue, the depth of social resistance to change cannot be minimized. The concept of battering is deeply threatening. It strikes at our most fundamental assumptions about the nature of intimate relations and the safeness of family life. The concept of male battering of women as a private issue exerts a powerful ideological pull on our consciousness; by seeing woman abuse as private, we affirm it as a problem that is individual and involves only a particular intimate relationship, for which there is no social responsibility to remedy. We need to deny its seriousness and pervasiveness in order to distance ourselves from the possibility of it in our own lives, to deny the interconnectedness of battering with so many other aspects of family life and gender relations. As a result, instead of focusing on the batterer, we focus on the battered woman, scrutinize her conduct, examine her pathology, and blame her for remaining in the relationship, in order to maintain our denial and our failure to confront the more basic and disturbing issues of power and control in intimate relationships. Focusing on the woman, not the man, perpetuates the power of patriarchy. Denial supports and legitimates this power, and the concept of privacy is a key aspect of this denial.

This process of denial takes many forms and operates on many levels. Men deny battering in order to protect their own privileges.[18] Women need to deny the pervasiveness of the problem so as not to link it to their own lives. Individual women who are battered tend to minimize the violence in order to distance themselves from some internalized negative concept of a "battered woman." I see denial in the attitudes of jurors, who try to remove themselves from the experiences of the battered and think "this could never happen to me; if it did, I would handle it differently."[19] I see denial in the public engagement in the 1988 case involving Hedda Nussbaum and Joel Steinberg, which focused on Nussbaum's complicity for the death of their child and involved feminists in active controversy over the boundaries of victimization.[20] The reports of the many state task forces on gender bias in the courts have painstakingly recorded judicial attitudes of denial.[21] Clearly, there is serious denial on the part of state legislators, members of Congress, and members of the executive branch who do not discuss battering as a public issue. In battering, we see both the power of denial and the denial of power. The concept of privacy is an ideological rationale for this denial and serves to maintain it.

For these reasons, the concept of privacy has encouraged, reinforced, and supported violence against women. Privacy says that violence against women is immune from sanction, that it is acceptable and part of the basic fabric of American family life. Privacy says that what goes on in the violent relationship should not be the subject of state or community intervention. Privacy says that battering is an individual problem, not a systemic one. Privacy operates as a mask for inequality, protecting male violence against women.

Shifting Parameters of Private and Public for Battered Women

As work on battered women has evolved, social meanings of what is private and public, and the relationship between them, have become more complex. Traditionally, battering was viewed as within the private sphere of the family, and therefore unprotected by law. Yet, as Martha Minow has suggested, this social failure to intervene in battering on grounds of privacy should be seen not as separate from the violence but as part of the violence: "When clerks in a local court harass a woman who applies for a restraining order against the violence in her home, they are part of the violence. Society is organized to permit violence in the home; it is organized through images in mass media and through broadly based social attitudes that condone violence. . . . Society permits such violence to go unchallenged through the isolation of families and the failures of police to respond. Public, rather than private, patterns of conduct and morals are implicated. Some police officers refuse to respond to domestic violence; some officers themselves abuse their spouses. . . . Some clerks and judges think domestic violence matters do not belong in court. These failures to respond to domestic violence are public, not private, actions."[22]

Although social failure to respond to problems of battered women has been justified on grounds of privacy, this failure to respond is an affirmative political decision that has serious public consequences. The rationale of privacy masks the political nature of the decision. Privacy thus plays a particularly pernicious role in supporting, encouraging, and legitimizing violence against women and other battered partners or family members. The state actively permits this violence by protecting the privileges and prerogatives of the batterer and failing to protect the battered women, as well as by prosecuting battered women for homicide when they act to protect themselves. These failures to respond, or selective responses, are part of "public rather than private patterns of conduct and morals."[23]

As legal reform efforts for battered women have developed, the border between public and private, concerning issues of battered women, has shifted. In some sense the public dimension of the problem has expanded. Courts have rendered legal decisions holding police officers liable for money damages for failure to intervene to protect battered women; we have experienced an explosion of state legal remedies to protect battered women; and advocates have secured federal legislation to assist battered women in implementing remedies. These gains suggest at least a recognition by governmental bodies, speaking with a public voice, that they must acknowledge and address the problem. Some of the rhetoric surrounding issues of battering has shifted from the language of private to the language of public.

Yet, on the level of practice, it is questionable which remedies, if any, are likely to provide real protection for those women who are abused or leverage to change their lives. Some aspects of the legal process may be significant because it may be important for a battered woman to be able to state in a public forum what happened and to be taken seriously by the judge. But none of these legal processes—neither orders of protection nor arrest alone—protect the woman, change her partner's intimate behavior, or create life support and alternatives to enable her to be safe. In addition, because most women who are abused in any of these contexts lack legal representation, meaningful access to these remedies is severely limited, especially for women without financial means.

Even as legal remedies and public perceptions have changed, the notion of family violence as relegated to the private sphere was given additional support by the Supreme Court's 1989 decision in *DeShaney v. Winnebago County Department of Social Services*. In *DeShaney*, the Court held that the state had no affirmative responsibility to protect a child who had been permanently injured as a result of abuse committed by his custodial father, even when the state had been investigating the child abuse for several years. The majority opinion reflects a crabbed view of the world that reasserts a clear distinction between public and private: family violence is private and therefore immune from state scrutiny because, implicitly, the state had no business to be there in the first place and no responsibility to intervene at all. *DeShaney* has been interpreted by courts around the country to limit police liability in civil suits brought by battered women.[24]

The tension between public and private also is evident in the issue of what legal processes are available to battered women and what the social meaning of those processes is to battered women and to society at large. For example, civil remedies known as restraining orders, or orders of protection, are court orders with flexible provisions that a battered woman can obtain to stop a man from beating her, prevent him from coming to the house, or evict him from the house. Criminal statutes provide for the arrest of batterers, either for beating or for violation of protective orders.[25] Although serious problems in the enforcement and implementation of these orders remain, the fact that these formal legal processes exist is evidence of a developing understanding of the public dimension of the problem. By giving battered women remedies in court, the need for public scrutiny, public control, and public sanction has at least theoretically been acknowledged. In addition, some states impose marriage license fees to generate funds for battered women's services, thus making a statement about the public impact of purportedly private conduct as well as implying an ideological link between marriage and violence. Some of these state statutory provisions have been challenged by battering men.[26]

At the same time that these remedies have been developing, a move toward more private and informal processes, notably mediation, has been under way. Most battered women's advocates are critical of mediation, because they believe that informal modes of dispute resolution substantially hurt battered women who are disadvantaged with respect to power, money, and resources. Mediation is viewed as signaling that battering is the women's individual "problem" that should be "worked out," and that the state has no role in it. The general mood in legal circles that favors alternative dispute resolution has helped to legitimate mediation and obscure its problematic implications in this context. The move to mediation and other more informal processes can also be understood as a reflection of the low priority that the law accords family issues generally and battered women's problems in particular.[27]

Criminal remedies for battering, particularly mandatory arrest provisions, are now widespread. Activists have argued that criminal remedies generally, and mandatory arrest in particular, send a clear social message that battering is impermissible and that because criminal remedies are prosecuted by the state, they give more public force to the sanction. Yet even civil remedies, such as orders of protection and tort suits brought by individual women against batterers, send a social message. The lawsuits use formal court processes and are subject to public scrutiny, and the legal decisions they produce make a public statement. Tort actions in particular may carry a greater social meaning in light of the demise of interspousal immunity, the social dimension of the claimed harm, and the affirmative nature of the claim for damages.[28] Other examples of alternative procedural frameworks that have a public meaning include the articulation of battering as a civil rights violation, as an international human rights violation, and as involuntary servitude.[29] There is a fundamental contradiction, however, in the gap between the articulation of these approaches on the "grand" level of theory and their implementation on the "ground" level of practice. Here, both theory and practice necessarily reflect our fundamental ambivalence about privacy.

Reva Siegel's documentation of the historical evolution of legal rationales concerning domestic violence supports this view of social ambivalence toward, and tenacity of, privacy rationales in legal reform. She suggests that although treatment of domestic violence in the law has moved from a rule of chastisement to views that protect domestic violence as within the "veil of privacy," this reform of legal status has largely legitimated violence, made it more palatable and more invisible. Even reforms that appear to revise the law dramatically, such as VAWA I, contain the seeds of ambivalence toward violence that characterize what she calls "prerogative and privacy." Siegel's work underscores the importance of critical analysis of the inevitable role of privacy in shaping legal reform on domestic violence.[30]

Indeed, this ambivalence has been made manifest in the Supreme Court decision in *Morrison*, which reflects the pervasiveness of concepts of privacy. *Morrison* held that domestic violence was a "local" not a "national" problem, and therefore Congress had exceeded its authority in passing the Civil Rights Remedy, which permitted victims of "gender motivated violence" to bring actions for damages in federal court under the Commerce Clause and the Fourteenth Amendment. In *Morrison* the Supreme Court rejected extensive congressional findings on the seriousness and pervasiveness of the problem of domestic violence and extensive documentation of the harms. Yet the Supreme Court's perception of domestic violence as "local" can be understood as a reaffirmation of the private.[31]

At the same time the development of more formal processes has promoted public education and helped to redefine violence as a public issue. Because of the availability of these legal remedies, more court proceedings take place and participants, judiciary, court personnel, and the public are educated about the problem of domestic violence. Public participation in these disputes may well have contributed to changing attitudes concerning the acceptability of violence against women.[32] The media frequently focus on court cases, producing many newspaper articles and television programs about cases involving violence against women.[33] Further, analysis of the actual implementation of these legal remedies, and of the failure of the courts to enforce their provisions, has been widely publicized in many state reports on gender bias and has expanded the educational process within the states.

The development of these more formal processes has also been important to battered women themselves. One empirical study of battered women's experiences in obtaining restraining orders in New Haven, Connecticut, concluded that temporary restraining orders help battered women in ways other than increasing police responsiveness or deterring violent men; "the process is (or can be) the empowerment." The authors of the study, Molly Chaudhuri and Kathleen Daly, stress that "this occurs when attorneys listen to battered women, giving them time and attention, and when judges understand their situation, giving them support and courage." They also observe: "As important, although unfortunately less frequent, women's empowerment can occur when men admit to what they have done in a public forum. Such conversations and admissions can transform the violence from a private familial matter, for which many women blame themselves, to a public setting where men are made accountable for their acts.[34]

The New Haven study underscores the importance of legal representation, another issue that reveals the tension between public and private. Although battered women now have remedies that are available to them "on the books," they have no assured access to lawyers to represent them. Many battered women cannot afford to hire a lawyer. Moreover, few lawyers are sensitive to their particular problems. State statutory schemes do not provide for counsel; indeed, many of the protective-order statutes specifically provide the option for battered women to represent themselves.[35] Battered women's advocates—formerly battered women or shelter workers themselves, usually without formal legal training—are now the link between battered women and the legal system, as well as between battered women and the child welfare and social service systems. For battered women, access to advocates shapes their satisfaction with the legal process.[36] Although battered women's advocacy has played a critical role for battered women and has contributed a woman-centered form of representation, it is necessarily limited. Even what may appear as the narrowest legal question concerning restraining orders may involve complex legal issues that affect divorce, support, and custody. Lack of skilled legal representation to assist in these necessarily interrelated matters has a deleterious impact on battered women's lives and safety.

None of the plethora of new state and federal legal remedies provide free counsel, so battered women's advocates assist many battered women who would not otherwise have had legal representation. Many battered women cannot use these legal remedies. If counsel were required but not provided by the state, those battered women who could not pay for representation would be severely disadvantaged. Only the provision of free counsel by those who are knowledgeable about these issues would make a substantial difference. Thus although in theory more formal legal process for battered women might be preferable, in practice, under the present conditions, of scarce legal resources and cutbacks in legal services, it may not be realistic.

Finally, the complex interrelationship between the private and the public can be seen within the battered women's movement itself. The terms "woman abuse" and "battered woman" did not exist before the movement developed. As Nancy Fraser has observed, "Linguistically, [wife beating] was classified with the disciplining of children and servants as a 'domestic,' as opposed to a 'political' matter." Feminist activists in the battered women's movement named the problem in a different way; they claimed that battering was not a personal, domestic problem but a systemic, political problem. Fraser notes that feminist redefinition of battered women's needs transcended the "conventional separation of sphere": "In order to be free from dependence on batterers, battered women needed not just temporary shelter but also jobs paying a 'family wage,' day care and affordable permanent housing."[37]

The battered women's movement, then, began with a clearly political and public agenda. Battered women were viewed primarily not as individual victims but as potential feminist activists. Activists organized battered women's shelters, which functioned as woman-centered refuges as well as sites of consciousness-raising; the organization of shelters was nonhierarchical and egalitarian, and many formerly battered women went on to become counselors or advocates. Many battered women who blamed themselves for having been abused developed a more political perspective and began to identify with other women rather than with the men who battered them.[38]

As woman abuse became a more legitimate political issue, battered women's organizations and shelters began to receive government funding.

Fraser recounts that "a variety of new, administrative constraints ranging from accounting procedures to regulation, accreditation and professionalization requirements" were imposed.[39] Many organizations began to develop a service perspective rather than to consider themselves activists. This had a substantive impact on the earlier, more explicitly political vision:

> As a consequence, publicly funded shelters underwent a transformation. Increasingly, they were staffed by professional social workers, many of whom had not themselves experienced battery. Thus a division between professional and client supplanted the more fluid continuum of relations that characterized the earlier shelters. Moreover, many social work staff have been trained to frame problems in a quasi-psychiatric perspective. This perspective structures the practices of many publicly funded shelters even despite the intentions of individual staff, many of whom are politically committed feminists. Consequently, the practices of such shelters have become more individualizing and less politicized. Battered women tend now to be positioned as clients. . . . They are only rarely addressed as potential feminist activists. Increasingly, the language game of therapy has supplanted that of consciousness raising. And the neutral scientific language of "spouse abuse" has supplanted more political talk of "male violence against women." Finally, the needs of battered women have been substantially reinterpreted. The very far-reaching earlier claims for the social and economic prerequisites of independence have tended to give way to a narrower focus on the individual woman's problems of "low self esteem."[40]

The battered women's movement has thus experienced the tension between a systemic "public" definition of the problem and an individualistic "privatized" vision. Within the movement and within the service and advocacy community, internal pressures propel the move to a more privatized definition and experience of battering. Claims of privacy encourage a focus on the individual, and they discourage collective definition, systemic analysis, and consequent social responsibility. This tendency has also affected public definitions of battering. The phenomenon of denial, which functions to keep individuals from acknowledging battering as a potential ingredient of all intimate relationships, is at work here as well.

Concepts of public and private have thus had a considerable impact on feminist lawmaking on battering. Rationales invoking privacy pervade and constrain feminist lawmaking. Privacy rhetoric continues to shape law reform and activism in a subtle but powerful way.

Feminist Lawmaking, Violence, and Equality

Generated by visions of women's equality, full citizenship and participation, autonomy, freedom from abuse, and liberty, the legal struggle for battered women has sought to transform the law of intimate violence. Activists and lawyers have used women's diverse experiences of violence, of physical abuse, of coercion and control, of economic threats, and of threats of harm to children and family members as the starting point for the development of legal doctrine and legal theory in courtrooms, legislatures, and classrooms.

The process of feminist lawmaking began with this vision. Lawyers and activists took it as their starting point for the assertion of legal claims. Thirty years later, there have been tremendous accomplishments: public recognition of the seriousness of the problem and legal recognition of many of the harms that generated this work. *Planned Parenthood v. Casey,* and many other cases that are decided every day in courts but never reported, have recognized the harms of intimate violence in a way that did not seem possible thirty years ago. Public education on these issues has been significantly advanced through legal decision making, through the media, and through courses in grade schools, colleges and universities, law schools, medical schools, and in popular culture. Assertion of legal claims concerning battering has advanced "political conversation" concerning women's rights and gender equality. Legal claims concerning battering have exposed new harms, expanded public understanding by labeling what was previously private as public, and made important statements concerning women's autonomy.

Yet, in the dialectical process of lawmaking, these cases have only highlighted political contradictions and emphasized the deeply political nature of these claims. The Supreme Court's decision in *Morrison* is an example. As feminist lawmaking has developed and more directly confronted issues of gender equality, intimate violence has in many ways become more decontextualized. In the very assertion of claims to equal treatment, tensions of victimization and agency and privacy consistently reemerge in the form of resistance to equality. There has been tremendous subversion of the fundamental vision of equality that generated this work.

This process of subversion happens in many ways—in major legal decisions such as *Morrison* and in everyday cases. In order for feminist lawmaking to be successful, lawyers who handle these claims, and judges who rule on them, must be genuinely able to hear them. Yet for lawyers the process of hearing experiences that may be threatening or unfamiliar, of really listening to those experiences and "taking them in" in order to reshape factual examination or theory of the case, is complex and difficult. Lawyers who do not know about the complexity of intimate violence, or who bring to the process of representation biases and misconceptions concerning battered women, are not going to be able to listen. They will dismiss the woman's story as trivial or see the woman as "difficult." Lawyers such as Marcia Clark, the lead prosecutor in the O. J. Simpson case,[41] who have their own demons of violence in their past, may not be able to make important decisions about choice of defense, or the need to pursue certain areas of investigation, because of biases that they have about intimate violence. Judges, too, need to recognize myths and misconceptions concerning battered women; judges who have a history of or experience with violence have their own biases and limitations in ruling on legal claims. For this reason, legal education plays a crucial role in shaping the attitudes of future lawyers and judges who will be handling these cases and in directing the future of feminist lawmaking.

Case studies of battered women who kill and battered women who are mothers highlight generic dimensions of this process of subversion. For battered women generally, but particularly battered women in these situations, it is difficult for both lawyers and judges to see them as "reasonable." Because the experience of battering may be so foreign to many legal decision makers, the fact of being battered alone may make a woman unreasonable in the eyes of her lawyer or the judge ruling on the case. Yet for a woman to kill her male partner brings back the historic view of "treason." A comparison of her situation in killing her partner ("representative of the state" in the household) with that of a man who kills the woman he has beaten (who is viewed as having no independent legal identity), underscores the underlying views of appropriate female conduct that shape these perceptions. Battered women who are mothers are equally maligned, and their circumstances are viewed with horror; they could not have acted "reasonably" if they did not, first and foremost, intervene to protect their child.[42] In both examples we see similar patterns of legal subversion, tendencies toward pathologizing battered women rather than viewing them as reasonable, uses of expert testimony on "battered woman syndrome" that individualize the harm rather than explaining a broader systemic pattern of gender socialization and "coercive control." At the same time there is a tendency to isolate the particular legal circumstance, the fact of the homicide or the relationship between the mother and her child, within a framework that renders invisible the interrelated webs of inequality: the woman's role within the family, her responsibility for children, her economic circumstances.

In the area of innovative law reform, we see similar problems. Current controversies concerning criminal prosecution and mandatory arrest reveal how the criminal justice system removes the woman from this larger context of gender. The legal discourse of "crime control" minimizes the liberatory discourse of inequality. Intimate violence becomes just one other "crime" problem that is unmoored from its social, historical, and cultural context. At the same time, the promise of the civil rights remedy of the Violence against Women Act—to put violence within a framework of equality and gender subordination—has been destroyed. The Supreme Court's decision in *Morrison* reflects similar resistance to the "public" nature of the problem, to the link between violence and liberty, violence and autonomy, violence and women's full participation and citizenship. VAWA II begins to address these issues, linking women's violence to homelessness, housing, and the host of larger gender issues.

Intimate violence has now been recognized as a "public" harm, but it is significant that this recognition is, in a sense, conditioned on a view that intimate violence is an individual problem, not a systemic or social one. Of course, in some sense it is always both an individual and a social problem. Intimate violence is shaped by a larger culture of social violence and is affected by a range of psychosocial factors. It arises in individual circumstances that belie the broader context. But just as feminist reformers in the past viewed male violence as linked to alcohol, our culture wants a quick-fix explanation and denies the link to gender.

What would it take to make things different, to make domestic violence subject to social sanction, to shift the burden of social response from acceptance—even that painful and resigned acceptance that still functions as complicity—into affirmative public rejection? Could feminist lawmaking that describes battered women's experiences with greater accuracy and complexity make a difference and be more effective in making change? Will feminist legal advocacy that more carefully explains women's acts of resistance to violence, and seeks to shift cultural and legal discourse from exclusive focus on the woman's exit to the woman's "resistant self-direction," help? Problems of distancing and denial of domestic violence, reinforced by traditional concepts of privacy and resistance to gender equality, stand in the way of social change.

A conservative interpretation of the reasons for social passivity toward domestic violence is that it is widely viewed as both inevitable and intractable. Intimate violence is at once too personal–because it has the potential to affect all intimate relationships–and too deeply political–because gender roles are so deeply ingrained in our social structure. In 1995 the National Organization for Women held a demonstration in Washington, D.C., protesting violence against women.[43] The demonstration's slogan, "The Power to STOP VIOLENCE Against Women Begins with Me," highlights this contradiction between the private and public dimensions of violence and the dilemma it poses for those who wish to accomplish social change. On the one hand, this slogan is a useful ideological step, for it places the responsibility on individuals to act to stop violence in their own daily lives. On the other hand, it takes the pressure off government to declare domestic violence a public problem, reinforces the historic link between domestic violence and privacy, and affirms individual solutions, individualism generally, and, perhaps inadvertently, individual self-blaming at the expense of collective action. Individuals do have the power to stop violence in individual circumstances, and to actively participate in social condonation, but government has the power and responsibility to transform social norms, provide resources, and ensure safety. So while the slogan stresses the necessity for personal responsibility, it also seems to endorse the privatization "solutions" for social problems that have characterized the last decade.

We deny that battering and woman abuse is the inevitable product of a culture that raises young girls to "stand by their man" no matter what, to put men first, and to make the "magic of love" the most important thing. Given a culture that still emphasizes marriage as far more important for women than for men, that places primary responsibility on women to keep the family together, that blames mothers for any problem in the family, it is a miracle that women ever leave abusive and controlling relationships when the risk to their lives and their children's lives may be so great. And when women stay in abusive relationships, as our culture has told them to do, we render invisible their heroic efforts to keep themselves and their children alive. Until we acknowledge and seek to change this broader cultural complicity and frame legal and social remedies for abuse within the problem of gender socialization and appropriate gender roles, little will change.

The thirty-year history of feminist lawmaking on battering reveals both the affirmative vision of equality, liberty, and freedom that has shaped legal strategy and decision making and the inevitable limitations of legal reform that does not take gender into account. Until we see violence squarely linked to gender and situate the problem of abuse within broader problems of gender subordination, thus reaffirming this historic link between violence and equality and making the promise of equality real, we will not and cannot move forward.

NOTES

1. Much of this chapter is excerpted from Elizabeth M. Schneider, *Battered Women and Feminist Lawmaking* (New Haven: Yale University Press, 2000). Copyright © 2000 Yale University Press. Reprinted with permission. It has been updated in light of recent developments. The section "The Violence of Privacy" is taken from "The Violence of Privacy" 23 *Connecticut Law Review* (1991): 973.

2. *Planned Parenthood v. Casey*, 505 U.S. 833, 891–2 (1992).

3. Wendy Webster Williams, "Fixing Locke: Liberal Orthodoxies and the Feminist Challenge to Intimate Violence" (manuscript on file with the author, 1998).

4. Clare Dalton and Elizabeth M. Schneider, *Battered Women and the Law* (New York: Foundation Press, 2001).

5. The Violence Women Act of 1994 provided for criminal offenses against interstate stalking and domestic abuse, a civil rights remedy for gender-motivated violence, and grants for community programs on domestic violence, battered women's shelters, and rape prevention and education. VAWA II grants money for programs preventing on-campus sexual assaults, provides transitional housing for domestic violence victims, has a host of provisions that affect battered immigrant women, and increases funding services for battered women. For a discussion of VAWA I and VAWA II, see Angela M. Killian, "Mandatory Minimum Sentences Coupled With Multi-Facet Interventions: An Effective Response to Domestic Violence," *UDC/DSCL Law Review* 6, no. 1(2001): 51, 61, 63; Leslye Orloff and Janice Kaguyutan, "Offering a Helping Hand: Legal Protections for Battered Immigrant Women: A History of Legislative Responses," *American University Journal of Gender, Social Policy and the Law* 10 (2001): 95.

6. 529 U.S. 598 (2000).

7. Reva Siegel, " 'The Rule of Love': Wife Beating as Prerogative and Privacy," *Yale Law Journal* 105 (1996): 2117, 2196–2206. See also Victoria Nourse, "Passion's Progress: Modern Law Reform and the Provocation Defense," *Yale Law Journal* 106 (1997): 1331.

8. 489 U.S. 189 (1989).

9. Nadine Taub and Elizabeth M. Schneider, "Women's Subordination and the Role of Law," in David Kairys, ed., *The Politics of Law*, 3rd. ed. (New York: Pantheon, 1982), 117, 118–24.

10. Id. at 121–22.

11. Linda Kerber, "Separate Spheres, Female Worlds, Women's Place: The Rhetoric of Women's History," *Journal of American History* 75 (1988): 9, 17; Alan Freeman and Elizabeth Mensch, "The Public-Private Distinction in American Law and Life," *Buffalo Law Review* 36 (1987): 237; Martha Minow, "Adjudicating Differences: Conflicts Among Feminist Lawyers," in Marianne Hirsch and Evelyn Fox Keller, eds., *Conflicts in Feminism* (New York: Routledge, 1990), 156–160 (; Symposium, "The Public/Private Distinction," *University of Pennsylvania Law Review* 130 (1982): 1289.

12. Frances Olsen, "The Family and the Market: A Story of Ideology and Legal Reform," *Harvard Law* Review 96 (1983): 1497, 1507, n. 39; 1537.

13. The dichotomy of women as private and men as public changes when women are childbearers. In *Muller v. Oregon*, 208 U.S. 412, 421 (1908), the Supreme Court emphasized that "as healthy mothers are essential to vigorous offspring, the physical well-being of woman becomes an object of public interest and care in order to preserve the strength and vigor of the race."

14. Taub and Schneider, "Perspectives on Women's Subordination," 122–23.

15. Catharine M. MacKinnon, *Toward a Feminist Theory of the State* (Cambridge: Harvard University Press, 1989); Rhonda Copelon, "Unpacking Patriarchy: Reproduction, Sexuality, Originalism and Constitutional Change," in Jules Lobel, ed., *A Less Than Perfect Union: Alternative Perspectives on the U.S. Constitution* (New York: Monthly Review Press, 1988), 303; Minow, "Adjudicating Differences."

16. Anita Allen's work has explored the importance of privacy to women. See Anita Allen, *Uneasy Access: Privacy for Women in a Free Society* (Totowa, N.J.: Rowman and Littlefield, 1988): 70–72. Allen has subsequently emphasized that these aspects of privacy must be preserved in legal remedies for intimate violence. Anita Allen, "Coercing Privacy," *William and Mary Law Review* 40 (1999): 723, 746.

17. Frank Michelman, "Private, Personal but Not Split: *Radin v. Rorty*," *Southern California Law Review* 63 (1990): 1783, 1974.

18. Martha Mahoney's article "Legal Images of Battered Women: Redefining the Issue of Separation," *Michigan Law Review* 90 (1991): 1, shaped my development of this section. For an exploration of the phenomenon of denial and the importance of naming violence generally, see Liz Kelly, "How Women Define Their Experiences of Violence," in Kersti Yllö and Michele Bograd, eds., *Feminist Perspectives on Wife Abuse* (Newbury Park, CA: Sage, 1988), 114–31.

19. For a discussion of jurors' attitudes toward battered women, see Elizabeth Bochnak, Elissa Krauss, Susie McPherson, Susan Sternberg, and Diane Wiley, "Case Preparation and Development," in Elizabeth Bochnak, ed., *Women's Self - Defense Cases: Theory and Practice* (Charlottesville, Va.: Michie, 1981); Neil Vidmar and Shari Seidman Diamond, "Juries and Expert Evidence," *Brooklyn Law Review* 66 (2001): 1121, 1165–66. See also Regina A. Schuller, "The Impact of Battered Women Syndrome Evidence on Jury Decision Processes," *Law and Human Behavior* 16 (1992): 597; Regina A. Schuller and Janice Cripps, "Expert Evidence Pertaining to Battered Women: The Impact of Gender of Expert and Timing of Testimony," *Law and Human Behavior* 22 17 (1998): 22; Neil Vidmar and Regina A. Schuller, "Juries and Expert Evidence: Social Framework Testimony," *Law and Contemporary Problems* 52 (1989): 133.

20. The Joel Steinberg-Hedda Nussbaum case involved the murder of their daughter, Lisa Steinberg, who was beaten to death by Joel Steinberg. This case focused on examination of Hedda Nussbaum as both a victim of abuse and a bad mother. See Ronald Sullivan, "Defense Tries to Show Nussbaum Liked Pain" *New York Times*, December 9, 1988, B2.

21. See, e.g., "Report of the New York Task Force on Women in the Courts," *Fordham Urban Law Journal* 15 (1986): 11; "First Year Report of the New Jersey Supreme Court Task Force on Women in the Courts," *Women's Rights Law Reporter* 9 (1986): 129; "Report of the Gender Bias Study of the Court System in Massachusetts," *New England Law Review* 24 (1990): 745. See also Ariella Hyman and Sarah Eaton, "The Domestic Violence Component of the New York Task Force Report on Women In The Courts: An Empirical Evaluation and Assessment of New York City Courts," *Fordham Urban Law Journal* 19 (1992): 391.

22. Martha Minow, "Words and the Door to the Land of Change: Law, Language, and Family Violence," *Vanderbilt Law Review* 43 (1990): 1665, 1671–72.

23. Id. At 1671.

24. *Deshaney v. Winnebago County Department of Social Services*, 489 U.S. 189 (1989). For a thoughtful analysis of *DeShaney*, see Minow, "Words and the Door," 1666–1676. *DeShaney* has made it difficult for victims of woman abuse to bring §1983

claims against the state for failure to protect them from battering. Courts have rejected substantive due-process claims, which are typically based on the alleged existence of a "special relationship" between the victims and the state (whether as a result of previous knowledge of the harm women faced at the hands of their abusers or because the state had issued a protective order), as incompatible with *Deshaney*. See, e.g., *Hynson v. City of Chester*, 731 F.Supp. 1236, 1239 (E.D. Pa. 1990); *Dudosh v. City of Allentown*, 722 F.Supp. 1233, 1235 (E.D.Pa. 1989). As a result of the diminishing availability, after *DeShaney*, of §1983 due-process claims based on the notion of a special relationship, battered women have had to develop alternative theories to sue the state for its failure to protect them, such as equal protection, claims that the state had failed adequately to train its agents in domestic violence situations, or claims based on state tort law. See *Soto v. Flores*, 103 F.3d 1056 (1st Cir. 1997), *cert. denied* 522 U.S. 819 (1997).

25. On civil remedies, see Peter Finn, "Statutory Authority in the Use and Enforcement of Civil Protection Orders Against Domestic Abuse," *Family Law Quarterly* 23 (1989); on criminal remedies, see Marion Wanless, "Mandatory Arrest: A Step Toward Eradicating Domestic Violence, But Is It Enough?" *University of Illinois Law Review* 1996 (1996): 533, 554–57.

26. For example, Mo.Rev.Stat. §488.445 (Supp. 1997) authorizes a surcharge of five dollars for a marriage license, to go toward domestic violence shelters. Fees have been imposed on marriage licenses to establish, maintain, and fund shelters for battered women or domestic violence programs in several other states. See Ala. Code §§30–6-11 (1999); N.J. Stat. Ann. §§37:1–12.2 (West 1999). Some marriage license statutes have been upheld in the face of constitutional challenges on a range of grounds. See, e.g., *Villars v. Provo*, 440 N.W.2d 160 (Minn. Ct. App. 1989). Others have been struck down as unconstitutional. See, e.g., *Safety Net for Abused Persons v. Seglura*, 692 So.2d 1038 (La. 1997).

27. See Karla Fischer, Neil Vidmar, and Rene Ellis, "The Culture of Battering and the Role of Mediation in Domestic Violence Cases," *Southern Methodist University Law Review* 46 (1993): 2117; Barbara Hart, "Gentle Jeopardy: The Further Endangerment of Battered Women and Children in Custody Mediation," *Mediation Quarterly* 7 (1990): 317; Lisa Lerman, "Mediation of Wife Abuse Cases: The Adverse Impact of Informal Dispute Resolution on Women," *Harvard Women's Law Journal* 7 (1984): 57, 88–89. For a more general analysis of the problems that mediation poses for women, see Trina Grillo, "The Mediation Alternative: Process Dangers for Women," *Yale Law Journal* 100 (1991): 1545. But see Donna Coker, "Enhancing Autonomy for Battered Women: Lessons from Navajo Peacemaking," *UCLA Law Review* 47 (1999): 1, arguing that methods of informal adjudication, such as Navajo peacemaking, should be considered. See generally Dalton and Schneider, *Battered Women and the Law* (2001).

28. See Clare Dalton, "Domestic Violence, Domestic Torts and Divorce: Constraints and Possibilities," *New England Law Review* 31 (1997): 319. See also *Giovine v. Giovine*, 663 A.2d 109 (N.J. 1995) (holding that a wife can sue for prolonged acts of battering throughout a marriage, and that damages may take into account both physical and emotional injury).

29. Several states have civil rights statutes that protect citizens from violence motivated by the victim's gender. It is arguable that these statutes may provide civil rights remedies for victims of domestic violence. See CA Pen. Code § 422.6 (West 1992); Mass. Gen. Laws Ann ch. 265 § 37 (West 1990); Wash. Rev. Code Ann. § 9A.36.080 (West 1998). The Violence Against Women Act of 1994 also defined gender bias as a civil rights violation in Title III of the act. For discussion of domestic violence as an international human rights violation, see generally Dorothy O. Thomas and Michele E. Beasley, "Domestic Violence as a Human Rights Issue, *Albany Law Review* 58 (1995): 1119; Joan Fitzpatrick, "The Use of International Human Rights Norms to Combat Violence Against Women," in Rebecca J. Cook, ed., *Human Rights of Women: National and International Perspectives* (Philadelphia: University of Pennsylvania Press, 1994), 532–571. For the articulation of battering as involuntary servitude, see Joyce E. McConnell, "Beyond Metaphor: Battered Women, Involuntary Servitude and the Thirteenth Amendment," *Yale Journal of Law and Feminism* 4 (1992): 207.

30. Siegel, "Rule of Love," 2117, 2206–2207.

31. See Sally F. Goldfarb, "Violence Against Women and the Persistence of Privacy," *Ohio State Law Journal* 61 (2000): 1; Sally F. Goldfarb, " 'No Civilized System of Justice': The Fate of the Violence Against Women Act," *West Virginia Law Review* 102 (2000): 499; Judith Resnik, "Categorical Federalism: Jurisdiction, Gender and the Globe," *Yale Law Journal* 111 (2001): 619.

32. Judith Resnik, "Due Process: A Public Dimension," *University of Florida Law Review* 39 (1987): 405, 419.

33. Nevertheless, the media have focused on cases involving battered women who have killed their assailants rather than on the "ordinary" cases of battered women who cannot get into shelters, cannot get restraining orders, or may risk losing custody of their children for failing to protect them from the batterer. Emphasis on these situations would direct public attention on the battering man and on the failure of social responsibility. See Molly Chaudhuri and Kathleen Daly, " 'Do Restraining Orders Help?' Battered Women's Experience with Male Violence and Legal Process," in Eve Buzawa, ed., *Domestic Violence: The Changing Criminal Justice Response* (Westport, Conn.: Auburn House, 1992).

34. Chaudhari and Daly, id.

35. Most civil restraining order statutes have no provisions for counsel and are designed for *pro se* applicants. Though legal advocates are bridging the representational gap in new and creative ways, battered women are still in desperate need of adequate legal representation because civil restraining order litigation inevitably involves issues of custody, support, and visitation. See Elizabeth M. Schneider, "Legal Reform Efforts to Assist Battered Women: Past Present, and Future" (1990), unpublished manuscript on file with author; Kathleen Waits, "Battered Women and Family Lawyers: The Need for an Identification Protocol," *Albany Law Review* 58 (1995): 1027; Linda Mills, "On the Other Side of Silence: Affective Lawyering for Intimate Abuse," *Cornell Law Review* 81 (1996): 1225. For a discussion of the problem of legal representation in restraining order litigation, see Finn and Colson, *Civil Protection*

Orders (Washington, D.C.: U.S. Department of Justice, National Institute of Justice, Office of Justice Programs, 1990).

36. James Ptacek, *Battered Women in the Courtroom: The Power of Judicial Response* (Boston: Northeastern University Press, 1999), 177–178. Ptacek's study of battered women and the restraining order process in Massachusetts found that "fully 70 percent of the women in Quincy mentioned advocates . . . as the most helpful aspects of the restraining order process" (177). Ptacek emphasizes the importance of woman-defined advocacy, which "builds a partnership between advocates and battered women and ultimately has each battered woman defining the advocacy and help she needs" (citing Jill Davies, Eleanor Lyon, and Diane Monti-Catania, *Safety Planning for Battered Women: Complex Lives, Difficult Choices*, Sage Series on Violence Against Women, vol. 7 [Newbury Park, CA: Sage, 1998]).

37. Nancy Fraser, "Struggle Over Needs: Outline of a Socialist-Feminist Critical Theory of Late-Capitalist Political Culture," in Linda Gordon, ed., *Women, the State, and Welfare* (Madison: University of Wisconsin Press, 1990), 199, 213–214.

38. Id. at 214.

39. Id.

40. Id. at 214–225.

41. See Schneider, *Battered Women and Feminist Lawmaking*, chapter 11, for a discussion of the Simpson case and Marcia Clark's admission concerning her own experience with domestic violence and the way in which it impacted on the prosecution of the case.

42. See id., chapter 9 on motherhood and battering; see generally Dalton and Schneider, *Battered Women and the Law.*

43. The National Organization for Women estimated the number of demonstrators to be 250,000, making this the largest rally ever held protesting violence against women. Jennifer Gonnerman, "Lights, Camera, Protest," *Village Voice* 14 (April 18, 1995).

CHAPTER 13

Infringements of Women's Constitutional Rights in Religious Lawmaking on Abortion

The legitimacy of enacting, validating, interpreting, applying, or enforcing legally binding regulations on the basis of religious considerations ("religious lawmaking") has been debated since the founding of our nation. Yet neither the Supreme Court nor scholars who have considered the matter have developed an approach to addressing religious lawmaking that accords due consideration to, and respect for, the constitutional rights and interests of *women* who are involved in the issue (what I will refer to here as "citizenship rights"). Instead, judicial and scholarly approaches share a virtual blindness to the significance of gender and power inequalities embedded in the practice of religious lawmaking. Although the most blatant forms of gender inequality have been eliminated from law and from many religious traditions as well, more subtle forms of exclusion, marginalization, and subordination of women are still operative in both institutions.

These injustices are magnified in religious lawmaking because the coercive power of the state is brought to bear to enforce a gender ideology often proclaimed to be divinely ordained or sanctioned, if not mandated, by religious institutions. In order to consider such rights, I will focus in this chapter on the debate over religious lawmaking as it has involved the issue of reproductive rights. Citizenship rights relevant to religious lawmaking on abortion especially include those rights protected by the Fourteenth Amendment's substantive due process and equal protection clauses and the First Amendment religion clauses, which protect the free exercise of religion and prohibit "the establishment of religion."

In this chapter I begin by briefly describing some of the ways in which religion has influenced the process of lawmaking on abortion, with the consequence of infringing upon women's citizenship rights. I then describe how the Supreme Court's decisions in this area have failed to protect these rights from infringement by religious lawmaking on abortion. Finally, I propose a practical legal framework for addressing the constitutional problems that religious lawmaking engenders for women. These problems are indicative of the inadequacies of the U.S. Constitution for addressing women's rights more generally.

Religious Influences on Abortion Lawmaking

Religious influences on abortion lawmaking are often conspicuous. For example, among Supreme Court cases involving abortion lawmaking, three stand out as notable. First, in *Harris v. McRae*,[1] religious influence is evident in the legislative history and background to the Hyde Amendment, an abortion law that significantly restricts women's exercise of their citizenship rights. In a second case, *Webster v. Reproductive Health Services*,[2] religious assumptions are evidenced in the language used to frame abortion restrictions in a state abortion statute. And in a third case, *Bowen v. Kendrick*,[3] religious influence is suggested in the provisions of the federal Adolescent Family Life Act (AFLA) statute related to religiously affiliated grantees.

The history of restrictive abortion laws illustrates that they were premised on views that are central in several world religions—views of women as "child rearers" and as "destined solely for the home and the rearing of the family."[4] The identification of abortion with religious morality has, to a great extent, been due to efforts by the Roman Catholic Church to outlaw abortion.[5]

Among the many religiously influenced restrictions on abortion that Congress has enacted since *Roe v. Wade*, which established a woman's constitutional right to choose whether or not to terminate a first or second trimester pregnancy in 1973, one of the most striking and controversial has been the Hyde Amendment. First enacted in 1976, the initial version of the Hyde Amendment prohibited the use of Medicaid funds for abortions "except where the life of the mother would be endangered if the fetus were carried to term."[6] Some form of the amendment has been enacted every subsequent year as a rider to an appropriations bill, generally permitting exceptions only if the woman's life is endangered or the pregnancy is the result of rape or incest. Since Medicaid is provided only to those living in poverty, the effect of the Hyde Amendment has been to enhance discrimination against poor women.

The legislative history of the congressional debates on the Hyde Amendment clearly reflects the role that religion played in passage of the law.[7] A research study of votes by members of the House of Representatives on the original Hyde Amendment revealed that religion was the second most significant factor influencing voting behavior, following party affiliation.[8] Several congresspersons during the hearings on the Hyde Amendment made explicit reference to religion and religious themes in expressing their opposition to abortion.[9] Many pro-life congresspersons used explicit references to God in their arguments. Pro-choice congresspersons also used religious references to argue to a contrary conclusion. They also referred to their own religious convictions, as well as those of their constituents.

The tendency of religious lawmakers to discount or denigrate women's experience is also evident in these congressional debates. Consideration of women was almost completely absent from their testimony. When women were mentioned, it was generally in negative terms, reflecting the lawmakers' opinions that women are untrustworthy, irresponsible, and even dangerous.[10]

In addition to the impact of religion *within* the congressional debates on the Hyde Amendment, religious groups lobbied hard from the outside, in favor of the proposed amendment. For example, pursuant to the Catholic Church's Pastoral Plan for Pro-Life Activities, Church leaders encouraged their parishioners to support the amendment and to lobby their legislators in favor of it. Evidence suggests that these efforts were partially responsible for the amendment's passage.[11] In addition to the Hyde Amendment, Congress has enacted a number of other religiously influenced restrictions on abortion in the years following *Roe v. Wade*, including the legislation at issue in the Supreme Court cases I will discuss shortly. Conservative Christian congresspersons were instrumental in the passage of much of this legislation.[12]

Infringements of Religious Lawmaking on Women's Constitutional Rights and Interests

Religious lawmaking presents two general types of constitutional problems. First, it may raise the problems of alienation, exclusion, coercion, and political divisiveness that principles of church-state separation underlying the Establishment Clause (what I here call "establishment concerns") were designed to address. Second, it may abridge other citizenship rights protected by the Constitution. In the abortion cases involving religious lawmaking that the Supreme Court has decided, it has failed to give adequate consideration to the extent to which religious lawmaking implicates citizenship rights. I will discuss four of these in particular, the first two under the First Amendment's religion clauses.

1. *Establishment Clause*: The Establishment Clause is relevant to religious lawmaking in two ways: one, when core principles of the Establishment

Clause have been violated; and two, when religious lawmaking infringes upon the establishment concerns of alienation, exclusion, coercion, and political divisiveness, factors that alone may not rise to the level of a full-fledged violation of the Establishment Clause.

The Supreme Court originally stated that the purpose of the Establishment Clause was "to erect a wall of separation between Church and State."[13] In *Walz v. Tax Commission*, the Supreme Court characterized the three main evils against which the Establishment Clause was intended to protect as "sponsorship, financial support, and active involvement of the sovereign in religious activity."[14] Religiously influenced laws may implicate the state in all three of these prohibited activities. The latter is especially pertinent to religious lawmaking, which involves government in religious activities.

In *Lemon v. Kurtzman*, the Court added that the Establishment Clause was also designed to protect against "political division along religious lines,"[15] another danger presented when laws are based on or influenced by religious considerations. The Court in *Lemon* noted that the history of many countries "attests to the hazards of religious intrusion into the political arena."[16] Justice O'Connor's oft-quoted statement in *Lynch v. Donnelly* recognized that "direct government action endorsing religion or a particular religious practice is invalid . . . because it sends a message to nonadherents that they are outsiders, not full members of the political community, and an accompanying message to adherents that they are insiders, favored members of the political community."[17]

Thus the Court has recognized in a general way that religious lawmaking presents establishment concerns, although it has seldom invalidated such lawmaking in the context of abortion regulation. In *Webster v. Reproductive Health Services*,[18] the Supreme Court upheld a Missouri abortion statute against a challenge to its constitutionality based on the Establishment Clause. The preamble to the Missouri abortion law at issue in *Webster* contained "findings" of the legislature that "The life of each human being begins at conception" and "unborn children have protectable interests in life, health, and well-being."[19] The act required that all Missouri laws be interpreted to provide "unborn children" with the same rights as "other persons" and included a number of restrictions on abortion. The Court found the preamble's language facially unobjectionable, since it "does not by its terms regulate abortion" and merely expresses Missouri's legitimate "value judgment favoring childbirth over abortion."

Bowen v. Kendrick[20] involved a constitutional challenge to the Adolescent Family Life Act brought by a group of federal taxpayers, clergymen, and the American Jewish Congress on Establishment Clause grounds. AFLA includes a restriction on abortion rights that indicates religious influences factored into its enactment in providing that grants may be made only to programs or projects that do not provide abortions or abortion counseling or referral "or subcontract with anyone who does," except where a pregnant adolescent and her parents request such referral.[21] The influence of religion is not apparent in the language of the statue; rather, it is apparent in its effects, since AFLA enables religious organizations to receive grants and requires that grant applicants specify how they will "involve religious and charitable organizations" in their provision of services.

A number of grants funded pursuant to the act have been given to organizations affiliated with religious institutions, raising potential Establishment Clause concerns about excessive entanglements between church and state. In particular, the act as written "makes it possible for religiously affiliated grantees to teach adolescents on issues that can be considered 'fundamental elements of religious doctrine'" and "the teaching of 'religion qua religion,'"[22] thereby involving government in financially supporting and endorsing religious influences on the adolescents served pursuant to the act.[23] The district court in *Bowen* upheld the plaintiffs' Establishment Clause challenge, but the Supreme Court reversed in *Bowen v. Kendrick*.[24]

2. *Free Exercise Clause*: In addition to raising establishment concerns, and potentially violating the Establishment Clause's core requirement of government neutrality toward religion, religious lawmaking often infringes upon rights protected by the First Amendment's Free Exercise Clause. In an oft-quoted passage, the Supreme Court declared that the Free Exercise Clause means that "no official, high or petty, can prescribe what shall be orthodox in politics, nationalism, religion, or other matters of opinion or force citizens to confess by word or act their faith therein."[25] The principle underlying this constitutional provision—that citizens should not be disadvantaged by government on the basis of their religion— is directly applicable to protecting citizens against the disadvantaging effects of religious lawmaking.

Any government policy that promotes, endorses, or disadvantages religion, or involves an excessive entanglement in religious matters, may infringe upon the free exercise rights of nonbelievers and disbelievers.[26] Although this principle has seldom been applied by the Court to invalidate religious lawmaking, the disproportionate representation of certain dominant Christian faiths in government suggests that religious lawmaking is likely to infringe upon the free exercise and other citizenship rights and interests of citizens from minority religious traditions, who are more likely to be lacking in political power, as the historical legal treatment of Mormon and Native American Indian religious beliefs illustrates.[27]

Regarding abortion cases, the majority of the Court in *Planned Parenthood v. Casey*[28] recognized the coercive function of restrictive abortion laws on women's free exercise rights by referring to the pregnant women's suffering as "too intimate and personal for the state to insist, without more, upon its own vision of the woman's role, however dominant that vision has been in the course of our history and our culture."[29] As noted, the coercion is more likely to result in women's disempowerment and disrespect when the state's decision is made by a male lawmaker and is based on the tenets of a patriarchal religious tradition.

Nonetheless, courts have seldom recognized women's reproductive rights as having Free Exercise Clause dimensions. One exception is the federal district court in *McRae v. Califano*, which invalidated the constitutionality of the Hyde Amendment under the Free Exercise Clause,[30] finding that it prevented some women from making abortion decisions in accordance with their religious beliefs or conscience. The Supreme Court reversed in *Harris v. McRae*,[31] ruling that in order to be eligible to claim that her Free Exercise rights had been violated by state restrictions on Medicaid funding for abortions, a pregnant woman must be able to show "that she sought an abortion under compulsion of religious belief" while pregnant and eligible to receive Medicaid.[32] Although the district court had determined that an organized effort of institutional religions to influence the vote on the amendment may have been decisive, the Supreme Court held that this was irrelevant since the Church lacked a monopoly on influencing passage of the Amendment. Despite the Supreme Court's ruling in this case, it seems evident that religious lawmaking is constitutionally problematic under both of the First Amendment religion clauses.

Other Citizenship Rights

In addition to the potential to run afoul of the First Amendment religion clauses, religious lawmaking may infringe upon or even directly violate citizenship rights protected by other constitutional provisions, especially the Fifth and Fourteenth amendments' guarantees of equal protection and due process.[33] The Due Process and Equal Protection clauses bar government from enacting laws that infringe on fundamental rights or classify persons in certain "suspect classes" without a compelling state interest for doing so. Religious lawmaking on abortion may infringe upon both of these rights.

1. *Substantive Due Process*: The Due Process Clause protects individual rights of liberty and privacy from unwarranted interference by government. In general, when government regulations burden rights deemed to be "fundamental," the state must show that it has a "compelling interest" for imposing the regulation, one that cannot be satisfied by less restrictive or burdensome means. The Supreme Court has interpreted the Due Process Clause to pro-

vide protection for individual rights not specifically enumerated in the Bill of Rights, including procreative decisions relating to contraceptive use, abortion, and marriage.[34] These cases are similar to those the Court has decided under the Free Exercise Clause in extending protection to personal decisions involving matters of integral importance to self-identity, which certainly includes the religious convictions of other citizens.

Among the most important of these personal decisions is a pregnant woman's decision whether or not to carry the fetus to term. In *Roe v. Wade*,[35] the Supreme Court determined that this right to privacy is a fundamental constitutional right, itself an aspect of the liberty guaranteed by substantive due process. In *Casey v. Planned Parenthood*, the Court stated that "the destiny of the woman must be shaped to a large extent on her own conception of her spiritual imperatives and her place in society," rather than "formed under compulsion of the State."[36] Restrictive abortion laws based on traditional religious patriarchal understandings about the proper status and roles of women are especially likely to discount or ignore women's rights and interests, and thereby run afoul of these constitutional protections.

2. *Equal Protection Clause.* In addition to implicating due process rights, religious lawmaking may infringe upon constitutional rights to the "equal protection of the laws." If government actions that classify or differentiate among individuals burden a fundamental right or involve a "suspect" classification, then they are subject to the "compelling state interest" test described above.[37]

The Court has recognized that restrictive abortion laws infringe upon women's rights to equal protection, especially when they are premised on the underlying stereotyped assumption that women can be forced to accept motherhood as a natural aspect of their role,[38] a view of women held by many religious traditions. As Justice Blackmun's dissent in *Casey* recognized, restrictive abortion laws "force upon women the physical labor and specific and direct medical and psychological harms that may accompany carrying a fetus to term," thereby forcing women to seek illegal abortions or self-abortions at the risk of physical injury or even death, "all in the name of enforced morality or religious dictates or lack of compassion, as it may be."[39]

Such restrictions violate the Equal Protection Clause because they impose roles on women that have historically contributed to their subjugation while not imposing comparable controls on men, without a compelling basis for doing so.[40] In addition, the exclusion of women from the formulation and interpretation of religious views on the morality and legality of abortion has meant that these views have in general not reflected careful consideration of the needs and interests of those persons most significantly affected by the legality of abortion, contrary to the principles of equal representation embedded in the Fourteenth Amendment.

Problems With Supreme Court Decisions on the Constitutionality of Religious Lawmaking

The Supreme Court has confirmed the relevance of both the First and Fourteenth Amendments to the issue of religious lawmaking. Yet its decisions in cases involving religiously influenced abortion regulations have not adequately upheld the rights of citizens protected by these constitutional provisions. The three cases discussed above—*Harris v. McRae, Webster v. Reproductive Health Services,* and *Bowen v. Kendrick*—illustrate the range of problems in the Supreme Court's analysis of religious lawmaking.

The problems with the Court's decisions in these three cases can be roughly categorized into the following types: first is a failure to uphold citizenship rights against infringements by religiously influenced lawmaking. Second is a lack of recognition or acknowledgment of the relevance of establishment concerns to the violation of citizenship rights. And third is the imposition of unduly burdensome standing requirements, which has the effect of obstructing access to the courts to challenge instances of religious lawmaking when it infringes upon citizenship rights.

Evidence of the first problem is the Court's unwillingness in these cases to consider evidence that the efforts of religious institutions had a direct influence on passage of legislation, in violation of the Establishment Clause. In addition, the Court failed to further interrogate the possible religion clause violations of laws that "happen . . . to coincide or harmonize with the tenets of some or all religions."[41] Instead, the Court merely assumed, rather than substantiated, its position that the government's stated interest in the protection of potential life reflected a valid secular purpose rather than a religious one, as required by the Court's interpretations of the Establishment Clause. Contrary to the majority opinion, Justice Stevens's dissent in *Webster* found the Missouri abortion statute's preamble invalid under the Establishment Clause, as endorsing "the theological position that there is the same secular interest in preserving the life of a fetus during the first 40 or 80 days of pregnancy as there is after viability."[42] Stevens characterized the preamble as "an unequivocal endorsement of a religious tenet of some but by no means all Christian faiths, [which] serves no identifiable secular purpose."[43]

With respect to the values protected by the Establishment Clause, in *Webster* the Court failed to examine how explicitly religious language in abortion legislation infringes on interests in maintaining secular laws.[44] Similarly, in *Bowen*, the Court declared a statute regulating abortion—which evidenced both religious and secular motivations—to have a "primary secular purpose" rather than investigating whether it could be *fully* supported on the basis of secular reasons.[45] The *Bowen* Court also failed to recognize the potential of government subsidies in the federal Adolescent Family Life Act for programs that include explicit religious teachings to result in entangling government with religion by supporting the dissemination of religious messages.

The second major problem with the Court's decisions in the cases we have considered thus far is their failure to recognize establishment concerns. First, the decision in *Bowen* overlooks the risk of alienation of nonbelievers in connection with legislation enabling religious organizations to receive grants and encouraging grant applicants to involve religious organizations in their provision of services to adolescents, especially those alleged to be teaching religious values under the auspices of a federally funded program. The Court also has ignored the establishment concerns of alienation and exclusion created when the religious character of legislation is linked to a specific religious tradition, such as with those of the Roman Catholic Church underlying the Hyde Amendment in the *Harris* case. These cases are inconsistent with the Court's earlier decisions on public funding of religious schools, which held that the Establishment Clause prohibits "government-financed or government-sponsored indoctrination into the beliefs of a particular religious faith."[46] In addition, the Court also has ignored the symbolic link created between government and religion (and thus the potential for political divisiveness and other establishment concerns) when legislation is directed to or involves specifically religious organizations[47] or is coercive of pregnant women who do not share the state's religiously defined views of fetal life (*Webster*), especially given the Court's recognition of symbolic linkages between government and religion as a ground for invalidating laws in other Establishment Clause cases.[48] As Justice Stevens's dissent in *Webster* recognizes, "the preamble read in context threatens serious encroachments upon the liberty of the pregnant woman."[49] The Court's failure adequately to take account of the damaging effects of religiously influenced legislation signals a need to revise how religious lawmaking is assessed under the Constitution.

A third problem with the Court's decisions in cases involving religious lawmaking is its failure to protect the citizenship rights protected by constitutional provisions other than the religion clauses. In the cases we have considered, the Court has ignored how religiously motivated legislation may violate pregnant women's liberty and privacy interests, protected by the Due Process guarantees, in deciding whether to terminate their pregnancies. In addition, the Court in *Webster* and *Harris* has refused to recognize the equal protection violations in statutory prohibitions on funding abortions for indigent women.[50]

In sum, the Court's approach to religion clause jurisprudence, especially in the area of abortion regulation, has been inattentive to the distinctive harms that religiously based or influenced laws may cause to the free exercise and other citizenship rights of women and religious minorities. In the following section I suggest some ways that these deficiencies in the Supreme Court's jurisprudence on religious lawmaking might be remedied.

Practical Legal Framework for Addressing Religious Lawmaking

To address adequately the constitutional problems raised by religious lawmaking, the Court's traditional test for Establishment Clause violations should be expanded so as to invalidate religiously influenced laws in a limited range of circumstances when establishment concerns are present and infringements upon citizenship rights cannot be fully justified by a secular rationale. The detailed description of this proposed model for adjudicating cases involving religious lawmaking can be found elsewhere.[51]

A few features, however, deserve note here. First, once a complainant has met his or her burden of establishing that a law has been based on or influenced by religious considerations *and* has effects that are alienating, exclusionary, coercive, and/or politically divisive, *i.e.*, raises establishment concerns, the state should be required to show that it has a substantial secular justification or rationale for the proposed law, analogous to the middle-tier level of scrutiny that the Court applies in gender discrimination cases. The purpose of requiring that laws bear a specifically *religious* influence is to justify the use of liberalized standing requirements and lower burdens of persuasion than are required in cases not presenting issues of religious lawmaking. The contention here is that religious influences add an additional risk that the challenged lawmaking may infringe (or has already infringed) upon citizenship rights, thereby justifying lowered standing and burden of proof requirements.

In addition, requiring that the party challenging the law show how religion was implicated serves the purpose of ensuring that whatever establishment concerns are present—risks of alienation, coercion, exclusion, or political divisiveness—have resulted from specifically *religious* influences. Restrictive abortion regulations that are *not* based on religious considerations, such as the AFLA at issue in *Bowen v. Kendrick*, certainly may be alienating, coercive, and politically divisive. However, it is the *combination* of religion with restrictive regulations, not *either* religious influence or restrictiveness alone, that justifies the application of a higher degree of scrutiny than the Court has traditionally accorded under its interpretations of the Establishment Clause.

Second, if the petitioner is not only successful in satisfying this requirement, but is also able to show that the religious lawmaking infringes upon a constitutionally protected right of citizenship, the enactment should be considered presumptively invalid and the burden of proof should shift to the state. Requiring that complainants show that the challenged law results in some burden on, interference with, or disadvantage to, their citizenship rights, does not—in contrast with the "violation" or "compulsion" standards traditionally applied by the Supreme Court—require them to demonstrate that the law makes their exercise of Citizenship Rights *impossible*.

Thus, when establishment concerns are present, petitioners should only be obligated to demonstrate that their citizenship rights have been *abridged* rather than completely denied or violated. In effect, the presence of establishment concerns reduces the burden of evidence that plaintiffs must present in order successfully to challenge the constitutional validity of religious lawmaking. The lower standard provides protections for women and subordinate religious groups from coercive treatment by politically and socially dominant religious influences on lawmaking. It is justified because the petitioner's demonstration of Establishment Concerns already provides some grounds for invalidating a religiously influenced enactment.

For a challenged law to be upheld once it has been shown to infringe upon Citizenship Rights, the government should be required to show that its challenged law can be supported on the basis of a compelling state interest that cannot be achieved through the use of less restrictive means. Many challenged abortion regulations would be suspect under the first step of the proposed assessment model, since the influence of religion can easily be demonstrated. However, the proposed assessment model does not invalidate every religiously influenced law that has alienating, exclusionary, coercive, or politically divisive effects. Such laws are valid, notwithstanding their religious character, if they can be justified by a substantial secular interest.

Requiring that the government's interest be a *secular* one is to prevent a lawmaking body from claiming that it had a compelling *religious* interest for passing a particular law, such as to prevent the apocalypse or to avoid the wrath of God. Application of the proposed model to a set of facts such as those in the *Bowen* case demonstrates that the proposed test does not invalidate *all* lawmaking in which religion has some bearing. In *Bowen*, for example, there was no evidence to suggest that the legislation itself was influenced by religious considerations. However, just as the existence of a *religious* purpose alone is not enough to invalidate a law, so also the existence of *a* secular purpose (whether substantial or compelling) should not be enough to validate a religiously-based law (especially where citizenship rights are at stake) unless the *effects* can be shown to not harm citizenship rights or unless the state has a compelling interest in the challenged regulation.

The appropriate focus of adjudications involving religious lawmaking should be on whether the government can justify a challenged law on the basis of a substantial secular state interest, not on whether the lawmaker's actual purpose or motivation or particular structure was religious. That is, the proposed test requires asking: "*Could* the law have been enacted without reference to religion?" If so, then the religious influence has not been the proximate cause of any harms to citizenship rights. Even though the effects of a law motivated by religious considerations (but sustainable on a secular rationale) may infringe upon citizenship rights, that infringement should be addressed on the basis of the Court's traditional tests, rather than on one designed to address the distinctive harms of religious lawmaking.

Under the proposed model for assessing religious lawmaking, if the religious dimension cannot be shown to have influenced the outcome of lawmaking, the justification for applying an interpretive model that diverges from the Court's traditional interpretations disappears. Thus, the *availability* of a substantial government interest for a law will be sufficient to satisfy the government's burden, regardless of whether individual lawmakers *actually* raised or relied on such grounds. This avoids problems of proof associated with having to ascertain "legislative intent" and also better protects the free exercise rights of religious lawmakers than does the Court's traditional test.

I have suggested that religiously influenced laws are constitutionally problematic. Religiously influenced abortion laws are especially troublesome with respect to protecting women's citizenship rights. The Supreme Court's traditional jurisprudence for adjudicating religious lawmaking is deficient in several respects, especially in failing to establish adequate protections for women's constitutional rights. As an alternative, I have proposed a legal strategy for resolving issues of religious lawmaking that better protects women's constitutional rights and interests. Just as the Constitution should not be "color blind," so should it not be blind to the disparate and disadvantaging impacts of religious lawmaking on its female citizens.

NOTES

1. 448 U.S. 297 (1980).
2. 492 U.S. 490 (1989).
3. 487 U.S. 589 (1988).
4. See Riva Siegel, "Reasoning From the Body: A Historical Perspective on Abortion Regulation and Questions of Equal Protection," *Stanford Law Review* 44 (1992): 261–381, at 356 (citing *Mississippi University for Women v. Hogan*, 458 U.S.718 [1982] at 726 n.11).
5. Immediately following the Court's decision in *Roe v. Wade*, 410 U.S.113 (1973), several religiously affiliated groups, many of them associated with the Roman Catholic

Church, mobilized their ranks in a highly developed, well organized, and generously funded campaign to reverse its effect through legislation and constitutional amendment; see Rosiland Petchesky,, *Abortion and Woman's Choice: The State, Sexuality, and Reproductive Freedom* (Boston: Northeastern University Press, 1990), 241–42; Laurence Tribe, *Abortion:The Clash of Absolutes* (Cambridge: Harvard University Press, 1990), 143–47. The "Pastoral Plan for Pro-Life Activities" issued in 1975 by the National Conference of Catholic Bishops (NCCB) specified that a "comprehensive pro-life legislative program" must include "passage of a constitutional amendment providing protection for the unborn child to the maximum degree possible," as well as "passage of federal and state laws and adoption of administrative policies that will restrict the practice of abortion as much as possible" (*McRae v. Califano*, 491 F. Supp. 630, 704 [S.D.N.Y. 1980]); see Timothy Byrnes, ed., *The Catholic Bishops in American Politics* (Princeton: Princeton University Press, 1991), 58–59.

6. The first version of the amendment Hyde introduced included no exceptions to the prohibition on funding abortions (*see Congressional Record* 122 [daily ed., June 24, 1977], H. 6646–6647).

7. See *McRae v. Califano*, 491 F. Supp. 630, 742–844 (E.D.N.Y. 1980).

8. Tatalovich, Raymond, and David Schier, "The Persistence of Ideological Cleavage in Voting on Abortion Legislation in the House of Representatives, 1973–1988," in Malcolm Goggin, ed., *Understanding the New Politics of Abortion* (Newbury Park, CA: Sage, 1993), 109–22, at 112.

9. See *McRae v. Califano*, 491 F. Supp. at 756–835.

10. See id., 491 F. Supp. at 773; see also 753. Representative Hyde argued more than once that "when the mother, who should be the natural protector of her unborn child becomes its deadly adversary, then it is the duty of this legislature to intervene on behalf of defenseless human life" (491 F. Supp. at 773). Senator Bartlett reasoned that "to defer to the moral judgment of the mother who does not want the child and a doctor paid by the government forces the fetus to have its life taken, and ignores the moral question of the unborn child" (491 F. Supp. at 748).

Representative Rudd argued that a woman should choose not to become pregnant and that "she should not ask the taxpayer to pay for her failure to exercise that choice" (491 F. Supp. at 775). Representative Bauman asserted that "the death of one unborn child was as important as the life of the mother who does not want the child" (491 F. Supp. at 825). Congressman Oberstar objected to the Supreme Court's focus on the mother in *Roe v. Wade*, criticizing it for ignoring the "vital issue" of the "rights of the unborn" (491 F. Supp. at 757).

11. See Brenda Hofman, "Political Theology: The Role of Organized Religion in the Anti-Abortion Movement," *Journal of Church and State* 28 (1986): 25–47, 39–40; Petchesky, supra n. 2, at 253 and n. 25.

12. See Matthew Moen, *The Christian Right and Congress* (Tuscaloosa: University of Alabama Press, 1989), 56–58.

13. See *Everson v. Board of Education*, 330 U.S. 1, 15–16 (1947); *McDaniel v. Paty*, 435 U.S. 618, 637 (1991) (Brennan, J., concurring).

14. 397 U.S. 664, 668 (1970).

15. 403 U.S. 602, 622–23 (1970).

16. 403 U.S. at 622–23.

17. 465 U.S. 668, 687–88 (1984) (O'Connor, J., concurring).

18. 492 U.S. 490 (1989).

19. Quoted in 492 U.S. at 501.

20. 487 U.S. 589, 597 (1988).

21. 42 U.S.Code Section 300z-10.

22. 487 U.S. at 599.

23. Congress was aware of the potential constitutional problems raised by AFLA's involvement with religious groups even before it passed the act. As if in anticipation of future challenge, the report accompanying the 1981 bill states the Senate committee's view that "provisions for the involvement of religious organizations do not violate the constitutional separation between church and state."

24. 657 F. Supp. 1547 (1987), reversed, 487 U.S. 589 (1988).

25. *West Virginia Board of Education v. Barnette*, 319 U.S. 624, 642 (1943).

26. See, e.g., *Larson v. Valente*, 456 U.S. 228 (1982).

27. See *Lyng v. Northwest Indian Cemetery Protective Association*, 485 U.S. 439 (1988); *Employment Division v. Smith*, 494 U.S. 872 (1990).

28. 505 U.S. 833 (1992).

29. 505 U.S. at 877.

30. 491 F. Supp. 630 (E.D.N.Y. 1980).

31. 448 U.S. 297 (1980).

32. 448 U.S. at 320.

33. The relevant part of the Fourteenth Amendment provides: "No State shall . . . deprive any person of life, liberty, or property, without due process of law; nor deny to any person within its jurisdiction the equal protection of the laws." The Fifth Amendment provides analogous guarantees that are binding on the federal government.

34. See *Griswold v. Connecticut*, 381 U.S. 479 (1965); *Eisenstadt v. Baird*, 405 U.S. 438 (1972); *Roe v. Wade*, 410 U.S. 113, 168 (1973); *Planned Parenthood v. Casey*, 505 U.S. 833 (1992).

35. 410 U.S. 113 (1973).

36. 505 U.S. at 852–53.

37. In addition, religious lawmaking may violate the principle of equal protection by discriminating between citizens on the basis of their religious beliefs. As noted earlier, according the binding authority of law to certain religious beliefs suggests that citizens not holding those beliefs are political outsiders, and unequal citizens.

38. *Planned Parenthood v. Casey*, 505 U.S. 833 at 852 (Stevens and Blackmun, dissenting); *Thornburgh v. American College of Obstetricians*, 476 U.S. 747, 772 (1985). See Siegel, supra n. 1, at 348–49; Tribe, supra n. 2, at 135; Ruth Bader Ginsburg, "Some Thoughts on Autonomy and Equality in Relation to *Roe v. Wade*," *North Carolina Law Review* 63 (1985): 375–95, at 375.

39. 492 U.S. at 557–58 (Blackmun, J., dissenting).

40. Not allowing autonomous decision making by pregnant women concerning whether or not to have an abortion "denigrates women as moral decision makers, and

it reinforces their role as sexual objects by undermining their ability to act as sexual agents" (Fran Olsen, "Unravelling Compromise," *Harvard Law Review* 103 (1989): 105–35, at121). In these respects, restrictive abortion laws also deprive women of their free exercise rights. In contrast, the law generally does not hold men responsible for giving any part of their own body to another, even if necessary to save the life of one of their offspring. *See Winston v. Lee*, 470 U.S. 753 (1985); *Rochin v. California*, 342 U.S. 165 (1952); Dawn Johnsen and March Wilder, "*Webster* and Women's Equality," *American Journal of Law and Medicine* 15 (1989): 178–84, 179.

41. *Harris v. McRae*, 448 U.S. 297 (1980); *McRae v. Califano*, 491 F. Supp. at 691; *Webster v. Reproductive Rights*, 492 U.S. 490, 572 n.17 (1989).

42. *Harris*, 448 U.S. at 319, *quoting McGowan v. Maryland*, 366 U.S. 420, 442 (1961); *Bowen*, 487 U.S. at 622.

43. 492 U.S. at 567–68.

44. 492 U.S. at 566–71.

45. *Webster*, 492 U.S. at 501, 506.

46. *Bowen*, 487 U.S. at 604.

47. 487 U.S. at 611–12, citing *Grand Rapids School District v. Bell*, 473 U.S. 373, 385 (1985).

48. *Bowen*, 487 U.S. at 617 n. 14.

49. See *Grand Rapids School District v. Ball*, 473 U.S. 373 (1985).

50. *Webster; Harris*.

51. 492 U.S. at 563 (Stevens, J., dissenting).

52. See Lucinda Peach, *Religious Lawmaking in a Secular State: Philosophical, Legal, and Feminist Perspectives on a Persistent Dilemma* (New York: Oxford University Press, 2002).

Martha Albertson Fineman

CHAPTER 14

What Place for Family Privacy?

The Separate Sphere

Society has devised special laws to apply to the family. The unique nature of these rules has been justified by reference to the family's relational aspects and intimate nature. In fact, "family law" can be thought of as a system of exemptions from the everyday rules that would apply to interactions among people in a nonfamily context. These exemptions are complemented by the imposition of a set of special family obligations. Family law defines the responsibilities of members toward one another and the claims or rights they have as family members. The typical focus of family law literature has been on how to use law to redefine, reform, or regulate intrafamily dynamics.

But family law does more than confer rights, duties, and obligations within the family. It also assumes and reflects a certain type of relationship between family and state. During the nineteenth century this relationship was typically cast as one of "separate spheres." Family (the private sphere) and state (the public sphere) were perceived as largely independent of one another. This metaphor of separation reflected an ethic or ideology of family privacy in which state intervention was the exception.

The characterization of the family as distinct and separate from the state still resonates in our rhetoric about families. The family is designated the quintessential "private" institution. Family is distinguished by its privateness

An earlier version of this article appeared in *George Washington Law Review* 67 (1999): 1207–24.

from both the market (a chameleon institution, public vis-à-vis the family but "private" vis-à-vis the state) and the state (the quintessential public institution). In a sense, privacy is what defines the family, gives it coherence as a concept. For the modern private family, protection from public interference remains the publicly stated norm—state intervention continues to be cast as exceptional, requiring some justification.

What are the contours of the family that are protected by privacy? Historically, it was a reproductive unit—husband and wife and their children—complemented by other household members such as apprentices or servants or extended family members. Today there is much less agreement about just who should be considered "family." The traditional unit of husband and wife (with or with out children) seems to qualify in all definitions. In fact, this reproductive family is considered by many people to represent the "natural" form of the family. However, others argue that the marital family should also be considered an exclusive vision of family in terms of policy and law.

This nuclear unit is thought to be in "crisis" because of the tendency of many marriages to dissemble and dissolve. It is also claimed that society is in a state of crisis as a result of instability in marriage. Many are concerned by the assembling of "deviant" and competing intimate entities, whose members claim they are entitled to the benefits and privileges previously extended to married couples. The family has become the symbolic terrain for the cultural war in which our society is increasingly mired.

If one believes the family is not inherently limited to any essential or natural form but is, rather, as contrived as any other societal institution, it affects one's perspective on the relationship between state and family. Under this conceptualization, the family cannot be viewed as separate. The metaphor of "symbiosis"[1] seems more appropriate than the separate spheres imagery to describe the family in relationship to the state. The family is located within the state. In this conceptualization, family and state are interactive—they define one another. Alterations in the scope or nature of one institution will correspondingly alter the scope or nature of the other. While it is true that initially law defines the family, controlling entry into the status and determining the consequences of family, once it is formed the family is a powerful constituency within the state. The expectations for the family relieve the state of some obligations. Family actions (or inactions) can place pressure on the state and require adjustments and accommodation that alter the nature of the state. The family will demand societal resources and, the more favored the family is, the more pressure builds from outsiders, demanding entry into the coveted status of family.

If this model of the family/state relationship is accurate, it has important implications for public policy. This reconfiguration of our concept of family indicates that the family is a dynamic institution. It is dynamic in the sense that its relationship with state is not fixed or static. Correspondingly, the family is not a natural entity with a form and set of functions that are constant and essential.[2]

Family and state can be reconfigured, and have been reconfigured, to reflect different sets of expectations and aspirations for both institutions. These expectations and aspirations are reflected in law and can also be determined as an empirical matter and traced in ideology about the family. This way of considering the family suggests that the family has a definite function within the state and also suggests that society would benefit from periodic self-conscious considerations about the continued viability and desirability of historic assumptions about the family as an institution. Currently we seem to be in a period of reconfiguration—there is certainly a sense of crisis surrounding the family as an institution and the question arises as to the direction we should take our families.

Expectations for the Private Family

In recent work, I have been rethinking the arrangement between family and state by articulating a theory of collective responsibility for dependency.[3] In this process I reconfigure certain core concepts in American policy discourse. The objective is to make an argument for the redistribution of responsibility for dependency among what I call the "coercive institutions"[4] of family, state, and market. Our current (and historic) stated national ideology glorifies self-sufficiency and independence, both for the individual and for the family. Within this ideology, the primary responsibility for the developmental or physiological dependence of children and some elderly, disabled, or ill persons, what I have previously labeled "inevitable dependency" is placed on the family. Dependency, which is seen, at least partially, in many other systems as a collective responsibility, in ours is privatized through the institution of the family. In our late capitalist system the state is perceived as having a role only in the case of family default. In such instances, the state might provide highly stigmatized assistance (welfare) for those (deviant) families unable to provide for their members' needs. Market institutions have few, if any, direct responsibility for the family, even for the families of their own workers.

My argument is that a more appropriate and equitable scheme would evenly distribute the burdens for inevitable dependency, with the market as well as the state assuming some up-front share of the economic and social costs (the subsidy) inherent in the reproduction of society. There is also a need for structural changes and institutional accommodation of the demands of caretaking. I articulate this claim as a "right," based on the argument that caretaking is societal preserving and perpetuating work. Dependency work produces things of benefit to society in general. It is the labor that generates citizens and workers, consumers and voters. As things are now structured, the costs of doing dependency work are hidden in the family where, due to gendered role divisions, they are borne primarily by women. Further, this caretaking labor, which is performed for the good of the society, has individual costs for caretakers who often find themselves sacrificing career development, forgoing economic opportunities, and becoming derivatively dependent upon others for resources in order to accomplish their tasks.

One conceptual problem with the idea of collective responsibility is that it opens the door to a corresponding argument that assumption of such responsibility must be accompanied by collective control over the circumstances leading to dependency. It will be argued that if society has obligations to subsidize and support caretakers because there is a collective responsibility for dependency, then society should have a correlative right to control intimate decisions that produce or effect dependency, for example decisions concerning reproduction or related to family formation and function.

It is in resisting assertions about the appropriateness of collective control that a reconfigured concept of "privacy" will be useful. In fact, weaving privacy into the arguments for collective responsibility strengthens both. Collective responsibility accompanied by a well-developed notion of privacy for the caretaking unit can provide autonomy for that unit. Collective resources provide the ability, while the norm of nonintervention provides the freedom for families to perform the societal tasks they have been assigned.

In regard to our current social scheme, we perceive a line of privacy drawn around certain intimate units, distinguishing them as family. The privacy line alters the relationship of individuals within the family entity and mediates their relationship to the state.[5] They are placed in the special category of family. This line of privacy, while it currently shields few entities beyond the traditional family for most purposes, could be drawn around caretaking or dependency units.

In fact, my project of rethinking our ideas about dependency and self-sufficiency mandates a corresponding reconsideration of other assumptions about the family as an institution and a reconceptualization of the family's relationship with the state. As part of this process the question is whether we can "modernize" the concept of family privacy, making it a complement to our restructured vision of the family. This will involve looking at both intrafamily ties and the place or location of the family within the state. The task of reconfiguring privacy has two related components: a shift in our understanding of what privacy attaches to, privileging family function and not family form, and the development of the idea of family privacy as an entity-based entitlement to self-government or autonomy. Thus conceived, privacy would not be a right to separation, secrecy or seclusion but the right to autonomy or self-determination for the family even as it is firmly located within a supportive and reciprocal state.[6]

In the pages that follow, after an initial disclaimer about my constitutional law prowess, I distinguish family from constitutional or individual privacy. Recognizing the typical critiques of family privacy, I argue that we must think beyond the historic manifestations of the concept. My construction of family privacy is more ideological than doctrinal and is dependent on, and essential to, the revisioning of family in functional terms.

Privacies

Most commentators focus on privacy as a matter of federal constitutional doctrine. This strand of privacy jurisprudence is individualistic in nature and has been the basis for some important decisions protecting choices concerning reproduction. This individual or constitutional notion of privacy is certainly necessary to deter impulses toward collective control of sexuality and reproduction. [7]

There has been quite a bit of debate in recent years about the effectiveness, as well as the wisdom, of using privacy to secure individual rights. I am not a constitutional scholar and remain an agnostic on questions such as whether equality or privacy is the most potent concept with which to try to preserve individual reproductive rights or whether sexual privacy is essential for the development of individual personhood.

My interest in the legal or doctrinal idea of privacy is focused on its use in consideration of the institution of the family—privacy in its common law sense. The idea of the entity of the family as something "private" predates, and is analytically separate from, the constitutional idea of individual privacy, although this "new" arena of privacy seems rooted in older notions about family relations. For example, *Griswold v. Connecticut*[8] is often cited as the bedrock case for the development of our constitutional concept of individual privacy regarding reproductive decisions. But the *Griswold* opinions articulating the concept of privacy are clearly looking beyond the individual, referencing an entity or marital concept of privacy.

The question *Griswold* explicitly presented was whether there was a constitutional right for married couples to use contraception.[9] Justice Douglas's majority opinion may have characterized the right to this type of privacy as located in the famous penumbras, but its presence transcended those shadows.

The privacy interests at issue were deemed "older than the Bill of Rights— older than our political parties, older than our school system."[10] And there was little ambiguity about what was being protected: "marriage is a coming together for better or worse, hopefully enduring, and intimate to the degree of being sacred."[11] Justice Goldberg's concurring opinion reiterated the point that it was marriage that was deserving of protection, stating that the statute at issue dealt "with a particularly important and sensitive area of privacy—that of the marital relation and the marital home."[12]

From the family law perspective, it is *Eisenstadt v. Baird*[13] that is the radical departure—*Eisenstadt* is the case that takes the idea of entity or marital privacy and expands constitutional protection beyond the common law limitations of the family relationship:

> It is true that in *Griswold* the right of privacy in question inhered in the marital relationship. Yet the marital couple is not an independent entity with a mind and heart of its own, but an association of two individuals each with a separate intellectual and emotional makeup. If the right of privacy means anything, it is the right of the individual, married or single, to be free from unwarranted governmental intrusion into matters so fundamentally affecting a person as the decision whether to bear or beget a child.[14]

This articulation of the principles in *Griswold* established the individual as the relevant subject. *Eisenstadt* effectively threw a constitutional cloak of privacy over certain individual decisions involving sex and reproduction.[15]

If we were to return to the doctrine of family or marital privacy we would see that it is distinguishable from the new individual variety in several significant ways. The obvious difference is in the designation of the relevant unit for protection, entity vs. individual. Also important, however, is the historic fact that family privacy operated as a generalized form of protection. What was shielded from state intervention and control were not only specific, weighty intimate decisions such as the decision to beget or bear a child but also mundane day-to-day family interactions.

Despite the Supreme Court's recent activity in bringing some aspects of family privacy into constitutional law, the cases that are most relevant in discerning the characteristics of family privacy are state not federal decisions.[16] The task of the state in family privacy cases is not to pronounce grand principles or figure out how to make family privacy mesh with other constitutional limitations. These cases address expectations and aspirations for families, articulating in the process what might be characterized as an ethic or ideology of family privacy. This ideology is rooted in idealizations but also references the perceived pragmatics of family relationships and the acknowledged limitations of legal (particularly judicial) systems as substitutes for family decision-making. The ideology expresses the norm of nonintervention in ongoing families—a principle of state restraint because of the needs of the functioning family.

The facts of *McGuire v. McGuire*[17] illustrate the contours of the common law doctrine of family privacy. Mrs. McGuire had asked the court to intervene and require her husband to provide suitable maintenance and support for her. She did not want a divorce or legal separation, just the enforcement of the terms of the state defined marriage contract, which required husbands to support their wives. Her complaints about her husband's lack of adequate support were rather compelling. For example, in spite of the fact that her husband was a fairly wealthy man, she had not received money to buy clothing for several years. She lived in a house with no indoor bathroom, kitchen sink, or functioning central heating. The Nebraska Supreme Court, while indicating that the husband's behavior was inappropriate, nonetheless held that his marital obligations could not be enforced if Mrs. McGuire chose to remain in her family relationship:

> The living standards of a family are a matter of concern to the household, and not for the courts to determine, even though the husband's attitude toward his wife, according to his wealth and circumstances, leaves little to be said in his behalf. As long as the home is maintained and the parties are living as husband and wife it may be said that the husband is legally supporting his wife and the purpose of the marriage relation is being carried out. Public policy requires such a holding.[18]

Mrs. McGuire's petition for a level of support consistent with the family wealth and income would be granted only if she left the relationship. As long as the marriage lasted, the courts would not intervene even if asked to by one of the partners to the marriage and even if all that was requested was enforcement of state imposed family obligations.

Of course, children present a more problematic situation. We are less certain that children can protect themselves within the family, or that they can protect themselves *from* the family. The nature of the parent-child relationship has occupied state and federal courts' attention. Parental conduct, be it discipline or decision-making, is generally protected unless it constitutes abuse or neglect of the child. Courts consistently reiterate the common law presumption that parents act in the best interests of their children. The law's concept of the family rests on the presumption that parents possess what children lack in maturity, experience, and capacity for judgment.[19] Consistent

with the search for sources in *Griswold*, the opinions about parent-child relationships also have found rights not in explicit textual provisions but in the
history and functioning of the family itself.[20]

Both individual and entity versions of privacy have limitations.[21] For example, family privacy is limited in two important senses. First, there is the historic doctrinal limitation that it applies primarily to family units that conform
to ideological conventions about appropriate form and function—to intact
nuclear families. Second, in recent decades, the idea of family privacy has
been severely criticized by feminists, children's rights proponents, and others
concerned by the potential for physical, emotional, or psychological abuse of
some family members by others. Family privacy was charged with obscuring
and fostering inequality and exploitation.

The Problem With Family Privacy

Somewhat of a dilemma is presented for those of us who view "privacy" as
essential to the concept of family while simultaneously conceding the more
modern notion that privacy can conceal, even foster, situations dangerous to
the individuals who comprise the family unit. The focus on the necessity of
privacy for family formation and functioning arises from concern with abuses
associated with state intervention and regulation of intimacy. By contrast,
those who are attuned to potential abuses within the family remind us that
hidden beneath the cloak of privacy are power imbalances, perhaps even incentives for the strong to prey upon or exploit the weak. When we consult the
empirical information, it seems both perspectives are warranted. Therefore,
the obvious course is found in trying to reconcile both concerns and balance
family privacy with protection for family members. Too often, however, advocates discard one (particularly family privacy) for the sake of the other.

In trying to reconcile the need of the family for privacy with the obligation
of the state to protect its citizens, we should first resolve the question of family population. How are we going to define the "family" that will be entitled to
privacy protection? Existing law defines the family through legal affiliations.
Only certain ties are significant for the establishment of the status of family.
Some ties are purely legally contrived, such as those in the construct of marriage, while others are considered to be reflective of a more "natural" nature,
such as the parent-child bond.[22]

The legally conceived family presumptively is, or has been, a reproductive
unit. The primary tie is the heterosexual affiliation of husband and wife, and
this gives the family its form.[23] Theirs is a connection considered basic to
family and to state, therefore historically legally mandated to be permanent,

exclusive, and stable.[24] This traditional family was hierarchically organized with well-defined gendered divisions of labor. It is this family that is criticized in much of the feminist jurisprudence of recent years. The feminist critique of privacy and the family begins with the assertion that it obscures private, often labeled "domestic," violence and abuse. For example, Catherine MacKinnon criticized liberal thinkers, along with cases such as *Roe v. Wade*, by characterizing "the ideology of privacy" as "a right of men to be let alone to oppress women one at a time."[25]

McKinnon understands privacy to be rooted in the concept of seclusion and separation from the protections that might be afforded by the state. Privacy is seen as the source of women's inequality, the location of her domination and subordination.[26] In fact, she asserts that to even complain about inequality in the private arena is inconsistent with the whole idea of privacy. To her, privacy cannot be understood outside of its historic manifestations of female subordination. [27]

Anita Allen begins her discussion of privacy in the same place as MacKinnon—within the confines of the historic nuclear family home. Her major concern is not with violence but with exploitation—the sacrifices compelled by "marriage, motherhood, housekeeping, dependence, and women's own moral ideas of caretaking and belonging."[28] Allen disagrees with MacKinnon, disputing the assertion that privacy poses an inherent threat to women, and argues that women are finally in a position to "expect, experience and exploit real privacy within the home and within heterosexual relationships."[29]

Allen views privacy as having many dimensions, referring to "family life within the home, and to the kinds of intimate personal relationships and activities commonly associated with them."[30]

While recognizing past abuses, Allen sees a use for "real" privacy in providing seclusion and solitude for women, in restricting access to information and preserving confidentiality, and in securing decisional privacy. Allen makes an important argument for retaining the constitutional, individualized notion of privacy and making sure that the conditions for its use and enjoyment are afforded to women. However, her analysis does not transcend the individual woman to consider the family.[31]

In fact, both MacKinnon's critique and Allen's defense of privacy assume there is danger in the domestic. The danger is located in the operation and expectations associated with heterosexuality (and subsequent reproduction). Women's interests are to be asserted independent of the family unit—typically against men who with greater or lesser degrees of ill will take advantage of women in families. Allen does bring children into the consideration, but retains an individualized analysis. Children mean caretaking, and caretaking precludes "real" privacy.[32] The object is to have a personal sense of privacy that permits women's resistance to reproduction and caretaking. Her notion of privacy in this regard is as a tool to "put an end to the psychological predisposition of women to care themselves into oblivion—a defense to intrafamily abuse."[33]

A second source of criticism of the idea of family privacy is those who focus on the rights of children. Under this analysis, family privacy protects parental authority.[34] In this area the tendency of privacy critics who see abuses has been to individualize the family, by separating children out for special concern and state protection. Some child advocates focus on physical and psychological abuse of children within families, advocating for intervention in these instances. These seem to me to be easy (problems of definition aside) cases. Privacy should never condone or obscure abuse.

What are of concern, however, are the more sweeping claims of some advocates—those who focus on the very basic question of how children are described and treated in law. The discomfort in this regard seems to be with the hierarchical or unequal nature of the parent-child relationship. The charge often leveled is that the law treats children as though they are the "property" of their parents, an inflammatory characterization that does more to obscure than illuminate the issues.

There are a number of suggestions for recasting the relationship between parent and child, substituting concepts such as "stewardship" or "trustee" for the more traditional notion of parental authority, thus leveling out the relationship.[35] These ideals, amorphously appealing on a rhetorical level, seem harmless enough as aspirations. The problems arise when they are implemented into laws that can be used at the relatively unfettered discretion of various state actors to undermine, even usurp, parental decision-making authority.

From the perspective of my project, notions of child advocacy can raise some interesting issues. How might a general and broadly construed norm of child advocacy (advocacy and activism absent abuse or neglect) relate to the concepts of collective responsibility without collective control? Perhaps advocacy may be of benefit to the project. For example, noted child advocate Barbara Woodhouse has urged the idea of stewardship. She uses the child advocates' claim that children must be treated as "people in their own right" to argue for laws and policies that focus on children's welfare.[36]

Woodhouse reaches for more than control over parents. With the objective of children's welfare as the organizing tools, she advocates for a more extensive sense of children's rights, which she terms "needs-based rights." These rights are not associated with children's rights to autonomy or independence but are the basis for a positive claim to basic nurture and protection.[37] This right is not only against parents but mandates community and political responses.

To some extent Woodhouse's concern with basic needs rights reflects my own call for collective responsibility for dependency. However, the identity of the rights holder and the source of the right are different in important ways. My claim is a communal one—entity focused and based on a claim of entitlement or right originating as a result of the societal work performed by caretakers. Woodhouse's model is not a compensatory one but is based on the status of the child as a future citizen. She positions the child as the claimholder and, in doing so, sets up the potential (perhaps inevitably) for collective, child protective supervision over and control of parental stewardship. The family is conceived in terms of individual (therefore potentially competing) interests.[38]

Autonomy for Family Functioning

As indicated earlier, rethinking the family and its relationship to the state requires a corresponding rethinking of other primary institutions and foundational concepts. As part of this process I suggest that we can and should rethink privacy in such a way as to confer autonomy on caretaking or dependency units. The beneficiary of this privacy is the unit, defined through its functioning not its form. In fact, the caretaking unit could adopt a multitude of possible forms. The unifying idea that creates the "new family" is the significance of the caretaker-dependent relationship.

Autonomy (my version of the "new" privacy to complement the new family) would protect entity decision-making, giving the unit the space and authority to self-government, including the right to self-definition. Autonomy does not presuppose that the family would be separate from society. The family would be anchored firmly within society, subsidized and supported by market and state but retaining authority within its parameters.[39] Privacy, just like subsidy, should attach to units performing societally necessary and essential functions, such as caretaking.[40]

This version of a reconceived family, entitled to privacy or autonomy, is responsive to some of the criticism of old forms of family privacy. For example, if the family is defined functionally, focused on the caretaker-dependent relationship, the traditionally problematic interactions of sexual affiliates (formerly designated spouses) are not protected by notions of family privacy. MacKinnon's charge that men will exploit women in an intimate context may still be a problem, but it will no longer be a privacy problem. The fact that privacy is refocused removes from the special or family context the entire range of relationships between sexual affiliates, opening them to public scrutiny.[41]

This opening up of some relationships to scrutiny does not mean that my reconfigured family model is going to escape feminist criticism, however. The criticism is most likely to be that a notion of collective responsibility (and therefore social subsidy) and privacy protection for the caretaking-dependent relationship will permanently enthrall women as dependency laborers. I think such arguments are based, in part, on assumptions about women's false consciousness.

In any case, my objective is not social engineering. I do not consider it my place to persuade women not to undertake caretaking. Rather, my objective is to work to ensure that if they do undertake caretaking, they will not be systemically disadvantaged and rendered economically dependent on men or on highly stigmatized state assistance as a result. I do believe in the possibility of women's agency; although we all operate within societal and cultural constraints, we can determine direction and decide to take one path rather than another. Women should have the ability (subsidy and privacy) to undertake a caretaking role.

The second line of family privacy critiques, those presented by the child advocates, will be more on point for the family I envision. This is true because the exemplar of the caretaker-dependent relationship is the parent-child relationship. One significant aspect of these relationships is that they are of inherent inequality, reflecting the fact that one role is that of child or dependent, while the other is that of parent or caretaker.

To point out that the parent-child relationship is one of dependency is not to make an assertion as to how we should value children. Children (or any other inevitably dependent persons) are equally important or equally valuable but typically not "equals" in the sense that society does not presume that they are equivalent to adults in capability or in their ability to make judgments. Therefore it is more appropriate to view the parent-child relationship, not as one of equality (as with sexual affiliates) but as one of responsibility. It is not about individuals but about a relationship. And a relationship defined by responsibility requires privacy or autonomy for the caretaking entity.

It is this distinction between equality and responsibility—individuals and relationship that many child advocates fail to make. In fact, some child advocacy attempts seem like efforts to equalize the relationship between parent and child by adding the leavening (in order to level) force of the advocate (as stand-in for the state). My argument about autonomy for the caretaking unit is an assertion that some relationships should be considered outside of the equality paradigm that so dominates liberal legal scholarship. The reasoning of some in the child advocacy community presents the danger that, under the rubric of protecting the child, we facilitate state intervention and control and potentially undermine the autonomy of caretaking units.

The fact that we can think that some intimate relationships are inherently unequal does not mean that they will inevitably be exploitative and oppressive or that the "less equal" participant will have no voice and no power within the relationship.[42] I explicitly make mention of this fact because it seems that many child advocates assume that exploitation necessarily follows once the inequality of the child is posited.

In the same way, the lack of a legal voice is equated with the lack of an actual voice. Of course, the determination of typical and atypical modes of operation in caretaker-dependent units presents an empirical question. My assumption is that a careful study would show that the relationship between typical caretakers and dependents is dynamic (it is in motion), fluid (easily changing shape), and interactive (the participants act upon each other). The reciprocal interactive nature of the relationship ensures that it will not be fixed. The reciprocity also means that in regard to family decision-making the dependent will seldom, if ever, be absent.

Caretakers typically consider dependents' needs; often dependents are an explicit part of the process of decision-making; and at times they even control it. Just as the relationship is fluid within daily interaction, it is dynamic over time. While the authority of a parent over a child will decline as the years pass, an adult child's authority over (and responsibility for) an elderly and ill parent may increase. This is not to assert that there will never be "wrong" decisions made by caretakers or even that there will never be outright abuse. On the other hand, no system of child advocacy no matter how interventionist and regulatory, can deliver only optimal, nonabusive caretaking.

It is important in this regard to realize that the debates about child advocacy are, to a large extent, only arguments about legal relationships and how legal authority is distributed. As a practical matter, they are arguments about the relationship between state and family more than attempts to define and regulate intrafamily interactions. By contrast, if we focus, as I urge, on entity autonomy and responsibility, we are at least attempting to understand and respond to how family units function. Legal relationships capture only some things about "real" families, often distorting a family's reality in the process. Legal relationships set up adversariness.

One danger of imposing an equality aspiration on relationships of responsibility is pertinent for the ideas of subsidy and collective responsibility discussed earlier. If we look at the child as the recipient of the subsidy and not the unit (in which the caretaker is the "head"), several issues arise. Foremost is the very real possibility that if the child is seen as the object of social policy and justification for subsidy, some form of quality control will be considered appropriate. Standardization and normative judgments in a diverse and pluralistic society can be problematic and contentious.

If, by contrast, subsidy is perceived as going to the caretaker-dependent entity or unit, it is more likely that autonomy over decision-making will follow. Units may make "mistakes," but if it is not abuse or neglect (we can argue about where to draw those lines later), then the unit, as recipient of the subsidy, should decide how it is to be used. This way of looking at what is the appropriate focus for policy also gives value to caretaking labor. The dependant may be the beneficiary, but the labor of the caretaker is what has societal value.

To protect caretaking relationships, the right to privacy must be extended beyond individuals. A concept of individual privacy, particularly in regard to the formation of intimate connections can complement family privacy, but some protection that transcends the interests of individual members of the entity is essential. When a caretaking-dependent unit has formed, family privacy would serve to shield and protect the functioning relationships within it. The protection would dissolve only if the entity grossly fails in the performance of its responsibilities or because the underlying relationship is itself dissolved.[43]

Entity privacy would denote a line of nonintervention drawn around ongoing functioning relationships. This version of privacy can provide a barrier between an entity performing family functions, such as the caretaker/dependent unit, and the potentially overreaching state seeking to impose collective standards or controls. Properly conceived, privacy as a principle of self-government allows the caretaker/dependent unit to flourish, supported and subsidized by the larger society without the imposition of conformity.

NOTES

1. I use this term to indicate a reciprocity or mutualism, although the term "containment" might also be appropriate. Containing family within its traditional form and function is certainly the goal of some political actors.

2. I use family here as a legal concept, the entity set aside for the special treatment historically given families.

3. See Martha Albertson Fineman, *The Neutered Mother, the Sexual Family, and Other Twentieth Century Tragedies* (New York, London: Routledge, 1995) and *The Autonomy Myth: A Theory of Dependency* (New York: The New Press, 2003).

4. I use the term "coercive" to distinguish these highly regulated, legally defined institutions from more voluntary social structures such as philanthropy, religion, or charity.

5. The common law privacy doctrine is not an individualized concept but is founded on the nature of the protected relationship: it attaches to the entity of the family not to the individuals that compose it. Historically, this has meant that in certain cases the doctrine operates to shield the family unit from state interference even when the request comes from one of the family members. Supra note 1, at 966. See

also *State v. Black*, 60 N.C. 274 (1864) (a case demonstrative of the court's reticence to interfere in an allegedly abusive marital relationship). For further analysis, see Stedman, "Right of Husband to Chastise Wife," *Virginia Law Review* 3 (1917): 241.

6. Of course abuses within real-life families will occur. However, the issue in those cases should be how to address such abuse within the parameters of a family privacy ethic. The existence of abuse should not be sufficient to launch an attack on privacy as applied to the family. See supra note 5 at 87–88.

7. I do argue, however, that individual concepts of privacy are not sufficient effectively to resist the impetus toward collective control in many areas of intimate and family life that the imposition of collective responsibility might provoke — for example, in the case of paternity actions, modification, and custody awards. See Fineman, supra note xx at 189–91.

8. 381 U.S. 479 (1965).

9. This limitation on the right was clearly on the mind of a number of Justices. In his concurrence, on behalf of the Chief Justice and Justice Brennan, Justice Goldberg asserted that our "concept of liberty protects those rights that are fundamental." Infra note 8 at 486. In delineating which rights rise to the status of being fundamental, Justice Goldberg noted that judges must look at the "traditions and (collective) conscience of our people to determine whether a principle is so rooted . . . as to be deemed fundamental." Infra note 8 at 493. Although not explicitly in the Constitution, to the dismay of Justice Stewart (see Stewart, J., dissenting), marital privacy was embraced as a fundamental right.

10. Id. at 486.

11. Id.

12. Id. at 495.

13. *Eisenstadt v. Baird*, 405 U.S. 438 (1972).

14. Id. at 453.

15. The fact that the cloak as it was spun out had certain holes does not detract from the basic point that it was tailored for individual not entity protection. See *Planned Parenthood of Central Missouri v. Danforth*, 428 U.S. 52 (1976). ("The obvious fact is that when the wife and the husband disagree on this decision [abortion], the view of only one of the two marriage partners can prevail. Inasmuch as it is the woman who physically bears the child and who is the more directly and immediately affected by the pregnancy, as between the two, the balance weighs in her favor.")

In cases subsequent to *Eisenstadt* various doctrinal limitations and exceptions have been fashioned to curb the reach of this modern un-family-fettered form of privacy. At the same time that *Eisenstadt* expanded the notion of who was protected by privacy, it seems to have contracted the possibilities of what was protected, focusing primarily on decisions concerning reproduction. Further, language about traditions deeply rooted from Goldberg's opinion in *Griswold* has proved constricting, limiting protection to the traditional. See: *Bowers v. Hardwick*, 106 S. Ct. 2841 (1986).

16. Federal courts have relied consistently on the domestic relations exception to decline jurisdiction in family law matters. This exception to diversity jurisdiction was established in *Barber v. Barber*, 21 How. 582, 16 L. Ed. 226 (1859). The overrid-

ing attitude of the federal bench is that state courts are and continue to be better equipped to handle domestic matters. *Simms v. Simms*, 175 U.S. 162, 20 S.Ct. 58, 44 L.Ed. 115 (1899); *McCarty v. McCarty* 453 U.S. 210, 101 S.Ct. 2728, 69 L.Ed. 2d 589 (1981). This general reluctance on the part of the federal judiciary may give way to increased federal activity in family law matters however. Judith Resnick argues that federal intervention in family law is inevitable however because an "interlocking en-meshed regulatory structure covers the host of human activity." For additional dis-cussion of federal intervention in family law matters see generally Judith Resnick, " 'Naturally' Without Gender: Women, Jurisdiction, and Federal Courts," NYU *Law Review* 66 (1991): 1682, 1750–1757.

17. *McGuire v. McGuire*, 157 Neb. 226, 59 N.W.2d 336 (1953).

18. See: Elizabeth M. Schneider, "The Violence of Privacy," *Connecticut Law Review* 23 (1991): 973, 976. There were many other contemporary cases embodying this principle of family privacy. Tort law has traditionally been held inapplicable to injuries inflicted by one family member on another. Under doctrines of interspousal and parent-child immunity, courts have consistently refused to allow recoveries for injuries that would be compensable but for the fact that they occurred in the private realm. In the same way, criminal law has failed to punish intentional injuries to fam-ily members. Common law and statutory definitions of rape in most states contin-ued to carve out a special exception for a husband's forced intercourse with his wife. In addition, wife beating was initially omitted from the definition of criminal assault on the ground that a husband had the right to chastise his wife.

19. 1 William Blackstone, *Commentaries*, 447.

20. It is this sense of privacy that I refer to as an ethic or ideology. It transcends law as such and informs the way that laws are interpreted and understood. Law can be utilized in the ideological project, but it cannot be a substitute for it. On the gen-eral question of the interaction of law and ideology, see generally Fineman, *The Neutered Mother*, supra, note 3 at part I.

21. The far reaching potential of the individual, constitutional version of privacy to protect a wide range of intimate decisions has been limited in subsequent cases. Privacy has been limited to conventional, heterosexual expressions of sexuality (*Bowers v. Hardwick*), eroded from its initial expansive application in the abortion context (*Planned Parenthood V. Casey*), and generally not applied to much beyond a narrow category of intimate decision making, notably—family (*Meyer v. Nebras-ka*), marriage (*Griswold v. Connecticut*), and procreation (*Skinner v. Oklahoma* and *Roe v. Wade*).

22. The contrived ties are those the law constructs between biological "strangers" through such devices as marriage (which creates husband and wife) or adoption (which creates parent[s] and child). Ties of a "natural" nature are those of consan-guinity, although only some of these family ties are reinforced by law in modern so-cieties.

23. The Supreme Court recognized this conception of family in *Maynard v. Hill*, 125 U.S. 190, 8 S.Ct. 723, 31 L.Ed. 654 (1888). Marriage "is an institution in the main-tenance of which in its purity the public is deeply interested, for it is the foundation

of the family and of society, without which there would be neither civilization nor progress," *Maynard v. Hill,* 125 U.S. 190, 211 (1888).

24. I am not asserting that this is how families actually operate. Image is aspirational or ideal. Law certainly reflects a bias for the reproductive unit as the appropriate family form. The basic family relationships in our jurisprudence are those of husband and wife and of parent and child. Those outside of these statuses will often analogize their intimate relationships to one of these paradigmatic ones in order to argue for benefits conferred upon the traditional family.

25. Catherine A. MacKinnon, "Roe v. Wade: A Study in Male Ideology," in *Abortion and Legal Perspectives* , Jay L. Garfield et al. eds. (Amherst: University of Massachusetts Press, 1985), 53.

26. See generally Catherine A. Mackinnon, *Toward a Feminist Theory of the State* (Cambridge: Harvard University Press, 1989). In an early critique of the liberal ideal, MacKinnon argued that privacy doctrine "is most at home, the place women experience the most force, in the family" (id. at 190). For women she asserts, "the measure of the intimacy has been the measure of the oppression," (id. at 191). When the law of privacy restricts intrusions into intimacy, it bars changes in control over that intimacy through law. "The existing distribution of power and resources within the private sphere are precisely what the law of privacy exists to protect" (id. at 193), the subordination and domination of women.

27. See generally Martha Fineman and Roxanne Mykitiuak, *Abortion: Moral and Legal Perspectives* (New York: Routledge, 1994). Increasingly, such critiques have been accepted and intervention in certain domestic situations has become more common. There is a change in the way society reacts to spousal violence. Marital exemptions to rape statutes have been successfully attacked and repealed in many states. Police are trained to respond to domestic calls and to take them seriously or risk legal responses. Sexual intimacy is no longer considered to carry with it a corresponding license to rape or batter. This change in societal perception about male family prerogative is largely the result of the feminist movement and its egalitarian premises.

I do not mean to imply that there is now freedom from abuse in intimate situations, merely to indicate that the ideological underpinnings for such violence have been successfully challenged.

28. See Anita Allen, "Privacy at Home: The Twofold Problem," in Nancy J. Hirschmann et al., eds., *Revisioning the Political: Feminist Reconstructions of Traditional Concepts in Western Political Theory* (Boulder, CO: Westview Press, 1996).

29. Id. at 194

30. Id. at 209, note 1.

31. Although I see Allen's project as consistent with mine, she may disagree. Hers is an individualistic model. The demands of the home are seen as having robbed women of meaningful personal privacy. She is skeptical about "shared privacy" (represented by a "love affair") and terms it dangerous when "it replaces individual privacy." Id. at 201.

32. Id. at 205. Privacy is both a negative and a positive force. As a negative, it provides for resistance to the imposition of reproduction and caretaking responsibilities

that can subvert women's positive liberty interests in private pursuits such as solitude, self-satisfaction, and fulfillment.

33. For a historical account of parental rights see generally Barbara Bennett Woodhouse, "Who Owns the Child?: Meyer and Pierce and the Child as Property," *William and Mary Law Review* 33 (1992): 995. For a discussion of the modern trend in parental rights see Barbara Bennett Woodhouse, "A Public Role in the Private Family: The Parental Rights and Responsibilities Act and The Politics of Child Protection and Education," *Ohio State Law Review* 57 (1996): 393.

34. "In Hatching the Egg: A Child Centered Perspective on Parents Rights" (*Cardozo Law Review* 14 [1993]: 1747), Barbara B. Woodhouse first advocated this new approach to the parent-child relationship, terming it the "generist perspective." It is based on the view that nurturing of the next generation is the touchstone of the family. An adult's relationship with children is one of trusteeship rather than ownership. Adult's "rights" of control and custody yield to the less adversarial notions of obligation to provide nurturing, authority to act on the child's behalf, and standing to participate in the collaborative planning to meet the child's needs. For more on the generist perspective, see Barbara Bennett Woodhouse, "Out of Children's Needs, Children's Rights: The Voice Defining the Family," *Brigham Young University Law Review* 8 (1994): 321.

35. Woodhouse, "Out of Children's Needs, Children's Rights," 321.

36. Id.

37. See generally Woodhouse, "Hatching the Egg," supra note 35 at 1051–1060; Linda Gordon many years ago warned of the danger of building policy around children isolated from their mothers. Such measures often end up hurting the mothers (and through them, the children). Linda Gordon, "Putting Children First: Women, Materialism, and Welfare in the Early Twentieth Century," in L. K. Kerber et al., eds., *U.S. History as Women's History* (Chapel Hill: University of North Carolina Press, 1995).

38. This is the position of the nuclear family today. It is afforded privacy and there has to be sufficient justification for intervention.

39. Privacy and subsidy are here conceived as intertwined rights that support an entity against the state. As such, they would actually facilitate a move away from form to function. Autonomy carries with it the ability to define the unit.

40. For example, there would be no tolerance of marital rape or so-called "domestic" violence. Both would be treated under the same set of rules that would apply to legal strangers (which is what they become without or outside of the family label).

41. I recognize that this will happen in some cases, but this realization should not provide the operative assumption for parent-child relationships. If it becomes the operative assumption, it creates a culture for state intervention and control.

42. A clear concept of entity-focused privacy could make a difference in a number of areas. For example, in custody determinations the initial decision would be made under a primary caretaker standard because it is this standard that respects the autonomy and decision making of the prior unit and that gives respect to decisions

that were made within the marital family by validating them at divorce. In addition, entity privacy would require that once a determination was made, it would be final. Modification, absent abuse or neglect findings that apply to all entities, would not occur simply because there were "changed circumstances" as is now the rule in most jurisdictions. Entity privacy would require the same respect for postdivorce caretaking units as is shown to two-parent units. There would also be implications for the welfare context. Certainly the current official coercive conduct and investigation of sexual activities associated with paternity proceeding would be affected.

43. A functional approach to the family is a process. Each generation must struggle with the question of what public expectations and aspirations are to be placed on the family. Further, we must explicitly consider not only the roles or functions we want our families to play but also ask what resources they will need to perform those functions. The question of what sources can be tapped to supply necessary family resources must also be addressed. This process places the family in the context of other societal institutions. Finally, the question of family privacy must be addressed. Society must resolve how porous the family will be, how much autonomy it is to be ceded.

David A. J. Richards

CHAPTER 15

The Right to Privacy and Gay/Lesbian Sexuality

Beyond Decriminalization to Equal Recognition

Liberal constitutional democracies increasingly acknowledge that claims of gays and lesbians are based on fundamental constitutional rights that are, in turn, grounded in respect for human rights required by arguments of justice. Two kinds of arguments have been prominent: first, arguments appealing to basic liberties (including that to an intimate life); second, arguments for an equal respect free of irrational prejudices (such as racism and sexism) that dehumanize and degrade. For example, the European Court of Human Rights has found laws criminalizing gay sex to be unconstitutional violations of applicable guarantees of the right of private life;[1] and the United States Supreme Court, which had earlier declined (5–4) to hold comparable laws unconstitutional,[2] later found state constitutional provisions, that forbade all laws protecting gays and lesbians from discrimination, an unconstitutional violation of the right to be free of dehumanizing prejudice,[3] a decision that casts doubt on the continuing authority of the earlier privacy decision. In this chapter I will first argue that a certain normative conception of how these rights are to be understood and related explains both the constitutional decriminalization of gay/lesbian sexuality and the more recent arguments for forms of legal recognition of same-sex partnerships; later, I will argue that a further elaboration of this argument explains why commercial sexual services should be decriminalized.

Decriminalization

Serious argument for the protection of the human and constitutional rights of gay and lesbian persons understandably first centered on the laws criminalizing gay/lesbian sex acts. Such argument arose in the United States, for example, as an interpretation of the underlying principle of law that protected what the Supreme Court called the right of constitutional privacy. In 1965 the Supreme Court of the United States in *Griswold v. Connecticut*[4] had interpreted this right as the basis for a right to contraception that had been persistently and eloquently defended and advocated by Margaret Sanger for well over forty years, a decision that Sanger lived to see.[5] The Court extended the right to abortion services in 1973 in *Roe v. Wade*[6] (reaffirming its central principle in 1992[7]); the Court narrowly denied the application of the right to consensual homosexual sex acts in *Bowers v. Hardwick*;[8] but, the legitimacy of that decision is now, as I earlier observed, in some real doubt.[9] I develop here the normative argument for the protection of such a right to intimate life, as well as its reasonable application to contraception, abortion, and, most recently, gay/lesbian sexuality.

Sanger's argument for the right to contraception was very much rooted in rights-based feminism.[10] Sanger's argument had two prongs, both of which were implicit in the Supreme Court's decisions in *Griswold* and later cases: first, a basic human right to intimate life and the role of the right to contraception as an instance of that right; and second, the assessment of whether laws abridging such a fundamental right met the heavy burden of secular justification that was required.

The basis of the fundamental human right to intimate life was, as important American feminists had argued in the nineteenth century,[11] as basic an inalienable right of moral personality (respect for which is central to the argument for toleration) as the right to conscience. Like the right to conscience, it protects intimately personal moral resources (thoughts and beliefs, intellect, emotions, self-image and self-identity) and the way of life that expresses and sustains such convictions in facing and meeting rationally and reasonably the challenge of a life worth living—one touched by enduring personal and ethical value. The right to intimate life centers on protecting these moral resources.

The human right of intimate life was not only a right in the argument for toleration central to American constitutionalism, but a right interpretively implicit in the historical traditions of American rights-based constitutionalism. In both of the two great revolutionary moments that framed the trajectory of American constitutionalism (the American Revolution and the Civil War), the right to intimate life was one of the central human rights the abridgment of which rendered political power illegitimate and gave rise to the Lockean right to revolution.[12] For example, the background literature on human rights, known to and assumed by the American revolutionaries and founding constitutionalists, included what the influential Scottish philosopher Francis Hutcheson called "the natural right each one to enter into the matrimonial relation with any one who consents."[13] Indeed, John Witherspoon, whose lectures Madison heard at Princeton, followed Hutcheson in listing even more abstractly as a basic human and natural right a "right to associate, if he so incline, with any person or persons, whom he can persuade (not force)—under this is contained the right to marriage."[14] And, at the time of the Civil War, the understanding of marriage as a basic human right took on a new depth and urgency because of the antebellum abolitionist rights-based attack on the peculiar nature of American slavery; such slavery failed to recognize the marriage or family rights of slaves[15] and indeed inflicted on the black family the moral horror of breaking them up by selling family members separately.[16] One in six slave marriages thus were ended by force or sale.[17] No aspect of American slavery more dramatized its radical evil for abolitionists and Americans more generally than its brutal deprivation of intimate personal life, including undermining the moral authority of parents over children. Slaves, Weld argued, had "as little control over them [children], as have domestic animals over the disposal of their young."[18] Slavery, thus understood as an attack on intimate personal life,[19] stripped persons of essential attributes of their humanity.

It is against this historical background (as well as background rights-based political theory) that it is interpretively correct to regard the right to intimate life as one of the unenumerated rights protected both by the Ninth Amendment and the Privileges and Immunities Clause of the Fourteenth Amendment, as Justice Harlan may be regarded as arguing in his concurrence in *Griswold*.[20] The Supreme Court quite properly interpreted the Fourteenth Amendment in particular as protecting this basic human right against unjustified state abridgement and, as Sanger had urged, regarding the right to use contraceptives as an instance of this right. The right to contraception was, for Sanger, so fundamental a human right for women because it would enable women, perhaps for the first time in human history, reliably to decide whether and when their sexual lives would be reproductive. Respect for this right was an aspect of the more basic right of intimate life in two ways. First, it would enable women to exercise control over their intimate relations to men, deciding whether and when such relations would be reproductive. Second, it would secure to women the right to decide whether and when they would form the intimate relationship to a child. Both forms of choice threatened the traditional gender-defined role of women's sexuality as both exclusively and mandatorily procreational and maternally self-sacrificing.

Abridgment of such a basic right (as by criminalizing sale and use of contraceptives) can only be justified by a compelling secular reason in contemporary circumstances, not on the grounds of reasons that are today sectarian (internal to a moral tradition no longer based on public reasons available and accessible to all). In fact, the only argument that could sustain such laws (namely, the Augustinian[21] and Thomistic[22] view that it is immoral to engage in nonprocreative sex) is not today a view of sexuality that can reasonably be enforced on people at large. Many people regard sexual love as an end in itself and the control of reproduction as a reasonable way to regulate when and whether they have children consistent with their own personal and larger ethical interests, those of their children, and those of an overpopulated society at large. Even the question of having children at all is today a highly personal matter, certainly no longer governed by the perhaps once compelling secular need to have children for necessary work in a largely agrarian society with high rates of infant and adult mortality.[23] From the perspective of women in particular, as Sanger made so clear, the enforcement of an anticontraceptive morality on society at large not only harms women's interests (as well as that of an overpopulated society more generally) but also impersonally demeans them to a purely reproductive function. Women are deprived of the rational dignity of deciding as moral agents and persons, perhaps for the first time in human history, whether, when, and on what terms they will have children consistent with their other legitimate aims and ambitions (including the free exercise of all their basic human rights). Enforcement of such a morality rests on a now conspicuously sectarian conception of gender hierarchy in which women's sexuality is defined by a mandatory procreative role and responsibility. That conception, the basis of the unjust construction of gender hierarchy, cannot reasonably be the measure of human rights today.[24]

Similar considerations explain the grounds for doubt about the putative public, nonsectarian justifications for laws criminalizing abortion and homosexual sexuality. Antiabortion laws, grounded in the alleged protection of a neutral good such as life, unreasonably equate the moral weight of a fetus in the early stages of pregnancy with that of a person and abortion with murder; such laws fail to take seriously the weight that should be accorded a woman's basic right to reproductive autonomy in making highly personal moral choices central to her most intimate bodily and personal life against the background of the lack of reasonable public consensus that fetal life, as such, can be equated in the early stages of pregnancy with that of a moral person.[25]

Antihomosexuality laws have even less semblance of a public justification (such as fetal life) that would be acceptably enforced on society at large and brutally abridge the sexual expression of the companionate loving relationships to which homosexuals, like heterosexuals, have an inalienable human right. Certainly, the interests expressive of sexual orientations must reasonably be understood in contemporary circumstances as aspects of the underlying right to intimate association, a right that persons may pursue in the empowering terms of autonomously reflective reasonable standards and judgments expressive of conviction. The arguments, traditionally supposed to rationalize abridgment of this fundamental right, cannot reasonably be defended as compelling secular interests today.

To be clear on this point, we need to examine critically the grounds traditionally supposed to rationalize the condemnation of homosexuality. Plato in *The Laws* gave influential expression to the moral condemnation in terms of two arguments: its nonprocreative character and (in its male homosexual forms) its degradation of the passive male partner to the status of a woman.[26] Neither of these two traditional moral reasons for condemning homosexuality can any longer be legitimately and indeed constitutionally imposed on society at large or any other person or group of persons.

One such moral reason (the condemnation of nonprocreational sex) can, for example, no longer constitutionally justify laws against the sale to and use of contraceptives by married and unmarried heterosexual couples.[27] The mandatory enforcement at large of the procreational model of sexuality is, in circumstances of overpopulation and declining infant and adult mortality, a sectarian ideal lacking adequate secular basis in the general goods that can alone reasonably justify state power; accordingly, contraceptive-using heterosexuals have the constitutional right to decide when and whether their sexual lives shall be pursued to procreate or as an independent expression of mutual love, affection, and companionship.[28]

And the other moral reason for condemning homosexual sex (the degradation of a man to the passive status of a woman) rests on the sexist premise of the degraded nature of women that has been properly rejected as a reasonable basis for laws or policies on grounds of suspect classification analysis.[29] If we constitutionally accept, as we increasingly do, the suspectness of gender on a par with that of race, we must, in principle, condemn, as a basis for law, any use of stereotypes expressive of the unjust enforcement of gender roles through law. That condemnation extends, as authoritative case law makes clear, to gender stereotypy as such whether immediately harmful to women or to men.[30]

Nonetheless, although each moral ground for the condemnation of homosexuality has been independently rejected as a reasonable justification for coercive laws enforceable on society at large (applicable to both men and women), these laws unreasonably retain their force when brought into specific relationship to the claims of homosexual men and women for equal justice under constitutional law.[31] These claims are today in their basic nature arguments of principle made by gay men and lesbians for the same respect for their intimate love life and other basic rights, free of unreasonable procreational and sexist requirements, now rather generously accorded men and women who are heterosexually coupled (including, as we have seen, even the right to abortion against the alleged weight of fetal life). Empirical issues relating to sexuality and gender are now subjected to more impartial critical assessment than they were previously; and the resulting light of public reason about issues of sexuality and gender should be available to all persons on fair terms. However, both the procreational mandates and the unjust gender stereotypy, constitutionally condemned for the benefit of heterosexual men and women, are ferociously applied to homosexual men and women.[32] It bespeaks the continuing political power of the traditional moral subjugation of homosexuals that such a claim of fair treatment (an argument of basic constitutional principle if any argument is) was contemptuously dismissed by a majority of the Supreme Court of the United States (5–4) in 1986 in *Bowers v. Hardwick*.[33] No skeptical scrutiny whatsoever was accorded state purposes elsewhere acknowledged as illegitimate. Certainly, no such purpose could be offered of the alleged weight of fetal life that has been rejected as a legitimate ground for criminalization of all forms of abortion; any claim of public health could be addressed, as they would be in comparable cases of heterosexual relations involving the basic constitutional right of intimate life, by constitutionally required alternatives less restrictive and more effective than criminalization (including use of prophylactics by those otherwise at threat from transmission of AIDS).[34]

Traditional moral arguments, now clearly reasonably rejected in their application to heterosexuals, were uncritically applied to a group much more exigently in need of constitutional protection on grounds of principle.[35] Reasonable advances in the public understanding of sexuality and gender, now constitutionally available to all heterosexuals, were suspended in favor of an appeal to the sexual mythology of the Middle Ages.[36] It is an indication of the genre of dehumanizing stereotypes at work in *Bowers v. Hardwick*, stripping a class of persons (blacks, women, Jews, homosexuals) of moral personality by reducing them to a mythologized sexuality, that the Court focussed so obsessionally on one sex act (sodomy); as Leo Bersani perceptively observed about the public discourse (reflected in *Bowers*), it resonates in images (inherited from the nineteenth century) of homosexuals as sexually obsessed prostitutes.[37] The transparently unprincipled character of *Bowers*[38] in such terms thus suggests a larger problem, which connects such treatment of homosexuals with the now familiar structural injustice underlying racism and sexism. Understanding that connection explains, I believe, the recent emergence of arguments for equal recognition of gay/lesbian relationships on more equal terms with recognition of heterosexual relationships, including claims to same-sex marriage.

Equal Protection

As I have observed, arguments for gay/lesbian rights rest on two kinds of arguments: first, arguments appealing to basic liberties; and second, arguments for an equal respect free of irrational prejudices (such as racism and sexism) that dehumanize and degrade. I have already defended the constitutional decriminalization of gay/lesbian sexuality as an aspect of the basic right to intimate life. Equal respect for such a basic right requires that its exercise not be subject to dehumanizing prejudices that, in their nature, cannot be reasonably justified in terms of compelling secular state purposes (as opposed to purposes acceptable only in sectarian terms). Once we agree that gay/lesbian sexuality cannot reasonably be criminalized on grounds of compelling secular state purposes, we need to ask whether such purposes might justify not extending to gays and lesbians legal recognition of their unions.

In this connection, a Catholic moral conservative such as John Finnis has argued that, even if *Bowers* were properly overruled (as he suggests it should be), it would still be appropriate to make the exclusively procreational model of sexuality the measure of the right to marriage.[39] On this view, as another moral conservative put it, the right to marriage is determined not solely by commitments arising from love as such but by "the natural teleology of the body."[40] There is, however, no difference of principle between the sectarian character of such arguments in the one context (*Bowers*) as opposed to another (the right to marriage). Heterosexual couples who are childless, whether by design or by force of circumstances, are not for that reason disqualified from the right to marry, nor could they reasonably be.[41] If the natural teleology of the body made any sense as a basis for public law, such childlessness as much violates the natural teleology of the body as that of a homosexual couple. But, the natural teleology of the body, whatever its legitimate force within sectarian moral and religious traditions, is not a publicly reasonable basis for law. The natural teleology of the body (like the teleology of nature more generally) cannot reasonably be a basis for public law in a morally and religiously pluralistic society that lacks any reasonable common ground to ascribe to such natural facts a politically enforceable normative purpose.[42] The imposition, on either heterosexual or homosexual love, of the model of mandatory procreational sex is surely, in contemporary circumstances, constitutionally unjust because it politically remakes reality in its own anachronistic sectarian image. In particular, it conspicuously fails to acknowledge what any reasonable understanding of modern life, not hostage to such a sectarian conception, must acknowledge: the force in human life of sexual love as an end in itself that sustains intimate relations of loving and being loved central to giving meaning to personal and ethical life.[43] From this perspective, the political demand that human love, to be maritally legitimate, must conform to the natural teleology of the body usurps the moral sovereignty of the person over the transformative moral powers of love in intimate relations and the identifications central to sustaining personal and ethical value in living, in effect, dehumanizing human sexuality to its purely biological, reproductive aspect. As a Catholic critic of his church's condemnation of homosexuality recently put this point (against, among others, Finnis), "it is extraordinary that so many branches of Christianity should have now degenerated into fertility cults."[44] Such a view, dubious even today on internal religious grounds, can hardly reasonably be the measure of rights and responsibilities in a secular society.[45] The role of human sexuality in the plastic imaginative life and transformative moral passions and identifications of free personality would, by force of law, be unreasonably degraded to the procrustean sectarian measure of a purely animal sexuality.[46]

Opposition to same-sex partnerships rests, on critical examination, on sectarian terms not on compelling secular purposes. Such opposition appeals to sectarian arguments that fail to treat gays and lesbian as persons, degrading them in terms of stereotypes of sexuality and gender that dehumanize. Indeed, at bottom, the insistence on opposite sexes, as the legitimate measure of the right to marriage, indulges, as the Hawaiian Supreme Court saw,[47] constitutionally illegitimate gender stereotypes. The prohibition of same-sex marriage, on this view, is to the unjust political construction of sexism and homophobia what the prohibition of racial intermarriage was to the unjust construction of racism.[48] The condemnation of same-sex marriage is one of the crucial aspects of the cultural construction of the dehumanization of the homosexual as a sexualized fallen woman; homosexuals on this view can no more marry than animals. Such dehumanizing prejudices, targeted against homosexuals, violate equal respect to be free of prejudices directed against their basic rights. Both the right to private life and the right against unjust subjection of basic rights to unjust prejudice, properly understood, thus require legal recognition of same-sex partnerships as they also require other protections for gays and lesbians against unjust discrimination.

Such dehumanization retains popular appeal when brought into relation to claims for same-sex marriage because, consistent with Freud's observation of the narcissism of small differences,[49] it enables a culture, with a long history of uncritical moral subjugation of women and homosexuals, not to take seriously, let alone think reasonably about the growing convergences of heterosexual and homosexual human love in the modern world. These include not only shared economic contributions to the household and convergent styles of nonprocreational sex and elaboration of erotic play as an end in itself but the interest in sex as an expressive bond central to companionate relationships of friendship and love as ends in themselves; several partners over a lifetime; when there is interest in children, only in few of them; and the insistence on the romantic love of tender and equal companions as the democratized center of sharing intimate daily life.[50] Indeed, some studies suggest that, if anything, homosexual relationships more fully develop features of egalitarian sharing that are more often the theory than the practice of heterosexual relations.[51] The uncritical ferocity of contemporary political homophobia draws its populist power from the compulsive need to construct Manichean differences where none reasonably exist, thus reenforcing institutions of gender hierarchy perceived now to be at threat. In particular, as Whitman argued,[52] democratic equality in homosexual intimate life threatens the core of traditional gender roles and the hierarchy central to such roles. Consistent with the paradox of intolerance, the embattled sectarian orthodoxy does not explore such reasonable doubts, but polemically represses them by remaking reality in its own sectarian image of marriage, powerfully deploying the uncritical traditional stereotype of the homosexual as the scapegoat of one's suppressed doubts (excluding the homosexual from the moral community of human rights, including the basic human right to intimate life). Homosexuals are the natural scapegoat for this uncritical feminist backlash,[53] because they, unlike women, remain a largely marginalized and despised minority. Advocates of the traditional sectarian orthodoxy object as strongly to many of the achievements of the feminist movement (some to the decriminalization of contraception, others to that of abortion, still others to now mainstream feminist issues such as equal rights[54]), but they have lost many of these battles, and the sectarian hard core of the orthodoxy, in fact hostile to feminism and civil rights measures in general,[55] takes its stand strategically where it still can against members of a traditionally stigmatized and silenced minority who are, like the Jews in Europe, easily demonized.[56]

The Scapegoating of Commercial Sex Today

If you have followed my argument so far, I would briefly mention, in conclusion, its further implications. I have argued for a robust understanding of the right to intimate life in a number of areas (contraceptive use, abortion services, consensual adult homosexuality) and indeed suggested that this interpretation should be grounded in the claims of rights-based feminism. I have elsewhere argued at length that the right to intimate life extends to commercial sex, and the kinds of compelling secular purposes required elsewhere (as we have seen) cannot reasonably justify criminalization as under current

American law (forms of reasonable regulations are a different matter).[57] In effect, in the United States prostitutes remain and are the ideological scapegoats whom most people (both on the left and right) love to hate.

Both the rights of intimate life and of equal respect require, in my judgment, protection of commercial sex from the continuing uncritical political force of gender stereotyping in our law and social and economic practices. Such sex workers are, in their claims to basic rights of intimate life and of work, no different from the rest of us. If we regard our rights to intimate life to compass sexual imaginations and lives that answer to our personal erotic needs and rebel against mandatory gender roles (for example, that our sexuality must be procreational or conventionally masculine or feminine or whatever), surely sex workers must equally have the right to explore their own sexual lives in the same way and to render sexual services to others on the same fair terms. Sex workers, on this view, challenge today, as they have in the past, the structural injustice of gender inequality precisely by insisting on both sexual and economic independence. Americans cannot reasonably understand, let alone remedy, such injustice if we continue to acquiesce in the anachronistic contempt for persons who may most reasonably challenge the unjust political force gender stereotypes continue to enjoy in a constitutional culture now committed to the condemnation of such stereotypes.

NOTES

1. See *Dudgeon v. The United Kingdom* (1981) 4EHRR 149 (Ct.); *Norris v. Ireland*, 142 Eur. Ct. H.R. (ser. A), at 186 (1988); *Modinos v. Cyprus*, 259 Eur. Ct. H.R. (ser. A), at 485 (1993).

2. See *Bowers v. Hardwick*, 478 U.S. 186 (1986).

3. See *Romer v. Evans*, 116 S.Ct. 1620 (1996).

4. See *Griswold v. Connecticut*, 381 U.S. 479 (1965).

5. See Ellen Chesler, *Woman of Valor: Margaret Sanger and the Birth Control Movement in America* (New York: Anchor, 1992), 11, 230, 376, 467.

6. See *Roe v. Wade*, 410 U.S. 113 (1973).

7. See *Planned Parenthood of Southeastern Pennsylvania v. Casey*, 505 U.S. , 112 S.Ct. 2791, 120 L.Ed.2d 674 (1992).

8. See *Bowers v. Hardwick*, 478 U.S. 186 (1986).

9. See, for example, *Romer v. Evans*, 116 S.Ct. 1620 (1996).

10. For elaboration of this point, see Richards, *Women, Gays, and the Constitution: The Grounds for Feminism and Gay Rights in Culture and Law* (Chicago: University of Chicago Press, 1998), 178–81.

11. For citations and discussion, see Richards, *Women, Gays, and the Constitution*, ch. 4.

12. See, on American revolutionary constitutionalism as framed by these events, Richards, *Foundations of American Constitutionalism* (New York: Oxford University Press, 1989); *Conscience and the Constitution: History, Theory, and Law of the Reconstruction Amendments* (Princeton: Princeton University Press, 1993).

13. See Francis Hutcheson, A *System of Moral Philosophy* , 2 vols. in 1 (1755; reprint, New York: Augustus M. Kelley, 1968), 299.

14. See John Witherspoon, *Lectures of Moral Philosophy* Jack Scott ed. (East Brunswick: N.J.: Associated University Presses, 1982), 123. For further development of this point, see Richards, *Toleration and the Constitution*, 232–33.

15. See Kenneth M. Stampp, *The Peculiar Institution* (New York: Vintage, 1956), 198, 340–49; Eugene D. Genovese, *Roll, Jordan, Roll: The World the Slaves Made* (New York: Vintage, 1974), 32, 52–53, 125, 451–58.

16. See Stampp, *The Peculiar Institution*, 199–207, 204–06, 333, 348–49; Herbert G. Gutman, *The Black Family in Slavery and Freedom, 1750–1925* (New York: Vintage, 1976), 146, 318, 349.

17. See Gutman, *The Black Family in Slavery and Freedom*, 318.

18. See Theodore Weld, *American Slavery as It Is* (1839; reprint, New York: Arno Press and The New York Times, 1968), 56.

19. See Ronald G. Walters, *The Antislavery Appeal: American Abolitionism after 1830* (New York: Norton, 1978), 95–96.

20. Justice Harlan, in fact, grounds his argument on the Due Process Clause of the Fourteenth Amendment, but the argument is more plausibly understood, as a matter of text, history, and political theory, as based on the Privileges and Immunities Clause of the Fourteenth Amendment, for reasons I give in Richards, *Conscience and the Constitution*, ch. 6. For further elaboration of this interpretation of *Griswold*, see Richards, *Toleration and the Constitution* (New York: Oxford University Press, 1986), 256–61.

21. See Augustine, *The City of God*, Henry Bettenson, trans. (Harmondsworth, England: Penguin, 1972), 577–94.

22. Thomas Aquinas elaborates Augustine's conception of the exclusive legitimacy of procreative sex in a striking way. Of the emission of semen apart from procreation in marriage, he wrote: "After the sin of homicide whereby a human nature already in existence is destroyed, this type of sin appears to take next place, for by it the generation of human nature is precluded." Thomas Aquinas, *On the Truth of the Catholic Faith: Summa Contra Gentiles*, Vernon Bourke, trans. (New York: Image, 1956), pt. 2, ch. 122(9), 146.

23. On how personal this decision now is, see, in general, Elaine Tyler May, *Barren in the Promised Land: Childless Americans and the Pursuit of Happiness* (New York: Basic Books, 1995).

24. For further discussion of the right to privacy and contraception, see Richards, *Toleration and the Constitution*, 256–61.

25. For further discussion, see Richards, *Toleration and the Constitution*, 261–69; Ronald Dworkin, *Life's Dominion: An Argument about Abortion, Euthanasia, and Individual Freedom* (New York: Knopf, 1993), 3–178.

26. See Plato, *Laws*, book 8, 835d-842a, in Edith Hamilton and Huntington Cairns, eds., *The Collected Dialogues of Plato* (New York: Pantheon, 1961), 1401–1402. On the moral condemnation of the passive role in homosexuality in both Greek and early Christian moral thought, see Peter Brown, *The Body and Society: Men, Women, and Sexual Renunciation in Early Christianity* (New York: Columbia University Press, 1988), 30, 382–83. But, for evidence of Greco-Roman toleration of long-term homosexual relations even between adults, see John Boswell, *Same-Sex Unions in Premodern Europe* (New York: Villard, 1994), 53–107; I am grateful to Stephen Morris for conversations on this point. Whether these relationships were regarded as marriages may be a very different matter. For criticism of Boswell's argument along this latter line, see Brent D. Shaw, "A Groom of One's Own?" *The New Republic*, July 18 and 25, 1994, 33–41.

27. See *Griswold v. Connecticut*, 381 U.S. 479 (1965); *Eisenstadt v. Baird*, 405 U.S. 438 (1972).

28. For further discussion, see Richards, *Toleration and the Constitution*, 256–61.

29. See, for example, *Frontiero v. Richardson*, 411 U.S. 677 (1973); *Craig v. Boren*, 429 U.S. 190 (1976). On homophobia as rooted in sexism, see Elisabeth Young-Bruehl, *The Anatomy of Prejudices* (Cambridge: Harvard University Press, 1986), 143, 148–51.

30. For cases that protect women from such harm, see *Reed v. Reed*, 404 U.S. 71 (1971) (right to administer estates); *Frontiero v. Richardson*, 411 U.S. 677 (1973) (dependency allowances to servicewomen); *Stanton v. Stanton*, 421 U.S. 7 (1975) (child support for education). For cases that protect men, see *Wengler v. Druggists Mutual Ins. Co.*, 446 U.S. 142 (1980) (widower's right to death benefits); *Craig v. Boren*, 429 U.S. 190 (1976) (age of drinking for men).

31. On the continuities among heterosexual and homosexual forms of intimacy in the modern era, see, in general, John D'Emilio and Estelle B. Freedman, *Intimate Matters: A History of Sexuality in America* (New York: Harper and Row, 1988), 239–360; Anthony Giddens, *The Transformation of Intimacy: Sexuality, Love, and Eroticism in Modern Societies* (Cambridge, U.K.: Polity, 1992). See also Barbara Ehrenreich, Elizabeth Hess, and Gloria Jacobs, *Remaking Love: The Feminization of Sex* (New York: Anchor, 1986); Anne Snitow, Christine Stansell, and Sharon Thompson, eds., *Powers of Desire: The Politics of Sexuality* (New York: Monthly Review Press, 1983); Carole S. Vance, ed., *Pleasure and Danger: Exploring Female Sexuality* (Boston: Routledge and Kegan Paul, 1984).

32. On the unjust gender stereotypy uncritically applied to homosexual men and women, see Susan Moller Okin, "Sexual Orientation and Gender: Dichotomizing Differences," in David M. Estlund and Martha C. Nussbaum, eds., *Sex, Preference, and Family: Essays on Law and Nature* (New York: Oxford University Press, 1997), 44–59.

33. *Bowers v. Hardwick*, 478 U.S. 186 (1986).

34. The argument applies, in any event, only to those forms of sex by gay men likely to transmit the disease; it does not reasonably apply to lesbians, nor does it apply to all forms of sex (including anal sex) by gay men. So, the argument that sex

acts as such can be criminalized on this basis is constitutionally overinclusive and inconsistent with the basic right thus abridged. The regulatory point is that even gay men at threat by virtue of their sexual practices can take preventive measures against this threat (by using condoms). For a recent discussion of what further such reasonable preventive measures the gay men at threat might also take, see Garbriel Rotello, *Sexual Ecology: AIDS and the Destiny of Gay Men* (New York: Dutton, 1997).

35. For further criticism, see Richards, *Foundations of American Constitutionalism*, 209–47.

36. Justice Blackmun put the point acidly: "Like Justice Holmes, I believe that 'it is revolting to have no better reason for a rule of law than that so it was laid down in the time of Henry IV. It is still more revolting if the grounds upon which it was laid down have vanished long since, and the rule simply persists from blind imitation of the past.' " *Bowers*, 478 U.S. at 199 [quoting Oliver Wendell Holmes, "The Path of the Law", *Harvard Law Review* 10 (1897): 457, 469.

37. See Leo Bersani, "Is the Rectum As a Grave?" in Douglas Crimp, *Cultural Analysis/Cultural Activism* (Cambridge: MIT Press, 1988), 197–222, 211–12, 222.

38. I develop this argument at greater length in Richards, *Foundations of American Constitutionalism*, ch. 6; and in Richards, "Constitutional Legitimacy and Constitutional Privacy,"*N.Y.U. Law Review* 61 (1986): 800. See also Anne D. Goldstein, "History, Homosexuality, and Political Values: Searching for the Hidden Determinants of *Bowers v. Hardwick*," *Yale Law Journal* 97 (1988): 1973; Nan D. Hunter, "Life After *Hardwick*," *Harvard Civil Rights-Civil Liberties Review* 27 (1992): 531; Janet E. Halley, "Reasoning About Sodomy: Act and Identity In and After *Bowers v. Hardwick*," *Virginia Law Review* 79 (1993): 1721; Anne B. Goldstein, "Reasoning About Homosexuality: A Commentary on Janet Halley's 'Reasoning About Sodomy: Act and Identity In and After *Bowers v. Hardwick*,' " *Virginia Law Review* 79 (1993): 1781; Kendall Thomas, "The Eclipse of Reason: A Rhetorical Reading of *Bowers v. Hardwic*," *Virginia Law Review* 79 (1993): 1805.

39. See John Finnis, "Law, Morality, and 'Sexual Orientation' "*Notre Dame Journal of Law, Ethics, and Public Policy* 9 (1995).

40. See Hadley Arkes, "Testimony on the Defense of Marriage Act, 1996," Judiciary Committee, House of Representatives, 1996 WL 246693 (F.D.C.H.)at p.l1; see also Hadley Arkes, "Questions of Principle, Not Predictions," *Georgia Law Journal* 84 (1995): 321; and, to similar effect, Robert P. George and Gerard V. Bradley, "Marriage and the Liberal Imagination," id., 301. For cogent criticism, see Stephen Macedo, "Homosexuality and the Conservative Mind," id., 261; and, "Reply to Critics," id., 329.

41. Cf. *Turner v. Safley*, 482 U.S. 78 (1987) (denial of marriage right to prison inmates, on ground could not procreate, held unconstitutional). For discussion, see William N. Eskridge, Jr., *The Case for Same-Sex Marriage* (New York: Free Press, 1996), 128–30.

42. Arguments of such sorts are based on appeals to nature of the same sort that David Hume considered for similar reasons an illegitimate basis for public laws, including laws prohibiting suicide: "'Tis impious, says, the *French* superstition to

inoculate for the small-pox, or usurp the business of providence, by voluntarily pro-ducing distempers and maladies. 'Tis impious says the modern *European* superstition, to put a period to our own life, and thereby rebel against our creator. And why not impious, say I, to build houses, cultivate the ground, and sail upon the ocean? In all these actions, we employ our powers of mind and body to produce some innovation in the course of nature, and in none of them do we any more. They are all of them, therefore, equally innocent or equally criminal." David Hume, "Of Suicide," in Eugene F. Miller, ed., *Essays Moral Political and Literary*, (1777; reprint, Indianapolis: LibertyClassics, 1985), 585.

43. See, in general, Anthony Giddens, *The Transformation of Intimacy: Sexuality, Love, and Eroticism in Modern Societies* (Cambridge, U.K.: Polity, 1992); John D'Emilio and Estelle B. Freedman, *Intimate Matters: A History of Sexuality in America* (New York: Harper and Row, 1988), 239–360; Barbara Ehrenreich, Elizabeth Hess, and Gloria Jacobs, *Remaking Love: The Feminization of Sex* (New York: Anchor, 1986); Ann Snitow, Christine Stansell, and Sharon Thompson, eds., *Powers of Desire: The Politics of Sexuality* (New York: Monthly Review Press, 1983); Carole S. Vance, ed., *Pleasure and Danger: Exploring Female Sexuality* (Boston: Routledge and Kegan Paul, 1984).

44. See Mark D. Jordan, *The Invention of Sodomy in Christian Theology* (Chicago: University of Chicago Press, 1997), 174.

45. As Mark Jordan observes: "The Christian criterion of fertility, of parenting, of filiation, is not bodily. That much was worked out with painstaking care in the early Trinitarian debates," id., 174.

46. For important studies of the differences between human and animal sexuality, see Clellan S. Ford and Frank A. Beach, *Patterns of Sexual Behavior* (New York: Harper and Row, 1951); Irenaus Eibl-Eibesfeldt, *Love and Hate: The Natural History of Behavior Patterns*, Geoffrey Strachan trans. (New York: Holt, Rinehart, and Winston, 1971). The insight is also central to Freud's exploration of the imaginative role of sexuality in human personality; see Sigmund Freud, " 'Civilized' Sexual Morality and Modern Nervous Illness," in *The Standard Edition of the Complete Psychological Works of Sigmund Freud*, ed. and trans. James Strachey (London: Hogarth Press, 1961), 9:81, 187: "The sexual instinct . . . is probably more strong developed in man than in most of the higher animals; it is certainly more constant, since it has almost entirely overcome the periodicity to which it is tied in animals. It places extraordinarily large amounts of force at the disposal of civilized activity, and it does this in virtue of its especially marked characteristic of being able to displace its aim without materially diminishing its intensity. This capacity to exchange its originally sexual aim for another one, which is no longer sexual but which is physically related to the first aim, is called the capacity for sublimation."

47. See *Baehr v. Lewin*, 852 P.2d 44 (Haw. 1993); for discussion, see Richards, *Identity and the Case for Gay Rights: Race, Gender, Religion as Analogies* (Chicago: University of Chicago Press, 1999), 154. See also *Baker v. Vermont*, 1999 Vt. Lexis 406 (gay/lesbian couples entitled to same benefits as heterosexual married couples under Vermont Constitution).

48. See Andrew Koppelman, "The Miscegenation Analogy: Sodomy Laws as Sex Discrimination," *Yale Law Journal* 98 (1988): 145.

49. See Sigmund Freud, *Civilization and Its Discontents*, in *The Standard Edition of the Complete Psychological Works of Sigmund Freud*, ed. and trans. James Strachey (London: Hogarth Press, 1961), 21: 114; see also *Moses and Monotheism* (1964), 23: 91.

50. See, on the continuities among heterosexual and homosexual forms of intimacy in the modern world, in general, Giddens, *Transformation of Intimacy*; D'Emilio and Freedman, *Intimate Matters*, 239–360; Philip Blumstein and Pepper Schwartz, *American Couples* (New York: William Morrow, 1983), 332–545. On declining fertility rates, see Claudia Goldin, *Understanding the Gender Gap: An Economic History of American Women* (New York: Oxford University Press, 1990), 139–42; on childlessness, see, in general, May, *Barren in the Promised Land*; on rising divorce rates, see Degler, *At Odds*, 165–68, 175–76. See also Ehrenreich, Hess, and Jacobs, *Remaking Love*; Snitow, Stansell, and Thompson, eds., *Powers of Desire*; Vance, ed., *Pleasure and Danger*.

51. On this point, see Susan Moller Okin, "Sexual Orientation and Gender: Dichotomizing Differences," in David M. Estlund and Martha C. Nussbaum, eds., *Sex, Preference, and Family: Essays on Law and Nature* (New York: Oxford University Press, 1997), 44–59.

52. See, for development of this point, Richards, *Women, Gays, and the Constitution*, 297–310.

53. See, in general, Susan Faludi, *Backlash: The Undeclared War Against American Women* (New York: Doubleday, 1991); Marilyn French, *The War Against Women* (London: Penguin, 1992).

54. For some sense of the range of such views and their supporting reasons, see Sherrye Henry, *The Deep Divide: Why American Women Resist Equality* (New York: MacMillan, 1994); Elizabeth Fox-Genovese, *"Feminism Is Not the Story of My Life": How Today's Feminist Elite Has Lost Touch with the Real Concerns of Women* (New York: Doubleday, 1996); Elizabeth Fox-Genovese, *Feminism Without Illusions: A Critique of Individualism* (Chapel Hill: University of North Carolina Press, 1991).

55. For its antifeminism, see Didi Herman, *The Antigay Agenda: Orthodox Vision and the Christian Right* (Chicago: University of Chicago Press, 1997), 103–10; for its opposition to the civil rights agenda in general, see id., 111–36, 140.

56. On the analogy of such contemporary homophobia to anti-Semitism, see Didi Herman, *Antigay Agenda*, 2–91, 125–28; cf. Elaine Pagels, *The Origin of Satan*, (New York: Random House, 1996), 102–5. See also, for a useful study of the reactionary populist politics of this group, Chris Bull and John Gallagher, *Perfect Enemies: The Religious Right, the Gay Movement, and the Politics of the 1990's* (New York: Crown, 1996).

57. See, on this point, David A. J. Richards, "Commercial Sex and the Rights of the Person: A Moral Argument for the Decriminalization of Prostitution," *University of Pennsylvania Law Review* 127 (1979): 1195.

Women and Work

Eileen Boris

CHAPTER 16

The Gender of Discrimination

Race, Sex, and Fair Employment

Rejecting the claim that black women composed a "special class to be protected from employment discrimination," the United States District Court, Eastern District of Missouri argued in 1976 that the Civil Rights Act of 1964 permitted charges of "race discrimination, sex discrimination, or alternatively either, but not a combination of both." Though subsequent courts have looked more favorably upon black women as a legal category, the *Degraffenreid* decision reflected the historical trajectory of antidiscrimination law, which silenced the gendered nature of race and the racialized nature of gender.[1] Its adherence to unitary notions of race and sex, in which a part stood for the whole, neglected the "interactive discrimination" faced by black women, whose experiences could not be subsumed completely under a "sex plus race" doctrine that still separated composite identity or limited the additional identities of women who claimed race as well as gender discrimination.[2]

This outcome hardly surprises. From the origins of the American Republic, "race" and "sex" have stood as distinct categories in law and social policy. "Women" entered the law as a silence, either because constitutions and statues specifically mentioned "men," or the legal fiction of marital unity collapsed their standing into that of the male household head.[3] "Women," however, meant "white" women. For women of African descent stood with their men as racial others under the laws of slavery and segregation. The category of "race" subsumed their experiences into those of their men.

Reconstruction-era civil rights acts applied to race, not "sex." The Fourteenth Amendment placed "male" in the Constitution and subsequent courts interpreted citizenship to restrict women's independent participation in the polity and link her nationality status upon marriage to that of her husband.[4] In the early twentieth century, wage, hour, and other labor standards covered "women," but domestic service and agricultural labor—the occupations of most black women—remained outside of the law.[5] The Nineteenth Amendment brought votes to women but not to black ones living in the Jim Crow South.[6]

This division into race and sex was not a biological inevitability but rose out of the interplay of intellectual and political forces. The great social movements of the nineteenth and twentieth century—abolitionism, women's rights, and civil rights—nearly always demanded rights on the basis of race or sex. Early social science constructed the category of race without focusing on the different experiences of men and women. Government statistics counted by race or sex, not by race and sex.[7] The state itself reflected the overall gender and racial division of labor. So the Women's Bureau—an agency that rarely considered nonwhite women—took responsibility for women within the Department of Labor; the World War I Division of Negro Economics and the 1930s Division of Negro Labor focused on black workers.[8] While black civil rights struggles inspired the second wave of feminism as much as the first, movements of African Americans of both sexes and those of predominantly European American women remained apart. Essentialism gripped the second wave of feminism no less than did masculinism pervade the civil rights struggle of the 1960s, with black men standing for African Americans.[9]

Title VII of the Civil Rights Act of 1964 appeared to bring "sex" and "race" together. It prohibited workplace discrimination on the basis of race, color, religion, sex, or national origin.[10] Popular accounts, along with older scholarly ones, portray the addition of "sex" as a decoy, though we now know that amender Howard K. Smith, a conservative Virginia Democrat, was a staunch proponent of the Equal Rights Amendment (ERA). These accounts perpetuate the beliefs of many liberals at the time that the act was really about race and that Southern legislators introduced "sex" merely to obstruct passage.[11] Certainly the resulting enforcement agency, the Equal Employment Opportunity Commission (EEOC), initially pursued race cases more vigorously than sex ones.[12] The statute's "bona fide occupational qualification" provided a greater loophole for sexual discrimination on the basis of female difference; so did the question of when a classification was sex-based, as with pregnancy. After 1964 courts deployed the Fourteenth Amendment to subject race to a stricter scrutiny than sex. That is, they allowed a lower threshold for the government to prove the necessity for distinctions on the basis of sex, for which pregnancy and privacy offered justification for different treatment, than they did for race, for which there was nearly no excuse for discrimination.

Based on an equal protection doctrine that developed from the race-based struggle against slavery, antidiscrimination law ended up treating different

people (i.e., men and women) as if they were the same (just black). It has privileged "race" over "sex" in so far as courts have been more inclined to accept
distinctions on the basis of "sex." Yet the relation of "race" to "sex" is much
more complicated than legal categories suggest. Law inadequately mirrors social life, even though its decisions and procedures reinforce existing hierarchies of authority and subordination. When historians move from legislation
and case law to social history, the law appears an imperfect instrument to ad-
judicate the complexity of experience and identity. After all, we possess not
only a race or gender,[13] but both these social constructions merge with other
social factors to define being.

Inspired by critical race feminism, this paper contributes to the ongoing
discussion of intersectionality and the failure of law and social policy to recognize harms to racial/ethnic women as racial/ethnic women. It does so by investigating the opening act of modern employment discrimination law during
World War II. Through Executive Order 8802 in June 1941, Franklin D. Roosevelt created the President's Committee on Fair Employment Practice
(FEPC) to end discrimination in government contracts and employment related to the war effort. The FEPC covered African Americans and other racial
minorities, Jews and other religious minorities, and noncitizens or those not
of United States nationality. However, most cases involved African Americans.[14] Though "sex" was absent from the FEPC's mandate, discrimination
wore a gendered face.

The forms of discrimination recognized by the FEPC undoubtedly shaped
the stories told to it. Women had to couch their complaints in the language
of race, religion, or nationality to gain redress. They had to charge race discrimination even if their experience proved much more complex than the
committee's reading of "race." Racialized gendered bodies mattered—and not
only to Southern demagogues who portrayed the FEPC as the first step toward "racial amalgamation."[15] Women's encounters with discrimination at
the hiring gate and on the shop floor differed from those of men of their group
because cultural notions of racialized womanhood and manhood shaped
both employer and coworker reactions to individuals from racial/ethnic
groups who sought employment in war industry.

My concern here lies less with the shortcomings of the FEPC than with
the inability of law and social policy to embody the multidimensionality that
shapes the nature of discrimination. The categories of antidiscrimination
were too crude to measure the jeopardy of women. This is not to claim that
black women during World War II wanted to charge sex discrimination or that
they experienced refusal to hire or promote (or prejudicial dismissal) as anything but race discrimination.[16] Comparing their situation to white women,
whose race offset disadvantage from gender, African American women found

that race discrimination knew no sex but that black womanhood distinguished their experience. Employers considered African American women as replacements for black men, viewing them as black but not as women, relegating them to dirty, arduous tasks rather than selecting them for clerical work and other positions held by white women. But, at the same time, perceptions of black women as Mammy, Sapphire, or Jezebel, as over-sexed temptresses and disheveled beasts of burden, distinguished them in terms of black womanhood rather than their blackness alone.[17] Constructed through contradictions—the most sexual but also the least womanly—black women faced discrimination that overflowed the boundaries of the law.

The FEPC

During World War II, African Americans viewed the FEPC as their agency. They lodged over 90 percent of complaints, with women bringing just under a third during the agency's most active period, July 1943 to December 1944.[18] Indeed, African Americans had forced its creation through the March On Washington Movement (MOWM), spearheaded by labor leader A. Philip Randolph of the Brotherhood of Sleeping Car Porters (BSCP). MOWM sought to open better-paying defense industry jobs and end segregation in the armed forces. For Randolph, the FEPC would be the means to cement the Double V campaign, victory against fascism and "empire over subject peoples" abroad and against Jim Crow and "white supremacy" at home.[19]

Established to contain protest as much as to address racial discrimination, the FEPC lacked enforcement powers. It remained an embattled agency for its entire life, attacked by both Southern segregationists and Northern defenders of the free market. While it could hold hearings, publicize abuses, and jawbone employers, it relied on individual complaint rather than investigations of patterns of abuse. Always without sufficient resources, the FEPC suffered from a hostile Congress that curtailed its funds in 1944 and, during reconversion, refused to legislate permanent status in 1946.[20]

The initial committee consisted of part-time commissioners drawn from business, labor, religion, the press, and politics. Even after agency reorganization under Executive Order 9346 in May 1943 and expansion into twelve regional offices, it never had the power to issue seek and desist orders or to hold defense production hostage to rectify discrimination. But an integrated staff of militant liberals, where black men supervised white men and women, pushed the limits of its mandate to investigate discrimination in industry, unions, and government.[21] Working with local race advancement organizations, especially the National Association for the Advancement of Colored People (NAACP) and the BSCP (whose vice president, Milton Webster, was a commissioner), the FEPC negotiated 5,000 cases and stopped forty strikes. Perhaps most significantly it legitimized black protest, expressed by letters to the agency in which working people confided their grievances.[22] Black workers increased war-related employment from 2 to 8 percent; black women began to leave domestic service and agricultural labor for industrial, non-household service, and some white-collar jobs. Dependent on labor shortages, however, these wartime economic gains proved temporary.[23]

Not On Account of Sex

The mandate of the FEPC did not encompass direct or indirect discrimination on account of sex. If an employer hired a black man over a black woman, there was no legal cause for action. Supervisors also might embrace the idea of equality with a vengeance, firing women out of the belief that they were incapable of doing men's work or holding them to standards of performance reached by few men.[24] Concepts of women's difference also influenced the FEPC. According to one FEPC investigator, "home conditions suggested that in the interests of the war effort, it would be much better for the complainant to take care of her infant child and assist in the management of the home" than take up employment.[25]

How the FEPC defined its jurisdiction reflected gendered understandings of which industries were essential to the war effort. Nursery schools failed to meet the mandate of "necessary for the maintenance of production of war materials." The FEPC dismissed cases in which women charged discrimination when either denied employment or fired from such jobs. Discrimination against black women took the form of refusal to hire; German women lost positions for being citizens of a belligerent nation. The federal government provided funds for nursery schools through the Latham Act, but FEPC lawyers argued in February 1944, "while the school is for children of mothers working in war industries, . . . it could not for that reason alone be considered a 'war industry' itself." Such schools did not "engage in 'vocational or training for war production.' " Moreover, local school districts ran the schools for the children of war workers in ways similar to those for other children. Teachers were local or state, not federal, employees. A later ruling held that even if the nurseries could fall under war industry, the FEPC lacked jurisdiction because the nondiscrimination clause in the Latham Act applied to construction projects, not to "aid to community services" or "employment pursuant to grants made under the law." In the six months between the first and second ruling on nursery schools, Congress had prohibited the FEPC from interfering with acts of Congress, removing any possible jurisdiction.[26]

There was no question that transportation was a war industry. Smoothly functioning railroads and streetcars facilitated wartime efficiency. Unlike childcare, a benefit identified with women, the FEPC recognized transit lines as necessary to the war effort. It pursued cases against transit companies throughout the country, including Los Angeles, Philadelphia, and Washington, D.C., while the military intervened in transit strikes to keep the trains rolling. Convenient and reliable public transit certainly made it easier for increased numbers of mothers to enter the labor force; women often "preferred work" in a locality "as it was near my home" or "to avoid the inconvenience of transportation."[27] But childcare was perhaps more essential if mothers were to engage in paid labor, and it lay outside agency purview.

Lines between race and sex discrimination were often murky. FEPC resolution of a May 1944 case lodged against a Detroit Plymouth plant illuminates the tangled relationship that derived from the structure of the labor market, as well as from discriminatory behavior. Here cultural notions of white and black womanhood came into contact with union understandings of the woman worker. A labor shortage led managers to rearrange work assignments so that men gave up work designated as "light" for tasks considered "heavy," with some women transferred to "light" work. But when it came to the janitorial department, where nearly all employees were black and more than half were women, women were to haul chips, "heavy" work customarily provided to men. United Automobile Workers (UAW) Local #51 protested because this job was "too heavy for female help as prescribed by law." The union claimed that the assignment violated existing protective labor legislation, restrictions on heavy lifting that often excluded women from better-paying jobs. The company counted that it had "installed new, lighter equipment" to comply with the legal weight maximum and the State Department of Labor already had approved women for this classification at other Chrysler plants.

Unable to accuse the company with breaking laws relating to the sex of a worker, the union charged management with "discrimination against Negro workers" because it "has taken white women off heavy jobs and placed them on light machines and light work," while putting black women on heavy work. Three black women, who refused the new task, received disciplinary lay-off. Black male workers responded by calling upon the union leadership "to either remove the women from this job-capacity or call a sympathy strike." The black men also demanded that the regional FEPC office take immediate action to avert a work stoppage.[28]

The FEPC promptly met with both management and union. It concluded that the union should drop this complaint for "a more substantial one" that charged employer discrimination in hiring because personnel had directed blacks, no matter their sex, to janitorial work but told whites about openings at higher grades. The investigator concluded, "although Negro women were involved in the complaint, the Union was actually concerned because of the job assignment, and in this instance, there was no discrimination between white and colored women." The job became "racial only to the extent that only Negro women worked" in the janitorial department.[29] Thus the regional office of the FEPC dismissed the complaint against Plymouth, claiming "no jurisdiction."[30]

But Will Maslow, FEPC Director of Field Operations and later Director of the American Jewish Congress, changed the disposition. His reasoning highlights how fair employment doctrine during the war considered only one axis of discrimination. "In as much as the complaint properly alleges discrimination because of race and in an industry subject to our jurisdiction it should be marked *dismissed* on merits," he concluded. For the union, which judged seniority to be "more important than a man's skin," black women were women, and thus threatened men's work and pay levels if they took over men's jobs, even the least skilled. For Maslow, the "facts" of the case failed to sustain the charge of race discrimination. The case was about dismissing women workers because they were women.[31]

Embodied Discrimination at the Hiring Gate and on the Shopfloor

The body became a site upon which discrimination took place. Physical appearance, age, or personal behavior justified refusal to hire or promote, actions protested against by African American women. Drawing upon the stereotype of the fat black woman, a Kaiser personnel manager explained to the FEPC "that black women were too large to climb, walk around, and get into difficult positions and places. 'Size cuts down adaptability.' " The LA Transit Lines told a Mrs. Franklin "that she was too heavy and her eyesight was bad." A Detroit employer pronounced not only the appearance of a newly hired black woman unacceptable but reported that "her language was such that I immediately received complaints from our shipping department that this would never do."[32]

Employers, however, were not the only ones to judge working-class black women by middle-class standards of appearance and decorum. Like an earlier generation of clubwomen, FEPC examiner Lethia W. Clore, a black woman herself, embraced a politics of respectability, forged in reaction to demeaning images, which demanded conformity to modesty and Christian womanhood. All black women had to meet the expectations of employers for the betterment of the race. To one rejected Detroit woman, she explained "that personal appearance is prerequisite number one in the search for employment and particularly so in the plants where the hiring of Negro women is a new experiment." She advised, "much needed attention to the hair" and "dark tailored clothing and a less conspicuous hat." About another case, she was more graphic: "Fact #1 to prohibit the upgrading of this complainant is her personal appearance. On the day she visited the office, this was not enhanced by her wearing slacks that were too tight and too short, a vivid coat, dark nail polish and no hat. In some departments her size would definitely prohibit her employment."[33] Black women themselves interpreted job rejection through the lens of respectability. A New York mother of a child fathered by a man other than her estranged husband wondered, "Is it my private life that keeps me from getting a [sic.] defense work?"[34]

When employers hired black women, they placed them on the dirtiest, hardest, and least healthful jobs. A Vancouver woman explained, "I realize that scaling is an important part of ship construction but if only negro girls are given the dirtiest and unhealthiest jobs in the war production, it is a most unjust practice in a country where ever race is supposed to have equal opportunities." Another women pointed to differential treatment of white and black women after they were hired based on white men's attitudes toward their bodies. Not only were the black women the only women made to do "a man's work," lifting hundred-pound iron ducts, but the foreman "stopped one of the white girls from doing anything because he could go around with her."[35]

White women reported what we now name sexual harassment on the job; black women experienced racial harassment and sexual insult. Both remained defined by their bodies.[36] White women, according to black women complainants, received more help and greater instruction; black women often seemed set up to fail. Black woman protested how white men aided white women but their "leadermen never helped us pull our leads." Moreover, black women "were timed in going to the rest rooms. While the white girls sat and read papers and powdered from quarter to half and an hr." Returning within fifteen minutes from the restroom was difficult when a woman had to navigate the ladders of a shipyard and pull off overalls and pants when she previously only "wore dresses." Objecting to differential treatment of white and black women, one black woman earned the animosity of the foreman, with the FEPC classifying her dismissal as a personality clash and thus outside its jurisdiction. But here inability to get along stemmed from the woman's protest of the foreman's treatment of other black women and her solidarity with them—that is, gendered race discrimination.[37]

Women, no matter their race, faced job difficulties in part because they still cared for children without the social structures that would allow them to combine family with waged labor. Lacking adequate childcare, women could not attend nighttime vocational training, a first step toward a defense job. When they did find a defense job, they often asked for the graveyard or swing shift because they could arrange childcare only for that time. They remained home to nurse the sick or left work early to carry a child to the doctor. This double day led to higher absenteeism among women than men.[38]

While white women also suffered from inadequate childcare and burdensome family responsibilities, the consequences of absenteeism for black women appeared harsher.[39] Only black women could charge, "they are hiring the white women but they won't hire the colored" in asking President Roosevelt "for a job."[40] The tale of Mrs. Geraldine Robinson—absenteeism for family reasons, a hostile foreman, and discriminatory rehiring procedures—resembled countless others. "I had to be off of work to help at home for Xmas and was off five days," she reported to the FEPC. "Apparently the foreman didn't like this, for when I came back . . . he gave me my discharge slip. He made the excuse about my leaving the boat before the whistle blew, but this is not so, for we couldn't leave until the whistle blows, because we have to get our cards from him."[41] Thus women's family labor provided the context in which some African American women found themselves in conflict with supervisors, which eventually led to their dismissal—and a complaint brought before the FEPC.

That discrimination derived from multiple factors appears in a complaint by Mrs. Julia Hughes, who claimed "that the U.S. Employment Service [USES] . . . refused to refer her to the Richmond Shipyards because she was too fat and her baby too young." Her doctor advised "that I was perfectly healthy and strong enough to work in the shipyards if I would dress properly." Still she crafted her charge in the language of race, believing "it was because she is a Negro." Though Hughes claimed, "I have just as much right to work in the shipyards as the next person," USES offered her domestic labor instead.[42]

Such slotting of black women into household labor reflected a longstanding practice, intensified by wartime shortages of servants. A personnel officer at the Port of Oakland automatically answered "janitress" when Esterline Davis sought to apply for a clerical job. The number of black women in clerical work actually quadrupled during the war, due to employment in government agencies, but they still composed a mere 2 percent of this fastest growing sector of women's work. The FEPC had some success in convincing employers to overcome their "hesitancy . . . in hiring Negroes in clerk jobs," especially "well-qualified" people. But by the time the understaffed FEPC investigated a specific complaint, discrimination had taken its toll. The FEPC often no longer could reach the complainant, who had perhaps moved to another job or city.[43]

Discrimination against men also reflected gendered practices, disrupting understandings of manhood. Whites regarded black men as sexual predators and knife wielders whose threat to workplace order had to be contained through exclusion or, if they were necessary as laboring bodies, separation from white women.[44] Men referred to discrimination as depriving them of manhood rights, central to which was the ability to support wives and children, to be breadwinners.[45] They further protested discrimination against wives. One Michigan man, about to be inducted into the army, asked, "how do you think i feel going to lose my life for freedom an my wife back here been push an shelve around from one factory to another an talk to as if she was a dog."[46] He recognized the same irony that countless women lamented when they questioned why their men should die for a nation that refused to hire them. Gendered embodiments of race, then, shaped the experience of discrimination for both men and women, but race discrimination remained too narrow to capture the harms done to black women as black women because men's lives stood for the "race."

Toward 1964 and Beyond

To understand why the FEPC failed to address sex, we must shift analytical gears, away from an internalist reading of FEPC complaints and shopfloor experiences to the political landscape as a whole. Just as white women's position during wartime mobilization varied from that of African Americans, so women's rights activists stood in a different relationship to the Democratic Party than did the black struggle for equality. Though white women would face female-typed employment following demobilization, their access to jobs was greater than that of black women. Employer resistance to the hiring of black workers proved a powerful legacy.[47] But African Americans, who were being incorporated into the Rooseveltian majority, were more favorably situated politically than were advocates of sexual equality. Many of the latter supported the Equal Rights Amendment (ERA) and were identified with the National Woman's Party (NWP).[48] A women's movement fragmented over the ERA produced no feminist onslaught to match the March on Washington Movement that had agitated for the FEPC's birth.[49]

New Deal liberals had embraced civil rights as the next arena of welfare state development; they drafted the language of the FEPC to address race discrimination.[50] But banning sex discrimination in employment was available to those who formulated the FEPC from other places than just the NWP. Black New Dealer Robert Weaver, the National Defense Advisory Commission official who developed the first wartime nondiscrimination policies, included "sex" in his nondiscrimination clause for defense training under the United States Office of Education. A 1940 job-training act also prohibited discrimination on the basis of "sex, race, or color," even as it accepted separate but equal training facilities.[51] That year NAACP lawyers analogized from "sex" to "race" in making a Fourteenth Amendment claim for equal pay for black schoolteachers. Among trade unions, the American Federation of Teachers, with its large female membership, promoted a broad fair practices doctrine prior to the war that "opposed salary discrimination based on Sex, Race, or Marital status."[52]

The wartime increase in women wage earners, especially whites in the industrial workforce, led the most progressive trade unions—notably the UAW and the United Electrical Workers—to include "sex" in contract nondiscrimination clauses, though unequal pay, dismissal of married women, and sex-typed work persisted into the postwar period. Perhaps reflecting the influence of the UAW, the Fair Employment Practice Council in Detroit, formed in support of the FEPC, included "sex" in its 1942 mandate. Even the American Federation of Labor (AFL), with affiliates that still barred women and non-white men, in 1944 put both "sex" and "race" in its nondiscrimination creed, though it did little to enforce such pronouncements.[53]

"Sex" entered the FEPC debate itself during the mid-1940s. Conservative Republican Clare Hoffman of Michigan, who denounced the FEPC for curtailing employer prerogatives, proposed adding "sex" as well as "ancestry and union membership" in 1946 to a bill for a permanent FEPC. Georgia Senator Richard Russell, a leading opponent of civil rights, suggested inclusion of "age" and "sex" in a "voluntary" FEPC. Most within the civil rights coalition dismissed "this chivalrous proposal," though some union women sought to ban "sex" as well as "race" discrimination in government contracts and state law. But when other supporters feared that adding "sex" would kill state FEPC legislation, those women retreated. Before a major Women's Bureau conference in 1948, women from the UAW and the Amalgamated Clothing Workers of America listed a "sex"-less FEPC among items, such as equal pay and fair labor standards, necessary for women in the postwar world. Part of the overall liberal agenda, fair employment remained identified with the industrial unions, the NAACP, and the American Jewish Congress.[54]

Women's organizations presented a mixed record when it came to endorsing the FEPC. During the war, the Young Women's Christian Association monitored compliance with fair employment, while the National Consumers' League, by then a Washington lobby fighting for fair labor standards, and the League of Women Shoppers, a more militant, Communist-influenced group, championed FEPC legislation.[55] In contrast, the largest social feminist organization, the League of Women Voters, belatedly acknowledged "public policies which recognize no discrimination because of race, creed or color" in its 1944 platform under "Civil Liberties." Individual chapters championed a permanent FEPC, but the National League exhibited a more tepid response, counseling education and then action on a state-by-state basis. Indeed, in 1945 its National Board rejected "an independent [antidiscrimination] agency with mandatory powers and enforcement penalties" even though it hired as its Washington lobbyist a white woman who had been on FEPC staff.[56] That year, the president of the United Council of Church Women spoke out against endorsing the FEPC and for the Equal Rights Amendment. Over the next few years, the American Association of University Women, another group with a diverse political and regional membership, refused to endorse legislation for a permanent FEPC.[57]

The NWP had no such qualms about adding "sex" to the FEPC. A shadow of its former self, this small group of elite feminists had gained their staunchest champions among Republicans. In rejecting protective labor legislation for women, the NWP had incurred the wrath of women's groups around the Democratic Party, Eleanor Roosevelt, and trade unionists, an important component of the New Deal coalition.[58] In its single-minded pursuit of sex equality, the NWP both competed for political attention against and tried "to "piggy-back" on the struggles of the black rights movement from 1945 to the 1964 act itself. It demanded that "sex" become part of any law upholding equal rights, including employment.

When such laws ignored "sex," NWP members attacked proposed legislation for promoting rights for blacks and Jews over that of white women like themselves—much as had Elizabeth Cady Stanton in debating the Fourteenth and Fifteenth amendments. Nora Stanton Barney, Stanton's granddaughter, condemned a proposed New York FEPC bill in 1945 by explicating her grievances in racialist terms. "Other elements in our population, notably the Hebrews and the Negroes, are asking to have teeth put in the civic rights that they are fully guaranteed by the Constitution, well knowing that women have no civic rights," she contended. Informing Governor Thomas Dewey that "the resentment of women is mounting day by day as they find themselves being pushed around and placed on the lowest economic level, below the Negroes and Jews," she felt threatened by black women, whom she viewed as "demanding" jobs that white women held. (Black women certainly wanted to be considered for such better jobs.) At the same time, she claimed to be a "champion of equality and justice for all races, creeds and colors" and only wanted "sex" added to the FEPC bill.[59]

With defense buildups, the Cold War and the Korean conflict gave new life to the FEPC idea, though no national board emerged on the model of the

World War II agency. In 1949 Secretary of Defense Louis Johnson outlawed for his department discrimination in civilian employment: "There shall be no discrimination because of race, sex, color, religion, national origin, lawful political association, or physical handicap." His rules went beyond most union contracts as well as a tepid FEPC that Truman had announced in July 1948 that only covered federal agencies. Johnson's policy reflected the ways that liberals viewed antidiscrimination as a labor standard, connected as it was to "the right to join any lawful union," occupational health and safety rules, and civil rights on the job in terms of grievances and promotions.[60] Later antidiscrimination efforts under Eisenhower and Kennedy relied on presidential committees to evaluate government contracts, but these continued to omit "sex." Approached by the NWP, Eisenhower's committee on contract compliance rebuffed inclusion of "sex" "on the grounds that the addition would make enforcement difficult."[61] Finally in 1956, the NWP maneuvered the House to include "sex" under the purview of a proposed Civil Rights Commission, but this bill passed too late in the term for Senate action.[62]

Trade unions continued to appear more inclined to outlaw "sex" discrimination than they did to enforce such declarations. Though rejecting the blanket ERA, the UAW pursued nondiscrimination on the basis of "sex." At biannual conventions during the 1950s, it resolved that nondiscrimination clauses in government contracts required "strengthening by the inclusion of the words 'sex' and age'." Sensitive to the plight of "Negro women, who are always the last hired and, consequently, the first laid off," the union attacked discrimination at the hiring gate. Nonetheless, the general categories—"womanpower, Negro workers, and older workers"—in which it couched demands for equity separated "sex" and "race." Of greater import, its equal treatment policy—"all workers are entitled to equal justice, equal job opportunity, equal job protection and equal pay for equal work"—failed to compensate for past discrimination that made seniority continue the work of exclusion.[63] Indeed, trade union champions of race-based civil rights did not necessarily wish to extend such protections to women in their own ranks. The United Packinghouse Workers, for one, sought to maintain discriminatory job classifications even as its endorsement of Title VII galvanized rank and file women to demand equal rights at work.[64]

On the eve of the Civil Rights Act of 1964, Congressional debates over Title VII reveal how gender was racialized in the process of a discussion centered on "race" or "sex" but not both. Feminist Martha Griffiths of Michigan (D), no less than civil rights opponent Smith, argued that the omission of "sex" would place "white women . . . last at the hiring gate." Most liberals clung to the separation of race and sex discrimination.[65] The President's Commission on the

Status of Women had reported in 1963 that "discrimination based on sex . . . involves problems sufficiently different from discrimination based on the other factors listed"—that is, "race."[66] New York's powerful Democratic congressman Emanuel Celler continued to believe, as he explained back in 1956, that "distinctions based on sex have never been considered within the purview of [the] prohibition[s of] . . . the 14th amendment."[67]

After *Degraffenreid,* courts looked more favorably upon black women as a legal category, especially when it came to hiring, firing, and promotion. In the 1980 *Jeffries v. Harris Community Action Ass'n,* the Fifth Circuit contended that "sex discrimination against black females can exist even absent discrimination against black men or white women and employer was not to escape liability . . . by a showing that it had not discriminated against blacks and did not discriminate against females."[68] But century's end still saw employers discriminating against black women as black women. Like the "unacceptable" behavior and deportment exposed in FEPC complaints, cases over appearance (especially braided hair) reflected employer and coworker responses to black women as culturally or socially different from norms of conduct or beauty that assume whiteness.[69] Similarly, as with sexual harassment, though black women plaintiffs have stood for "women" and have shaped the law for all,[70] courts have had a difficult time having them stand for the class of "women" or of "blacks." Courts tend to evaluate their stories as incidents of "race-based gender discrimination" rather than gender discrimination.[71] Now black women sometimes count as "women," but the category of black woman remains more a subject of theory than of judicial practice. The law continues to dismiss "how race and gender operate in concert," as lawyer Judith Winston has noted.[72]

In 1945, when the wartime FEPC was about to expire, supporters of a permanent agency argued that it "had made a major contribution to the winning of the war through enforcing the American principle that all men and women should have an equal opportunity to earn a living and to contribute to the nation's productive power."[73] But the FEPC actually failed women at a time when hiring hall and shop-floor practices disadvantaged black women as black women. The history of the wartime FEPC suggests the ways that administrative structures and judicial processes can normalize inequality, even while attempting to combat other forms of discrimination. The chasm between "race" and "sex" in antidiscrimination law testifies to the persistent power of binary oppositions within legal and cultural thought. In this tale men and women inhabited racialized bodies, which served as a terrain of struggle, a location of the symbolic that had material consequences that law and social policy have only partially recognized.

NOTES

1. *DeGraffenreid v. General Motors Assembly Div., Etc.*, 413 F. Supp. 142, 143 (1976).

2. Reggie R. Smith, "Separate Identities: Black Women, Work, and Title VII," *Harvard Women's Law Journal* 14 (Spring 1991): 21–75.

3. Linda Kerber, *No Constitutional Right to Be Ladies: Women and the Obligations of Citizenship* (New York: Hill and Wang, 1999).

4. Ellen Carol DuBois, "Outgrowing the Compact of the Fathers: Equal Rights, Woman Suffrage, and the United States Constitution, 1820–1878," *Journal of American History* 74 (December 1987): 836–62.

5. Vivien Hart, *Bound By Our Constitution: Women, Workers, and the Minimum Wage* (Princeton: Princeton University Press, 1994).

6. Ann D. Gordon et al., eds., *African American Women and the Vote, 1837–1965* (Amherst: University of Massachusetts Press, 1997).

7. Gary Gerstle, "The Protean Character of American Liberalism," *American Historical Review* 99 (Oct. 1994): 1043–73; Margo Anderson, *The American Census: A Social History* (New Haven: Yale University Press, 1988).

8. Eileen Boris and Michael Honey, "Gender, Race, and the Policies of the Labor Department," *Monthly Labor Review* 111 (February 1988): 26–36.

9. Elisabeth Spelman, *Inessential Woman* (Boston: Beacon Press, 1988).

10. Civil Rights Act of 1964, par. 703(a), 42 U.S.C.A. par 2000e-2(a).

11. Introducer Howard W. Smith (D-VA) was a fierce opponent of fair employment, even in World War II. Jo Freeman, "How Sex Got Into Title VII: Persistent Opportunism as a Maker of Public Policy," *Law and Inequality: A Journal of Theory and Practice* 9 (March 1991): 163–85.

12. Cynthia Harrison, *On Account of Sex: The Politics of Women's Issues, 1945–1968* (Berkeley: University of California Press, 1988): 187–91; Hugh D. Graham, *The Civil Rights Era: Origins and Development of National Policy* (New York: Oxford University Press, 1990), 205–32.

13. Though the law speaks of "sex," feminist theory refers to "gender".

14. Merl E. Reed, *Seedtime for the Modern Civil Rights Movement: The President's Committee on Fair Employment Practice, 1941–1946* (Baton Rouge: Louisiana State University Press, 1991).

15. "It Can. . . . Did Happen Here On The Floor of the Senate," Excerpts from Remarks of Senator Eastland, *Pittsburgh Courier*, July 7, 1945, 5.

16. Melinda Chateauvert, *Marching Together: Women of the Brotherhood of Sleeping Car Porters* (Urbana: University of Illinois Press, 1998), 129.

17. K. Sue Jewell, *From Mammy to Miss America and Beyond: Cultural Images and the Shaping of US Social Policy* (New York: Routledge, 1993).

18. Table 9, "Comparison of Docketings with Closings . . . Involving Total and Negro women Complainants by Region," *First Report: Fair Employment Practice Committee: July 1943—December 1944* (Washington: GPO, 1945), 133. My analysis comes from reading closed cases from the key wartime centers of Detroit and California.

19. A. Philip Randolph, "Why Should We March?" *Survey Graphic* (November 1942), 488; Paula F. Pfeffer, *A. Philip Randolph, Pioneer of the Civil Rights Movement* (Baton Rouge: Louisiana State University Press, 1990), 45–132.

20. Reed, *Seedtime for Reform*.

21. Ibid, 350–57.

22. *Final Report: Fair Employment Practice Committee*, June 28, 1946 (Washington: GPO, 1947), 8.

23. Susan Hartmann, *The Home Front and Beyond: American Women in the 1940s* (Boston: Twayne, 1982), 77–82; George Lipsitz, *Rainbow At Midnight: Labor and Culture in the 1940s* (Urbana: University of Illinois Press, 1994), 73.

24. Harry Kingman to Will Maslow, "Final Disposition Report," Dec. 18, 1943, 12-BR-186, reel 110F, folder "Marinship Corporation." Microfilm edition of FEPC Papers, RG228, National Archives. All documents are from this collection unless noted.

25. Memo To Will Maslow from Edward Lawson, Dec. 28, 1943, 2-BR-408, reel 14F.

26. E. G. Trimble to George M. Johnson, Feb. 15, 1944; Frank D. Reeves to George M. Johnson, "Jurisdiction over Maritime Nursery Schools, 12-BR-335," Sept. 27, 1944; George M. Johnson to Hugh B. Cox, June 16, 1944, reel 63H, folder "Rulings."

27. Herbert Hill, *Black Labor and the American Legal System: Race, Work, and the Law* (Madison: University of Wisconsin Press, 1985), 274–333; letter from Raymond and Jeanne R. Dobard to Harry Kingman, Jan. 29, 1944, in C. L. Dellums Papers, 72/132, Carton 32, Bancroft Library, University of California, Berkeley.

28. E. J. Lambert to the FEPC, May 15, 1944, with attached letter of May 12 to C. C. Hopkins; office memorandum from Morris Weitz to Edward M. Swan, June 21, 1944; conference check sheet, Plymouth Div., Chrysler Corp, 5-BR-1328, Supplemental, 1–4, all in reel 59F, folder "Chrysler, Plymouth Division."

29. "Final Disposition Report," 5-BR-1328, June 19, 1944, reel 59F, folder "Chrysler, Plymouth Division;" conference check sheet, 3.

30. Memorandum from Will Maslow to William T. McKnight, Aug. 22, 1944, reel 59F, folder "Chrysler, Plymouth Division."

31. Ibid.

32. Reed, *Seedtime*, 306; Mrs. Mary Ruth Franklin, 12-BR-1452, 1/12/45, reel 106F; deposition from Elsie Charity, Feb. 3, 1943, State of Michigan, County of Wayne, reel 58F, folder "Briggs #3."

33. Clore's race from Congressman John Rankin, D-Mississippi, *Congressional Record-House*, May 26, 1944, 5056. Memo to William T. McKnight, Regional Director from Lethia W. Clore, examiner-in-charge, Oct. 12, 1943, reel 58F, folder "Briggs #2;" Memo to McKnight from Clore, Oct. 21, 1943, 5-BR-1233, reel 60F, folder "Hudson Motor Car Company."

34. Ella Hamilton to NAACP, New York City, Feb. 15, 1943, in pt.13, ser. A, reel 10, "NYC, General, 1941–49," NAACP Papers.

35. Letter to president from Miss Rosa M. Cawson, Vancouver, July 1, 1943; letter to president from Mrs. Jackie Miller, San Mateo, Cal., 1943, both in reel 112F, folder: "Boilermakers' Auxiliary Union Issue, Aug. 29, 1943, Exhibit C," in file: "Moore Drydock," FEPC-San Bruno Branch, the National Archives.

36. Amy Kesselman, *Fleeting Opportunities: Women Shipyard Workers in Portland and Vancouver During World War II and Reconversion* (Albany: SUNY Press, 1990), 55–63.

37. Letter to president from Mrs. D. X. Young, Oakland, Cal., Dec. 5, 1942, in file: "Moore Drydock;" letter to Mr. Routledge from Mrs. Doris Mae Williams, Vancouver, Washington, May 4, 1944, No. 12-BR-339, reel 110F, folder "Kaiser Company;" Edith Brown to the Department of Justice, July 30, 1943, no. 12-BR-31, reel 112F; United States of America Before the FEPC, "Complaint," 8/9/1944, 12-GR-432, reel 111F, folder "Oakland Naval Supply Depot;" office memo, 2/18/44, 5-BR-1298, reel 60F, folder "Kelsey-Hayes, Plymouth, Mich." For white women breaking rules without punishment but black women being disciplined, see "Complaint," Feb. 19, 1945, 12-GR-590, reel 111F, folder "Oakland Naval Supply Depot."

38. Kesselman, *Fleeting Opportunities,* 69–70, 71–89.

39. I am unable to document whether black women suffered from changes in shifts more often than white women.

40. Letter to President Roosevelt from Bernice McFadden, Oct. 12, 1944, reel 108F, 12-UR-311, folder "Boilermaker's Local 513, Richmond."

41. Harry Kingman to Will Maslow, "Final Disposition Report," Sept. 21, 1944, 12-GR-456; Harry Kingman to Will Maslow, "Final Disposition Report," Sept. 28, 1944, and USA Before the FEPC, "Complaint," 8/9/1944, both 12-GR-432, reel 111F, folder "Oakland Naval Supply Depot;" complaint by Mrs. Geraldine Robinson, Richmond, California, Dec. 30, 1944, 12-BR-552, reel 112F, "Richmond Shipyards."

42. Hughes to Roosevelt; Harry L. Kingman to Will Maslow, "Final Disposition Report," March 18, 1944, 12-GR-6, reel 112F, folder "Richmond Employment Service."

43. Affidavit, Esterline Davis, March 4, 1942, carton 32, folder, "FEPC Jan. 1942," Dellums Papers; Harry Kingman to Will Maslow, final disposition report," 12-BR-341, July 15, 1944, reel 112F, folder "Richmond Shipyard #1."

44. "Minutes of Meeting with Grievance Committee of the United Steelworkers of America Affiliated with the USA Local 1131," box SG12417, folder 9, Governor Sparks Papers, Alabama Department of Archives and History.

45. Dear Sir, from Lairrie White, Vancouver, Washington, Jan. 9, 1945 received, 12-BR-566, reel 110F.

46. Dear Mr. President, from Mark Pruitt Jr. (not legible), n.d., reel 58F, file: "Budd Wheel"; Harry Kingman to Will Maslow, "Final Disposition Report," July 15, 1944, 12-BR-122, reel 112F, folder "Richmond Shipyards' Employment Offices."

47. H. Langerhans and L. F. Manfred, "Manpower Is Competence," *Manpower Mobilization,* 6, in Papers of the NAACP, pt. 13, ser. B, reel 21, file: War Manpower Commission, 1943, microfilm edition.

48. Nancy Weiss, *Farewell to the Party of Lincoln: Black Politics in the Age of FDR* (Princeton: Princeton University Press, 1983).

49. Nancy Cott, *The Grounding of Modern Feminism* (New Haven: Yale University Press, 1987), 117–42.

50. Patricia Sullivan, *Days of Hope: Race and Democracy in the New Deal Era* (Chapel Hill: University of North Carolina Press, 1996), especially 133–68.

51. As cited in Andrew E. Kersten, *Race, Jobs, and the War: The FEPC in the Midwest, 1941–1946* (Urbana: University of Illinois Press, 2000), 12.

52. "Passed at AFT Executive Council Meeting, Chicago Dec. 27–Jan. 2, 1941," in papers of the NAACP, pt. 3, ser. B, reel 11, "Virginia, Norfolk-Marshall, Thurgood, 1940–41."

53. "RWLB Approves Race Clauses in Contracts," *Pittsburgh Courier*, July 14, 1945, 5; "UAW-CIO Official Urges Vigilance in Combating Job Discrimination," ibid., Sept. 8, 1945, 2; Lucius L. Jones, "AFL Awaits Action on Anti-Bias Resolution," ibid., Dec. 2, 1944, 1.

54. Freeman, "How Sex Got into Title VII," 170; Herbert R. Northrup, "Progress Without Federal Compulsion: Arguing the Case for Compromise Methods," *Commentary*, Sept. 10, 1952, 207; "Women's Bureau Conference: The American Woman, Her Changing Role," *Women's Bureau Bulletin*, no. 224 (Washington: GPO, 1948): 104, 151.

55. Landon R. Y. Storrs, *Civilizing Capitalism: the National Consumers' League, Women's Activism, and Labor Standards in the New Deal Era* (Chapel Hill: University of North Carolina Press, 2000); Minutes of the Seventh Annual Membership Meeting of the League of Women Shoppers, Inc., May 9 and 10, 1944 —New York City, 5, 9, box 1, LWS Papers, Smith College, Sophia Smith Collection.

56. Anna Lord Strauss to Dear President, March 28, 1945; Marcia S. Foote to Anna Lord Strauss, Nov. 8, 1945; *Government and Our Minorities: Government's Role in Helping to Equalize Opportunities for Minorities in the United States* (Washington: NLWV, August 1945), 12–3, all in box 659, folder, "FEPC;" "Miss Muriel Ferris," January 1955, folder "Muriel Ferris," all in part 3, Papers of the National League of Women Voters, Library of Congress (LWVP).

57. *Manuscript: A Washington News Letter*, Nov. 12, 1945, no. 35, 5, in reel 3H, office files of Malcolm Ross, FEPC Papers; Susan Lynn, *Progressive Women in Conservative Times: Racial Justice, Peace, and Feminism, 1945 to the 1960s* (New Brunswick: Rutgers University Press, 1992), 62–63, 65; Susan M. Hartmann, *The Other Feminists: Activists in the Liberal Establishment* (New Haven: Yale University Press, 1998).

58. Storrs, *Civilizing Capitalism*, passim.

59. Leila J. Rupp and Verta Taylor, *Survival in the Doldrums: The American Women's Rights Movement, 1945 to the 1960s* (New York: Oxford University Press), 159–62; Ellen Carol Dubois, *Feminism and Suffrage: The Emergence of An Independent Women's Movement in America, 1848–1869* (Ithaca, N.Y.: Cornell University Press, 1978).

60. "The NAACP's Fight for an Executive Order Against Discrimination in Federal Employment," Aug. 25, 1948, pt. 13, ser. B, reel 13, "FEPC, General, 1948," NAACP Papers; "Johnson Policy: Defense Job Bias Outlawed," *Pittsburgh Courier*, Oct. 22, 1949, 11.

61. Graham, *The Civil Rights Era*, 16–73. On the rebuff, Freeman, "How 'Sex' Got Into Title VII," 171.

62. Freeman, "How 'Sex' Got Into Title VII," 171–72.

63. Proceedings Fifteenth Constitutional Convention of the International Union United Automobile, Aircraft and Agricultural Implement Workers of America (UAW-CIO), March 27–April 1, 1955, Cleveland, Ohio, 52; Report of UAW-CIO President Walter P. Reuther to the Fourteenth Constitutional Convention, March 22–27, 1953, Atlantic City, 194; Caroline Davis, "Women's Department," Report of UAW President Walter P. Reuther to the Sixteenth Constitutional Convention, April 7–12, 1957, Atlantic City, 174-D, 170-D, all in author's possession.

64. Dennis A. Deslippe, *"Rights , Not Roses": Unions and the Rise of Working-Class Feminism, 1945–80* (Urbana: University of Illinois Press, 2000), 146–65.

65. *Congressional Record*, v. 110, pt. 2, 88th Congress, 2nd Sess., Feb. 8, 1964, 2578. Alice Kessler-Harris, *In Pursuit of Equity: Women, Men, and the Quest for Economic Citizenship in 20th-Century America* (New York: Oxford University Press, 2001), 239–89.

66. Cynthia Harrison, "A 'New Frontier' for Women: The Public Policy of the Kennedy Administration," *Journal of American History* 67 (December 1980): 644.

67. Freeman, "How 'Sex' Got Into Title VII," 172.

68. *Jeffries v. Harris Community Action Ass'n.*, 615 F.2d. 1026 (5th Cir. 1980).

69. *Rogers v. American Airlines* 527 F. Supp. 299 (S.D.N.Y. 1981).

70. Gwendolyn Mink, *Hostile Environment* (Ithaca, N.Y.: Cornell University Press, 1999).

71. *Brooms v. Regal Tube Co.*, 881 F2d 412 (7th Cir. 1989); *Mumford v. James T. Barret Co.*, 441 F. Supp. 459 (E.D. Michigan 1977).

72. 42 U.S.C. Section 1981; 42 U.S.C. 2000e. Judith A. Winston, "Mirror, Mirror on the Wall: Title VII, Section 1981, and the Intersection of Race and Gender in the Civil Rights Act of 1990, *California Law Review* 79 (1991): 775–805, quoted at 798.

73. *What Score Do You Have on FEPC*, [1945], reel 3H, Ross office files: "National Federation for Constitutional Liberties."

Susan Sturm

CHAPTER 17

Second Generation Employment Discrimination

A Structural Approach

The project of pursuing workplace equality has reached a new stage. Racial and gender inequality persists in many places of employment while the explanations and solutions for these conditions have become more complex and elusive. Smoking guns—the sign on the door that "Irish need not apply" or the rejection explained by the comment that "this is no job for a woman"—are largely things of the past. Many employers now have formal policies prohibiting race and sex discrimination, as well as procedures to enforce them. Cognitive bias, structures of decision making, and patterns of interaction have replaced deliberate racism and sexism as the frontier of much continued inequality.

Judges, advocates, and commentators focused initially on eradicating first generation discrimination, which concerns deliberate exclusion or subordination based on race, gender, ethnicity, or age. Relatively easy to define, it violates widely shared norms of formal equality. It can easily be labeled discrimination once surfaced and frequently gives rise to clear, rule-like remedies, such as sanctioning discriminatory conduct, hiring or promoting previously excluded individuals, adopting numerically based ("goal") programs, and increasing the representation of previously excluded groups in the applicant pool.

First generation forms of exclusion continue but have become increasingly intertwined with, and in some contexts supplanted by, more complex, interactive, subtle, and structural forms of bias. Increasingly, sexual harassment and

This is a revised version of an article by the same name in the *Columbia Law Review* 101 (2001): 458.

discriminatory exclusion involve issues that depart from the "first generation" patterns of bias. Unequal treatment may result from cognitive or unconscious bias rather than intentional exclusion.[1] Second generation claims frequently involve social practices and patterns of interaction among groups within the workplace that, over time, exclude nondominant groups. Exclusion is frequently difficult to trace directly to intentional, discrete actions of particular actors, and may sometimes be visible only in the aggregate. Structures of decision making, opportunity, and power fail to surface these patterns of exclusion and themselves produce differential access and opportunity.[2]

As an example, consider a large law firm in which complaints have surfaced about a series of issues involving gender. Almost half of the firm's associates are women, but the representation of women drops off precipitously at the senior associate/junior partner level. The firm's senior management is almost entirely male and several departments, such as tax and mergers and acquisitions, have particularly low numbers of women. Lawyers "work around the clock" and frequently collaborate on large and complex cases. Decision making about personnel issues is largely subjective and discretionary, with little systemic assessment of its efficacy or fairness. Advancement depends upon informal decisions involving assignment of cases, access to training, and exposure to significant clients. Mentoring of new lawyers, crucial to professional success, blurs the line between personal and professional interaction.

A group of women have questioned recent decisions denying women promotion to partnership, the firm's general failure to retain and promote women despite comparable entry credentials, and a series of individual incidents that triggered complaints of sexual harassment and gender bias. In part because the firm aggressively recruits women at the entry level and fails to track patterns in work assignment and promotion, the firm's management has been largely unaware of any problem. The complaints involved a range of issues: differences in patterns of work assignment and training opportunities among men and women; tolerance of a sexualized work environment by partners who are otherwise significant "rainmakers"; routine comments by male lawyers, particularly in the predominantly male departments, on the appearance, sexuality, and competence of women; harsh assessments of women's capacities and work styles based on gender stereotypes; avoidance of work-related contact with women by members of particular departments; and hyperscrutiny of women's performance by some and invisibility of women's contributions to others. These complaints coincide with a concern about low morale and productivity among diverse work teams. Upon examination, the firm discovers dramatic differences in the retention and promotion rates of men and women in the firm.

The complex and dynamic problems inherent in second generation discrimination cases pose a serious challenge for a "first generation" system that is jurocentric—that relies solely on courts (or other external governmental institutions) to articulate and enforce specific, across-the-board rules. Any rule broad enough to embrace the variety of contexts and conduct that might arise will inevitably be quite general and ambiguous and will produce considerable uncertainty about the boundaries of lawful conduct. Ambiguous rules will provide inadequate guidance to shape conduct and will undermine efforts at anticipatory compliance. This uncertainty in turn tends to induce gestures of compliance with the legal norm, without necessarily inducing any change in the underlying behavior causing the problem.[3] Employers' fear of sanctions if internal evaluation reveals previously unrecognized bias has the perverse effect of discouraging them from inquiring into or addressing second generation problems.

Efforts to reduce the uncertainty of general and ambiguous legal norms by articulating more specific and detailed rules produces a different but equally problematic result. Specific commands will not neatly adapt to variable and fluid contexts. Inevitably, they will be underinclusive, overinclusive, or both. Moreover, the process of designing and implementing effective remedies for second generation bias is inseparably linked to that of defining the very nature of the problem itself. Separating problem definition from its institutional context undermines the efficacy of the resulting legal norm as well as the remedy designed to achieve it.

Thus, second generation cases are resistant to solution through after-the-fact adjudicative sanctions for rule violations. Yet these types of problems will persist if left solely to the discretion of employers to address, in response to market incentives. Although there often is an overlap between concerns about efficiency and fairness, many firms have not developed the organizational systems that would enable them to identify these connections. Firms tend to undervalue the importance of human resource issues generally and avoid addressing the messy problems of managing human relationships until those problems surface as crises. Many firms use short-term measures of productivity, which frequently fail to make visible the longer-term patterns of inefficiency that underlie second generation bias. Moreover, there may be situations in which the values of nondiscrimination and efficiency conflict, such as when firms perceive the exclusion of particular groups to serve or reflect rational economic goals. In the absence of continued legal regulation, firms will lack adequate incentives to address bias in those situations.

Over the last decade an interesting and complex regulatory pattern has emerged. Multiple public, private, and nongovernmental actors are actively and interactively developing systems to address sexual harassment, glass ceiling, and other second generation problems. The judiciary, key stakeholders within workplaces, and nongovernmental actors have begun to approach these questions as posing essentially issues of problem solving. Each has, to varying degrees, linked its antibias efforts with the more general challenge of enhancing institutional capacity to manage complex workplace relationships. These multiple actors have, perhaps unwittingly, begun to carve out distinctive roles and relationships that form the outlines of a dynamic regulatory system for addressing second generation discrimination.

This chapter sketches out a framework that makes visible these emerging and converging patterns of response to second generation discrimination. It explores the potential for a decentered, holistic, and dynamic approach to these more structural forms of bias. This new regulatory approach shifts the emphasis away from primary reliance on after-the-fact enforcement of centrally defined, specific commands. Instead, normative elaboration occurs through a fluid, interactive relationship between problem solving and problem definition within specific workplaces and in multiple other arenas, including but not limited to the judiciary. In this framework, compliance is achieved through and evaluated in relation to improving institutional capacity to identify, prevent, and redress exclusion, bias, and abuse. This approach expands the field of "regulatory" participants to include the long neglected activities of legal actors within workplaces and significant nongovernmental organizations, such as professional associations, insurance companies, brokers, research consortia, and advocacy groups.

The motif of this second generation regulatory approach is that of structuralism. By this, I mean an approach that encourages the development of institutions and processes to enact general norms in particular contexts. "Legality" emerges from an interactive process of information gathering, problem identification, remediation, and evaluation. Regulation fosters dynamic interactions that cut across established conceptual, professional, and organizational boundaries in reaction to observed problems. This approach encourages experimentation with respect to information gathering, organizational design, incentive structures, measures of effectiveness, and methods of institutionalizing accountability as part of an explicit system of legal regulation. Workplaces and nongovernmental institutions influencing workplace practice are treated within this regulatory regime as lawmaking bodies, rather than simply as objects of state or market regulation. The role of nongovernmental actors is particularly interesting and striking.

In this chapter I discuss and strive to move from the background to the foreground emerging and converging patterns in multiple arenas that address sexual harassment and subjective employment practices. The methodology focuses on the sites of innovation and creative reconfiguration of relations. This approach seeks to expose patterns and possibilities that emerge from creating regulatory architecture that encourages their development. I briefly summarize the judiciary's important but decentered role in this emerging regime and then examine the developments in workplace and mediating institutions that have transformed possibilities for this structural regime.

The Courts: General Norm Elaboration and Context-Based Problem Solving

Recent Supreme Court decisions can—I do not say must—be read to encourage workplace structures that provide for contextual norm elaboration and problem solving.[4] The Court moves in this direction by (1) embracing contextualization as part of the process of determining the impact and legal significance of particular discriminatory conduct; (2) defining the underlying legal violation as a condition or problem that must be effectively addressed; (3) encouraging institutional innovation within workplaces by prescribing an approach that enables employers to avoid liability by effectively preventing or redressing harassment and bias problems; and (4) providing accountability by evaluating the effectiveness of internal processes in addressing conduct properly identified as problematic. Two areas have emerged in which the courts have provided for this crucial engagement between generally articulated norms and local conditions and practices: sexual harassment and subjective employment practices.

Hostile Environment Sexual Harassment

In the area of sexual harassment, the Supreme Court adopted an open-ended, general norm and provided incentives for employers to develop mechanisms for ongoing elaboration and revision of the norm as it applies to particular problems and contexts.[5] Instead of adopting a particular theory or set of rules governing meaning of sexual harassment, the Court articulates an open-ended norm: The critical issue is whether members of one sex are exposed to disadvantageous terms or conditions of employment to which members of other sex not exposed. The Court thus rejects the possibility of a unitary, specific, or precise set of rules.

The Supreme Court adds two doctrinal features that prompt institutional innovation as the method for producing contingent normative specificity: First, the Court specifically calls for a contextual approach to determining the meaning and significance of the general norm. Second, the Court articulated a standard of employer liability that induces workplaces to develop internal mechanisms to engage with the meaning of and possible solutions to the problem of sexual harassment. Elaborated most recently in *Burlington Industries, Inc. v. Ellerth* and *Faragher v. City of Boca Raton*, the Court holds employers liable for hostile environment harassment involving supervisors unless the employer has "exercised reasonable care to avoid harassment and to eliminate it when it might occur."[6]

Of crucial importance here, the Court evaluates the adequacy of those steps by their effectiveness. These cases offer employers an affirmative defense to a hostile environment harassment claim if the employer has shown that it took reasonable steps to prevent harassment and to eliminate it when it does occur. This is not simply a good faith standard that substitutes formal process for meaningful results. Instead, it ties the adequacy of problem-solving processes to demonstrated elimination of the discriminatory condition. Such an approach blurs the line between internal and external legal regulation and between formal and informal legal process. Because they will be held accountable for the effectiveness of their efforts, employers have incentives to create internal processes that address sexual harassment in ways that can be shown to be legitimate and effective when assessed in relation to other workplaces and to the underlying principles reflected in the general norm articulated by the Supreme Court.

While technically specified as an affirmative defense, the Court's employer liability approach moves in the direction of linking problem definition and resolution. In effect, the Court's approach makes the creation of an administrative problem-solving process a part of an employer's legal obligation. Thus it is not only jurors and judges who will be struggling to define sexual harassment as part of a determination of liability for past conduct. As part of their responsibility for preventing and redressing workplace harassment, employers must determine the meaning and causes of harassment as it occurs on an ongoing and continuous basis. The Court's emphasis on effective problem solving encourages employers to define sexual harassment in terms of its impact and cause rather than to engage solely in after-the-fact legal line drawing. Because their efforts will only be rewarded if they prevent or eliminate serious problems, employers must at least identify whether the challenged conduct presents a problem important enough to warrant change at an individual or organizational level.

Legal Regulation of Subjective Employment Practices

The legal regulation of subjective employment practices offers another example of legal norms that focus on addressing a problem through improving the capacity of organizations to make fair decisions rather than on specifying a unitary rule for compliance. In this area the structural approach is built into the definition of the legal harm rather than, as in the sexual harassment area, introduced through the articulation of an independent employer liability defense. In fact, applying a structural lens to the subjective employment practices cases helps resolve a dilemma, described below, that has stymied courts and commentators struggling to define the proper approach to these systems of discretionary decision making.

Employers engage in subjective decision making whenever they make employment decisions that require the exercise of judgment and discretion. These practices could involve individuals, such as promotion and job assignment decisions resulting from interviews, references, and collective or individual assessments of the relative merits of candidates, or groups, such as decisions about defining the pool from which to select employees for a particular position.[7] For a variety of reasons, decisions requiring the exercise of individual or collective judgment that are highly unstructured tend to reflect, express, or produce biased outcomes.[8] This bias has been linked to patterns of underrepresentation or exclusion of members of nondominant groups.[9]

The Supreme Court has recognized this relationship between unstructured discretionary employment decisions and discrimination. In *Watson v. Fort Worth Bank & Trust*, the Court held that disparate impact analysis applies to subjective employment practices, including "an employer's undisciplined system of subjective decision making."[10] This decision reflected a recognition that systemic factors, namely the structure (or lack thereof) of decision making, caused exclusion, as well as the expression of bias by individuals or groups operating within those structures.

Some lower courts have framed their legal analysis of subjective employment practices to take account of the systemic and structural determinants of bias.[11] Their decisions, interpreting the Supreme Court's decision in *Watson* in light of the Civil Rights Act of 1991,[12] focus on the adequacy of employers' internal decision-making processes and systems as the basis for determining the business necessity of subjective employment practices with adverse impact. If subjective employment practices produce a disparate impact on women or people of color, this disparity is a signal of the possibility that the system is contributing to the production or expression of bias. The court then assesses the subjective decision-making process to determine whether it provided adequate steps to minimize or eliminate the expression of bias in those decision-making processes. The emphasis is on whether the degree of unaccountable or unstructured exercise of discretion is warranted. To make this determination, courts will look at the available alternatives. Are there systems of decision making that will permit the exercise of discretion but will institute standards and processes that minimize the expression of bias? Thus the signal of a potential problem is the statistical disparity between the composition of the pool of applicants and the composition of those selected.

But this disparity does not in and of itself constitute a violation. It instead prompts an inquiry into the adequacy, fairness, and accountability of the decision-making processes that produced the initially suspect outcome. This legal standard does not establish a set of rules specifying how employers should set up their systems of decision making. Instead, it establishes a requirement that an employer take steps to minimize the likelihood that its subjective decision-making processes will produce bias. The results of the process are not the only measure of success; they are a trigger that suggests the need for employers to engage in a process of self-evaluation to establish fair systems and mechanisms of accountability. Employers who engage in this process, with demonstrable results showing that they are addressing the problem and will continue to do so, would ostensibly be found to satisfy the business necessity requirement. These employers would, in theory, also be less likely to have subjective employment practices that produce pronounced discriminatory effects.

Shaping an Effective Internal Workplace Regime: Examples from the Field

At least in some contexts, the Supreme Court's recent cases have converged with a more structural and dynamically oriented approach to second generation bias within workplaces as well. Some employers have responded to patterns of bias, exclusion, turnover, and glass ceiling by redesigning their systems of decision making, work assignment, and conflict resolution to address simultaneously concerns about equity and effectiveness. Sexual harassment and glass ceiling jurisprudence has encouraged and reinforced widespread organizational development of internal problem-solving and dispute-resolution processes.

I present below a description of two workplaces that exhibit attributes of an ongoing, continually revised, and accountable problem solving system: Deloitte & Touche and Home Depot.[13] Although the systems vary considerably in their design and implementation, they share several features. They have (1) adopted a process of data gathering and analysis to identify the patterns of decision making that risk producing bias; (2) instituted effective problem-solving strategies at both the individual and systemic level, and functionally integrated those processes with day-to-day operations; (3) generated process and outcome measures of effectiveness; and (4) built in systems to hold these processes accountable. These examples offer a starting point for identifying how internal workplace processes can meet concerns about accountability, legitimacy, and effectiveness.

Deloitte & Touche

Deloitte & Touche, America's third largest accounting, tax, and management consulting firm, implemented a major women's initiative that dramatically increased women's advancement in the company and reduced the turnover rate of women in particular and employees in general.[14] The women's initiative resulted not from the threat of litigation but, rather, from the CEO's perception that a gender gap in the promotion and turnover rate signaled a problem with the firm's capacity to compete effectively for talent. The firm addressed this problem by forming ongoing, participatory task forces with responsibility for determining the nature and cause of a gender gap in promotion and turnover, making recommendations to change the conditions underlying these patterns, developing systems to address those problems and to make future patterns transparent, and monitoring the results. The task force recommendations were implemented through ongoing data gathering and analysis, operational change through line management, and accountability in relation to benchmarks.

The task force approached this challenge the same way it would address a project for a client: What is the problem, who has the information needed to understand why it is happening, and how do we fix it? They hired Catalyst, a nonprofit research organization, to help them better understand and respond to the patterns they observed. Catalyst identified three problem areas: a male-dominated culture, fewer career-advancement opportunities for women, and a companywide need for a more balanced work-life approach. In response, Deloitte created an external task force to monitor its progress, with Lynn Martin, the former head of the Glass Ceiling Commission, as its head. It also created an internal task force responsible for implementing recommendations, headed by a respected partner and supported by a full-time staff position.

The task force undertook the process of translating Catalysts' findings into an agenda for change. Three basic principles guided the implementation process. First, line management, rather than Human Resources, would drive the operational changes. Second, accountability and commitment had to be expressed both internally and externally to assure follow-through. Finally, an accountability structure was developed to make the women's initiative matter to each partner's success.

One of the changes made by the task force was to make the assignment process and its results visible by instituting annual assignment reviews. The task force also made changes to make flexible work arrangements viable without threatening an individual's advancement. Deloitte worked with a consulting firm to develop a two-day workshop, called "Men and Women as Colleagues," to raise awareness of gender dynamics in the firm. The initiative also introduced succession and formal career planning for women. The process encouraged the formation of women's management groups, "in which women would assemble to identify issues in their own offices, as well as to provide another opportunity for networking." Deloitte & Touche now compares offices to one another and to benchmarks the firm has established, and it provides reports to management that are used in evaluations and tied to compensation.

The women's initiative produced swift and observable results, both in women's participation and in the firm's overall retention rate. The combination of increased communication and programmatic change contributed to what many called a culture change. Flexible work has become acceptable at Deloitte for women and men. "By 1995, 23% of senior managers were women, the percentage of women admitted to partner rose from 8% in 1991 to 21%; the turnover rate for female senior managers dropped from 26% to 15%." In 1993, the U.S. firm had 88 women partners; in 1999, the total was 246.[15] The turnover rate fell for both men and women between 1995 and 1998. The firm's CEO "credits his firms 30% growth rate last year—the best among the Big Five . . . —to lower turnover." Deloitte's success has attracted attention and awards and has itself become an effective recruitment tool.

Home Depot

Home Depot is a home improvement company that pioneered the concept and, in many ways, the market for do-it-yourself home improvements. It was the subject of a class action lawsuit, brought in 1994 by a group of female employees and applicants in the Western Division, alleging that women experienced sex segregation and discrimination in gender discrimination in hiring, initial assignments, promotions, compensation, and training, with women receiving assignments to lower-paying, dead end jobs.[16] They attributed these disparities to a highly arbitrary, subjective decision-making process, operating in "a working environment that is heavily male-oriented" and encouraging personnel decisions based on stereotypes. These gender problems coincided with concerns that the company's informal employment practices were inefficient, arbitrary, and unworkable.

The court certified a class of female applicants and employees. On the eve of trial, a court-ordered mediation process produced a global settlement, embodied in a consent decree. The mediation process involved sophisticated plaintiffs' counsel, in-house counsel, senior human resource officials, and experts in systems design. The challenge was to develop a system that would work in a company that was dynamic, decentralized, and entrepreneurial. The solution was to achieve accountability through technology, information systems, and systematizing discretion rather than through rules. The design and implementation of this innovative solution was possible in no small part because of a mutual recognition (by the company and plaintiffs' counsel) that this system must be designed to link equity and effectiveness, as well as a commitment at the top of the organization to its successful implementation.

The keystone of the new system is a companywide automated hiring and promotion system, called JPP, for Job Preference Process.[17] This process virtually eliminates the possibility for managers to steer applicants to particular roles based on stereotypes, expands the pool of applicants for every position, and opens up avenues for advancement that applicants themselves may not otherwise have considered. The JPP also brokers and tracks information at both the individual and the system level. A system of exception reporting was instituted as a "trip wire," to indicate problems with managers' decision making or applicants' advancement. This system integrates the process of hiring and promotion with data gathering and analysis.

This information is used both to increase the effectiveness of the personnel system in matching applicants to positions and to identify trends or patterns of underutilization that warrant further inquiry. The aggregate demographic data serves a similar diagnostic function for locating and correcting problems concerning the inclusion of women, people of color, and older workers. Home Depot has established benchmarks for each position. The benchmarks "are not quotas; they are Benchmarks designed to afford guidance as to whether Home Depot is making selection decisions in such a way as to afford equal employment opportunity." Failure to achieve a benchmark triggers further inquiry and a "constructive dialogue" aimed at understanding whether a problem exists and if so, how to correct it.

Thus Home Depot achieves meaningful accountability through technological design, management systems, and information transparency. It combines rationalization of the employment process with managerial accountability through internal and external monitoring.

The current system involves individuals who are not part of the day-to-day personnel process in holding the system accountable in relation to its goals. Accountability also depends on developing measurable but flexible standards of effectiveness for the process and its outcomes. In addition to the benchmarks established in the consent decree, Home Depot has developed several other indicators of the effectiveness of their new personnel system. These indicators refer both to the impact on women's participation in the company and on the company's ability to attract and retain high-quality employees. According to these measures, Home Depot's system has been strikingly successful in both increasing women's participation at all levels of the company and retaining high quality personnel more efficiently.

Since the JPP was introduced, the number of female managers and the number of minority managers has increased by 30 percent and 28 percent respectively. More women are expressing interest in merchandising positions, receiving serious consideration, and being hired or promoted into those positions. The process has also tangibly improved the effectiveness of Home Depot's personnel process.

The two employers described here have self-consciously designed or revised their systems of conflict resolution and problem solving to address their particular culture, power dynamics, and patterns of daily interaction. Notwithstanding important differences, the companies share several characteristics that seem important to the effectiveness of their internal problem solving regimes. They are: (1) *problem oriented*—each company developed a customized system to address its particular culture and problems; (2) *functionally integrated*—the systems linked but did not entirely merge processes for addressing interrelated domains, such as principle (e.g., bias, access, fairness) and productivity (e.g., recruitment, turnover), individual employment decisions, and systemic patterns; (3) *data driven*—problem resolution generates and is informed by ongoing analysis of information-revealing patterns of dysfunction; and (4) *accountable*—each system builds in methods of assessing its effectiveness, and evaluating those responsible for its effective implementation.

Law's Role in Shaping Internal Problem-Solving Processes

Law interacted with internal change initiatives in these two workplaces in both complementary and contradictory ways. It served as a catalyst, and provided legitimacy, clout, and regular consideration for human resource concerns that are typically neglected or undervalued. At the same time, however, "legal" came to symbolize the risk involved in taking proactive steps to address problems with legal implications. Law helped make the vocabulary of norms a part of the day-to-day language of the workplace and to inject normative considerations into decisions about how to structure the day-to-day operations of the business. But it also threatened to relegate these same concerns to the category of liability avoidance and thus marginalize both their ethical and economic dimensions. Law encouraged the development of internal systems of accountability, even as it sometimes, out of concern that revealing problems or mistakes would fuel legal "punishment," stifled creativity and risk taking.

The hard regulatory question involves the large middle group of employers that are neither in the forefront—developing innovative ways to link inclusion and productivity—nor in the backwaters, actively excluding members of nondominant groups. How can regulation encourage this middle group to learn from and improve upon the efforts of the frontrunners? In the examples described above, individual and organizational intermediaries played a crucial role in mediating this tension between the coercive and aspirational character of law, as well as in building stakeholders' capacity and incentive to address complex workplace bias.

The Pivotal Role of Intermediaries in a Structural Regime

The structural approach to second generation problems calls for a dynamic and reciprocal relationship between judicially elaborated general legal norms and workplace-generated problem-solving approaches, which in turn elaborate and transform the understanding of the general norm. This interactive dynamic is important because of the limitations of both judicially managed *and* completely decentralized regimes. If the courts assume direct responsibility for elaborating specific standards for effective problem solving, they risk reproducing the limitations of a rule-enforcement dynamic. The systems described in the previous section work because they are tailored to their context and functionally integrated into the incentive structure and culture of the organization. These same systems might fail miserably if introduced in a different organizational or cultural context. Efforts to define comprehensive and adequately directive standards that still account for differences in context face insurmountable obstacles. Judicially defined codes for effective process are likely to mimic adversarial processes that fail to respond to the complexities of second generation employment discrimination. Or, they will embrace minimal standards that do not provide any meaningful accountability. Judicially developed and imposed systems frequently trigger strong resentment and resistance, which invites strategic behavior aimed at minimizing the impact of the law. This tendency discourages employers from analyzing their practices to identify problems. In any case courts are often reluctant to dictate unilaterally how employers should manage their employees.

But if the regulatory project remains entirely local and context specific, the structural move risks sacrificing accountability to public norms. Many employers lacking the capacity or incentive to develop effective systems would face little pressure or support to change. Internal processes that emerged from gross inequalities or power imbalances would lack an external reference point that would bring those problems to light. A decentralized approach to defining effective problem-solving systems would also provide no way of learning from the successes and failures of other companies or elaborating the meaning of the nondiscrimination principle in light of changing circumstances, except at the most local level. The complete privatization of responsibility for problem-solving processes would thus undermine the law's normative impact.

This dilemma seems intractable if framed as a choice between employers on the one hand and government on the other. How can there be external accountability without externally imposed rules? How can the law shape internal problem-solving processes without taking over the process of defining their features? How can standards of effectiveness be developed that are flexible enough to account for variability and still comparable across different locations?

Nongovernmental organizations and professional networks play a crucial role in mediating the relationship between legal institutions and workplaces. A set of intermediate actors, operating within and across the boundaries of workplaces, have emerged as important players in the implementation of workplace innovations to address bias.[18] At least some of these intermediaries have begun to play an ongoing role of: (1) building the capacity and constituencies needed to operate effective, accountable systems within organizations; (2) pooling and critically assessing examples across institutions; (3) generating effectiveness norms; and (4) constructing communities of practice to sustain this ongoing, reflexive inquiry. These nongovernmental actors are shaping courts' approach to defining effective workplace problem solving, and translating legal norms into organizational systems and standards. Indeed, the long-term viability of a structural regulatory regime may depend on the effectiveness of intermediaries in translating and mediating between formal law and workplace practice.

The case studies illustrate the importance of intermediaries in bridging conventional dichotomies such as public/private, legal/nonlegal, general/contextual, coercive/cooperative. These intermediaries are individuals and organizations who do not directly act for the state but who have the authority to articulate and vindicate legal norms without directly deploying coercive state power. Their participation sets up regular occasions for evaluating and revising day-to-day practices.[19] They are also connected to a broader community of practice that provides some form of accountability for the actions of the intermediary. This affiliation with a broader network enables these intermediaries to pool information within and across contexts, to identify problems without directly triggering punitive legal action, and to navigate the challenges of sharing information about best practices without revealing trade secrets to business competitors or breaching confidentiality in individual cases. This section briefly sketches out the individual and organizational actors that mediate the relationship between law and the workplace.

Individual Change Agents: Redefining the Role of Problem Solver

One category of intermediaries consists of individuals and organizations with some form of professional knowledge and an affiliation with a larger community of practice who function as interdisciplinary, intergroup problem solvers. This group includes the human resource professionals, lawyers, industrial psychologists, and organizational consultants who have redefined their roles to translate legal norms into organizational terms and then convey to formal legal bodies the organizational practices that effectuate and elaborate legal principles. Many of these individual and organizational actors are repeat players, either within one organization or across a variety of contexts. They straddle an insider/outside role. Their effectiveness as intermediaries lies not with their professional expertise per se but, rather, with the pattern of relationships and experiences their professional or organizational position enables them to aggregate.

Organizational Mediators of Change

Regional, industry-based, and national research/policy/practice consortia have emerged in the area of workplace practice, inclusion, and organizational change. These organizations are well-situated to perform a mediating role between law and the workplace. The Deloitte & Touche example is illustrative. As part of its women's initiative, Deloitte & Touche retained the services of several nonprofit research organizations to help figure out why women were leaving the firm and what to do about it. One such organization was Catalyst, a nonprofit research organization that advises corporations on how to move women ahead. It conducts internal assessments of employment practices and helps companies devise long-term, structural approaches that address glass ceiling issues.[20] Its staff includes an interdisciplinary group of researchers with different kinds of expertise who work as a problem-solving team. In addition to its corporate services, Catalyst conducts aggregate research on problems and best practices and shares this information both with its corporate membership and in published reports. It also sponsors conferences and distributes awards for exemplary initiatives.

Problem-Solving Lawyers

Creative lawyers on both sides of the employment discrimination divide also play an important role as catalysts, poolers of information, and sources of accountability. The roles of plaintiffs' counsel and in-house counsel have intersected and blurred in interesting ways, particularly in the process of developing effective remedies. Again, the case studies illustrate this development. In-house counsel at Home Depot report to the vice president for human resources, rather than to the general counsel. They sit at the table during process of system analysis and redesign. A substantial portion of their role involves translating the problems identified through the problem-solving process into ongoing training, system redesign, and policy revision. Their knowledge and power to mobilize law makes them legitimate and influential participants in shaping but not dictating practice, unless a crisis erupts.

The evolution of the role of plaintiffs' counsel who function as repeat players in structural reform regimes is particularly striking. The involvement of plaintiffs' counsel in the negotiation of the Home Depot consent decree illustrates this development. The firm that represented plaintiffs in the West Coast litigation—Saperstein, Goldstein, Demchak, & Baller—is one of the nation's most visible and successful firms handling plaintiffs' discrimination cases. This track record equipped Barry Goldstein and the firm to play a significant structural role.

In the Home Depot case participants on all sides of the litigation describe Goldstein's role as crucial to the development of a flexible, accountable remedy that by all accounts has been extremely effective in increasing women's participation and improving productivity. Once settlement negotiations began in earnest, Goldstein participated in setting up a process that would generate the information needed to address the problem and involve the people with the expertise and responsibility within the organization in implementing the newly devised system. He sat at the table with the actual operations people, the psychologists who were developing the tests, and the systems engineers who were designing the computer system. His role was not to design the system himself or to hire an expert who would manage implementation. Instead, his role was to help those who would have to implement one to develop a system that would work, that would be sufficiently transparent so that the information would provide a continual check on the process and that would institutionalize regular occasions for evaluating the system's effectiveness. Built into the consent decree process was the assignment of responsibility for internal compliance monitoring to high-level company officials, backed up by regular compliance reports to plaintiffs.

This arrangement vividly illustrates the convergence for lawyers of entrepreneurialism and justice seeking. Management lawyers prod and enable their clients to adopt more functional and fair human resource systems. Employees' advocates work with corporations and insurance companies to develop effective structures for minimizing bias within organizations. Problem-solving lawyers on both sides can play an important role as catalysts and resources for effective problem solving.

Employee Groups: Constituencies for Change

Groups such as employee caucuses and self-help groups, civil rights and women's advocacy organizations, and progressive labor unions have also emerged as catalysts for and partners in developing workplace policy and monitoring workplace practices.[21] These employee organizations, informal and formal, provide regular opportunities for employees to mobilize around issues of second generation bias. By bringing together employees with common experiences, these groups facilitate the identification of patterns of dysfunction. They also enable employees to interact with their employer as a group, which both elevates the importance of responding and diffuses the target of any retaliation. For example, at Deloitte & Touche, networks of women managers have developed both within the company and among a local group of professional women in financial services and management. These groups identify issues of shared concern, evaluate the effectiveness of internal initiatives, and design effective strategies for new types of problems.

Unions have in some settings provided an established institutional framework to support employees in collective efforts to address second generation bias and build inclusive work environments.[22] Finally, workplace, women's rights, and civil rights advocacy groups have begun to play a role in building the capacity of employee groups to hold employers accountable and to participate in shaping their workplace cultures and practices. Organizations such as 9 to 5, the National Employment Law Project, the Workplace Project, and national civil rights groups have, to varying degrees, used their legitimacy, resources, and track record to document patterns of exclusion, create networks among local groups interested in pooling information and strategies, and build the capacity of employee groups to push for and participate in effective, structural change.

Insurance Companies and Brokers: Gatekeepers of Legal Norms

The insurance industry is an increasingly important player in the overall workplace regulatory field. Until recently, firms could not purchase insurance for sexual harassment and discrimination claims. Now more than seventy insurance companies nationwide offer sexual harassment insurance to their clients.[23] Advocates have expressed concern about the impact of insurance on discrimination law's effectiveness, but insurance companies could turn out to be a significant player in the move to encourage structural workplace responses.

Insurers have begun to require employers to adopt a proactive approach to sexual harassment and discrimination as a prerequisite for obtaining and maintaining a liability policy.[24] In the wake of decisions requiring them to pay for injuries arising from sexual harassment, "insurance companies are likely to start requiring clients to have the kind of anti-harassment policies and remedies that were outlined . . . by the United States Supreme Court."[25] "The underwriting process is likely to include an evaluation of a firm's existing employment practices," including a review by an outside lawyer or consultant to assess the adequacy of current conditions and decision-making processes.[26] Once a policy is in place, most underwriters offer and encourage the use of loss control services.

Insurance brokers also act as gatekeepers for clients seeking employment practices liability (EPL) insurance by advising clients about the kinds of changes needed to get coverage or to reduce their premium. In addition, insurance companies have expanded the services they offer in order to compete with consulting firms that provide advice to companies on how to lower their risk of liability. They now offer free or reduced-fee consulting services to interested account holders. These services include employment practices audits, assistance in designing effective human resource systems, and review of policies and manuals for compliance and effectiveness in risk reduction.

Thus, a spectrum of mediating actors and organizations has fostered the development of hybrid forms of relationships between public and private norms, legal and informal incentives, and contextual and general learning.

Conclusion: Strengthening the Infrastructure for Effective Workplace Problem Solving

The movement I have described toward an integrated, holistic, and continually evolving goverance system is currently only partial and incomplete. Countertendencies and patterns that undercut its viability continue to exist. Many lower courts have watered down the Supreme Court's linkage of institutional innovation and effective outcomes and threaten to allow formal gestures to substitute for effective problem solving. Many employers have internal grievance mechanisms that are more symbolic than substantive. The crucial sector of mediating actors is underdeveloped, lacks resources, and has yet to develop ways of assuring its own accountability. The infrastructure necessary to facilitate the information pooling and accountability that is crucial to the legitimacy of a structural approach is not yet adequately developed. Unsurprisingly, therefore, the conception of discrimination regulation has not yet shifted sufficiently to match or guide the emergent practice at present. An inadequate understanding of the dynamic relationships among private, governmental, and intermediate actors also exists.

At its best, the current regime encourages and rewards effective, context-specific problem solving and dispute resolution within workplaces, informed by information about more general patterns and examples of effective processes. Incomplete implementation, however, threatens both to dilute the law's normative impact and to interfere with employers' economically motivated initiatives to address second generation bias. We thus face a watershed moment in the regulation of workplace practices.

I have identified three focal areas to realize more fully the regulatory shift to a structural approach: (1) the judiciary—by shoring up the judicial commitment and elaboration of the structural approach; (2) individual change agents—by developing their role as problem solvers; and (3) nongovernmental organizations—by building their capacity to play an effective mediating role.

For the judiciary, the Supreme Court has already laid the foundations of this role, by defining the norm as a problematic condition and encouraging employers to remedy that condition through institutional innovation. What is missing is (1) clear judicial expression of the commitment to effectiveness in remedying violations; (2) a method for generating and revising standards for evaluating the effectiveness of a particular problem-solving process, without reverting to command-specific rules; and (3) sufficient experience of the benefits of effective problem solving to overcome the prevailing culture of equating problem identification with liability.

Ideally, judicial actors collaborate in deliberating about the criteria of effectiveness, without assuming direct responsibility for formulating a code of conduct. They do this by insisting that employers, with the help of inside and outside collaborators, develop and justify working criteria for evaluating the effectiveness of their internal problem-solving mechanisms. Courts are then in a position to assess the employers' justification for their effectiveness criteria and their compliance with those criteria. This enables courts to function as a catalyst rather than as either a de facto employment director or a deferrer to employers' unaccountable choices.

Courts thus play an important role. They continue to apply coercion, but they separate coercion from an inflexible application of a fixed rule structure. They evaluate the adequacy of particular employers' internal efforts based on the information supplied by the litigants about the adequacy of the system established to address problems. This evaluation is based on both the process and the outcome of that process of conflict resolution. Courts also sanction the violations of norms that have been shown to be detectable and correctable and that were not detected or corrected by a particular employer.

Compliance is assessed based on the ability to respond to a problem of harassment or biased decision making, not just on the basis of the outcome of a particular conflict. Courts would continue to establish a floor of acceptable conduct. The floor would, however, rise, as the capacity to address problems effectively increases. The goal and standard would be to improve each time a conflict arises. The approach to compliance could also reward employers who develop effective, accountable, and inclusive decision-making processes by protecting them from liability for problems exposed and remedied by those processes. Employers who are engaged in an ongoing process of self-assessment and self-correction that can be evaluated by a standard of effectiveness, both in general and in relation to particular disputes or conflicts, would be subject to less stringent scrutiny for particular claims of discrimination. Employers who are continually improving are in compliance. This lowers the risk of pro forma compliance and gaming. It emphasizes improvement of the process and conditions, with individual disputes assessed in relation to the organization's effectiveness in addressing problems rather than as a basis in themselves for determining failure or noncompliance.

Thus, in this structural regulatory regime, courts create a framework that will generate the information, incentives, and opportunity to elaborate the meaning of a general norm in context and the development of contingent solutions in cases that do not lie on the normative boundary. This process would then generate information that would deepen our understanding of the general norm and perhaps better enable us to construct wise solutions in the cases closer to the normative line.

On my account, individual change agents are critical to the internal problem-solving process and the external aggregation of information and experiences because they are best positioned to spread learnings into communities of practice. If I am correct, that fact requires revising the roles of human resource specialists, employee advocates, organizational development specialists, ombudsmen, corporate counsel, and general line managers. In order for these actors to see themselves as change agents, they need to shift their focus from individual cases and complaints to a systemic viewpoint. They should define their roles to include the gathering of data across cases, looking for patterns, and making change based on those patterns. What is critical, here, is how these change agents address the patterns they identify.

Finally, it is crucial to devote energy, thought, and resources to the project of building the capacity and accountability of individual change agents to function as problem solvers. One important component of this shift is to focus academic attention on documenting and analyzing the emerging practice, assembling, in effect, an inventory of stories or case studies involving effective change agents. These stories would illustrate the importance of expanding the conception of advocacy beyond the courts and broadening the conception of professional role to include a focus on building institutional capacity to problem solve. This would help identify and foster the conditions that enable a variety of organizational professionals and managers to revise their roles in order to become reflective practitioners and innovators in dealing with deeply embedded gendered norms and work practices.

The workplace example would inform the work of both those concerned specifically with increasing workplace equality and those interested in the more general regulatory questions. It certainly invites further inquiry into the role of intermediary institutions and actors as enablers of complex regulatory regimes adequate to the challenge of complex problems. Perhaps it will encourage at least some companies to shift their focus toward learning from the innovators, instead of thinking simply about how to avoid becoming the next legal fiasco.

NOTES

1. See Linda Hamilton Krieger, "The Content of Our Categories: A Cognitive Bias Approach to Discrimination and Equal Employment Opportunity," *Stanford Law Review* 47 (1995): 1161, 1186–1188.

2. See Robin J. Ely and Debra E. Meyerson, "Theories of Gender in Organizations: A New Approach to Organizational Analysis and Change," in B. Staw and R. Sutton, eds., *Research in Organizational Behavior* 23 (2001); David B. Wilkins and G. Mitu Gulati, "Why Are There So Few Black Lawyers in Corporate Law Firms? An Institutional Analysis," *California Law Review* 84 (1996): 496–501.

3. See Lauren B. Edelman, "Legal Ambiguity and Symbolic Structures: Organizational Mediation of Civil Rights Law," *American Journal of Sociology* 97 (1992): 1531, 1538.

4. See *Burlington Industries, Inc. v. Ellerth*, 524 U.S. 742, 765 (1998); *Harris v. Forklift Sys., Inc.*, 510 U.S. 17, 21–23 (1993); *Watson v. Fort Worth Bank & Trust*, 487 U.S. 977, 990–91 (1988).

5. See *Faragher v. City of Boca Raton*, 524 U.S. 775, 786 (1998); *Harris v. Forklift Sys.*, 510 U.S. 17, 21.

6. 524 U.S. 742 (1988); 524 U.S. 775, 805 (1998).

7. See *Thomas v. Wash. County Sch. Bd.*, 915 F.2d 922 (4th Cir. 1990).

8. See *Thomas v. Eastman Kodak Co.*, 183 F.3d 38, 61 (1st Cir. 1999).

9. See Wayne Cascio, Applied Psychology in Personnel Management 77 (3d ed. 1987); Susan T. Fiske & Shelley E. Taylor, Social Cognition 159–67 (1984); Krieger, "Content of Our Categories," 1199–1211.

10. 487 U.S. 977, 990 (1988).

11. See, e.g., *Butler v. Home Depot, Inc.*, No. C-85–2182SI, 1997 U.S. Dist. LEXIS 16296, at *47 (N.D. Cal. Aug. 28, 1997); *Shores v. Publix Super Markets, Inc.*, No. 95–1162-CIV-T-25(E), 1996 WL 407850, at *5–6 (M.D. Fla. Mar. 12 1996); *Stender v. Lucky Stores, Inc.*, 803 F. Supp. 259, 335 (N.D. Cal. 1992).

12. 42 U.S.C. § 2000e-2(k)(1)(A).

13. Readers interested in a discussion of the problem-solving practices of a third workplace should consult the longer version of this chapter, cited supra, n. 1.

14. This case study draws heavily from an excellent, two-part case study prepared under the supervision of Professor Rosabeth Moss Kanter as part of the Harvard Business School case-study series. See Jane Roessner, Deloitte & Touche (A): A Hole in the Pipeline, N9–300–012 (September 28, 1999) and Deloitte & Touche (B): Changing the Workplace, N9–300–013 (September 28, 1999). It is supplemented by media coverage of Deloitte & Touche's women's initiative and selected interviews with Deloitte & Touche personnel.

15. "Deloitte & Touche CEO Explains Growth in Terms of Lower Turnover," *The CPA Journal* (March 2000): 10.

16. *Butler v. Home Depot*, 1997 U.S. Dist. LEXIS 16296 (N.D. Cal. 1997).

17. Consent Decree at 32, *Butler v. Home Depot, Inc.*, 1997 U.S. Dist. LEXIS 16296 (N.D. Cal. 1997) (No. C-95–2182 SI).

18. See Edelman et al., "The Endogeneity of Legal Regulation: Procedures as Rational Myths," *American Journal of Sociology* 105 (1999): 406, 412.

19. See Carol A. Heimer, "Competing Institutions: Law, Medicine, and Family in Neonatal Intensive Care," *Law and Society Review* 33 (1999): 17, 34.

20. See http://www.catalystwomen.org/about/advisory.html.

21. See Penda D. Hair, "Prayer and Protest: Bringing a Community Vision of Justice to a Labor Dispute," *University of Pennsylvania Journal of Labor and Employment Law* 2 (2000): 657, 660.

22. See, e.g., Doug Gamble and Nina Gregg, "Rethinking the Twenty-first Century Workplace: Unions and Workplace Democracy," *University of Pennsylvania Journal of Labor and Employment Law* 1 (1998): 429, 449–50; Charles C. Hockscher, *The New Unionism: Employee Involvement in the Changing Corporation* (Ithaca: ILR Press of Cornell University Press, 1996), 177.

23. Amy Joyce, "More Firms Are Buying Sexual Harassment Insurance Policies," *Los Angeles Times*, May 26, 1998, p. D3.

24. See Francis J. Mootz III, "Insurance Coverage of Employment Discrimination Claims," *University of Miami Law Review* 52 (1997): 78, n. 27.

25. Leslie Eaton, "State Insurers May Demand Stricter Harassment Policies," *NewY ork Times*, July 4, 1998, p. B6.

26. See Dave Pelland, "Exploring Employment Practices and Policies," *Risk Management* 45 (1998): 6; see also Dave Pelland, "Facing a Rising Exposure," *Risk Management* 44 (1997): 10.

CHAPTER 18

Our Economy of Mothers and Others

Women and Economics Revisited

A property lawyer coined the term "feminization of poverty" in the late 1970s to highlight the prevalence of women among the poor.[1] This take on the feminization of poverty, while important, is limited in a country with a poverty rate of 11.8 percent.[2] This chapter will argue that we need to fold the traditional debate on the proportion of women among the poor into a more sweeping analysis of the relationship between women and economics.

In doing this, we should follow the lead of the growing international awareness, which focuses more broadly on women's relationship to economic security. Statistics show that women are the poorest of the world's poor. Women are not only 59 percent of those in poverty and 70 percent of those in extreme poverty,[3] but they also "earn less than a tenth of the world's income and own less than one percent of the world's property."[4]

If our goal is an analysis of women's economic welfare, what better place to start than with Charlotte Perkins Gilman's *Women and Economics*?[5] This classic treatment, published in 1898, established the framework we still use today. Gilman's central focus is on women's dependence:

Women, as a class, neither produce nor distribute wealth . . . women, as individuals, labor mainly as house servants, are not paid as such, and would not be satisfied . . . if they were so paid . . . wives are not business

A slightly longer version of this essay was originally published in *Journal of Gender, Race, and Justice* 5 (2002): 411; reprinted with permission.

partners or co-producers of wealth with their husbands, unless they actually practice the same profession . . . they are not salaried as mothers, and that it would be unspeakably degrading if they were, what remains to those who deny that women are supported by men?[6]

Gilman has no doubt that women are supported by men. This support is both an affront to their dignity ("the pitiful dependence of the human female") and corrosive of their character ("the sluggish and greedy disposition bred of long ages of dependence"). Her solution is to restructure the tasks performed by wives along the industrial model. Even child care is professionalized under this model. The Gilman tradition, echoed virtually unchanged some sixty years later by Betty Friedan in *The Feminine Mystique*, dominates popular imagery of American feminism to this day.[7] Feminism today is still associated with an insistence on employment for women with day care centers as the solution for the conflict between work and family demands.

I have argued that the Gilman model[8] is flawed because it accepts too readily three basic elements of the housewife/breadwinner system historians call "domesticity."[9] First, it accepts the current construction of paid labor, which reflects the ideal of a worker who starts to work in early adulthood and works for forty years straight, taking no time off for childbearing or child rearing. Second, it accepts the dichotomy between home and work, as well as the notion that household work is not "work." Reva Siegel has documented that before the nineteenth century, society openly acknowledged the economic value of women's household labor.[10] However, the advent of domesticity's new sex/gender arrangements erased the economic value of household work. Consequently, today there is an attitude among homemakers that they "don't work."[11] Finally, the Gilman model embraces the privatized theory that reproductive work is a private responsibility and not a public necessity.[12]

We need to change each element of domesticity in order to create a new model for the analysis of women and economics. I will propose an analytic framework that changes gender arrangements in both market work and family work.

Discussions of women and poverty tend to focus on "welfare," the social safety net designed for the impoverished. Yet the social safety net affects only women's relationship to a small fraction of our economy. Welfare programs constitute a tiny fraction, 3 to 4 percent,[13] of the federal budget; much more important are "entitlement" programs such as social security, unemployment insurance, our elaborate system of tax and other social expenditures.

If the goal is to analyze women's relationship to the public distribution of wealth, it makes no sense to focus our attention only on a small fraction of government budgets. We need to bring the analysis of other government programs (now considered topics of interest only to specialists) into the mainstream of gender research. Thus far the only government program other than welfare that has received extensive gender analysis is tax. Critical tax theory can provide many of the tools we need for analysis of the public sector.[14] This is an important step, but we need to go further. To gain a balanced picture of women's relationship to economic security, we need to examine women's relationship to private as well as public wealth.

To the extent that we discuss women's relationship to the private economy, the tendency is to focus on women's workforce participation. Yet this approach itself is gendered. The economic security of most men depends on their employment status, but the economic security of many women does not. American women still do eighty percent of the child care,[15] and this family work often affects their participation in paid work.[16] For this reason, in order to analyze women's relationship to private wealth, we need to consider not only their paid but also their family work. In the United States this boils down to a discussion of divorce law, but the real issue is one of who owns what within the family.

To summarize, we need to widen our analysis of women and economic security to include the social safety net and the disproportionate percentage of women among the poor. We also need to consider how other government wealth-distribution programs, from social "entitlements" to the tax system, systematically favor men over women. Finally, we need to analyze women's relationship to private as well as public wealth through a consideration both of women's relationship to paid work and their entitlements based on family relationships.

Access to Economic Security through Market Work

Today two statistics frame the way we look at women and paid work. The first is women's workforce participation, a demographic measure that documents the demise of the breadwinner/housewife model as women entered the workforce. The second is the wage gap, which measures the gap between the wages of men who work full-time against the wages of women who work full-time. Both statistics reflect the Gilmore model; they are designed to measure the extent to which women are in the labor force working shoulder to shoulder with men, as ideal workers who become employed in early adulthood and remain employed, full-time and full-force, for forty years straight.

While the work patterns and wages of women without children are looking increasingly like those of ideal-worker men, the same is not true of mothers. If we look at mothers during the key years of career advancement, aged twenty-five to forty-four, two out of three do not perform as ideal workers even in the minimal sense of working forty hours per week all year. What is more dramatic is that 92 percent work less than fifty hours per week.[17] In an age where virtually all good jobs require full-time work, and many of the best jobs require overtime, mothers are cut out of the labor pool for many desirable jobs, blue- as well as white-collar.

Economy of Mothers in Comparison to Others

Jane Waldfogel has documented that women without children earn 90 percent of the wages of men, but mothers earn only 60 percent of the wages of fathers, and that this "family gap" between the wages of mothers and other adults increased during the 1980s[18] and may still be rising among the least privileged women. If we look not at women's workforce participation but at whether they perform as ideal workers along with men, what emerges is a picture of the fragile hold women have on market work in a society where nearly 90 percent of women become mothers during their working lives.[19]

In short, a focus on wage gap and workforce participation figures tends to exaggerate the extent to which women have reached economic equality. After all, two-thirds of working women work less than forty hours per week.[20] Therefore, the wage gap statistic comparing women who work full-time with men who work full-time grossly overestimates the extent of women's equality. Workforce participation statistics are equally misleading: consider the woman lawyer who dropped out of her legal career and ran a part-time quilt business from her home.[21] Though she was "in the workforce," she remained firmly marginalized and economically vulnerable. We need new economic measures that document our economy of mothers and others.

At a deeper level, we need to reassess Gilman's assumption that the key to economic equality is for women to perform as ideal workers along with men while child care is delegated to professional child care workers. As a model for economic equality this has proved to be morally troubling and of limited effectiveness.[22] Particularly in an age of high overtime, we need to go back and rethink how we define the "committed" or "responsible" worker.

The problem with pinning our hopes for women's equality on a strategy of having women perform as ideal workers, as June Carbone said long ago, is that "it leaves out the small matter of who will take care of the children."[23] The real issue is that our ideals at work do not fit with our ideals for family life. In a society with the longest hours of overtime in the industrialized world, longer even than Japan's, the ideal-worker norm clashes with our sense of what we owe to children. Fathers who work full-time work an average of forty-eight

hours per week.[24] This increases when combined with their average com-
mutes, meaning that they may well be gone from home ten or more hours
each weekday. We are caught in the clash of two social ideals: the ideal-worker
norm on the job and the norm of parental care at home. This clash combines
with gender performance norms that engender in most women the desire to
be a "real mother" (complete with milk, cookies, and carpool) and in most
men the desire to be a "real man" (which includes performing as an ideal
worker to the extent his race, class, and personality allow him to do so). The
end result is that gender has proved unbending. The economy of mothers and
others will not change until we redefine the ideal worker and restructure market work and thereby redefine our work ideals so that they are more in sync
with our traditions of nurturance. The key here is family-responsive policies.

Access to Economic Security through Family Work

One out of four mothers is still a housewife during the key years of career
advancement.[25] Economic security for many women does not depend on
paid work but on entitlements gained within the family. Moreover, homemakers are not the only ones whose economic security depends on entitlements gained through family life. Women who work part-time make a fraction
of what their husbands or ex-husbands make, given the depressed wages of
part-time workers. Even women who work full-time often have wages that are
comparatively low.[26] The end result is that, in the average American family,
the father still earns nearly 70 percent of the family income.[27] Thus economic security depends on entitlements gained within the family relationships not
only for homemakers but also for many women who work part-time or even
full-time outside the home.

The only existing conversation for discussing this topic is the "new theory
of alimony" debate in family law;[28] however, the issues at stake here require
more than a narrow focus on alimony, which has traditionally been based on
need rather than on ownership and has never been awarded to more than a
small fraction of women (currently around 8 percent).[29] Instead, we need a
more sweeping consideration of who owns what within the family.

To undertake this analysis, we need to examine domesticity's definition of
paid work as "real work," while defining equally important care work as "not
working." I like to quote one mother: "I get so sick of people asking me, 'Do
you work?' Of course I work! I've got five children under ten! I work twenty-
four hours a day! But of course they mean, 'Do you work for pay, outside your
home?' " A key tenet of domesticity is that wives are "supported" by men who

"work." In fact, the only reason a father can perform as an ideal worker is that he typically is supported by a flow of child care and other family work from his partner (whether they are currently married or ever have been). Once we notice the father's dependence on that flow of family work, we can see that the chief family asset in most households, the ideal-worker wage, reflects not only the father's paid work but also the mother's family work.[30]

Note how this analysis flips the traditional understanding of who is dependent upon whom; the common understanding, accepted by Gilman, is that women depend on men.[31] In order to change domesticity's erasure of household work, we need to place front and center the idea that family work is work, not leisure, and that it is an integral part of the overall economy.[32]

One would think that an asset reflecting the work of two family members would be jointly owned. In divorce courts, in the economy of gratitude in intact marriages,[33] and in many government benefits programs, the husband typically is treated as the sole owner of the ideal-worker wage.

There is a little bit of wealth redistribution throughout family law but not much;[34] alimony is rare, temporary, and generally low because most families have so little savings; no property distribution rule has much effect. Two prominent economists estimate that fathers as a group pay only 6 percent of their income in child support, although some fathers pay a lot more.[35] In this context, it should not be surprising that nearly 40 percent of divorced mothers end up living in poverty.[36] When we take a step back from this analysis, we can see that what we have, and what we are exporting through globalization, is a system in which men specialize in paid work, work linked with ownership, while women specialize in family work, leisure linked with economic vulnerability.

When you define the ideal worker as someone without responsibility for children, you set up a child-care system that pushes the primary caregivers to the margins of economic life. In a few European countries the government steps in to redistribute wealth to women and children.[37] However, the absence of such a system in most other regions leads to predictably high levels of child and maternal poverty. In the United States, 80 percent of those living in poverty are women and children.[38] Few governments in developed countries have the political desire to save women and children from the gendered logic of the private economy; some European countries have outstanding supports for caregivers,[39] but many other developed countries, notably the United States, do not.[40] Even fewer developing countries have the resources to do so. Unless we want to export our economy of mothers and others through globalization, we need to redefine the relationship of women to private wealth, not only in the United States but worldwide.

Access to Economic Security Through the Government

Completing our analysis of women and economic security requires an analysis of women's relationship not only to private wealth but also to government wealth. Scholars of the social safety net have led the way in delineating how government wealth distribution programs affect women.[41] The next step is to move from an analysis of women to an analysis of gender. When the series of programs commonly known as "welfare" is seen through the lens of domesticity, what emerges is a particularly pernicious example of how women's family work is erased and treated as leisure. Thus the impoverished mother who takes three buses at midnight to get her asthmatic child to the hospital is defined as lazy.[42]

The Linked Fate of Women and Children

An analysis that starts with domesticity also highlights the way our economic system links the fate of women and children. A system that provides for the care of children by economically marginalizing their caregivers is one that systematically impoverishes children as well as women. This is in sharp contrast to the view that women's equality will hurt children's chances. In fact, domesticity in a society allergic to government redistribution, such as the United States, is a sex/gender system that systematically impoverishes children. One out of five U.S. children and one out of two of African-American children are living in impoverished conditions.[43]

Domesticity and Government Redistribution Programs

In addition to providing the groundwork for an analysis of welfare that focuses on women, domesticity offers some significant insights into government redistribution programs other than those that form part of the social safety net. Mary O'Connell provides a particularly insightful analysis.[44] O'Connell points out that in the United States a three-tiered system of economic security exists. "The greatest security belongs to those whose attachment to paid work is lengthy, uninterrupted, and highly remunerative"—to workers, typically men, who conform to "career" ideals. This first tier, designed to replace the ideal-worker wage, often gives fairly robust benefits. The second tier gives benefits on a derivative basis to family members of ideal workers and yields a much more fragile claim on economic security: it offers only "a hodgepodge of entitlements, fraught with gaps, that frequently fails to provide needed protection to the recipient." Finally, those who do not engage in paid work, and who lack access based on a derivative basis, must look to statutes providing some benefits for their economic security. This third tier consists of means-tested benefits such as Temporary Assistance for Needy Families (TANF) given to a population, overwhelmingly female, that often remains impoverished even after receipt of the benefits. "This three-tier system is gendered," O'Connell points out, "with the upper tier inhabited predominantly by men, and the two lower tiers staffed almost exclusively by women."

The distribution of government benefits plays a great, if not greater, role in defining women's relationship to economic security.[45] As O'Connell points out, government benefits include more than the obvious candidates: Social Security, unemployment insurance, and worker's compensation. An analysis of how government actions allocate wealth needs to include the tax subsidies given to private health care and pension plans. Today these benefits reflect the model of an ideal worker who begins full-time work in early adulthood and works uninterrupted until retirement. This model is designed around men's bodies and life patterns; therefore, it discriminates against women. According to estimates by the Older Women's League, by 2030, a majority of women still will not work in the patterns required to receive Social Security.[46]

The solutions are complex, but two basic principles emerge. First, social entitlements should be based equally on the two important kinds of work most adults do: paid work and family work. Social security and other benefits should be earned not only through paid work, but also through family work. Second, benefits linked to paid work should not be limited to ideal workers as traditionally defined. Health insurance policy waiting periods, Employee Retirement Income Security Act (ERISA) vesting rules, Social Security recency requirements and the thirty-five-year work-life rule should be abolished or redesigned so that they are not disproportionately skewed toward men. Currently men earn social entitlements, such as Social Security, and private benefits such as health insurance and private pensions that are less available to women.[47]

Designing Policies to Change the Relationship of Women and Economics

This completes the basic analysis. The next question is this: How do we change the relationship of women and economic security? To change that relationship, we can change one or more of three basic relationships. First, we can change the relationship between employers and employees. Second, we

can change entitlements within the family. Third, we can change the configuration of the public and private spheres.

Changing the Relationship Between Employers and Employees.

One approach is to change the relationship of employers and employees.
We can accomplish these changes by requiring workplaces to take account of
the important family work responsibilities of their employees. To do this, we
need to go far beyond current "family friendly" policies and rethink how we
define the ideal worker. "When you work part-time or temporary," said one
secretary, "they treat you differently, they don't take you serious."[48] Many policies explicitly affect promotion, as when law firms take part-time attorneys off
the partnership track, a practice that is still very common.[49] Professional workers, who are disproportionately likely to have access to work/family benefits,[50]
also often find that "the only responsible way to work part-time is to work full-
time"; they find their hours creeping up despite the fact they are being paid
less, and many find themselves with less desirable work assignments to boot.[51]
Some employers enjoy a "family friendly" dividend when they pocket a percentage of a part-time worker's salary without hiring anyone else to handle the
part-timer's workload. Needless to say, this practice has fueled a backlash by
child-free workers against family friendly policies.[52]

What would restructured work look like if it did not carry the penalties it
now does? A baseline is the principle of proportionality: proportional pay, benefits, and advancement for part-time work. It is vitally important in white-collar
contexts, because the "executive schedule" has sharply limited the number of
women who survive in business (more than 95 percent of upper-level management is still men),[53] law (87 percent of law firm partners are still men),[54]
academics (more than 74 percent of tenured professors are still men),[55] and
many other traditionally masculine professions. The principle of proportionality is also important in good blue-collar jobs. Such jobs tend to have a high
benefit load (up to 40 percent of wages),[56] which gives employers the motivation to require long hours of existing employees rather than to hire new ones.
In addition, traditionally masculine blue-collar jobs rarely have part-time tracks
and, as we have seen, mothers rarely work jobs with lots of overtime. Consequently, scheduling plays a significant role in keeping women out of high-
paying, traditionally masculine blue-collar work (which is not to say that other
factors, notably sexual harassment, do not also play a role).[57] Finally, the principle of proportionality can offer significant benefits to the working poor, who
often can find only part-time work, with depressed wage rates, no benefits, and
no chance for advancement. At Shopper's Food Warehouse, for example, part-
timers are ineligible for promotion to management positions.[58]

To implement the principle of proportionality requires us to rethink the ways we define an ambitious, committed, valuable worker. But family-responsive workplaces require other changes as well. For example, in interviews with more than three hundred women in Iowa, sociologist Jennifer Glass found that the women she spoke with, many of them working-class, expressed the need for flextime so that their work hours would match with the hours of their child-care provider, as well as time off for medical appointments, child illnesses (infants average six doctor's visits a year),[59] and school plays and conferences. They also stated the need for an adequate supply of quality, affordable child care.[60]

Voluntary programs that persuade employers to change traditional ways of doing business hold significant promise, particularly in an age of high employment. The "business case" reflects the fact that current business practices impose steep costs on employers. Most dramatic are the costs of high attrition among mothers in full-time or overtime work and among fathers in high-overtime environments. Human resources professionals report that replacing a worker costs between 75 and 150 percent of the worker's annual salary, with more highly trained workers costing more to replace. Family responsive policies tend to reduce absenteeism. Productivity may rise as well. In 1930 the Kellogg Company implemented six-hour workdays as a coping strategy for Depression-caused unemployment.[61] After implementing the change, the company discovered that worker productivity increased an average of 3 to 4 percent. A final, and understudied, element of the business case for family-responsive policies is the correlation between employee satisfaction, employee loyalty, and client loyalty. Employers who have effective family-responsive policies in an era when employee loyalty is hard to come by find that employees who feel their family needs are being addressed can be fiercely loyal, as in the case of the moving company that experienced zero turnover when they offered telecommuting and other benefits,[62] or the dermatology company that experienced zero turnover once it provided a 20 percent discount to the neighboring family care unit, instituted flexible work hours, and provided parent education classes.[63] Employee loyalty is important in itself because it reduces attrition and increases motivation, but it is also important for another reason: study after study has shown a correlation between retaining employees and retaining clients.[64] For lawyers, of course, this is intuitive: we have all seen clients walk out the door when "their" lawyer leaves.

Here is a radical proposition: employers should reward productivity. We should choose and promote workers based on the quality of their work product not on the schedule they can keep. Why? In a society where schedule correlates tightly with gender, a system that systematically rewards people based on their ability to keep the schedule kept by most men, but few women, discriminates against women.

To explore this, let's return to the definition of the ideal worker who takes no time off for childbearing or child rearing. Who needs no time off for childbirth? And, in a society where women still do the large bulk of the child care, who needs no time off for child rearing? Designing workplaces around men's bodies and men's traditional lifestyles is discriminatory.

Note that this is gender, not sex discrimination: what is at issue is not a disadvantage that attaches to all women but one that attaches to all caregivers. Martin Malin has suggested that the Family and Medical Leave Act's prohibition on employer interference with leave rights is a possible tool for combating this workplace hostility toward paternal use of parental leave.[65]

The importance of adding this analysis to the business case is twofold. First, many employers are people of good will, who are shocked at the thought that they are systematically disadvantaging women. Take Jim Johnson, president of the moving company Johnson Storage & Moving Co., mentioned above. After Johnson heard me speak, he went right back and asked his human resources people whether his practice of not giving benefits to parttimers affected mostly women. He was horrified to hear that it did and immediately offered proportional benefits to part-timers to the extent his insurance company allowed him to do so.[66] We should not forget that, in the United States, discrimination language is a language of social ethics.

Second, of course, discrimination language shifts our sense of who is entitled to what. A sense that a failure to accommodate family responsibilities may constitute gender discrimination could change contract negotiations, if unions could point out the way that the systematic devaluation of part-time work systematically discriminated against women. Cumulatively, these cases can begin to change perceptions about work/family conflict from the view that it reflects only "mother's choice" to the view that it often signals gender discrimination against men as well as against women.

Changing Entitlements within the Family

The standard approach to changing entitlements within the family in this country has been to try to change the allocation of family work between men and women. This strategy has achieved some success. Men now contribute more family work: but women still do between 66 and 80 percent.[67]

Some men, notably in families that use the "tag team" approach, where both parents work but one parent cares for the children while the other is at work, do significant amounts of child care.[68] But other men still do very little.

This picture is further complicated by class differences, with less-privileged men doing significantly more child care than more privileged white men, presumably because the tag-team approach appears to be most common among working-class families.[69]

This picture suggests that statistics averaging the amount of child care performed by men are less than informative. What we need are statistics that break out tag teamers from other men. Forty years after women started bargaining for equality within the household, it is estimated that they continue to perform between 66 and 80 percent of the housework.[70] We need to be more thoughtful about why women continue to perform the majority of household work, and this is where three areas of literature should prove helpful. One is the booming literature on masculinity, which can help us understand the gender pressures on men that make them resist the hydraulic pressures within individual households to share work more equally.[71] The second is the growing literature on "gatekeeping" by women, including Naomi Cahn's important insight that mothers often refuse to let go of the sole-source supplier (primary caregiver) role because their identity as women is tied up with that particular gender performance.[72] Finally, there is another literature that does not, but should, exist: a literature that explores the relationship of gender and class. One reason gender has proved so unbending is because gender performances play a central role in class formation. Gender performances help create class status, as when the ideology and practice of intensive mothering create high-human-capital kids. The available cultural idioms for the performances of class are very gendered, as when families consider having the mother at home a signal of having "arrived" at middle-class status.[73]

The most basic fact about the typically privatized, psychologized, American strategy of solving the work/family conflict by changing the allocation of family work is that it has failed. It is time to shift attention away from women's psychology onto structural economic relations: the structure of market work and the issue of who owns what within the family. Both above and in other contexts,[74] I have discussed these issues as they relate to families in the United States. Here I only want to add that, although divorce law is the key locus for changing traditional notions of who owns what within the family in the United States, in other countries inheritance laws may be the key to gaining access to wealth for women. In many parts of Africa, inheritance laws are often guided by customary law, which often considers the woman to be the property of her husband and therefore ineligible to inherit anything.[75] In Latin America, as another example, inheritance laws focus on the children; the wife is effectively disinherited.[76]

Changing the Relationship between the Public and Private Spheres

In this context, once again, we need to recognize the extent to which conversations within American feminism have been framed within an intensely privatized frame. The United States stands virtually alone among developed nations in its conviction that child rearing is a private frolic rather than a social enterprise of vital importance. The National Partnership on Women and Families has taken the lead in its inexhaustible lobbying to persuade the American Congress to provide for American parents the kinds of parental leaves that are almost universal in developed nations outside the United States.[77] The limited nature of what has been achieved, an unpaid Family and Medical Leave Act that, at best, accounts for only three months of child rearing, a task that lasts twenty years, is attributable more to the inhospitableness of the soil than lobbyists' skill.

If the Scandinavian approach of mandating leaves is one approach to changing the configuration of the public and private spheres, the other is the approach articulated by Martha Fineman, Nancy Dowd, and others: to establish a new social entitlements program that provides social subsidies to all caregivers.[78] As I have argued elsewhere, social subsidies for caregivers are extremely important as a measure to alleviate our high levels of childhood poverty; they would also contribute to economic security for many women.[79]

Feminist Jurisprudence and Care Work

All three projects contribute to the deconstruction of domesticity both as an ideology and as a system of structuring market work and delivering child services. As feminists we need to be very thoughtful about what Deborah Tannen has called the "argument culture," the tendency to engage through attack.[80] Inevitably, we will disagree sometimes, and we need intellectual room to explore those disagreements. In conclusion, we need to move away from an emphasis on the disproportionate share of women among the poor, the wage gap, and the "new theory of alimony" debate toward a more sweeping analysis of women and economics. When we do, we will find ourselves rewriting Charlotte Perkins Gilman's approach by rejecting certain key elements of domesticity she adopted without comment. These include the breadwinner structure of market work, in which the ideal worker is someone who has few significant responsibilities for children; the assumption that homemakers are dependent and somehow lacking; and the notion that the costs of child rearing (in a system that provides for children's care by economically marginalizing their caregivers) are "naturally" privatized onto individual mothers without significant social support.

Like Gilman, we can only proceed by mobilizing certain elements of domesticity against others. Thus Martha Fineman urges socialization of the costs of child rearing in the name of Mother.[81] I urge a restructuring of work around the norm of parental care.

NOTES

1. Diana Pierce "The Feminization of Poverty: Women, Work and Welfare," *Urban and Social Chance Review* 11 (winter/spring 1978): 28.

2. U.S. Census Bureau, *Poverty Rate Lowest in 20 Years, Household Income at Record High, Census Bureau Reports* (cited Sept. 26, 2000], available from World Wide Web at http://www.census.gov/Press-Release/www/2000/cb00–158.html.

3. See Jane Lee Saber, "Women and the International Monetary Fund," *ILSA Journal of International and Comparative Law* 5 (Spring 1999): 335, 337 (stating that among the 1.2 billion people living in extreme poverty within undeveloped countries, 59 percent are female); Unifem, *Strengthening Women's Economic Capacity* (cited Apr. 2, 2001), available from World Wide Web at http://www.unifem.undp.org/economic.htm (stating women represent 70 percent of the 1.3 billion people that live in absolute poverty and when nearly 900 million women have less than $1 a day, the association between gender inequality and poverty remains a harrowing reality).

4. See Gillian Moon, "Trade and Women in Developing Countries," available from World Wide Web at http://www.caa.org.au/horizons/h13/trade.html (cited Sept. 17, 2000) (citing Erika Gottfried, Note, "Mercosur: A Tool to Further Women's Rights in the Member Nations," *Fordham Urban Law Journal* 25 [1998]: 923, 925, 953).

5. Charlotte Perkins Gilman, *Women and Economics* (1898; reprint, Mineola, N.Y.: Dover, 1998).

6. Gilman at 9.

7. Betty Friedan, *The Feminine Mystique* (1963; reprint, New York: Norton,).

8. See Joan Williams, *Unbending Gender: Why Family and Work Conflict and What to do About It* (New York: Oxford University Press, 2000).

9. Williams at 2.

10. See Reva B. Siegel, "Home as Work: The First Women's Rights Claims Concerning Wive's Household Labor, 1850–1880," *Yale Law Journal* 103 (1994): 1073, 1093.

11. See Siegel at 1092–1093.

12. For brilliant and forceful contestations of this premise, see Martha Fineman, "Cracking the Foundational Myths: Independence, Autonomy, and Self-Sufficiency," *American University Journal of Gender Social Policy & the Law* 8 (2000): 13

13. Office of the Assistant Secretary for Planning and Evaluation, U.S. House of Representatives, *The 2000 Green Book* (cited Apr. 2, 2001), available from World Wide Web at http://aspe.gov/2000gb/appeni.txt.

14. See, e.g., Nancy C. Staudt, "Taxing Housework," *Georgetown Law Journal* 84 (1996): 1571, 1574.

15. John P. Robinson and Geoffrey Godbey, *Time for Life: The Surprising Ways Americans Use Their Time* (University Park: Penn State University Press, 1997), 104.

16. See Williams, supra note 8, at 2.

17. Thanks to Suzanne Bianchi and Liana Sayer for calculating these figures from the Bureau of Labor Statistics & Bureau of the Census, *March 1999 Current Population Survey* (cited Jan. 27, 2002), available from World Wide Web at http://www.bls.census.gov/cps/cpsmain.htm.

18. Jane Waldfogel, "Understanding the 'Family Gap' in Pay for Women with Children," *Journal of Economic Perspectives* 12 (winter 1998): 137, 143, *see also* Jane Waldfogel and Susan E. Mayer, *Gender Differences in the Low-Wage Labor Market, in Finding Jobs: Work & Welfare Reform,* in David E. Card and Rebecca M. Blank, eds., (New York: Russell Sage Foundation: 2000), 214–15; Jane Waldfogel, "The Effect of Children on Women's Wages," *American Sociological Review* 92 (1997): 209.

19. Williams, supra note 8, at 2.

20. See id. (citing the computations of Professor Manuelita Ureta).

21. Id. at 1.

22. The model is morally troubling, in a society without the political will to provide publicly subsidized childcare, because it consigns many children to market child care of questionable quality. National Institute of Child Health and Human Development, The NICHD Study of Early Childcare (1998). Rather, the current system solves privileged women's gender troubles by taking advantage of their privileged position in class and racial hierarchies. See Williams, supra note 8, at 145–76.

23. June Carbone, "Income Sharing: Redefining the Family in Terms of Community," *Houston Law Review* 31 (summer 1994): 359.

24. James A. Levine and Todd L. Pittinsky, *Working Fathers: New Strategies for Balancing Work and Family* (Reading, Penn.: Addison-Wesley, 1997), 25.

25. Williams, supra note 8, at 2.

26. See Bureau of Labor Statistics, *Labor Force Statistics From the Current Population Survey* (cited Oct. 20, 2000), available from World Wide Web at http://www.bls.gov/news.release/wkyeng.t02.html.

27. Thanks to Steve Hipple for calculating these figures from the Bureau of Labor Statistics & Bureau of the Census, *Current Population Survey* (cited Mar. 1999), available from World Wide Web at http://www.bls.census.gov/cps/cpsmain.htm.

28. For a comprehensive listing of the contributions to this debate, see Joan Williams, "Symposium On Divorce and Feminist Legal Theory: Is Coverture Dead? Beyond a New Theory of Alimony," Georgetown Law Journal 82 (1994): 2227, 2228 n. 2.

29. See Williams, supra note 8, at 122.

30. The implication here is that a homemaker married to a rich man will receive more than one married to a poor one. Changing our notion of who owns what within the family, unfortunately, cannot address the unconscionably wide disparities of income in the United States.

31. Gilman, supra note 7, at 5.

32. See generally Jeanne Boydston, *Home and Work: Housework, Wages, and the Ideology of Labor in the Early Republic* (New York: Oxford University Press, 1990).

33. See Arlie Hochschild, *The Second Shift: Inside the Two Job Marriage* (New York: Viking, 1989), 110–27.

34. Hochschild at 121–22.

35. E-mail from Sara McClanahan, Professor of Sociology and Public Affairs, Princeton University, and Irv Garfinkel, Professor of Contemporary Urban Problems, Columbia University, to Joan Williams, Professor of Law, American University, Washington College of Law (Jan. 11, 2000).

36. Demie Kurtz, *For Richer For Poorer*: Mothers Confront Divorce (New York: Routledge, 1995), 3.

37. Joan Williams, "Afterword: Exploring the Economic Meanings of Gender," *American University Law Review* 49 (2000): 989

38. Williams, supra note 8, at 115.

39. *See* Ann Crittenden, *The Price of Motherhood: Why the Most Important Job in the World Is Still the Least Valued* (New York: Metropolis Books, 2001), 239–49, 264.

40. See Barbara R. Bergmann, *Saving Our Children from Poverty: What the United States Can Learn from France* (New York: Russell Sage Foundation), 91–116.

41. Katharine Silbaugh, "Turning Labor into Love: Housework and the Law," *Northwestern University Law Review* 91 (1996): 1, 23–26.

42. See Joan Williams, "Exploring the Economic Meanings of Gender," *American University Law Review* 49 (2000): 987, 1005

43. Curtis J. Berger and Joan C. Williams, *Property: Land Ownership and Use*, 4th ed. (Boston: Little, Brown, 1997), 40.

44. See Mary E. O'Connell, "On the Fringe: Rethinking the Link Between Wages and Benefits," *Tulane Law Review* 67 (May 1993): 1421; see also Mary Becker, "Patriarchy and Inequality: Towards a Substantive Feminism," *University of Chicago Legal Forum* 21 (1999); see also Silbaugh, supra note 41.

45. See Heidi Hartmann and Catherine Hill, *Strengthening Social Security for Women: A Report from the Working Conference on Women and Social Security* (Washington, D.C.: Institute For Women's Policy Research, 1999), 1, 7.

46. O'Connell at 1497.

47. O'Connell at 1454–1471.

48. O'Connell at 1472.

49. Interview with members of the Washington, D.C. legal community, for the Project on Attorney Retention (the PAR Project) funded by the Alfred P. Sloan Foundation and the Women's Bar Association of the District of Columbia (Oct. 11, 2000). The final report based on these interviews is available at PAR Project, Balanced Hours: Effective Part-Time Policies for Washington Law Firms http://www.pardc.org (hereinafter PAR Report).

50. Williams, supra note 8, at 33.

51. Williams, supra note 8, at 72–75; PAR Report at 18.

52. See, e.g., Elinor Burkett, *The Baby Boon: How Family Friendly America Cheats the Childless* (New York: Free Press, 2000).

53. Williams, supra note 8, at 67.

54. Williams, supra note 8, at 67.

55. Joan C. Williams, "How the Tenure Track Discriminates Against Women," *Chronicle of Higher Education* (cited Oct. 27, 2000), available from World Wide Web at http://chronicle.com/jobs/2000/10/2000102703c.htm.

56. O'Connell at 1425. Note that this statistic is for all jobs, not just blue-collar jobs.

57. Williams, supra note 8, at 78–81.

58. Julie McWilliams, Address at the Industrial Relations Research Association National Public Policy Forum (June 22, 2000).

59. Jody Heymann, *The Widening Gap: Why America's Working Families Are in Jeopardy and What Can Be Done About It* (New York: Basic Books, 2000), 73.

60. Interview with Jennifer Glass, Chair of the department of sociology, University of Iowa, in Iowa City, Iowa (Oct. 13, 2000).

61. Juliet B. Schor, *The Overworked American: The Unexpected Decline of Leisure* (1992), 154–55.

62. Interview with Jim Johnson, President, Johnson Moving and Storage, in Denver, Colo. (May 11, 2000) (hereinafter Johnson interview).

63. See Williams, supra note 8, at 88.

64. See Keith Hammonds, "Balancing Work and Family," *Business Week*, 16 Sept. 1996, 74; Patricia Sellers, "Keeping the Buyer you Already Have," *Fortune*, 22 Sept. 1993, 56; Patricia Sellers, "What Customers Really Want," *Fortune*, 4 June 1990, 58; Sue Shellenbarger, "Companies Are Finding It Really Pays To Be Nice to Employees," *Wall Street Journal*, 22 July 1998, B1; Wyatt Watson, *Strategy@Work* (cited Oct. 20, 2000), available from World Wide Web at http://www.watsonwyatt.com/strategy-atwork/editions/2000/2000_04_08.asp.

65. See Martin H. Malin, "Fathers and Parental Leave," *Texas Law Review* 72 (1994): 1047, 1049.

66. Johnson interview, supra note 62.

67. See Williams, supra note 8, at 2; see also Sharon Hays, *The Cultural Contradictions of Motherhood* (New Haven: Yale University Press, 1998), 100.

68. Jacqueline L. Salmon, " 'Hi, Dad! Bye, Mom'—Couples Try Parenting in Shifts," *Washington Post*, 2 Aug. 1998, A1; see also Kathleen Gerson, *No Man's Land: Men's Changing Commitments to Family and Work* (New York: Basic Books, 1993), 22–37.

69. Lillian B. Rubin, *Families on the Fault Line: America's Working-Class Speaks About the Family, the Economy, Race, and Ethnicity* (New York: HarperCollins, 1994), 93–94.

70. Estimates vary widely. See, e.g., Scott Coltrane, *Family Man: Fatherhood, Housework, and Gender Equity* 53 (1996); Hays, 100; Levine and Pittinsky, *Working Fathers*, 26; Joseph H. Pleck, *Are "Family Supportive" Employer Policies Relevant to Men?* in Jane C. Hood ed., *Men, Work, and Family* (Newbury Park, Cal.: Sage, 1993), 219–20.

71. See, e.g., Michael S. Kimmel, *Manhood in America: A Cultural History* (New York: Free Press, 1996).

72. See Naomi Cahn, "Gendered Identities, Women and Household Work," *Villanova Law Review* 44 (1999): 534–35.

73. Williams, supra note 8, at 153–61.

74. See Williams, supra note 27; see also Joan Williams, "Wives Own Half? Winning for Wives After Wendt," *Connecticut Law Review* 32 (fall 1999): 249.

75. See Celestine I. Nyamu, "How Should Human Rights and Development Respond to Cultural Legitimation of Gender Hierarchy in Developing Countries," *Harvard International Law Journal* 41 (spring 2000): 381.

76. See Steven Hendrix, "Property Law Innovation in Latin America with Recommendations," *Boston College International & Comparative Law Review* 18 (1995): 1, 13–14.

77. See The National Partnership on Women and Families, at http://www.nationalpartnership.org (cited Oct. 19, 2000).

78. Fineman, infra note 81, at 26–27; see also Nancy E. Dowd, *Redefining Fatherhood* (New York: New York University Press, 2000), 220–25 (discussing the disregard of the family in economic and public policies); Eva Feder Kittay, *Love's Labor: Essays on Women, Equality, and Dependency* (New York: Routledge, 1999), 140–46 (discussing the need to change public policy and liberal theory to take dependency into account).

79. See Williams, *supra* note 42, at 988–90.

80. Deborah Tannen, *The Argument Culture: Moving from Debate to Dialogue* (New York: Random House, 1998), 7–8.

81. Martha Albertson Fineman, *The Neutered Mother, the Sexual Family, and Other Twentieth-Century Tragedies* (New York: Routledge, 1995), 228.

PART 3

Practice

Citizenship and the
Equal Rights Amendment

CHAPTER 19

Women and Citizenship

The Virginia Military Institute Case

In 1839 John Logan was the first student to sign the register at the newly opened Virginia Military Institute (VMI). In 1997 Beth Ann Hogan added her name as well, becoming the first woman to do so. In between lies a tale about the Constitution, gender discrimination, and citizenship.

Hogan got to sign her name because in 1996 the Supreme Court told VMI that its refusal to admit women was a violation of the Constitution; specifically, the Fourteenth Amendment's Equal Protection Clause (*U.S. v. Virginia*).[1] The case gave Ruth Bader Ginsburg, who had created much of the country's gender equality law as a lawyer in the 1970s, a crowning moment in her career. Now a Supreme Court justice, she wrote the opinion for the Court, drawing upon the precedents she herself had set two decades earlier.[2] Her opinion both altered the standard for determining unconstitutional gender discrimination and suggested that it is wrong to read the Constitution as defining citizenship in terms only of rights rather than as a combination of rights and responsibilities.

VMI's stated mission is to produce "citizen-soldiers" who are engaged in civilian life but ready to assume responsibility for the defense of their country when necessary. It seeks to do so through the "adversative method," a system designed to strip students of their individuality and remake them in the image of VMI. First-year students are called "rats" because, as VMI's dean of students commented during the litigation in *U.S. v. Virginia*, the rat is "the lowest animal on earth and part of our humbling experience where we try to bring everybody into a basic commonality, everybody is very Spartan, very—they are all treated exactly alike and the rat term kind of defines that very appropriately."[3]

The equal treatment to which all rats are subjected is a particularly brutal form of hazing. The process begins on the first day of school, when the new students' heads are shaved. From then on they are at the mercy of both VMI's stringent rules and its upperclassmen, who are authorized to order the rats around at will. Any underclassman can stop a rat and penalize him (or, now, her) for any alleged infraction of the rules. This includes such things as not being able to recite verbatim from the booklet of school history and rules known as the *Rat Bible* or failing to follow deliberately conflicting orders barked out by different upperclassmen. The most frequent penalty is having to drop down to the ground and perform a hefty series of push-ups. Rats must walk at rigid attention outside their rooms, eyes straight ahead, chins tucked into their collarbones; failure to do so is another infraction. At any hour, day, or night upperclassmen can come pouring through a bedroom door, screaming, demanding push-ups, perhaps in the room, perhaps in the communal showers while water pours down.

VMI believes that visibly equal treatment is a perquisite for the creation of a sense of community and shared responsibility. One mechanism for assuring everyone that treatment is indeed equal is to eliminate privacy. Until 1997 the four-student bedroom doors had shadeless windows and a line to the back window that had to be unobstructed by furniture. Bathrooms are communal; again, until 1997 they boasted no partitions or stalls.[4] Before that it was only men who shared bathrooms and all other spaces and who endured VMI's adversative method together. The grueling four years became a male bonding ritual, emphasizing brotherhood and the otherness of women. No women were permitted to set foot in the barracks, where all students live, and a "gentleman's code" emphasized the respect that VMI men were always to show "ladies."[5]

In 1989 a northern Virginia female high school student asked to apply to VMI. The Institute responded that it did not accept applications from women. VMI is a publicly funded state institution, prohibited by both the Equal Protection Clause and the Civil Rights Act of 1964 from discriminating on the basis of sex. The student turned to the Department of Justice, which sued VMI and the state of Virginia on her behalf.

VMI would maintain through all the court appearances that followed that admitting women would "destroy" the Institute (the word was used repeatedly)[6] by making completely equal treatment and the lack of privacy impossible. There would have to be different physical standards for female students, VMI argued, and the sense of camaraderie that resulted from the public, communal mastering of the hurdles set by the Institute would no longer exist. VMI believed that the leveling adversative method could work only within a single-sex institution. If women were admitted, VMI insisted, the intense male bonding at the heart of its pedagogical system would be lost.

As the litigation progressed, Virginia offered a substitute for admitting women to VMI: the creation of another single-sex program for potential female citizen-soldiers at nearby Mary Baldwin College, where they could enjoy the setting of a gracious Southern college while taking courses in leadership. Unlike cadets at VMI, students at the Virginia Women's Institute for Leadership (VWIL) would not be given the opportunity to experience constant military-style discipline, nor would they live together as a community apart from everyone else, be offered courses in engineering and advanced math and physics, have access to substantial athletic facilities, or be taught by a faculty that was the qualitative equivalent of VMI's.

To the task force at Mary Baldwin that designed VWIL, the disparities between it and VMI were desirable and reflected real differences in the way men and women learn. Task force members undertook an "in-depth study of the published literature on the developmental psychology of women and the cognitive development of women," according to the college, and read the literature as demonstrating that "women tend to value cooperation and relationships"; "leadership is [a] process of working with and through people"; "women's identity is relationship"; and leadership is either "interactive" or "command and control," with women preferring the former.[7] Women would not benefit from VMI's strict hierarchy and "extreme adversarial environment"; instead, they required a single-sex setting based on cooperation, mutual nurturing, and an emphasis on the building up of esteem.[8] In differentiating all women from all men and postulating a uniquely female style of learning that had implications for the production of citizen-soldiers, VMI and VWIL implicitly raised the question of who ought to be entitled to full citizenship.

Historically, citizens have been defined as those members of a society who are prepared to fight in order to protect it. There have long been corollary citizens who don't fight, such as women married to soldier-citizens or their children, but full citizenship and all the respect implicit in the word have been reserved for citizen-soldiers themselves. Both the American and French revolutions, for example, emphasized the right as well as the responsibility of the citizen to be prepared to bear arms. The revolutionary nature of the two wars lay not only in the way they swept the old regimes out of power but in their insistence on the idea that political rights belonged to those who fought for the nation.[9]

That approach to citizenship has been an element of federal policy throughout American history. Male foreigners who arrived in the United States and subsequently served in its armed forces were thereby entitled to citizenship. There was no similar provision for women. Both native-born and foreign-born men had political rights because they fulfilled responsibilities viewed as beneficial to society. Women's contributions to communal life were so thoroughly taken for granted that no official recognition was considered necessary. While the production of children, for example, clearly is as important to the continuation and well-being of society as is its military defense, that has not been considered the kind of service that merits full citizenship. It is merely what women do.

The view of women's function as performed without effort or sacrifice is evident in the different value placed on the risks taken by men and women in their gender-specific responsibilities. Men faced the possibility of physical harm and death when they defended their country, and their willingness to assume that gamble was at the heart of the decision to grant them the title of citizen. Women faced the same possibility when they became pregnant and gave birth, but no concomitant honor was awarded them. And it was of course taken for granted that women did not belong in the military.

The consequences have been significant. For one, the military has been perceived throughout U.S. history as a training ground for civilian leadership. George Washington was only the first military hero whose combat experience was assumed to prepare him for high political office; others, such as Andrew Jackson, Ulysses S. Grant, George C. Marshall, Dwight D. Eisenhower, and John F. Kennedy would follow. If women could not fight, the reasoning went, neither could they understand crucial issues of foreign policy or the needs of the national defense; they therefore did not belong in the government. It is not a coincidence that there was no woman secretary of state until Madeleine Albright took up her new post in 1997 or that as of 2003 there still has been no female secretary of defense.

Beyond the military and the halls of government, women found themselves excluded from two other places where citizens performed their duties: the voting booth and the jury room. The presupposition, as Supreme Court Justice Joseph Bradley stated in 1873, was that "the natural and proper timidity and delicacy which belongs to the female sex evidently unfits if for many of the occupations of civil life."[10] That was still the case almost one hundred years later, when the Supreme Court declared in 1961 (*Hoyt v. Louisiana*) that women could not be expected to serve on juries because "woman is still regarded as the center of home and family life."[11] The decision was one that attorney Ruth Bader Ginsburg would seek to overturn, understanding that a perceived absence of responsibilities was inevitably tied to a real absence of rights.[12]

Another part of the history that fed into *U.S. v. Virginia* was the changing interpretation given by the Supreme Court to the Equal Protection Clause. The Supreme Court held in 1896 that the clause permitted states to provide "separate but equal" public services for white and black citizens.[13] The same court said in 1954, in *Brown v. Board of Education*, that the earlier justices got it wrong and that the clause forbade the states from treating the races differently.[14] The meaning of the Fourteenth Amendment had evolved, and it continued to do so after 1954. In a series of subsequent cases the Court gradually held that any statute or governmental action that differentiated among people on the basis of their race was presumptively unconstitutional and would be subjected to "strict scrutiny" by the nation's courts.[15] Race was declared a "suspect classification." The usual court rule is that a law is presumed legitimate unless someone proves otherwise. "Strict scrutiny" and "suspect classification" meant that where racial discrimination was alleged, the burden of proof would now be shifted to the state, which would have to convince the courts that its policy was constitutional. Race-based statutes would be presumed to be illegal.

The rule of thumb under the Equal Protection Clause for laws that differentiated between people on a basis other than race—such as gender—was called the "rational relation" test. If a state could demonstrate that a statute was enacted in an area over which the legislature had power—education, for example—and that it embodied a rational approach to whatever problem the legislature meant to address, the courts would rule that the law was not a violation of the Equal Protection Clause. When a court upheld a state policy as bearing a rational relation to a legitimate legislative concern, that court did not necessarily endorse the policy as good; rather, it stated in effect that the policy was within the bounds of legislative discretion.

One of Ginsburg's goals as an advocate was to get the courts to extend the more stringent strict scrutiny test to gender discrimination cases. As a result of litigative efforts by her and other attorneys in the 1970s, the Court declared gender equality to be a constitutional tenet, but it did not shift the burden of proof in the same way it had in race cases.[16] Ginsburg did manage to move the Court away from some of its earlier holdings about gender and citizenship, however: in two of the cases she argued, the Court struck down state laws based on the assumption that women should not be asked to fulfill the responsibilities of the jury room, and women and men now share that obligation.[17]

Shortly after Sandra Day O'Connor became the first woman on the Supreme Court in 1981, she articulated a new standard in gender discrimination cases (*Mississippi v. Hogan*).[18] The occasion was a challenge brought by a man who had been turned down by the all-female nursing program at the Mississippi University for Women. O'Connor declared for the Supreme Court that a state had to have an "exceedingly persuasive justification" for providing any benefit to only one sex. A single-sex classification could be validated "only by showing at least that the classification serves 'important governmental objectives and that the discriminatory means employed' are 'substantially related to the achievement of those objectives.'" In addition, classifications could not be justified by reference to "fixed notions" or "archaic and stereotypic notions" about men and women. "Thus, if the statutory objective is to exclude or 'protect' members of one gender because they are presumed to suffer from an inherent handicap or to be innately inferior, the objective itself is illegitimate."[19]

Mississippi v. Hogan added "exceedingly persuasive justification" to the legal lexicon, but it did not make clear whether future gender discrimination cases would be considered on the basis of the rational relation test, the strict scrutiny standard, or something in between. The criterion remained ambiguous even after the Court decided *J.E.B. v. Alabama*, a jury selection case, in 1994.[20] Without endorsing the strict scrutiny test, Justice Harry Blackmun wrote for the majority in *J.E.B.* that there was unconstitutional discrimination when a state categorized on the basis of "invidious, archaic, and overbroad stereotypes about the relative abilities of men and women."[21] Each side in *U.S. v. Virginia* thought that meant it would win the case. The Justice Department argued that such stereotypic notions were at the heart of VMI's objections to the prospect of admitting women. The institute replied that it was relying not on stereotypes but on social science research that showed women learned better in the absence of men. That finding, along with the alleged destruction of VMI that would follow from the admission of women, constituted an "exceedingly persuasive justification" for keeping the Institute all male. One issue, then, was whether a state could base its policies on generalizations about an entire group of people.

Ginsburg's opinion in *U.S. v. Virginia* addressed the issue by drawing on the doctrines articulated in *Hogan* and *J.E.B* and placing them in the dual context of U.S. history and the ideal of citizenship.[22] The historical background was particularly important because commentators throughout the long litigation had asked why women would want to do anything as bizarre as assault one of the last remaining male bastions and subject themselves to the rigors of its grueling routine. As it did in reporting the similar trials of Shannon Faulkner, the young woman who attempted to gender integrate The Citadel, much of the media suggested that such a woman was a less-than-feminine gender outlaw.[23] Ginsburg's language specifically rebutted the idea of a universal femininity that could claim constitutional endorsement. Her corrective took the form of a discussion of the country's centuries-long history of underestimating women and then forbidding them to prove themselves equal citizens.

"Today's skeptical scrutiny of official action denying rights or opportunities based on sex responds to volumes of history," Ginsburg wrote.[24] Noting that women had not been given the vote until 1920, she commented that "for a half century thereafter, it remained the prevailing doctrine that government, both federal and state, could withhold from women opportunities accorded men so long as any 'basis in reason' could be conceived for the discrimination."[25] Women had been kept out of law, medicine, and, more recently, the police, supposedly for their own protection and because the "experts" said they would undermine male solidarity. Ginsburg cited Dr. Edward H. Clarke of Harvard Medical School and his seventeen-edition *Sex in Education* to show that medical "experts" of the late nineteenth century had warned solemnly that "the physiological effects of hard study and academic competition with boys would interfere with the development of girls' reproductive organs" and that, in Dr. Clarke's words, "identical education of the two sexes is a crime before God and humanity, that physiology protests against, and that experience weeps over."[26] A Minnesota court relied upon the same kind of thinking when it declared in 1876, in response to a woman's petition to be permitted to practice law, "It cannot therefore be said that the opposition of courts to the admission of females to practice . . . is to any extent the outgrowth of . . . 'old fogyism.' . . . It arises rather from a comprehension of the magnitude of the responsibilities connected with the successful practice of law"—responsibilities that women could not possibly meet.[27]

Similarly, Virginia's sudden great desire to protect the women in its educational system by excluding them from the rigors of VMI seemed suspect in light of the history of higher education in the state. The schools for women that Virginia began supporting, decades after VMI came into existence, were later converted into coeducational institutions, but the all-male VMI remained single-sex—so Virginia taxpayers were once again funding all-male but not all-female public education. The flagship University of Virginia began admitting women undergraduates only at the astonishingly late date of 1970, and then only in the face of litigation.[28] "The historical record," Ginsburg stated, "indicates action more deliberate than anomalous: First, protection of women against higher education; next, schools for women far from equal in resources and stature to schools for men; finally, conversion of the separate schools to coeducation."[29]

But Virginia had not only "protected" women from the opportunities provided by its system of higher education. It, along with VMI, was also "protecting" them from assuming the full rights and responsibilities of citizenship. The institute, as noted, defined its mission as the production of citizen-soldiers, individuals whom it described as "imbued with love of learning, confident in the functions and attitudes of leadership, possessing a high sense of public service, advocates of the American democracy and free enterprise system, and ready . . . to defend their country in time of national peril."[30] "Surely," Ginsburg wrote, "that goal is great enough to accommodate women, who today count as citizens in our American democracy equal in stature to men."[31]

Ginsburg also brought the law of the land a step closer to extending the "strict scrutiny" test to gender equality cases. Some of her judicial colleagues were not prepared to apply the same test to racial and gender cases, however, and Ginsburg made it clear that the court's decision in *U.S. v. Virginia* should not be interpreted as doing so.[32] "Without equating gender classifications, for all purposes, to classifications based on race or national origin," she wrote, the Court's earlier decisions had "carefully inspected official action that closes a door or denies opportunity to women (or to men)." She labeled the new test "skeptical scrutiny," another version of "careful . . . inspect[ion]" of official action. Under it, and in keeping with the *Hogan* case, a state's rationale for treating men and women differently had to be "exceedingly persuasive." The burden of proof "rests entirely on the State," which must demonstrate that the classification "serves 'important governmental objectives and that the discriminatory means employed' are 'substantially related to the achievement of those objectives.' " And, Ginsburg added, the state's justification "must not rely on overbroad generalizations about the different talents, capacities, or preferences of males and females"—presumably including generalizations about women's capability and desire to carry out the burdens of citizenship.[33] From its description, skeptical scrutiny sounds very much like strict scrutiny, but Ginsburg explained the distinction. "Supposed 'inherent differences' " among people of various races or national origins, she suggested, were false, but "physical differences between men and women . . . are enduring. . . . 'Inherent differences' between men and women, we have come to appreciate, remain cause for celebration, but not for denigration of the members of either sex or for artificial constraints on an individual's opportunity." The Supreme Court had backed away from its early endorsement of *race*-conscious remedies for past discrimination such as affirmative action.[34] Ginsburg's language emphasized that *sex*-conscious remedies were nonetheless permissible if they were used "to compensate women 'for particularly economic disabilities [they have] suffered,' to 'promot[e] equal employment opportunity,' to advance full development of the talent and capacities of our Nation's people."[35]

The difference between "strict" and "skeptical" scrutiny, then, lay in the delineation of the circumstances under which sex-conscious government policies might be legitimate. Policies that kept women out of areas of life open to men were unconstitutional; policies that compensated them for past discrimination might be upheld by the courts. As strict scrutiny did not result in an automatic striking down of legislation, one might argue that the strict-skeptical divide was actually a distinction without a difference, but it was in part a way of circumventing the other justices' unwillingness to extend the strict scrutiny test to gender equality law.

Gender-specific classifications could not be used, "as they once were, to create or perpetuate the legal, social, and economic inferiority of women," including the idea that they were unable to fight for the nation. Ginsburg implicitly attacked the "outmoded stereotype" that women's service to the nation is to be performed through childbearing rather than in the military, arguing in effect that preventing any group of citizens from fulfilling what is commonly understood to be a major element of citizen responsibility necessarily and unconstitutionally confines that group to second-class citizenship. By placing the exclusion of women from a publicly supported military college in the context of the nation's historical discrimination against women, she both helped move the law even further away from a vision of women as dependent citizens and incorporated an important element of feminist theory into the Court's constitutional jurisprudence.

Feminist jurisprudence stresses that law must be understood in its historical context. It might, perhaps, be possible to view one exclusionary act as reasonable or logical under specific circumstances. When a number of exclusionary acts are viewed together, however, and are therefore recognized as constituting parts of a discriminatory pattern, then the reasonableness or logic of any one becomes discernibly suspect. When VMI's exclusion of women was placed in the context of a society that maintained that women could not perform the same citizenship functions as men, it could be seen as the kind of irrational and ultimately pernicious discrimination that is forbidden by the Equal Protection Clause.

A second feature of much feminist jurisprudence is an emphasis on the individual, and particularly the individual woman, rather than the group. Ginsburg's opinion acknowledged that "most women would not choose VMI's adversative method," any more than most men would. That was not the issue, however; "rather, the question is whether the State can constitutionally deny to women who have the will and capacity, the training and attendant opportunities that VMI uniquely affords."[36]

The new standard in gender equality litigation became "skeptical scrutiny," with the burden of proof now on the state to demonstrate that gender-specific laws have been enacted to fulfill an important governmental function, that they are a least-restrictive method of achieving it, and that they are not based on stereotypical notions about "the way women are"[37] rather than on individual capabilities.

As Ginsburg noted, drawing upon historian Richard Morris, "A prime part of the history of our Constitution . . . is the story of the extension of constitutional rights and protections to people once ignored or excluded."[38] *U.S. v. Virginia* not only reiterated the Constitution's extension of rights to women as

well as men; more, it emphasized that women are equally capable of fulfilling the responsibilities that society demands of all its citizens.

The first women cadets arrived at VMI in the fall of 1997. Two of them were
Erin Nicole Claunch and Kendra Russell. Claunch, who would become one
of the Institute's cross-country running stars, also began to outdo most of the
male cadets in physical fitness. Sixty sit-ups in one minute were required; she
did eighty-four. Cadets were supposed to be able to do five pull-ups; she did
fifteen. Her grades were equally impressive and in 2000 Claunch was chosen
as one of VMI's two brigade commanders—the students who run much of life
at VMI and serve as liaisons with the commandant's office.[39] Russell would
star as a physics and math major with minors in computer science, English,
philosophy, and writing, and after inventing the job of copy editor for the Institute's newspaper, would become its first woman editor-in-chief.[40]

The Constitution was no longer what it had been in 1839. Neither were the
women citizens of the United States, and neither was VMI.

NOTES

1. *U.S. v. Virginia*, 519 U.S. 515 (1996). The relevant section of the Fourteenth
Amendment reads, "No state shall . . . deny to any person within its jurisdiction the
equal protection of the laws."

2. *Reed v. Reed*, 404 U.S. 71 (1971); *Frontiero v. Richardson*, 411 U.S. 677 (1973);
Kahn v. Shevin, 416 U.S. 351 (1974); *Weinberger v. Wiesenfeld*, 420 U.S. 636 (1975);
Califano v. Goldfarb, 430 U.S. 199 (1977); *Taylor v. Louisiana*, 419 U.S. 522 (1974);
Duren v. Missouri, 439 US 357 (1979).

3. Testimony of Col. Norman Bissell, *U.S. v. Virginia*, 766 F. Supp. 1407 (W.D.
Va. 1992), Joint Appendix, pp. 101–2. Bissell's official title was Commandant, which
at VMI is the equivalent of dean of students.

4. The description in these paragraphs is of the rat line as it existed in 1989, when
U.S. v. Virginia began. Changes in the physical facilities have been made since
women were admitted in 1997.

5. "The Code of a Gentleman," as printed in the 1990 *Rat Bible*, said in part:

"The honor of a gentleman demands the inviolability of his word, and the in-
corruptibility of his principles. He is the descendant of the knight, the crusader; he
is the defender of the defenseless and the champion of justice . . .

"A Gentleman . . .

"Does not discuss his family affairs in public or with acquaintances.

"Does not speak more than casually about his girl friend.

"Does not go to a lady's house if he is affected by alcohol . . .

"Does not slap strangers on the back nor so much as lay a finger on a lady."

6. See, e.g., *U.S. v. Virginia*, Brief for Cross-Petitioners, pp. 34–36.

7. *U.S. v. Virginia*, 852 F. Supp. 471 (1994), joint transcript, p. 428; author's interview, Brenda Bryant, director of VWIL, July 16, 1999; "Women and Leadership: A Selected Bibliography" and list of task force members supplied by Dr. Bryant.

8. Mary Baldwin College, "The Virginia Women's Institute for Leadership at Mary Baldwin College," September 1994, p. 2.

9. Morris Janowitz, "Military Conflict," in *Essays in the Institutional Analysis of War and Peace* (Beverly Hills, Cal.: Sage, 1975), p. 435; Sebastian De Grazia, "Political Equality and Military Participation," *Armed Forces & Society* 7 (1981): 185.

10. *Bradwell v. The State* (usually cited as *Bradwell v. Illinois*), 83 U.S. 130 (1873) at 141 (concurring).

11. *Hoyt v. Louisiana*, 368 U.S. 57 (1961) at 62. By 1961, some states and the federal government permitted women to serve on juries, but it was still constitutional for states to exclude them.

12. See, e.g., Ruth Bader Ginsburg, "Remarks on Women's Progress in the Legal Profession in the United States," *Tulsa Law Journal* 33 (1997): 13.

13. *Plessy v. Ferguson*, 163 U.S. 537 (1896).

14. *Brown v. Board of Education*, 347 U.S. 483 (1954).

15. See, e.g., *McLaughlin v. Florida*, 379 U.S. 184 (1964); *Loving v. Virginia*, 388 U.S. 1 (1967). The Court's first use of the suspect classification doctrine for race-based government action came in *Korematsu v. United States*, 323 U.S. 214 (1944) at 216. *Korematsu*, however, upheld the government's detention of Japanese Americans during World War II. For the most part, the doctrine was not developed until after *Brown*.

16. See cases in note 2; *Wengler v. Druggists Mutual Ins. Co.*, 446 U.S. 142 (1980). An intermediate standard between rational relation and strict scrutiny was articulated in *Craig v. Boren*. A good compilation of the cases from the 1970s is Ruth Bader Ginsburg, "The Burger Court's Grapplings with Sex Discrimination" in Vincent Blasi, ed., *The Burger Court: The Counter-Revolution That Wasn't* (New Haven: Yale University Press, 1983), pp. 132–56.

17. *Taylor v. Louisiana*, 419 U.S. 522 (1974); *Duren v. Missouri*, 439 U.S. 357 (1979).

18. *Mississippi v. Hogan*, 458 U.S. 718 (1982).

19. *Hogan* at 724–25, quoting *Wengler v. Druggists Mutual Ins. Co.* at 150 and citing *Frontiero v. Richardson* at 684–85 (plurality opinion), among others.

20. *J.E.B. v. Alabama ex rel. T.B.*, 511 U.S. 127 (1994).

21. *J.E.B.* at 131, 135–37.

22. 518 U.S. 515 at 530–33.

23. *Faulkner v. Jones*, 10 F.3d 226 (4th Cir. 1993), 858 F. Supp. 552 (D.S.C. 1994). See Catherine S. Manegold, *In Glory's Shadow: Shannon Faulkner, The Citadel and a Changing America* (New York: Knopf, 2000). The phrase "gender outlaw" is in Valorie K. Vojdik, "At War: Narrative Tactics in The Citadel and VMI Litigation," *Harvard Women's Law Journal* 19, no. 1 (1996): 7.

24. 518 U.S. 515 at 531–33.

25. Id. at 531.

26. Id. at 537, quoting Edward H. Clarke, *Sex in Education; or, A Fair Chance for the Girls* (J. R. Osgood and Company, 1873), pp. 38–39, 62–63, 127.

27. 518 U.S. 515 at 543, quoting *In re Application of Martha Angle Dorsett to Be Admitted to Practice as Attorney and Counselor at Law* (Minn. C. P. Hennepin Cty., 1876), in *The Syllabi*, Oct. 21, 1876, pp. 5–6.

28. 518 U.S. 515 at 537–38, referring to *Kirstein v. Rector and Visitors of Univ. of Virginia*, 309 F. Supp. 184 (ED Va. 1970).

29. 518 U.S. 515 at 535–39.

30. Id. at 545, quoting Mission Study Committee of the VMI Board of Visitors, "Report," May 16, 1986.

31. Id.

32. In addition, as noted in note 33 and accompanying text, recent Court decisions in race discrimination cases had raised the question of whether the "strict scrutiny" standard might preclude affirmative action. If the Court seemed to be moving in the direction of interpreting strict scrutiny as meaning that almost all affirmative action for racial minorities was unconstitutional, might applying strict scrutiny to gender-related policies ultimately result in the negation of policies that were designed to compensate women for past and continuing discrimination? It was a possibility that had concerned many litigators for gender equality, including those involved in the VMI case, and Ginsburg shared the concern. See Philippa Strum, *Women in the Barracks: The VMI Case and Equal Rights* (Lawrence: University of Kansas Press, 2002), pp. 251–53, 283.

33. 518 U.S. 515 at 532–33, quoting *Wengler v. Druggists Mutual Ins. Co.*, 446 U.S. 142, 150 (1980).

34. *See*, e.g., the difference between *Regents of the Univ. of Cal. v. Bakke*, 438 U.S. 265 (1978) and *United Steelworkers of America v. Weber*, 443 U.S. 193 (1979) and *City of Richmond v. J. A. Croson Co.*, 488 U.S. 469 (1989), and *Adarand Constructors v. Pena*, 515 U.S. 200 (1995).

35. 518 U.S. 515 at 534, quoting from *Califano v. Webster*, 430 U.S. 313, 320 (1977); *California Federal Savings & Loan Association v. Guerra*, 479 U.S. 272, 289 (1989). Citations omitted.

36. 518 U.S. 515 at 542.

37. Id. at 550.

38. Id. at 557–58, citing Richard B. Morris, *The Forging of the Union, 1781–1789* (New York: Harper and Row, 1987), p. 193.

39. Author's interview, Col. Mike Strickler, VMI, May 5, 2000; John White, "Loudoun Woman, a Star Student, Athlete And Pioneer, Advances to a Top VMI Post," *Washington Post*, Mar. 23, 2000; n.a., "Woman rises to top post in VMI corps," *Seattle Times*, Mar. 23, 2000.

40. Author's interviews, Kendra Russell, VMI, May 5, 2000, and Col. Mike Strickler, op. cit.; Matt Chittum, "Female Cadet Chosen VMI Newspaper Editor," *Roanoke Times & World News*, March 30, 2000; n.a., "Metro in Brief: First Woman Chosen to Lead VMI Paper," *Washington Post*, Mar. 30, 2000.

Cynthia Harrison

CHAPTER 20
"Heightened Scrutiny"

An Alternative Route to Constitutional Equality for U.S. Women

In 1923, three years after the Suffrage Amendment had been ratified, the National Woman's Party (NWP) decided to seek an amendment to the Constitution guaranteeing full legal equality for women.[1] The NWP believed itself impelled toward this strategy by the refusal of the U.S. Supreme Court to find that the Fourteenth Amendment extended its promise of "equal protection" to women. Some five decades later a revitalized women's movement won both Congressional support for the Equal Rights Amendment (ERA) and a pronouncement from the Supreme Court that women could indeed rely upon the Fourteenth Amendment. In 1982 the attempt to ratify the amendment failed but, in response to cases brought by the ACLU women's rights project and other feminist litigants, the Court continued to strike sex distinctions in the law. In addition, relying upon its power to regulate commerce, Congress responded to the new women's movement by enacting a variety of measures that eliminated much of the bias in law that the NWP had targeted initially when it proposed a new constitutional amendment. State legislatures similarly added new provisions to their state codes, mirroring the new commitment to equal treatment on the federal level. By 1996 Associate

A longer version of this essay, "Constitutional Equality for Women: Losing the Battle but Winning the War," appeared originally in Sandra Van Burkleo, Kermit L. Hall, and Robert J. Kaczorowski, eds., *Constitutionalism and American Culture: Writing the New Constitutional History* (Lawrence: University Press of Kansas, 2002). I would like to thank Susan Deller Ross, Philippa Strum, Sarah Wilson, Elizabeth Symonds, and Vivien Hart for their comments on earlier drafts. All responsibility for errors is, of course, my own.

Justice Antonin Scalia, in a lone dissent in a sex discrimination case, accused his colleagues on the Supreme Court of making sex distinctions in the law all but impossible to sustain. Perhaps the goal of constitutional equality for women had been reached.

This chapter argues that the jurisprudence of sex-based discrimination under the Fourteenth Amendment, along with statutory changes on the federal and state level, has largely fulfilled the expectations of the proponents of the Equal Rights Amendment. As of 2000 the Court had provided sufficient legal foundation to satisfy in many respects both its original proponents in 1923 and even those feminists who in 1972 succeeded in winning the support of Congress for the amendment. Moreover, the level of review that the Supreme Court applied would accommodate sex-based differences of which even many feminists approve. It is unlikely that adjudication would have differed materially even with the addition of the ERA to the Constitution. By the end of the century, in fact, even feminists had decided that history had overtaken the old amendment: In 1995 the National Organization for Women (NOW) advanced a much more comprehensive—and politically daring—constitutional equality amendment, claiming rather than disclaiming coverage for gay men and lesbians and a right to abortion. (See note 58 for text.) Moreover, some feminists had grown disenchanted with the notion of simple legal equality, shifting their focus to the provision of institutional supports, such as child-care funding, as a right of women's citizenship and as a necessity to enable poor women, many of them women of color, to raise their families safely while performing wage-earning work. Finally, few still nurtured the illusion that even perfect laws would guarantee equal treatment, adequate means, or respect for individual needs and differences. As in the past, future decisions on the nature of constitutional and social equality will turn more on effective political activism of women than on specific constitutional text.

Early Decisions

In 1923 the National Woman's Party had only a handful of Supreme Court decisions concerning sex to assess in determining the next suitable step toward women's full constitutional rights, but the few decisions had powerfully confined women's ambit. During congressional consideration of the Fourteenth and Fifteenth Amendments to the Constitution, women's rights activists, who had worked ardently for the abolition of slavery and for the enactment of measures guaranteeing equality for the freedmen and women, tried hard to get a guarantee of suffrage for women included within their mandates; short of that objective, they sought at least to prevent the addition of the word "male" to the Constitution in the second section of the Fourteenth Amendment. But their former allies deserted them, and they failed on both scores. Once the amendments were part of the Constitution, women tried to insinuate themselves within the new legal protection, but the Court proved no more sympathetic than Congress had. The rift between advocates of equality was bitter.

In 1873,[2] 1875,[3] and 1908[4] the Supreme Court insisted that classification based on sex passed constitutional muster. By 1908, however, Progressive reformers welcomed the distinction. After the 1905 decision in *Lochner v. New York*,[5] wherein the Court struck down a state law limiting hours and cited a due process "right to contract" that states could not restrict, Progressives feared that the Court would invalidate any law regulating working conditions. They were therefore much relieved when the Court, in *Muller v. Oregon* (1908), let stand an Oregon statute that prohibited employers from requiring women to work in factories or laundries for more than ten hours a day. The protection seemed more important to women's well-being than a statement of legal equality. The Court echoed the famous brief submitted by Louis Brandeis, then lawyer for the National Consumers League (NCL): "Differentiated . . . from the other sex, [woman] is properly placed in a class by herself, and legislation designed for her protection may be sustained, even when like legislation is not necessary for men and could not be sustained."[6] Although the Court did uphold hours laws for male workers within the decade,[7] it did not renounce its earlier holding that state law could still place woman "in a class by herself." Whether women required special treatment or equal treatment under the law remained a contentious issue among advocates for women for another six decades.

The Next Amendment

Thus, although the Nineteenth Amendment to the Constitution in 1920 explicitly guaranteed women the right to vote, a universe of state legislation remained that delimited women's world. Confronted by this state of affairs, the National Woman's Party, the militant wing of the suffrage movement, decided in 1921 to broach a new amendment that would sweep away legal constraints even without the cooperation of the Supreme Court. Initially, the NWP hoped to accommodate the advocates of protective labor legislation and retain those laws that benefited women workers by preventing the bitterest forms of exploitation; indeed, many NWP members had fought to achieve such statutes. But the argument for both equal rights and special treatment collapsed under the weight of its internal contradiction as a legal principle and the resulting difficulties in wording such an amendment and in implementing such a policy.

After almost two years of discussion and a sobering demonstration of a state effort to both guarantee equality and safeguard protections,[8] the NWP elected to pursue straight legal equality and unveiled its proposed amendment at the party's national conference in July 1923. It read: "Men and women shall have equal rights throughout the United States and every place subject to its jurisdiction,"[9] and the party adopted it unanimously. It then began a decades-long campaign for support among women's organizations and elected officials. An extensive list of state and federal laws that discriminated arbitrarily against women served as the foundation of the Party's argument in favor of an equal rights amendment to the Constitution. Several of the women's organizations that opposed the ERA nevertheless supported eliminating many of these laws. They advocated a strategy that called for "specific bills for specific ills," which would target problems in the law but leave untouched legislation they deemed helpful to women, especially to the poorest working women. But, insisted NWP founder Alice Paul, "We shall not be safe until the principle of equal rights is written into the framework of our Government."[10] Meanwhile, between 1923 and 1971 the Supreme Court wavered in the few cases it decided in this period, sometimes referencing the constitutional amendment adopted in 1920 guaranteeing to women the right to vote and requiring equality but other times allowing differentiation by sex in the law to stand.[11] The Court's inconsistent rulings served as confirmation of the need for a clear directive.

The politics of World War II increased the number of ERA supporters, as had the widespread discrimination against married women during the Great Depression. A sympathetic member of Congress introduced the ERA into every Congress, but not until 1942, with the war under way, did a congressional committee report it favorably to the floor. Both the position of the United States as the avatar of democracy and the valor women displayed as workers and military personnel made their exclusion from protection of fundamental law seem both embarrassing and unfair. The amendment's first floor vote, in the Senate in 1946, drew a majority of the votes, although not the two-thirds needed.[12]

Had women's organizations coalesced around the amendment, its passage at least through Congress would likely have succeeded, but the increased support for the amendment spurred its opponents to new heights in defense of sex-specific labor laws. With the assistance of Senator Carl Hayden (D-Ariz.), the opponents hit upon an effective blockade: at every floor vote, the senator would offer his proviso, that the ERA would not "impair any rights, benefits, or exemptions now or hereafter conferred by law, upon persons of the female sex." In 1950 and 1953, delighted to be able to vote for both equal treatment for women and special protection, the Senate duly added the Hayden rider to the ERA; ERA supporters then killed the bill.[13]

New Support

If the fifteen years following the end of the war introduced little in the way of constitutional change for women, their own economic decisions altered the social landscape. The opportunities provided by both the war and the explosion of jobs in the sectors employing women during the 1950s made the waged work of white married mothers commonplace, following their black counterparts into the labor force. Like men, though in smaller numbers, women also took advantage of federally funded educational opportunities so that by the time of the election of John F. Kennedy as president, the stresses in the family-work dynamic had become visible enough among middle-class white families to warrant national examination.

In response Kennedy appointed a national commission both to explore the status of women and to deflate support for the ERA, which liberals continued to oppose. That commission, however, helped re-ignite a new women's movement, soon to be united in support of constitutional equality. In its final report the President's Commission on the Status of Women acknowledged the need for and the justice of a constitutional guarantee of equal protection under law. It favored a Supreme Court holding to this effect rather than the adoption of the Equal Rights Amendment, anticipating that the Court would know when to discard, and when to retain, laws that distinguished men from women. The commissioners hoped by this stratagem to preserve sensible laws that differentiated appropriately by sex (they had in mind certain labor laws) and to jettison the legislation that promoted invidious distinctions.[14]

The commission's work generated a new level of concern and activism focused on women's status, modeled on the parallel movement aimed at gaining the protection of the law for blacks. In gathering information to inform its wide-ranging recommendations, the commission accumulated copious documentation of the many obstacles women confronted on account of their sex. State commissions worked in tandem with the federal commission, and the federal government inspired further momentum by holding annual national meetings in Washington.

The creation of a new women's movement, based on these component parts, occurred after Congress in 1964 unexpectedly yielded to pressure from National Woman's Party activists (working through Congressman Howard Smith (D-Va.), an ERA supporter) and the National Federation of Business and Professional Women's Clubs to include women in civil rights legislation barring discrimination in employment based on race.[15] In lobbying for such legislation, activists used the information the President's Commission had collected (although the President's Commission had called a legislative ban premature and many proponents of a law protecting blacks from discrimination objected to adding protection for women). A ban on sex discrimination in employment immediately threw into question the status of state labor laws that applied only to women. The Equal Employment Opportunity Commission (EEOC), the agency created by Congress to enforce Title VII of the 1964 Civil Rights Act, found itself in the middle of the long-standing battle, but within five years feminist litigators had brought about a resolution of the issue. Federal courts held that the federal legislation superseded any state law, and though employers might comply with both, they could not protect themselves against a charge of discrimination by citing a state labor law. Although some of the old guard argued futilely in favor of retaining sex-specific laws, by and large feminists agreed that labor laws should apply to both male and female workers, a contention that few now disputed. The EEOC likewise adopted this position in August 1969,[16] and the old bone of contention was finally buried. With its interment came swift unanimity among women's organizations behind a constitutional amendment.

The burgeoning women's movement also incited change at an amazing pace in the lower federal courts, in state and federal legislatures, and in state courts. In 1966 a three-judge federal district court in Alabama threw out the state's jury service law that barred women from jury duty, citing the Fourteenth Amendment.[17] In 1968 a federal district court in Connecticut declared unconstitutional longer prison terms for women than for men convicted of the same crimes.[18] In 1970, courts in Illinois and New Jersey eliminated bans against women bartenders,[19] and that same year a federal district court in Virginia endorsed the proposal to open Mr. Jefferson's university to coeducation, also citing the equal protection clause of the Fourteenth Amendment.[20] It was a sign of the times that these decisions were not appealed to the Supreme Court, with the institutions instead capitulating to the changing legal standard. Even where courts upheld discriminatory practices, legislatures acted to remove the barrier.[21] In 1961 Wisconsin had become the first state to prohibit discrimination in employment within the state;[22] by 1973 the American Civil Liberties Union (ACLU) found only eleven states (eight of them in the South) without state fair employment practices (FEP) laws that included protection against sex discrimination as well as against race discrimination. (By 1983 nine states still had no FEP law, all southern except North Dakota; only Georgia had an FEP law that did not include sex bias.) The changes reflected a new presence on the part of feminists not only as lobbyists but, indeed, as jurists and as legislators.

Congressional resistance to the ERA dissolved in the face of the new consensus. In March 1972 ERA advocates succeeded in winning the two-thirds vote in both houses of Congress, and without any qualifying provisions for the amendment that now read: "Equality of rights under the law shall not be denied or abridged by the United States or by any State on account of sex."[23] The state of Hawaii ratified the amendment on the first day it went to the states, March 22, 1972. The alacrity of the response justified Calvin Coolidge's remark to Alice Paul in 1923 that Congress would approve the ERA if American women really wanted it.[24]

With newly sympathetic legislatures and courts, what did modern feminists seek in the ERA? Feminist representatives described a wide array of desired legal changes. Aileen Hernandez, NOW's president, argued that the ERA would create a "clear national policy that women should not be discriminated against" and in doing so would help in the enforcement of sex-discrimination statutes in employment and would generally open to women "the kind of first class citizenship which will permit them early in life to make career choices that are not now available."[25] Noted Martha Griffiths: "All this amendment asks could easily be done without the amendment if the Supreme Court were willing to do it, but they are not."[26] Perhaps the definitive assessment of the impact and benefits of the Equal Rights Amendment appeared in the *Yale Law Journal* in April 1971, a collaboration between three women law students (Barbara Brown, Gail Falk, and Ann Freedman) identified as "active in the women's movement" and Yale law professor Thomas Emerson. The Yale authors argued that under the ERA sex would be a prohibited classification except where unique physical attributes obtained (permitting, for example, laws relating to wet nurses or sperm donors, rape, and determination of paternity). Legislation providing, for example, leave for child rearing would have to be written in a sex-neutral way; classification based on pregnancy would have to be narrowly drawn. "Current mores" would govern sex separation for privacy purposes: laws could thus require employment of same-sex police officers for strip searches and permit segregated toilet and sleeping facilities.[27] Single-sex schools could exist, so long as they remained private.[28] But classification for "benign quotas" or "compensatory aid" would not pass muster under the ERA except as remedies for past discrimination.[29] In other ways the operation of the ERA would be both "obvious and direct,"[30] eliminating sex differences in jury service, qualifications to conduct business, age requirements, government benefits, and Social Security and enhancing the existing trends toward equality in marriage and divorce law and in employment doctrine as begun under Title

VII of the 1964 Civil Rights Law. The ERA would demand changes in criminal law where differences existed, most notably with respect to sexual conduct, although some differences might remain if they survived close judicial scrutiny to ensure their basis in "unique physical characteristics."[31] Brown and her coauthors noted that the Model Penal Code already incorporated such a stance.[32] With respect to the military, however, they warned that the amendment would have "a substantial and pervasive impact upon military practices and institutions," requiring "a radical restructuring of the military's view of women,"[33] including draft, enlistment, assignment, training, and veterans' benefits. But, they predicted, "changes in the law, where necessary to bring the military into compliance with the amendment will not be difficult to effect."[34] They concluded that the ERA would "establish fully, emphatically, and unambiguously the proposition that before the law women and men are to be treated without difference."[35]

In sum, then, it could be argued that feminists were asking for clarity—a clear legal standard of equal treatment without regard to sex, with the burden on the state to demonstrate a compelling reason for making the distinction—and permanence, a standard that would not be subject to the vagaries of changing political winds or even court personnel. But before the decade was out, two things were plain: first, an amendment to the Constitution would not come easily; second, legislative actions and court decisions would make many feminist arguments anachronisms. Phyllis Schlafly, the conservative Republican leader of the Eagle Forum who led the fight against ratification, used as one of her key points the idea that the constitutional amendment was simply unnecessary, a point that became harder to contest as the decade wore on. Despite the inability of feminists to wrest the final three states required for ratification (even with the deadline extended by Congress to June 1982), a dizzying array of new statutes and judicial holdings brought the goal of equality under law closer to reality.

"Heightened Scrutiny": A New Weapon

Among the first changes was alteration in Supreme Court doctrine. Although it did not initially acknowledge a departure, in 1971 (*Reed v. Reed*[36]) the U.S. Supreme Court found that a state law that preferred male executors to female executors had distinguished "irrationally" on the basis of sex and therefore denied to women the equal protection of the law. Reviewing a law under the standard of "rationality" meant that the Court presumed a state law to be constitutional; someone who objected had the obligation to show that the classification in the law had no rational relationship to any legitimate state objective. But the *Reed* decision was only the first of many, and the Court in 1976 (*Craig v. Boren*[37]) owned that it had taken to subjecting laws that differentiated on the basis of sex to a higher level of review than mere "rationality." Under the new standard of "heightened scrutiny," the state had to demonstrate not only that the law was "rationally related" to a "legitimate" state objective but also that it was "substantially related" to an "important governmental objective." The new standard did not pose as high a barrier as the "rigid scrutiny" applied to a race-based classification, which the Court declared to be a "suspect classification." The Court presumed race-based classifications unconstitutional unless the state could show that the law was narrowly tailored and closely related to achieving a "compelling" state interest—a very high burden of proof. Still, with *Craig*, the burden of proof to justify a sex-based classification had shifted to the state, as proponents had hoped. (Although four justices argued for a "strict scrutiny" standard in a 1973 case, that position never won a majority.[38])

Using the new intermediate standard, the Court proceeded to strike many more sex-based laws than it permitted to stand; at the same time, Congress enacted federal measures to prohibit forms of discrimination either not open to constitutional challenge or found by the Court to be free of constitutional taint. In 1978, for example, Congress passed the Pregnancy Discrimination Act in response to the Court's determination that discrimination against pregnant workers violated neither the Constitution's demand for equal treatment nor the ban against sex discrimination in employment in Title VII of the 1964 Civil Rights Act.[39] Simultaneous efforts to seek amendments to state constitutions, sixteen of them successful, and to amend state laws also wiped sex-based laws from the books. The U.S. Supreme Court had imposed equal protection requirements even on members of Congress and state judges not then covered by federal discrimination statutes.[40]

Thus, despite the failure of the ERA to win ratification, by June 1982 a substantial body of antidiscrimination law now rested in court reporters and codes of both the federal and the state governments. And though a Republican victory in the 1980 election checked the feminist juggernaut, throughout the 1980s the Supreme Court did not reverse its course. By 1997, of the feminist goals that an equal rights amendment would reach, few remained unfulfilled. Women and men had won virtual equality concerning domicile, age at marriage, marital surnames, ownership and control of marital property, child custody, divorce, and alimony.[41] In short, in the words of the ACLU's specialists in women's rights law, "Despite the loss of the ERA, the 1970s gave [women] the legal structure for eradicating discrimination."[42]

The Court continued to uphold sex distinctions in the law in only a few instances, usually justifying the action by reference either to privacy or to a need for compensatory treatment.[43] In a smaller set of cases, the Court provided rationales that recalled the paternalistic tradition one might have presumed abjured: In *Dothard v. Rawlinson*,[44] the Court splintered but upheld a prohibition on women prison guards in an Alabama maximum security prison based on the savage prison conditions obtaining in Alabama; in *Michael M. v. Sonoma County Superior Court*, by a 5–4 vote, the Court let stand California's "statutory rape" law on the unsupported basis that only a sex-specific law could effectively protect young women from unintended pregnancy.[45] Another area in which the Court countenanced sex differences concerned unmarried parents, holding in several cases that differential treatment between unmarried fathers and unmarried mothers could be justified, decisions that on the whole favored mothers.[46] The dispute over "maternity leave" found resolution eventually in the passage of sex-neutral leave legislation:[47] the federal Family and Medical Leave Act was signed by President William Jefferson Clinton on February 5, 1993, following exactly the legal formula laid out in the *Yale Law Journal* article. The area in which the Court endorsed the largest number of sex distinctions involved, predictably, the military. Citing Congress's differential treatment of men and women, it refrained from imposing a single standard. Most notably, in a 1981 case brought by a man protesting an all-male draft, *Rostker v. Goldberg*,[48] the Court declined to require Congress to equalize its treatment of men and women in the military, noting the "greater deference" the Court has always accorded to Congress in matters military.[49] The Yale authors had predicted incorrectly that changes in the law would come easily. But even the military could not operate with an entirely free hand: in 1973 the Court had insisted, by a margin of eight to one, that Congress treat married women equally with married men in the armed services with respect to benefits (in this case, a housing allowance).[50]

Still, in the years after *Rostker*, the actions of both Congress and the Pentagon continued to demonstrate the unsettled nature of the relationship between women and military service and the movement toward equal treatment. Most exclusions and exemptions obtaining in 1981 had been lifted by 1996.[51] Complete equality remained elusive: the regulation that prohibited women's participation in ground combat barred them from 32 percent of military jobs. Political scientist Jane Mansbridge has argued that the ERA lost crucial support because feminists insisted that the amendment would require equal treatment of women and men in the military,[52] and the pace of Congressional change suggested that prevailing sentiment had not yet endorsed full equality in this arena. Nevertheless, the exceptions of the Court and Congress in this area represented a departure from a new general rule of equality.

In 1996 the U.S. Supreme Court reviewed the status of women under the Fourteenth Amendment in a case many feminists called "as important a Constitutional gender-discrimination case as this Court has ever addressed."[53] On June 26, 1996, in *U.S. v. Virginia*,[54] the U.S. Supreme Court decided that the Virginia Military Institute (VMI), a state-supported all-male college founded in 1839, had to admit women. Associate Justice Ruth Bader Ginsburg wrote for the 7–1 majority. Although twenty-five years earlier, in a brief written on behalf of the ACLU in *Reed v. Reed*, Ginsburg had urged the Court to apply "strict scrutiny" to sex-based distinctions, in *U.S. v. Virginia* she based her decision on the "intermediate scrutiny" the Court had applied explicitly to sex-based distinctions since 1976. Presumably against Ginsburg's preferences, stated repeatedly in briefs written between 1971 and 1980 when she was directing the ACLU Women's Rights Project, the Court ignored the pleas of the United States Solicitor Gneral and many *amici* to raise the standard of review to "strict scrutiny."[55]

In her opinion, Justice Ginsburg now defended "intermediate scrutiny," although her interpretation of this standard was expansive:

> Without equating gender classifications for all purposes to classifications based on race or national origin, the Court, in post-*Reed* decisions, has carefully inspected official action that closes a door or denies opportunity to women (or to men). [Citations omitted.] To summarize the Court's current directions for cases of official classification based on gender: Focusing on the differential treatment or denial of opportunity for which relief is sought, the reviewing court must determine whether the proffered justification is "exceedingly persuasive." The burden of justification is demanding and it rests entirely on the State. . . . The State must show "at least that the [challenged] classification serves 'important governmental objectives and that the discriminatory means employed' are 'substantially related to the achievement of those objectives.' " . . . The justification must be genuine, not hypothesized or invented *post hoc* in response to litigation. And it must not rely on overbroad generalizations about the different talents, capacities, or preferences of males and females.
>
> The heightened review standard our precedent establishes does not make sex a proscribed classification. Supposed "inherent differences" are no longer accepted as a ground for race or national origin classification. . . . Physical differences between men and women, however, are enduring. . . .
>
> "Inherent differences" between men and women, we have come to appreciate, remain cause for celebration, but not for denigration of the

members of either sex or for artificial constraints on an individual's opportunity. Sex classifications may be used to compensate women "for particular economic disabilities [they have] suffered," . . . to 'promot[e] equal employment opportunity,' . . . to advance full development of the talent and capacities of our Nation's people. But such classifications may not be used, as they once were, . . . to create or perpetuate the legal, social, and economic inferiority of women." (15–16)

In a footnote, Justice Ginsburg appeared to reassure those concerned about the endurance of single-sex education, although her meaning is ambiguous: "We do not question the State's prerogative evenhandedly to support diverse educational opportunities. We address specifically and only an educational opportunity recognized . . . as 'unique' " (16, n. 7).

Not at all persuaded by this demurrer, Justice Antonin Scalia in his dissent indignantly accused his colleagues of changing the decision rule: "The rationale of today's decision," he wrote, "is sweeping: for sex-based classifications, a redefinition of intermediate scrutiny that makes it indistinguishable from strict scrutiny." Justice Scalia correctly observed that this decision marked an important bellwether. The majority of seven included not only the appointees of President Clinton (Justices Breyer and Ginsburg) but also all the "swing" justices named by Presidents Reagan and Bush (Souter, Kennedy, and O'Connor), as well as Justice Stevens, a Nixon appointee (although usually a reliable liberal). Even Chief Justice Rehnquist, a frequent ally of Justices Scalia and Thomas, joined the result (but not the reasoning of the decision). With Justice Thomas not participating, presumably because his son attended VMI, Justice Scalia was alone in his dissent.

The coalition of seven justices, important in part for its numerical strength but more so for its alliance across political boundaries, suggested that the decision was a durable one and one that, as Justice Scalia lamented, sustained the contemporary reach of "intermediate scrutiny." If not identical to "strict scrutiny," it nonetheless permitted few distinctions. In fact, the advocates of strict scrutiny in the briefs described a level of review with results very much like that of intermediate scrutiny as the Court was now applying it: it permitted compensatory programs for women and separate educational facilities for women and men (so long as comparable programs are available for each), it did not touch military limitations placed on women, and it left in place separate public accommodations in the way of sanitary facilities. But such exceptions plainly distinguished the impact of this level of scrutiny from that of the "strict scrutiny" sought and won by the civil rights movement from the 1940s on, which targeted exactly racial classifications in educational institutions, in public accommodations (including public rest rooms), and in the military.

A New Engagement?

Justice Ginsburg's opinion and Scalia's dissent notwithstanding, numbers of feminists continued to believe that the ERA remained essential to women's legal protection. Given the history of Supreme Court adjudication, what were amendment advocates seeking in 1997? In her January 1997 letter soliciting cosponsors,[56] Democratic Congress member Carolyn Maloney of New York told her colleagues that "without the ERA, laws can still perpetuate gender classifications that keep women from achieving their full potential." She offered no specific examples, although in the newsletter of the National Woman's Party she explained that the ERA would help "women . . . engaged in a constant struggle to maintain laws which protect equality in education and in the workplace." In the same issue the NWP itself contended: "Passage of the ERA can help to make equal pay a reality for women."[57] The article did not explain the nexus between the constitutional amendment and pay raises for women.

In any case, at the end of the century the ERA stood no chance of approval. Conservatives were in the majority in Congress, and the compromise of specific bills for specific ills and a compliant Supreme Court, assessing on an individual basis which laws should fall and which remain, had undercut many of the amendment's strongest arguments.

In fact, by 1995 the ERA as then composed satisfied not even feminists. Many now argued that the simple formal equality of the 1972 amendment asked for too little. In 1995 one of the most stalwart of the amendment's advocates, the National Organization for Women, promulgated a new "Constitutional Equality Amendment" that explicitly prohibited discrimination based on sexual orientation or indigence, guaranteed a woman's right to terminate a pregnancy, endorsed affirmative action programs, and stipulated "strict scrutiny" as the standard of judicial review. The new proposal implicitly acknowledged that most of the goals attainable under the old rubric of "equal rights for women" had been achieved and that feminists required a different strategy to effect a more comprehensive agenda, including the provision of social goods to enable poor women, many of them women of color, to live with adequate means and physical safety.[58]

But the constitutional status of women had changed dramatically in the preceding quarter of a century. Although vestigial forms of discrimination remained in the law, the plethora of state and federal statutes that distinguished arbitrarily on the basis of sex had been nullified. Even the symbolic battle had been won. Feminists claimed in 1923 and again in the 1970s that constitutional equality would generate a commitment to equality also in those areas formally untouched by government power. Such a commitment now existed in almost all quarters of American life, at least on paper. Moreover, the few remaining distinctions permitted, such as single-sex colleges and compensatory programs, had substantial feminist support as well.

What of significance was still missing from the constitutional status of women that the language of the 1972 amendment would provide? We can locate two major lacunae. The first was that women continued to be treated differently from men by Congress with respect to military service. The second was that, at least in theory, both the constitutional standard requiring equal treatment and the legislative foundation for equal opportunity could unravel; that is, the right to equal protection lacked permanence. Would the ERA make a difference?

The position of women in the military had consistently been a sticking point, and it remained so, with feminist insistence on absolute equality driving away potential supporters of a constitutional amendment.[59] Nevertheless, few ERA supporters would countenance an explicit exception for differences in military service. Women had lost their lives in the service of their country, and women soldiers argued vehemently that all roles in the military must be open to them.[60]

But one could not realistically predict that the ERA would settle this question before it was concluded in some other way. Historically the Supreme Court has deferred to Congress and to the military on military matters. In the face of congressional and military resistance, the argument that men and women are differently situated with respect to military service might serve to justify any difference the Court chose to permit, even with the ERA. A court that could require the arrest and detention of American citizens based on race and cite wartime necessity (*Korematsu v. United States*, 323 U.S. 214 [1944]), explicit constitutional language to the contrary notwithstanding, could well acquiesce to the military with respect to women in combat. If the army lifted the combat exclusion, much opposition to the ERA would disappear, as it did when Title VII eliminated single-sex labor laws. But this issue would need to be resolved in advance of ratification. With the possible exception of the civil war amendments, constitutional amendments are lagging indicators of change, not propellants.[61]

What about permanence? In 1996 seven justices of the Supreme Court affirmed that the Constitution does not abide invidious distinctions based on sex. Feminists argued nonetheless that the absence of explicit constitutional text rendered all decisions potentially unstable, vulnerable to reversal at the hands of new conservative justices. Perhaps explicit language in the Constitution enshrining sexual equality would prove a sturdier bulwark than a 7–1 decision; permanent language in the Constitution might well work to retard a backlash. On the other hand, as *Plessy v. Ferguson*[62] illustrates, the Court will not necessarily be deterred by the explicit language of the Constitution either. Given a profound enough period of conservative reaction, concepts such as "equality," "rights," or "compelling interests" do not foreclose reinterpretation. And the history of resistance to the Supreme Court's 1962 ruling concerning prayer in public schools[63] demonstrates that constitutional imperatives—textual or interpretive—do not perforce change local practice

By the end of the twentieth century ERA advocates had not achieved their goal, but they nonetheless had good reason to declare victory in the war for constitutional equality as proposed by the 1972 amendment. Few explicit distinctions remained in the law; those that did had general support, in some cases (such as affirmative action and single-sex education) even from feminists. Permanence, meanwhile, is always illusory. Both opponents and proponents pointed to conflicting judicial rulings under state ERAs. Construction of equality under the law for men and women would likely continue to turn on understandings by judges of appropriate distinctions rather than constitutional text. Their understandings would be shaped by the political, economic, and social behavior of women and the popular responses to those behaviors. In 1971 Margaret Eastwood, an attorney and fervent supporter of the ERA, laid out the changes she and other supporters assumed an ERA would bring about. However, she noted that the words of the Constitution would have no effect if women did not mobilize: "Unless women play a greater role in all forms of government, there is no assurance that their lack of equal status under the law will not continue indefinitely despite new constitutional mandates."[64] Regardless of the language in the Constitution, what matters is the political mobilization of women. With it, constitutional equality is safe; without it, the inscribed words of the ERA would be only, in James Madison's words, "parchment barriers."

NOTES

1. The original wording proposed by the NWP in 1923 reads: "Men and women shall have equal rights throughout the United States and in every place subject to its jurisdiction." The U.S. Senate Judiciary Committee changed the wording in 1943 to bring the amendment text in line with the suffrage amendment. The language adopted in 1972 read: "Equality of rights under the law shall not be denied or abridged by the United States or by any state on account of sex."

2. *Bradwell v. State of Illinois*, 83 U.S. (16 Wall.) 130, at 141–42 (1873).

3. *Minor v. Happersett*, 88 U.S. (21 Wall.) 162 (1875).

4. *Muller v. Oregon*, 208 U.S. 412 (1908).

5. 198 U.S. 45 (1905).

6. 208 U.S. 422 (1908).

7. *Bunting v. Oregon*, 243 U.S. 426 (1917).

8. The state of Wisconsin had passed an equal rights law in 1921 to clarify women's status in the wake of the suffrage amendment. The law promised women equality under law but permitted to stand those laws that offered "special protection and privileges." Under this legal regime, the state's attorney general had ruled acceptable a law that banned women from working for state legislators on the grounds that the hours were too long. J. Stanley Lemons, *The Woman Citizen: Social Feminism in the 1920s* (Charlottesville: University Press of Virginia, 1990), 187–89.

9. Susan D. Becker, *The Origins of the Equal Rights Amendment: American Feminism Between the Wars* (Westport, Conn.: Greenwood Press, 1981), 19.

10. Quoted in Becker, *Origins of the Equal Rights Amendment*, 19.

11. *Adkins v. Children's Hospital*, 261 U.S. 525 (1923) and *Morehead v. New York ex rel. Tipaldo*, 298 U.S. 587 (1936), striking down sex-specific minimum wage laws; *Radice v. New York*, 264 U.S. 292, (1924), upholding a night-work limitation for women; *Ballard v. United States*, 329 U.S. 187 (1946), at 193–94, striking down a jury-differentiation practice; *Goesaert v. Cleary, Liquor Control Commission of Michigan*, 335 U.S. 464 (1948), allowing a state to limit the right of women to tend bar; *Hoyt v. Florida*, 368 U.S. 57 (1961), at 62, allowing differentiation in jury service.

12. For a fuller discussion, see Cynthia Harrison, *On Account of Sex: The Politics of Women's Issues, 1945–1968* (Berkeley: University of California Press, 1988), chap. 1.

13. See ibid., chap. 2.

14. Ibid., chap. 7.

15. Much ink has been spilled over the question of Howard Smith's motives in introducing an amendment to add "sex" to the employment title of the Civil Rights Act of 1964. He would, no doubt, have happily seen the entire act go down in flames, but if it were to succeed (and surely he knew it would), his own preference was likely to have (white) women included in its purview. He was, in fact, a longstanding supporter of the Equal Rights Amendment, his amendment was urged on him by his pro-ERA Virginia constituents, and he bragged about his role in his next election campaign. Moreover, the survival of the amendment in the Senate, where many opportunities to expunge it existed, gives lie to the propaganda that this dramatic change in the law was inadvertent. See Harrison, ibid., 177–78, 295 n. 20.

16. 29 CFR sec. 1604.1 (1970).

17. *White v. Crook*, 251 F.Supp. 401 (M.D. Ala. 1966), at 408.

18. *United States ex rel. Robinson v. York*, 281 F.Supp. 8 (D. Conn. 1968).

19. *McCrimmon v. Daley*, 2 F.E.P. Cas. 971 (N.D. Ill. 19070; *Paterson Tavern & Grill Owners Ass'n, Inc. v. Borough of Hawthorne*, 57 N.J. 180, 270 A.2d 628 (1970).

20. *Kirstein v. Rector and Visitors of the University of Virginia*, 309 F.Supp. 184 (E.D. Va. 1970).

21. *State v. Hall*, 187 So. 2d 861 (Miss.); MISS. CODE ANN. sec. 1762 (Supp. 1968), cited in Mary Eastwood, "The Double Standard of Justice: Women's Rights Under the Constitution," *Valparaiso University Law Review* 5, no. 2 (symposium issue 1971): 290.

22. Sonia Pressman Fuentes, "Federal Remedial Sanctions: Focus on Title VII," *Valparaiso University Law Review* 5, no. 2 (symposium issue 1971): 395.

23. The amendment had been rewritten in the 1940s to conform to the language of the suffrage amendment. Alice Paul, the author of the first version, did the redraft. See Harrison, *On Account of Sex*, 16.

24. Becker, *Origins of the Equal Rights Amendment*, 93.

25. Hearings on S. J. Res. 61 Before the Subcomm. on Constitutional Amendments of the Senate Comm. on the Judiciary, 90th Cong., 2d sess. (May 1970), 43.

26. Ibid., 19.

27. Barbara A. Brown et al. "The Equal Rights Amendment," 889–902.

28. Ibid., 907.

29. Ibid., 903–04.

30. Ibid., 920.

31. Ibid., 954.

32. Ibid., 966.

33. Ibid., 969.

34. Ibid., 978.

35. Ibid., 980.

36. 404 U.S. 71 (1971).

37. 429 U.S. 190 (1976).

38. *Frontiero v. Richardson*, 411 U.S. 677 (1973). Perhaps ironically, Justice Lewis F. Powell declined to join his four colleagues in this case because the ERA was pending before the states and he thought it unwise for the Court "to pre-empt . . . the prescribed constitutional processes" (411 U.S. 677, 693).

39. *Geduldig v. Aiello*, 417 U.S. 484 (1974); *General Electric Co. v. Gilbert*, 429 U.S. 125 (1976).

40. *Davis v. Passman*, 442 U.S. 228 (1979); *Forrester v. White*, 484 U.S. 219 (1988).

41. Herma Hill Kay, *Text, Cases and Materials on Sex-Based Discrimination*, 3^d ed. (St. Paul, Minn.: West Publishing, 1988), passim.

42. Susan Deller Ross and Ann Barcher. *The Rights of Women: The Basic ACLU Guide to A Woman's Rights*, rev. ed. (New York: Bantam, 1983), xiv.

43. *Califano v. Webster*, 430 U.S. 313 (1977); *Heckler v. Mathews*, 465 U.S. 728 (1984).

44. 433 U.S. 321 (1977).

45. 450 U.S. 464 (1981).

46. See, e.g., *Parham v. Hughes*, 441 U.S. 347 (1979); *Caban v. Mohammed*, 441 U.S. 380 (1979); *Lehr v. Robertson*, 463 U.S. 248 (1983); *Clark v. Jeter*, 486 U.S. 461 (1988); *Nguyen v. INS*, No. 99–2071 (June 11, 2001).

47. *California Federal Savings & Loan Association v. Guerra*, 479 U.S. 272 (1987).

48. 453 US 57 (1981).

49. *Schlesinger v. Ballard*, 419 U.S. 498 (1975), upholding different promotion procedures for men and women; *Personnel Administrator of Massachusetts v. Feeney*, 442 U.S. 256 (1979), upholding veterans' preference laws.

50. *Frontiero v. Richardson*, 411 U.S. 677 (1973).

51. P. L. 102–190, December 5, 1991; *New York Times*, December 29, 1996, April 1, 1997; *Washington Post*, December 30, 1997.

52. Jane J. Mansbridge, *Why We Lost the ERA* (Chicago: University of Chicago Press, 1986), 85.

53. Robert N. Weiner et al., "Brief of *Amici Curiae* National Women's Law Center, American Civil Liberties Union [and 21 additional *amici*] in support of the petition for a writ of certiorari to the U.S. Court of Appeals for the Fourth Circuit, *U.S. v. Virginia*, Docket No. 94–1941, filed June 26, 1995, Law Library, Library of Congress, Washington, D.C., 2.

54. 518 U.S. 515 (1996).

55. Deborah L. Markowitz, "In Pursuit of Equality: One Woman's Work to Change the Law," *Women's Rights Law Reporter* 11 (summer 1989): 77–80.

56. Maloney to "Dear Colleague," January 13, 1997, in the author's possession.

57. *Equal Rights* 82, no. 1 (fall 1997): 1, 7.

58. The Constitutional Equality Amendment promulgated by the National Organization for Women, July 1995 reads as follows:

"Section 1. Women and men shall have equal rights throughout the United States and every place and entity subject to its jurisdiction; through this article, the subordination of women to men is abolished;

"Section 2. All persons shall have equal rights and privileges without discrimination on account of sex, race, sexual orientation, marital status, ethnicity, national origin, color or indigence (see also Sec. 4);

"Section 3. This article prohibits pregnancy discrimination and guarantees the absolute right of a woman to make her own reproductive decisions including the termination of pregnancy;

"Section 4. This article prohibits discrimination based upon characteristics unique to or stereotypes about any class protected under this article. This article also prohibits discrimination through the use of any facially neutral criteria which have a disparate impact based on membership in a class protected under this article.

"Section 5. This article does not preclude any law, program or activity that would remedy the effects of discrimination and that is closely related to achieving such remedial purposes;

"Section 6. This article shall be interpreted under the highest standard of judicial review;

"Section 7. The United States and the several states shall guarantee the implementation and enforcement of this article. (Source: NOW Web site: www.now.org)."

59. For elaboration of this argument, see Mansbridge, *Why We Lost the ERA*.

60. Lory Manning and Jennifer E. Griffith, *Women in the Military: Where They Stand*, 2d ed. (Washington, D.C.: Women's Research and Education Institute, 1998).

61. Other effects have been claimed for the ERA—for example, that it would affect abortion laws or protect homosexual unions—but they are less plausible.

62. 163 U.S. 537 (1896).

63. *Engel v. Vitale*, 370 U.S. 421 (1962).

64. Eastwood, "Double Standard of Justice," 298.

CHAPTER 21

Whatever Happened to the ERA?

—Equality of rights under the law shall not be denied or abridged by the United States or by any State on account of sex.

Why We Lost the ERA, written in 1986, made the point that actors in a social movement are deeply influenced by their own contexts and incentives.[1] Moreover, social movements are many headed, based on a "participatory decentralization" that facilitates the sometimes conflicting contributions of actors with different perspectives and incentives (including, for example, the incentives that lead me to write this chapter). In particular, many of the incentives of social movement actors lead them not to take as their audience the members of the public who must be convinced if a policy is to be voted into law. On the other hand, the very participatory decentralization that generates conflicts within the movement also brings intellectual challenge to that movement in ways not possible in organizations with a "party line." The present chapter reveals that many of the dynamics identified in the movement from 1972 to 1982 still operate in the current social movement activity around the ERA.

This final chapter has four parts, illuminating four separate perspectives on the Equal Rights Amendment (ERA) from different corners of the legal and political universe. It does not claim to represent all the important perspectives on the ERA currently or to recount the history of the ERA since 1982. It looks briefly at four separate "takes" on the ERA in 2001—those of: (1) feminist constitutional lawyers Martha Fineman and Mary Becker; (2) state courts interpreting state ERAs since 1982; (3) women activists still trying to get their states to ratify the original amendment in unratified states such as Missouri; and (4) the National Organization for Women (NOW), which has crafted a Constitutional Equality Amendment that might or might not replace the original

ERA. The exercise is "Rashomon"-like in character, for each take represents not only one side of the ERA struggle but also something of the piece of the universe from which that take comes.

1

In 1990 Nancy Fraser and I invited three feminist legal theorists, along with a feminist practitioner teaching a legal clinic at Northwestern University, to give a panel at Northwestern on "Women, Public Policy, and the Law." After a set of presentations in which the participants explained their stance toward the subject, I asked them all, "If you could simply push a button and put the ERA in the constitution right now, with no political struggle, would you do it?"

All three feminist constitutional scholars said no. The practitioner, surprised at the others' responses, produced a strong yes.

I was not surprised at the scholars' responses. In the period from 1972, when the ERA first went before the states, to 1982, when the deadline ran out, many feminist constitutional scholars had bitten their tongues. Few had voiced publicly any reservations about the wisdom of the amendment. Because the issues were not completely clear and the potential practical consequences of dissent were dire, few feminist academics wanted to raise questions that for them amounted not to vehement opposition but only to serious worries about the amendment's effects. But when the deadline for ratification ran out in 1982, the dam burst. The law journals exploded with articles on what soon came to be called the "equality/difference" controversy.[2]

That controversy, which still pits one group of feminist legal scholars against another, is by now well documented and well known, as is the move within it of Catherine MacKinnon and then others to replace "difference" with "dominance." I will not go into it here, except to point out the obvious, that the scholars who most wanted to maintain the power of the state to institute measures aimed specifically at reducing male dominance and addressing women's different needs had the most serious reservations about the "formal equality" embodied in the ERA.

I recently telephoned Martha Fineman and Mary Becker, two of the constitutional lawyers on the panel we held at Northwestern, to see if they would hold today to their conclusion in 1990. Both said they would.

Martha Fineman would continue to oppose the ERA because of the trouble formal equality has brought in its wake. She supports, for example, policies devised specifically to avoid the exploitation of caretaking labor, and worries that some of these policies might be ruled unconstitutional under the 1972 wording of the ERA. Nor would she favor an ERA worded to reflect the wording of the Fourteenth Amendment.[3] The Fourteenth Amendment, she points out, generates problems deriving from the way it has been interpreted to require either a "suspect class" or a "discrete and insular minority." The emphasis in the Fourteenth Amendment approach is on social disadvantage rather than on traditional and fundamental citizens' rights.

Instead, Fineman would propose something like the Common Benefit Clause of the Vermont Constitution (see the appendix at the end of this chapter for wording). It was under this clause that the Vermont judiciary legalized gay and lesbian marriage. Fineman points out that this clause was adopted as part of the Vermont Constitution in 1777, preceding the Fourteenth Amendment by nearly a century. It is therefore not tied to the specific historic circumstances and limitations of the Fourteenth Amendment, which stress disadvantage. Rather, the Vermont clause, as the Vermont Supreme Court has interpreted it, recognizes that the state gives benefits and mandates that those benefits be extended to all, not just a subgroup, of the citizens. Interpreting the clause in the gay/lesbian marriage case, the Vermont Supreme Court stated that the clause was part of the "powerful movement for social equivalence unleashed by the Revolution," and commented that it "mirrors the confidence of [citizens] aggressively laying claim to the same rights as their peers."

Mary Becker reaches the same result as Martha Fineman — a repudiation of the ERA as worded when it went before the states between 1972 and 1982. But she has a different emphasis. Whereas Fineman focuses on caretaking labor and the right to work (an economic and structural analysis of the work/family conflict), Becker focuses on issues of custody and maintenance at divorce and on issues of affirmative action.[4] In an important recent article Becker recounts, in sympathetic and convincing detail, the arguments of women on both sides of the ERA debate from 1961 to 1963, when Esther Peterson and Pauli Murray argued against the ERA and Marguarite Rawalt for it. As she explains how the formal equality of the ERA came to seem the better strategy, and as she lists the many successes of formal equality under the Fourteenth Amendment, however, Becker also argues against formal equality that the underlying patriarchal structure of our existing society makes affirmative action for women necessary as a tool of resistance:

Affirmative action may be appropriate with respect to child custody, for example, and in many employment settings, particularly those that regard masculine traits as essential for effective performance. Sex-specific rules might be appropriate in other areas as well. Perhaps, for example, we should encourage all-female schools, quotes of at least fifty percent women for various governmental entities, and an all-female all-volunteer combat unit.[5]

Instead of the 1972 version of the ERA, therefore, Becker suggests an ERA whose first section reflects the due process and equal protection clauses of the Fourteenth Amendment, whose second section requires that each state have at least one senator who is a woman, and whose third section rests ultimate responsibility for interpretation with Congress (see appendix for wording). The first section of Becker's amendment specifies due process and equal protection for "any woman or man," thus opening the door to legislation designed particularly for the specifically gender-related circumstances of men or women in order to guarantee them due process and equal protection. The second section, related to many of the European movements for legislative parity for women, directly contravenes the earlier ERA's mandate of neutral wording.

Fineman and Becker are only two of a number of sophisticated feminist theorists whose analysis today opposes the introduction of the Equal Rights Amendment of 1972. Any serious attempt to reintroduce the ERA to Congress would have to take account of arguments such as these.

2

Meanwhile, in state courts all over the country, people have been using their state equal rights amendments to bring cases charging abridgement of rights on account of sex. As far as I know, the only complete account of the effects of these cases consists of an analysis of cases brought under the Texas constitution's ERA.[6]

Texas is the most populous ERA state. It also has the largest judicial system of any state with an ERA in its constitution. Yet no one would claim that it was representative of all the other states. Among other things, in Texas, the words that constitute the state's ERA ("equality under the law shall not be denied or abridged because of sex, race, color, creed, or national origin"), adopted as an amendment to the state constitution in 1972, were not interpreted to require "strict scrutiny" until 1987.[7]

Of the twenty-seven cases decided by the Texas courts between 1972 and 1993, the claimants prevailed in only seven.[8] The beneficiaries were: (1) women college students who won the right to live off campus (and correspondingly men to live on campus) regardless of sex; (2) jilted female fiancées (and correspondingly jilted male fiancés) who won the right to sue for "heart balm" damages; (3) wives who won the right to sue for loss of consortium when a third party injured or killed their husband; (4) biological fathers who won parental rights to their children over the objection of the biological mothers; and (5) female topless dancers who won the right not to have the aureolas of their breasts covered (i.e., treated differently from the breasts of their male counterparts by city ordinances regulating sexually oriented business-es).[9] Of these, arguably the cases of the greatest substantive importance were those in which biological fathers won a set of rights: the right to prevent moth-ers from giving children born out of wedlock up for adoption, the right to at-tack the presumption of legitimacy and sue for paternity against parents in an existing marriage, and the right to a court-appointed attorney in paternal cases when indigent.

Of the 27 cases from 1972 to 1993 brought to the Texas Supreme Court under the state's ERA, men brought 16 and women 11. Of the seven claimants who prevailed, three were men and four women. The pattern is even more fa-vorable to men in the 28 equal protection sex discrimination cases brought be-fore the U.S. Supreme Court from 1971 to 1998. There men brought 18 of the cases and women 10. Of the 16 claimants who prevailed, nine were men and seven women. In both venues men have been more likely than women to bring cases. They have been about as likely or more likely to prevail.[10]

It is dangerous to generalize from state ERA cases to what might happen in the United States Supreme Court with an Equal Rights Amendment in the federal constitution. States with equal rights amendments in their constitu-tions are precisely the states most likely to have eliminated invidious discrim-inations against women through statutory changes. One would therefore ex-pect these states to be the most likely to generate cases that are either trivial in nature or benefit men.

More complete analyses of experiences with state ERAs may exist. I am re-lying in this analysis only on a Lexis-Nexis search based on the keywords "equal rights amendment" and "state."[11] If more complete analyses have *not* been done, however, it would be worth doing them ourselves before we try to bring a federal ERA before Congress and before the states again. If we do not do these analyses, I think we can be sure that the ERA opponents will do so.

3

Meanwhile again, in yet a third corner of the universe—the unratified states—women activists are continuing to try to get their state legislature to ratify the 1972 ERA. In 2000, for example, women in Missouri, Virginia, and Illinois succeeded in getting bills for ERA ratification introduced in their state legislatures, and in two cases out of committee and onto the floor. In no state have the activists and pro-ERA legislators succeeded in getting a vote. When-ever the amendment has reached the legislative floor, it has been tabled. But the fight goes on.

The legal strategy these women are using is worth attention.

The roots of this strategy lie in a series of events, seemingly unrelated to the ERA, that in 1992 culminated in putting the Twenty-Seventh Amendment in the constitution. That amendment, originally proposed by James Madison in 1789, required Congress to take a roll-call vote whenever it approved a pay raise. The amendment garnered six state ratifications in the three years from 1789 to 1791, then none for eighty-nine years. In 1873 one more state ratified. Then 105 years passed. In 1978 one more state ratified. Then five more years passed. An extraordinary push from 1983 to 1992, in which thirty-two more states ratified, taking the amendment over the top, was begun and entrepreneured by Gregory Watson, a student at the University of Texas, who discovered the languishing Madison amendment in 1982 when, ironically, he was doing research for a paper on whether Congress could extend the ratification deadline for the ERA. Enamored of the Madison amendment, he worked indefatigably to push for its passage in the state legislatures, spending $6,000 of his own money to sponsor the nationwide effort. Watson got a "C" on his research paper. But he is credited with influencing twenty-six state legislatures to ratify the Madison amendment.[12]

On May 7, 1992, Michigan became the thirty-eighth state to ratify the Madison amendment, 203 years after its initial proposal. On May 18, the archivist of the United States ruled the amendment ratified, and a day later it was published in the Federal Register, the official repository of statutes, regulations, and constitutional amendments.[13] Although some members of Congress were concerned about the procedure, criticized the archivist, and made abortive moves to declare invalid the four unratified amendments that still remain before the states, on May 20 Congress approved the Twenty-Seventh Amendment by votes of 99 to 0 in the Senate and 414 to 3 in the House.

In December 1992 Richard Bernstein of the NYU Law School analyzed the issues in this process. Bernstein pointed out that the controlling Supreme Court case, *Coleman v. Miller*, decided in 1939, had concluded that "the question of the efficacy of ratifications by state legislatures . . . should be regarded as a political question pertaining to the political departments, with the ultimate authority in the Congress in the exercise of its control over the promulgation of the adoption of the amendment."[14] Bernstein also pointed out that the now live possibility of reviving unratified amendments could have important implications for the still unratified ERA.

The key breakthrough, however, came with a 1997 article in the *William and Mary Journal of Women and the Law* by three women graduates of the T. C. Williams School of Law in Richmond, Virginia.[15] The law school's Women Law Students' Association sponsored the work. The three authors pointed out that the acceptance of the Madison amendment implies, in the words of the Department of Justice's recommendation to the national archivist at the time, that "there is no requirement of contemporaneous ratification."[16] Moreover, the time limit of seven years for the ERA, later extended to ten, is located in the proposing clause of the amendment, not in its text. "By separating the time limit from the body of the amendment," they argued, "Congress retains the authority to review the limit."[17] Congress thought it had power to intervene on the time limit when it granted the ERA extension in 1979 (although that power was never tested in the Supreme Court, because the case came before the court after the three-year extension had expired). In this analysis, if Congress has the power that the Court said it had in *Coleman* and that it exercised in 1979 by extending the ERA's first time limit, it can adjust or even repeal the time limit in the original proposing clause. In short, Congress can legally repeal or extend a deadline at will. It can also accept a running total. Apparently, the only thing it cannot do is accept a rescission. So if the legislatures of three more states ratify the ERA, Congress can simply adopt it, as it did the Madison amendment.

Accordingly, in Congress, Representative Robert Andrews (D.-N.J.) has introduced a resolution stipulating that Congress will approve the ERA when three more states finally ratify it.

In Missouri, Illinois, Virginia, Florida, Oklahoma and Arizona, activists have taken up the challenge. In Missouri, women active in the first ERA struggle are organizing again, district by district. They are driving to the rural districts and have energized young women in the universities and university towns. The new ERA movement has a national organization, the ERA Summit, affiliated with the National Women's Party. The movement's two main websites, providing legal and organizing information, call for "simple justice" for "all the citizens of the United States."[18]

As for the opponents, as Ellen Goodman wrote, it's "like deja vu all over again."[19] A flyer from Missouri Right to Life warns that "Under the wording of the ERA as passed by Congress in 1972, *any* state or federal restrictions on abortion, and *any* restrictions on government funding of abortion, would be invalidated as forms of 'illegal sex discrimination.' "[20] A flyer from Concerned Women for America of Missouri, which claims "over 5,000 members," states that the "ERA would prohibit Missouri or any other state from outlawing marriages and adoption of children by homosexuals."[21] The Eagle Forum, broadening the attack, not only urges the defeat of the Missouri ERA but adds that "Those who proclaim their liberation from men always go to Government as a replacement. . . . Trouble with husband? *Free housing*, accuse your husband of spousal 'rape.' "[22] With these arguments and their other resources, the "antis" have become sufficiently strong in each of the active states to keep the legislators from bringing the ERA to a vote.[23]

But the pro-ERA activists are undaunted. Shirley Breeze, who heads the Missouri campaign, says: "This time it's a different ballgame. A different mood in the country. The ERA is not as threatening as it was, but it's just as important."[24]

4

Meanwhile, back at the offices of the National Organization for Women, we find yet a fourth take on the ERA.

In the years 1978 to 1982, when the struggle for the ERA had shifted to the last unratified states, NOW took considerable trouble to make the feminist message palatable to middle America. In Illinois, for example, NOW opened a second office several blocks from its main office to house the ERA effort. The ERA office had no banners, posters, or pamphlets advocating lesbian or abortion rights. In a decision that split NOW and caused many activists to leave, the organization decided not to allow socialist, lesbian, or abortion banners in ERA demonstrations. Most of the longtime NOW activists who were lesbian consciously did not publicize their orientation.

The ERA issue appealed to women who had never been involved in any feminist cause. They took busses or carpooled to the state capital to lobby, organized coffee-and-cake district meetings with their representatives, sacrificed evenings when they would have been with their kids and families, wrote letters to the editor, and gave the first money they had ever given to a political cause. Every time they thought about the issue or talked about it with a neighbor, they got madder. They had experienced being second-class citizens all their lives, and with the ERA it came together for them. Women "weren't even in the constitution." And it was intolerable.

Some of the state ERA activists, of course, had always been involved in politics, usually but not always with the Democratic Party. A number of highly influential members of ERA Illinois were active in the Republican Party. The members of NOW were almost entirely Democrat or left-of-Democrat.

In this environment, where the ERA had to get votes in southern Illinois, rural Florida, and rural North Carolina (the most recalcitrant areas in the states where ratification was most likely), feminism had to have meaning to women whose political and lifestyle choices were neither cosmopolitan nor radical. Those women nevertheless supported the ERA because it spoke to them of the many ways they had been ignored, put aside, and counted as less all their lives. NOW, as the richest and most energetic feminist organization in America, threw itself into the ERA struggle. As a result, its membership soared from 55,000 in 1977 to 210,000 in 1982.

When the ERA deadline finally passed in 1982, however, the pent-up energy of all the other projects that had been put on the back burner for the ERA exploded and NOW activists turned to other things. The ERA never went off NOW's agenda, but it did not dominate as it had in the last few years of struggle before the deadline. The organization made the decision not to seek ratification again until it knew it had sufficient votes in the state legislatures.

Freed of the need to appeal to middle America, where does NOW stand on the ERA at this time? In 1993 the NOW annual national convention decided to form two committees, one to survey its chapter members about their current thinking on the direction the organization should take on the ERA and the other to study the history of the previous amendment and the impact of state ERAs. The next year an ERA Strategy Summit meeting was called for the purpose of "developing recommended language for a new ERA." The resolution calling for the strategy summit specified that "any proposed amendment must include the concepts of reproductive rights including abortion and non-discrimination on the basis of sexual orientation."[25] The next year, 1995, the national NOW conference produced a "working draft of an equal rights amendment," now called the "Constitutional Equality Amendment" (CEA). Section one of the CEA specifies that "Women and men shall have equal rights throughout the United States and every place and entity subject to its jurisdiction," and that "through this article, the subordination of women to men is abolished." Section two specifies that "All persons shall have equal rights and privileges without discrimination on account of sex, race, sexual orientation, marital status, ethnicity, national origin, color or indigence." (See appendix for wording.)[26] All other considerations aside, the simple inclusion of indigence makes the amendment impossible to pass in Congress or the states.

According to a NOW representative, NOW does not believe that the organization should continue to promote an ERA that embodies the meaning established when the amendment was originally introduced in 1972. The problem is not so much the wording of the original ERA as the understanding of it that prevailed during the 1972 legislative debate, which suggested that the amendment would not affect issues such as combat exemption, sex discrimination in insurance, taxation of single-sex schools, and abortion issues. Because that limited understanding would govern the attempted ratification of the remaining three states today, NOW objects to actions that would continue the ratification process by using the precedent of Madison to declare meaningless the time limit on the original ERA.[27]

Accordingly, NOW gives no support to the women in Missouri, Illinois, and elsewhere who are organizing to ratify the ERA.

The universe of feminism and feminist activists is big and varied. It is not for nothing that we have learned these days to speak of "feminisms" rather than "feminism." In many ways the ERA serves as a Rorschach test to illuminate the quite different perspectives of some of the many forms of feminism. In this chapter I have looked at only four of the different perspectives that might be taken on the Equal Rights Amendment. Each perspective sheds as much light on those who share that perspective as on the amendment itself.

There are many reasons to propose an amendment to the U.S. constitution. Actually having that amendment become law is only one of them. Of the three new versions of the ERA proposed by Fineman, Becker, and the National Organization for Women, not one has a realistic chance of passing in the next decade. Constitutional amendments need near consensus to pass. The process is designed that way, requiring the support of two-thirds of both houses of Congress and three-quarters of the states. The Fineman amendment, based on the Common Benefit Clause of the Vermont Constitution, would very plausibly legalize gay and lesbian marriages, as it did in Vermont. Today not even a mere majority of the U.S. public supports this policy. Indeed, arguments that the ERA would have this effect form the basis of many of the attacks on the 1972 ERA in the currently unratified states. The Becker amendment would require that each state have one woman senator. Given the strong opposition to any "quotas" in the U.S., it is inconceivable that a majority of the public today would support such a requirement in the Constitution. The NOW amendment abolishes women's subordination and forbids discrimination on the basis of sexual orientation or indigence. No state legislature today would give the Supreme Court the interpretive powers that the court might find in the concepts of "subordination" or discrimination against "indigence." Nor would a majority of the public support eliminating discrimination on the basis of sexual orientation in matters such as marriage.

Yet both Fineman and Becker's suggested amendments are consciousness-raising. Aimed primarily at legal theorists, they do what we want the work of our best legal theorists to do: they make us think critically and they set a target for our aspirations. NOW's new amendment also expresses aspirations, serving as a signal to its own members and others of the principles for which the organization stands. Each amendment addresses a particular audience. And each does an excellent job at its task. The audience for none of these amendments is a rural man or woman in Missouri, southern Illinois, Florida, Oklahoma, or Arizona. The task of none of them is to succeed in being passed in thirty-eight state legislatures in the near future.

At the moment the only people working for an ERA that might stand a chance of becoming part of the constitution of the U.S. in the next ten—or perhaps more—years are the lonely women in Missouri, Virginia, and Illinois, pouring their hours into organizing in the districts. If they begin to succeed, their actions will provoke a far fuller deliberation on this subject within the movement than has yet taken place. That will be good.

Appendix: Versions of and Substitutes for the Equal Rights Amendment (ERA)

A. *The "Alice Paul Amendment," introduced in Congress in 1923 (directly after suffrage) and in every subsequent congress for the next twenty years:*

Men and women shall have equal rights throughout the United States and in every place subject to its jurisdiction. Congress shall have power to enforce this article by appropriate legislation.

B. *The Equal Rights Amendment passed by the U.S. Congress in 1972 and ratified by thirty-five of the required thirty-eight states:*

1. Equality of rights under the law shall not be denied or abridged by the United States or by any State on account of sex.
2. The Congress shall have the power to enforce, by appropriate legislation, the provisions of this article.
3. This amendment shall take effect two years after the date of ratification.

C. *The "Fourteenth Amendment" version:*

Neither the United States nor any State shall, on account of sex, deny to any person within its jurisdiction the equal protection of the laws.

D. *The "Common Benefit" clause of the Vermont constitution (chap. I, art. 7):*

That government is, or ought to be, instituted for the common benefit, protection, and security of the people, nation, or community, and not for the particular emolument or advantage of any single person, family, or set of persons, who are a part only of that community.

E. *Mary Becker's suggestion for a new Equal Rights Amendment:*[28]

1. Neither any state nor the federal government shall deprive any woman or man of life, liberty, or property, without due process of law; nor deny to any woman or man within its jurisdiction the equal protection of the laws.
2. Each state shall have at least one senator who is a woman. Congress shall, through appropriate legislation, establish laws to enforce this provision and may determine that it becomes effective only upon the retirement of male incumbents.

3. Congress shall have the ultimate power to enforce this Amendment and to determine its scope and meaning."

F. The National Organization for Women, Constitutional Equality Amendment (CEA):[29]

Section 1. Women and men shall have equal rights throughout the United States and every place and entity subject to its jurisdiction; through this article, the subordination of women to men is abolished;

Section 2. All persons shall have equal rights and privileges without discrimination on account of sex, race, sexual orientation, marital status, ethnicity, national origin, color or indigence;

Section 3. This article prohibits pregnancy discrimination and guarantees the absolute right of a woman to make her own reproductive decisions including the termination of pregnancy;

Section 4. This article prohibits discrimination based upon characteristics unique to or stereotypes about any class protected under this article. This article also prohibits discrimination through the use of any facially neutral criteria which have a disparate impact based on membership in a class protected under this article.

Section 5. This article does not preclude any law, program or activity that would remedy the effects of discrimination and that is closely related to achieving such remedial purposes;

Section 6. This article shall be interpreted under the highest standard of judicial review;

Section 7. The United States and the several states shall guarantee the implementation and enforcement of this article.

NOTES

1. The Equal Rights Amendment was passed by the House of Representatives in 1971 (by a vote of 354 to 23) and the Senate in 1972 (by a vote of 84 to 8). Thirty of the required thirty-eight states ratified in 1972 and 1973, often with unanimous or nearly unanimous votes. Then the opposition rallied, spurred in part by the Supreme Court's 1973 decision in *Roe v. Wade*. Three more states ratified in 1974, one in 1975, and one in 1977, bringing the total to three short of ratification. Alabama, Arizona, Arkansas, Georgia, Louisiana, Mississippi, Missouri, Oklahoma, Utah, and Virginia were written off as hopeless, being either Southern or Mormon states. The struggle for the required last three states focused on Florida, Illinois, Nevada, and North Carolina. None had ratified by 1982, the deadline for ratification. (See,

inter alia, Jane Mansbridge, *Why We Lost the ERA* [Chicago: University of Chicago Press, 1986], for analysis of the reasons for the remaining states' failure to ratify.)

2. See articles collected in, e.g., Leslie Friedman Goldstein, ed., *Feminist Jurisprudence: The Difference Debate* (Lanham, Md.: Rowan and Littlefield, 1992), Patricia Smith, ed., *Feminist Jurisprudence* (New York: Oxford University Press, 1993), and D. Kelly Weisberg, *Feminist Legal Theory: Foundations* (Philadelphia: Temple University Press, 1993).

3. In 1971 Senator Birch Bayh proposed such a wording on the grounds that this wording would insure passage. (See appendix for wording.)

4. Mary Becker, "The Sixties Shift to Formal Equality and the Courts: An Argument for Pragmatism and Politics," *William and Mary Law Review* 40 (l998): 209–76.

5. Id., 265.

6. Wolfgang P. Hirczy de Mino, "Does an Equal Rights Amendment Make a Difference?" *Albany Law Review* 60 (1997): 1581–1609.

7. This standard, routinely applied in cases dealing with race, requires that laws drawing distinctions on the basis of the characteristic in question will be held unconstitutional unless they further a "compelling" state objective that cannot be accomplished otherwise. It is the standard that most observers expected the U.S. Supreme Court to adopt in interpreting the federal ERA, although the Court might have adopted an interpretation, urged by influential feminist constitutional lawyers, that flatly prohibited the use of sex as a basis for differential treatment except in the three cases of physical characteristics unique to one sex, laws guaranteeing privacy to the two sexes, and affirmative action. For the second, or "prohibition," interpretation, see Barbara A. Brown, Thomas I. Emerson, Gail Falk, and Ann E. Freedman, "The Equal Rights Amendment: A Constitutional Basis for Equal Rights for Women," *Yale Law Journal* 80 (1971): 955–962. For expectations regarding interpretation at the time of ratification, see Jane Mansbridge, *Why We Lost the ERA* (Chicago: University of Chicago Press, 1986), pp. 250–51, nn. 25–26, and accompanying text.

8. De Miro 1997, 1588.

9. Id., 1594.

10. Calculations from Becker 1998. See also Susan Gluck Mezey, *In Pursuit of Equality: Women, Public Policy, and the Federal Courts* (New York: St. Martin, 1992), 22).

11. I am indebted to Karen Taylor for this search.

12. Ruth Ann Strickland, "The Twenty-Seventh Amendment and Constitutional Change by Stealth," *P.S.: Political Science and Politics* 26 (l993): 716–22, 720.

13. Richard B. Bernstein, "The Sleeper Wakes: The History and Legacy of the Twenty-seventh Amendment," *Fordham Law Review* 61 (1992): 497–555, 539.

14. Chief Justice Hughes, joined by Stone and Reed, in 307 U.S. 433, 450 (1939), cited at id. 545.

15. Allison L. Held, Sheryl L. Herndon, and Danielle M. Stager, "The Equal Rights Amendment: Why the ERA Remains Legally Viable and Properly Before the States," *William and Mary Journal of Women and the Law* 3 (1997): 113–36.

16. Id., 121.

17. Id., 126.

18. The specific wording is from http://members.aol.com/ERACampaignWeb. See also http://www.equalrightsamendment.org.

19. Ellen Goodman, "A Glimmer of Hope for the Dormant Equal Rights Amendment," *Boston Globe* February 13, 2000, p. E7. See also Annys Shin, "Reviving the E.R.A.," *Ms.* (February/March 2000): 26–27.

20. Missouri Right to Life (PO Box 651, Jefferson City, MO 85102–0651), "To: Pro-Life Members of the Missouri House of Representatives."

21. Concerned Women for America of Missouri, "Equal Rights Amendment."

22. Missouri Eagle Forum, "HJR 35—Equal Rights Amendment—Not needed . . ."

23. Sarah A. Soule and Susan Olzak have shown that in the 1972–82 wave of the ERA movement, conservative sentiment in the states and anti-ERA protest both had large independent and interactive effects on state legislatures' failure to ratify ("State-Level Ratification of the Equal Rights Amendment, 1972–1982," unpublished ms., 2001, University of Arizona).

24. Goodman, 2000.

25. http://www.now.org/issues/economic/cea/history.html#1994.

26. A minority report from the strategy summit concluded that, "We wish the language to be concise, clear, simple, effective, focused and inclusive. Examples of such could be the Alice Paul language, or the 1982 language, or the following: 'Women and men shall have equality of rights, privileges and liberties throughout the U.S. and in every place and entity subject to its jurisdiction.' We insist that any form that is adopted include a full legislative history specifically including lesbian rights and protection of all categories as well as reproductive freedom" (http://www.now.org/nnt.05–95/era.html).

27. Telephone communication from Twiss Butler of NOW to Karen Taylor, February 5, 2001. *Why We Lost the ERA* discusses the 1972 legislative debate, concluding that it left the status of combat exemption ambiguous and that the possibility that the ERA would require women to be sent into combat on the same basis as men was a significant factor in the failure of the states to ratify.

28. Becker 1998.

29. http://www.now.org/issues/economic/cea/concept.html. This page also provides the rationales for each of the concepts and sections.

About the Contributors

ADJOA A. AIYETORO is chair of the Legal Strategies Commission of the National Coalition of Blacks for Reparations in America (N'COBRA) and co-coordinator of the Reparations Coordinating Committee. She is also Adjunct Professor at the American University, Washington College of Law, teaching Litigating Reparations for African Americans. Ms. Aiyetoro is past director of the National Conference of Black Lawyers and past director of administration for the Congressional Black Caucus Foundation, Inc.

NORMA BASCH is Professor of History at Rutgers University, Newark. She is the author of *In the Eyes of the Law: Women, Marriage and Property in Nineteenth-Century New York* (1982) and, more recently, *Framing American Divorce: From the Revolutionary Generation to the Victorians* (1999), which was awarded the Scribes Book Prize from the American Society of Writers on Legal Subjects.

CAROL BERKIN is Professor of History at The City University Graduate School and University Center and Baruch College, where she teaches American colonial, early Republic, and women's history. Her books include: *Jonathan Sewall: Odyssey of an American Loyalist*, which was nominated for the Pulitzer Prize; *First Generations: Women in Colonial America*; and most recently *A Brilliant Solution: Inventing the American Constitution* (2002).

EILEEN BORIS is the Hull Professor of Women's Studies at the University of California, Santa Barbara and the author of *Home to Work: Motherhood and the Politics of Industrial Homework* (1994), which won the Philip Taft Prize in Labor History. She is coeditor of *Complicating Categories: Gender, Class, Race, and Ethnicity* (1999) and editor of a special issue of *The Journal of Women's History* on "Women's Labors." She is finishing a book titled *Citizens on the Job: Race, Gender, and Rights in Modern America* and beginning a project tentatively called, *Defining Work, Revaluing Care.*

PEGGY COOPER DAVIS is Shad Professor of Law and director of the Lawyering Program at New York University. A former family court judge, she has written extensively about family and child welfare. Her book, *Neglected Stories: The Constitution and Family Values* links antislavery ideology concerning the family with the Reconstruction Amendments to establish the soundness of Supreme Court decisions recognizing a constitutional right of family integrity. Professor Davis's scholarship, which often employs methodologies of critical race theory, also addresses legal process and pedagogy.

MARTHA ALBERTSON FINEMAN is Dorothea S. Clarke Professor of Feminist Jurisprudence at Cornell Law School. In addition to numerous articles and book chapters on divorce law, child custody law, welfare reform, and feminist legal theory, she is author of *The Illusion of Equality: The Rhetoric and Reality of Divorce Reform* (1991) and *The Neutered Mother, the Sexual Family, and other Twentieth-Century Tragedies* (1995).

CAROL C. GOULD is Professor of Philosophy at Stevens Institute of Technology and Adjunct Professor of International and Public Affairs at Columbia University. She is the author of *Marx's Social Ontology* (1978), *Rethinking Democracy* (1988), and *Between the Personal and the Global: Democracy and Human Rights Reconsidered* (forthcoming). She has also edited seven books including *Women and Philosophy* (1976), *Beyond Domination* (1984), and *Gender* (1999) and has published more than forty articles in social and political philosophy, feminist philosophy, and applied ethics.

CYNTHIA HARRISON is Associate Professor of History and of Women's Studies at George Washington University in Washington, D.C., where she teaches U.S. women's history, constitutional history, and women and public policy. She is the author of *On Account of Sex: The Politics of Women's Issues, 1945–1968* (1988).

JAN LEWIS is Professor of History at Rutgers University, Newark. She is the author of *The Pursuit of Happiness: Family and Values in Jefferson's Virginia* (1983); coeditor (with Peter N. Stearns) of *An Emotional History of the Unit-*

ed States (1998); coeditor (with Peter S. Onuf) of Sally Hemings and Thomas Jefferson: History, Memory, and Civic Culture (1999); and coeditor (with James Horn and Peter S. Onuf) of The Revolution of 1800: Democracy, Race, and the New Republic (2002). She is completing a book on the connections among family, gender, race, and political thought in the early national era.

JANE MANSBRIDGE is Adams Professor at the John F. Kennedy School of Government, Harvard University. She is author of Beyond Adversary Democracy (1980) and Why We Lost the ERA (1986), as well as of many articles in political theory. Her most recent book is entitled Everyday Feminism (forthcoming).

MARTHA C. NUSSBAUM is Ernst Freund Distinguished Service Professor of Law and Ethics at The University of Chicago, appointed in the Philosophy Department, Law School, and Divinity School. She is an Associate in the Classics Department, an Affiliate of the Committee on Southern Asian Studies, a member of the Board of the Human Rights Program, and the coordinator of the new Center for Comparative Constitutionalism. Her most recent books are Women and Human Development (2000) and Upheavals of Thought: The Intelligence of the Emotions (2001).

LUCINDA JOY PEACH is Associate Professor in the Department of Philosophy and Religion at American University. Her areas of special interest are moral philosophy, applied ethics, and gender and religion. She is the author of Legislating Morality: Religious Identity and Moral Pluralism (2002) and the editor of both Women and World Religions (2002) and Women in Culture: An Anthology (1998).

FRANCIS FOX PIVEN is Distinguished Professor of Political Science and Sociology at the Graduate School and University Center of the City University of New York. She is coauthor with Richard Cloward of Poor People's Movements (1977), Regulating the Poor: The Functions of Public Welfare (1993), and Why Americans Still Don't Vote: And Why Politicians Want it That Way (2000).

JUDITH RESNIK is the Arthur Liman Professor of Law at Yale Law School, where she writes and teaches courses on adjudication, large-scale litigation, procedure, federalism, aspects of constitutional law, and feminist theory. She is the author of many essays addressing women's roles and rights, including "Asking Questions about Gender in Courts" (Signs, 1996); "Singular and Aggregate Voices: Law and Literature and Law and Feminism"; and " 'Naturally

Without Gender': Jurisdiction, Women, and the Federal Courts" (*New York University Law Review*, 1991).

DAVID A. J. RICHARDS is Edwin D. Webb Professor of Law at New York University School of Law, where he teaches constitutional law, criminal law, and (with Carol Gilligan) a seminar on gender issues in the culture and psychology of democratic societies. He is the author of ten books, including, most recently, *Women, Gays, and the Constitution: The Grounds for Feminism and Gay Rights in Culture and Law* (1998); *Identity and the Case for Gay Rights: Race, Gender, Religion as Analogies* (1999); and *Free Speech and the Politics of Identity* (1999).

ELIZABETH M. SCHNEIDER is the Rose L. Hoffer Professor of Law at Brooklyn Law School, and has been Visiting Professor of Law at Harvard and Columbia Law Schools. She was a civil rights litigator at the Center for Constitutional Rights in New York before entering teaching and has written many articles on gender and law. Her book, *Battered Women and Feminist Lawmaking* (2000), won the 2000 Association of American Publishers Professional-Scholarly Publishing Award in Law.

SIBYL A. SCHWARZENBACH is Associate Professor of Philosophy at The City University of New York (Baruch College and the Graduate School and University Center), and most recently an External Fellow at Stanford University's Humanities Center (2002–2003). In addition to numerous articles in the area of social and political philosophy, ethics, as well as feminist theory, she is author of the fourthcoming book *On Civic Friendship*.

PATRICIA SMITH is Professor of Philosophy at The City University of New York (Baruch College and the Graduate School and University Center). She is author of *Liberalism and Affirmative Obligation* (1998) and *Omission, Law, and Responsibility* (forthcoming), and has edited or coedited four anthologies: *The Nature and Process of Law* (1993), *Feminist Jurisprudence* (1993), *Marginal Groups and Mainstream American Culture* (2000), and *Legal Philosophy: Current Questions of Theory and Practice* (2002).

PHILIPPA STRUM is the director of the Division of U.S. Studies, Woodrow Wilson International Center for Scholars and the Broeklundian Professor Emerita of Political Science, Brooklyn College. Among her books are *Women in the Barracks: The VMI Case and Equal Rights* (2002), *When the Nazis Came to Skokie: Freedom for the Speech We Hate* (1999; honorable mention, American Bar Association Silver Gavel Award), *Privacy: The Debate in the*

United States Since 1945 (1998), *Brandeis: Beyond Progressivism* (1993), and *Louis D. Brandeis: Justice for the People* (l984; nominated for the Pulitzer Prize in biography).

SUSAN STURM is Professor of Law at Columbia Law School. She writes and speaks extensively on issues of race and gender in the workplace, judicial intervention and organizational change, and participation and deliberation. Her recent publications include "Lawyers and the Pursuit of Workplace Equity," *Wisconsin Law Review* (2002); "Second Generation Employment Discrimination: A Structural Approach," *Columbia Law Review* (2001); "Equality and Inequality," *International Encyclopedia of Social Sciences* (2001); and "Race, Gender, and the Law in the Twenty-First Century Workplace," *University of Pennsylvania Journal of Labor and Employment Law* (1998). She is also coauthor (with Lani Guinier) of *Who's Qualified? The Future of Affirmative Action* (Beacon Press, 2001).

JOAN WILLIAMS is Professor of Law at American University, Washington College of Law, as well as director of the Program on Gender, Work & Family, and codirector of the Project on Attorney Retention. She is author of *Unbending Gender: Why Work and Family Conflict and What To Do About It* (1999), which was awarded the Gustavus Myers Outstanding Book Award for the Study of Bigotry and Human Rights.

Index

abortion issue, xi, 1, 371; citizenship rights and, 226–27; Establishment Clause and, 223–25; Free Exercise Clause and, 225–27; *Harris v. McRae*, 226; Hyde Amendment, 222–23, 226, 229; infringement on women's constitutional rights, 223–27; *Planned Parenthood v. Casey*, 225–26; privacy and, 162–63, 168, 170, 179, 185. *see also* religious lawmaking; *Roe v. Wade*

Adams, John, 27

Adolescent Family Life Act (AFLA), 222, 224–25, 228–30, 234n.23

affection, 28–29

affirmative action, 139, 159, 342, 346n.32, 367

affirmative obligations, 112–13, 118–22, 183–84

African Americans, 282; Civil War soldiers, 61–62; feminist coalition, 53–54; myth of inferiority, 70–71, 73. *see also* black women; slavery

Aid to Families with Dependent Children (AFDC), 110, 116–18, 121, 133

alimony, new theory of, 318, 326

Allbright, Madeleine, 338

Allen, Anita, 244, 252n.31

Amendments to the Constitution: Third, 154; Fourth, 154, 159, 170; Fifth, 153, 159, 178, 226, 234n.33; Sixth, 178; Eighth, 159; Ninth, 154, 257; Nineteenth, xi, 180, 274, 349; Twenty-Seventh, 370; Reconstruction Amendments, xi, 16–17, 54, 64. *see also* Bricker Amendment; Constitutional Equality Amendment; Equal Rights Amendment; First Amendment; Fourteenth Amendment; Hyde Amendment; Thirteenth Amendment

American and Foreign Anti-Slavery Society, 62

American Civil Liberties Union (ACLU), 352

American Revolution, 38, 256–57, 337

Andrews, Robert, 371

Anti-Federalist writings, 14

antislavery activists, 16, 53–61

Aristotle, 3, 4, 5, 10, 19nn.12, 13, 162; view of legislators, 5–6